Max Planck Institute for Intellectual Property, Competition and Tax Law

MPI Studies on Intellectual Property, Competition and Tax Law

Volume 1

Edited by

Josef Drexl
Reto M. Hilty
Wolfgang Schön
Joseph Straus

Reto M. Hilty
Frauke Henning-Bodewig
(Editors)

Law Against Unfair Competition

Towards a New Paradigm in Europe?

Springer

Professor Dr. Reto M. Hilty
Dr. Frauke Henning-Bodewig
Max Planck Institute for Intellectual Property,
Competition and Tax Law
Marstallplatz 1
80539 Munich
Germany
hilty@ip.mpg.de
fhb@ip.mpg.de

ISBN 978-3-642-09096-7 e-ISBN 978-3-540-71882-6

Springer is a part of Springer Science+Business Media

springer.com

Softcover reprint of the hardcover 1st edition 2007

Cover-design: WMX Design GmbH, Heidelberg

Preface

Unfair competition law is concerned with fair play in commerce. It is generally regarded as necessary – together with antitrust law – in order to steer competition along an orderly course, and thereby to contribute to promoting an efficient market system that serves the interests of all participants.

Nevertheless the significance of unfair competition law varies from one country to another. Whereas in some countries, such as Germany, it is seen as one of the most effective commercial laws, in other countries, such as the United Kingdom, it leads rather a shadowy existence.

From the outset, this discrepancy laid in the differences in national legal systems. Whilst those continental European countries that possessed a written civil law when instances of unfair competition emerged, more or less successfully attempted to incorporate them in the existing tort law system, protection in the common law countries was restricted to some narrowly defined torts, in particular "passing off". At this stage one of the few shared convictions was, that the protection of "honest entrepreneurs" was at issue; on this basis, in 1900, the only regulation at the international level until now was enacted, Art. 10bis of the Paris Convention.

Yet even this foundation is increasingly fragile. The crucial factor is namely the controversial role of consumer protection in unfair competition law. Although the interest of consumers in the fairness of commercial practices was generally regarded as legitimate, the reaction to recognise this interest was quite different. Whilst some countries integrated this protection in their existing legal regulations against unfair competition – which thereby became a sort of "market law" – other countries continued to provide protection for competitors under tort law, and supplemented this by provisions on specific business practices, serving mainly consumers' interests.

Against this background it is not surprising that a comprehensive, coherent harmonisation at the level of the European Community has still not been successful. In 1984, a Directive on misleading advertising was accomplished, which was supplemented by comparative advertising in 1997; and there continues to be selective harmonisation by specific product and media regulations and a partial alignment of rights for the protection of intellectual property. Only in 2005 did an overarching regulation again succeed in the form of Directive 2005/29/EC, which concerns unfair commercial practices in general.

Yet at the same time the latter Directive clearly illustrates the shortcomings of previous European legal development, which can be attributed to the absence of a convincing legal foundation on which to base modern unfair competition law. Whilst, for instance, protection was initially focussed exclusively on competitors (and consumers merely as a reflex), the Directive on unfair commercial practices does exactly the opposite: it now only concerns protection of consumers in the so-called "B2C" relationship (and, at best, protection of competitors as a reflex).

There seems to be no rhyme or reason for this change of direction. Coupled with the enduring controversy about the principle of the country of origin and the Commission's "piecemeal approach" to regulation, it becomes evident that the foundations of modern law against unfair competition urgently require detailed academic scrutiny.

It is striking that so far – to the extent that any debate taken place at all – the opinions of only a few EU Member States have primarily attracted attention. This state of affairs can no longer be justified since 2004 at the latest, however, at which point in time the EU increased from only 15 Member States to 25, and in the meantime even to 27. Yet, in drafting the European law, the opinions of the new Member States have still largely not been considered – even for the Directive on unfair business practices enacted in 2005.

The Max Planck Institute for Intellectual Property, Competition and Tax Law therefore held a conference in Budapest on 16–18 June 2005, entitled "The law against unfair competition in the new Member States: Impulses for Europe?". The conference addressed the special problems of the law against unfair competition in the new Member States and their effects on future Community law. Renowned scholars from several "old" Member States, as well as from almost all the new ones, were enlisted as speakers. The aim of the conference, alongside general issues, such as those concerning the interfaces between competition law and other fields of law, was particularly to contrast the regulatory approaches of all the Member States. The aspects that will be foremost at the European level in future could thus be elaborated in a joint discussion. This conference continued the theme of two earlier conferences held by the Max Planck Institute, namely the symposium "Competition law and consumer protection in Central and Eastern Europe" in 1991, and the Ringberg Conference "Reorganisation of competition law" in 1994.

Munich, January 2007
Reto Hilty Frauke Henning-Bodewig

Table of Contents

List of Authors

Paolo Auteri	Prof. Dr. iur., Professor for Intellectual Property Law and Competition Law at the University of Pavia, Attorney at Law in Milan
Antonina Bakardjieva Engelbrekt	Dr. iur., LL.D., Associate Professor (Docent) in Civil Law, Stockholm University, Department of Law
Frauke Henning-Bodewig	Dr. iur., Head of Department at the Max Planck Institute for Intellectual Property, Competition and Tax Law, Munich
Jennifer Davis	Dr. iur., Newton Trust Lecturer in Intellectual Property Law in the Law Faculty, University of Cambridge, Fellow of Wolfson College, Cambridge
Judit Firniksz	Dr. iur., Head of the Consumer Section – Gazdasági Versenyhivatal (Hungarian Competition Authority)
Jochen Glöckner	Prof. Dr. iur., LL.M. (USA), Professor for German and European Private and Commercial Law at the University of Constance
Peter Grilc	Prof. Dr. iur., Professor of Competition Law and EU Law, University of Ljubljana
Petr Hajn	Prof. Dr. iur., Professor of Commercial Law, Faculty of Law, Masaryk University, Brno
Reto Hilty	Prof. Dr. iur., Director at the Max Planck Institute for Intellectual Property, Competition and Tax Law, Munich, Professor at the University of Zurich
Marcus Höpperger	Acting Director, Law and International Classifications Division, Sector of Trademarks, Industrial Designs and Geographical Indications, WIPO, Geneva
Vytautas Mizaras	Dr. iur., LL.M., Associate Professor and Head of the Department of Civil Law and Civil Procedure at the Faculty of Law of the Vilnius University, Lithuania

Wolfgang Schuhmacher	Prof. Dr. iur., Department of Labour Law, Commercial Law and European Law at the Law Faculty of Salzburg
Martin Senftleben	Dr. iur., Associate Officer, Law Section, Sector of Trademarks, Industrial Designs and Geographical Indications, WIPO, Geneva
Anton Škreko	Dr. iur., Researcher at the Faculty of Law of Trnava University in Trnava, Department of Civil and Commercial Law
Ryszard Skubisz	Prof. Dr. iur., Chair of the Jean Monet European Union Law Department at the Faculty of Law and Administration of the Maria Curie-Sklodowska University of Lublin, Poland
Jules Stuyck	Prof. Dr. iur., Professor of European and Economic Law at the K.U.Leuven and of European Law at the R.U. Nijmegen; Visiting professor at the CEU (Budapest)
Janusz Szwaja	Prof. Dr. iur., Jagiellonian University of Crakow, Poland

The Law Against Unfair Competition and Its Interfaces

*Reto M. Hilty**

1. Point of Departure: Competition Law in Its Widest Sense

In a constitutional state ("Rechtsstaat"), committed to liberal values, the intervention of the legislator in the market forces of free competition requires a specific justification.[1] Economically speaking, this justification rests on the consideration that,

---

* The author wishes to thank *Martin Pflüger*, Research Fellow at the Max Planck Institute for Intellectual Property, Competition, and Tax Law, for his valuable support, especially in document enquiry and analysis.

1 On the same basis rest *e.g.* BEATER, "Unlauterer Wettbewerb" Sec. 12, note 31 *et seq.* (2002); SCHÜNEMANN, in: HARTE-BAVENDAMM & HENNING-BODEWIG (eds.), "Gesetz gegen den unlauteren Wettbewerb, Kommentar" Sec. 1, note 34 (2004), (*see also*, however, Sec. 1, notes 20 and 24, as well as Sec. 3, note 163 *et seq.*, extremely cautious concerning intervention by the State, this being substantiated essentially with regard to the alleged lack of knowledge concerning the effects of intervention in "the highly complex system as a whole"); SAMBUC, in: HARTE & HENNING, *ibidem*, Intro. F, note 206; KÖHLER, in: HEFERMEHL, KÖHLER & BORNKAMM (eds.), "Wettbewerbsrecht" Intro. to the Law Against Unfair Competition, note 1.33 (25th ed. 2007).

without any such intervention, a market failure would ensue after a certain period of time.[2]

At first sight, this justification – the intervention in competition to avoid a potential market failure – appears to differ from the justification for intellectual property rights. For intellectual property rights it is customarily accepted that, by granting time-limited exclusive rights (as granted, for example, to the holders of patents or copyrights) incentives are created, ultimately aimed at optimising the allocation of resources.[3] On closer scrutiny, however, such a perception is not convincing. This is so for two reasons:

- Firstly, the stated objectives very quickly become blurred when they are applied to practical constellations. The two lines of justification are thus less in the nature of two distinct theoretical approaches, but rather different gravitational fields for possible ways of economic argumentation. Concrete legal norms may be at a greater or lesser distance from the one or the other gravitational field. However, it would be wrong to conclude from this that different approaches to legal regulation would necessarily pursue functionally different aims. In this way, exclusive rights may not only create incentives for the production of something new, but they may also contribute towards avoiding a potential market failure (thus, for example, trade marks, because they substantially reduce the consumer search

---

[2] With regard to the topic of a market failure also *infra* 3.4; *cf.* for definitions of the concept of a market failure GABLER, "Wirtschaftslexikon" L-Z, Vol. 2 (12th ed. 1988); GEIGANT, HASLINGER, SOBOTKA & WESTPHAL (eds.), "Lexikon der Volkswirtschaft" (7th ed. 2000); DICHTL & ISSING (eds.), "Vahlens großes Wirtschaftslexikon" L-Z, Vol. 2 (2nd ed. 1993); *see also* with regard to the topic as a whole FRITSCH, WEIN & EWERS, "Marktversagen und Wirtschaftspolitik: mikroökonomische Grundlagen staatlichen Handelns" 81 (6th ed. 2005); following essentially the same approach BRÜNING, in: HARTE & HENNING (eds.), *supra* note 1, at Intro. F, note 127; *see also* GORDON, "Systemische und fallbezogene Lösungsansätze für Marktversagen bei Immaterialgütern," in: OTT & SCHÄFER (eds.), "Ökonomische Analyse der rechtlichen Organisation von Innovationen" 328 *et seq.* (1994) (related to US intellectual property law); by the same author, "Asymmetric market failure and prisoner's dilemma in intellectual property," 17 Dayton Law Review 853 *et seq.* (1991-1992); BERGH & LEHMANN, "Informationsökonomie und Verbraucherschutz im Wettbewerbs- und Warenzeichenrecht," 1992 GRUR Int. 591 (market failure as a result of an information deficit); in a similar context HUNTLEY & STEPHEN, "Unfair Competition, Consumer Deception, and Brand Copying: An Economic Perspective," 15 International Review of Law and Economics 448 *et seq.* (1995).

[3] This has been analysed much more thoroughly with regard to patent law than with regard to copyright law; for a fundamental treatment, *see* in particular MACHLUP, "Die wirtschaftlichen Grundlagen des Patentrechts," 1961 GRUR Ausl. 373 *et seq.*, 473 *et seq.*, 524 *et seq.*; also in detail with regard to the mechanisms in general – however, with a strong emphasis on physical property – LEHMANN, "Eigentum, geistiges Eigentum, gewerbliche Schutzrechte – Property Rights als Wettbewerbsbeschränkungen zur Förderung des Wettbewerbs," 1983 GRUR Int. 356 *et seq.*, in particular 360; similarly critical BEATER, "Nachahmen im Wettbewerb" 357 (1995); *see also* OPPENLÄNDER, "Die wirtschaftspolitische Bedeutung des Patentwesens aus der Sicht der empirischen Wirtschaftsforschung," 1982 GRUR Int. 598 *et seq.*, in particular 599. More recently *e.g.* KRAẞER, "Patentrecht" 34, as well as 43 *et seq.* (5th ed. 2004); PRETNAR, "Die ökonomische Auswirkung von Patenten in der wissensbasierten Marktwirtschaft," 2004 GRUR Int. 776 *et seq.*

costs[4]). Conversely, as will be explained below,[5] specific incentives aimed at optimising the allocation of resources may also be created without granting exclusive rights.

- Secondly, the two (theoretically severable) lines of argumentation, i.e. the creation of incentives by means of exclusive rights, on the one hand, and the selective intervention of the legislator to avoid a market failure, on the other, by no means constitute opposites in a larger context; they rather function in an almost complementary manner. This is so because, in the final analysis, both are directed at optimising competition in a predefined desired form. This follows from the fact that competition should not be seen as a homogenous entity, but as a form of multilayered "state", entailing the most diverse facets.[6] One of these facets is, for example, competition between technologies, which as a whole may experience a significant encouragement exactly through the instrument of the law of patents – despite the fact that the individual patent (referring to the concrete invention) embodies an exclusive right.[7] Conversely, regulations genuinely pertaining to competition law may reinforce an individual position in competition and, in this way – at any rate selectively and functionally – approximate an exclusive legal position.

---

4 HUNTLEY & STEPHEN, 15 International Review of Law and Economics 448 *et seq.*, *see also* 452 (1995); for a fundamental treatment, *see* in particular LANDES & POSNER, "The Economic Structure of Intellectual Property Law" 167 *et seq.* (2003); correspondingly already by the same authors, "Trademark Law: An Economic Perspective," Vol. 30, No. 2 Journal of Law and Economics 265 *et seq.*, in particular 269 *et seq.* (Oct. 1978). *See also* COOTER & ULEN, "Law & Economics" 134 *et seq.* (4th ed. 2004); AKERLOF, "The Market for 'Lemons': Quality Uncertainty and the Market Mechanism," 84 Quarterly Journal of Economics 488 *et seq.* (1970); BERG & LEHMANN, 1992 GRUR Int. 588 *et seq.*, in particular 591.

5 *Infra* 4.3.

6 With regard to the nature of competition in particular *e.g.* KÖHLER, in: HEFERMEHL, KÖHLER & BORNKAMM, *supra* note 1, at Intro., note 1.23, in terms of which one deals with "an extremely complex set of facts which, on the one hand, presupposes certain circumstances so that it can take place and develop whatsoever, on the other hand, however, because of its manifold functions can be understood in terms of the most diverse aspects and in the light of different objectives". The concept of competition thus serves both the purpose of characterising the behavioural processes of various enterprises in a certain market and the relations inter se concerning them which arise therefrom and with the market partners on the opposite market side, as well as that of describing the market situation of a specific product including its substitute goods and characterising the organising principle dominating the economy as a whole.

7 With regard to the effect of encouragement through exclusive rights (in particular with regard to patent rights) KRAßER, *supra* note 3, at 34, 43 *et seq.* and 45 *et seq.*; LEHMANN, 1983 GRUR Int. 360; OPPENLÄNDER, 1982 GRUR Int. 599, 600 *et seq.*; PRETNAR, 2004 GRUR Int. 776 *et seq.*

This approach of complementary functions is, in fact, recognised by present-day commentators.[8] It prevents the drawing of artificial boundaries and, in this way, makes it possible to define competition law in its widest sense as the totality of all those legal instruments whose aim is to continuously approximate the actual behaviour of individual competitors in a constantly changing (i.e. dynamic) context to predefined target values. Competition law thus defined in its widest sense therefore constitutes the core of what will be termed "the law of market behaviour" ("Marktverhaltensrecht") here.[9]

It should be added that in a constitutional state ("Rechtsstaat"), committed not only to liberal values, but which also seeks to realise other socio-politically consolidated values, the stated target values need not only be of an economic nature. The law of market behaviour may, in fact, find its justification also in, for example, social

---

[8] Particularly clear KUR, "Funktionswandel von Schutzrechten: Ursachen und Konsequenzen der inhaltlichen Annäherung und Überlagerung von Schutzrechtstypen," in: SCHRICKER, DREIER & KUR (eds.), "Geistiges Eigentum im Dienst der Innovation" 23 *et seq.*, in particular 32 *et seq.* ("erosion of the limits of protective rights") (2001); by the same author, "A New Framework for Intellectual Property Rights – Horizontal Issues," 2004 IIC 1 *et seq.*, in particular 19; SAMBUC, in: HARTE & HENNING (eds.), *supra* note 1, at Intro. F, note 185 *et seq.*, 204 *et seq.*; by the same author, "Der UWG Nachahmungsschutz" note 35 *et seq.* (1996); KÖHLER, in: HEFERMEHL, KÖHLER & BORNKAMM (eds.), *supra* note 1, at Sec. 4 Law Against Unfair Competition, note 9.4; BEATER, *supra* note 1, at Sec. 1, note 71 (*cf.* with regard to the often inconcise approach of the courts, however, also note 76); WEIHRAUCH, "Der unmittelbare Leistungsschutz im UWG" 240 (2001); KELLER, "Der wettbewerbsrechtliche Leistungsschutz – Vom Handlungsschutz zur Immaterialgüterrechtsähnlichkeit," in: AHRENS, ET AL. (eds.), "FS Erdmann" 595 *et seq.* (2002); *see also* BEYERLEIN, "Ergänzender Leistungsschutz gemäß § 4 Nr. 9 UWG als „geistiges Eigentum" nach der Enforcement-Richtlinie (2004/48/EG)," 2005 WRP 1355, as well as generally WEBER, "Dritte Spur zwischen absoluten und relativen Rechten?," in: HONSELL ET AL. (eds.), "Aktuelle Aspekte des Schuld- und Sachenrechts, FS Heinz Rey" 591 *et seq.* (Zurich 2003). For a fundamental treatment in the context of antitrust law, *see* ULLRICH, "Lizenzkartellrecht auf dem Weg zur Mitte," 1996 GRUR Int. 565 *et seq.* ("The protective right is only a means to the end inherent in competition, a competence to act, which makes possible behaviour promoting competition, *i.e.* aimed at individually maximising profit, but it is not already an end, incentive or reward itself, neither as such nor as a system. ... [Intellectual property] ... permits ... only exploiting the forces of competition which may already be found in the market order." [translation]), as well as in particular also HEINEMANN, "Immaterialgüterschutz in der Wettbewerbsordnung" 619 *et seq.* (2002). *See* in this context also *e.g.* BGH, October 10, 1971, I ZR 12/70, 1972 GRUR 189 *et seq.* – *Wandsteckdose II.*

[9] Explanatory statement of the German Government to Sec. 1 of the Act Against Unfair Competition (BT-Drucks 15/1487) at 16; GLÖCKNER, "Europäisches Lauterkeitsrecht" 7 (2006); KÖHLER, in: HEFERMEHL, KÖHLER & BORNKAMM (eds.) *supra* note 1, at Intro., note 1.24 ("competition as a behavioural process"), as well as Sec. 1, note 43; by the same author, "Zur Konkurrenz lauterkeitsrechtlicher und kartellrechtlicher Normen," 2005 WRP 645 *et seq.*, in particular 646, 653; *see also* FEZER, "Modernisierung des deutschen Rechts gegen den unlauteren Wettbewerb auf der Grundlage einer Europäisierung des Wettbewerbsrechts," 2001 WRP 997. *See also* for a more precise definition of the concept of "a law of market behaviour", however, *infra* 5.2.

justice, cultural diversity or ecological sustainability.[10] In the following, the observation of these values is taken for granted as far as European law, which is presently being focused on, is concerned, without discussing the question whether the European Community actually has the necessary competence to implement these values at this point.

2. Definition of Topic: The Legal Protection of the Competitor

If the law of market behaviour is to be understood as a complete set of legal norms, this does not, of course, exclude defining specific fields forming part of the law of market behaviour, in which the objectives of statutory arrangements may quite legitimately vary, compared to those of other fields.[11] Nevertheless, it appears neither necessary nor reasonably possible to partition the law of market behaviour as an entirety into its separate fields in an abstract manner, for example, to draw a clear line between legal approaches to protect intellectual property on the one hand and competition on the other, since these fields overlap each other substantially, as will be shown later.[12] However, what is decisive against this background is not to loose sight of both the particularities of each field as well as its relations to other fields.

This finding becomes particularly important, if one looks for interfaces as presently required by the topic. In that respect, from the perspective of the law against unfair competition, two negative delimitations need to be made here, however, to define the topic more closely:

- The first one follows from the fact that the topic in the present context refers to "the law against unfair competition"; this gives rise to – at any rate in the tradition of those European states which know that term whatsoever – a counterpoint to antitrust law. Antitrust law covers those constellations in which individual com-

---

[10] *See also* FRITSCH, WEIN & EWERS, *supra* note 2, at 81; KÖHLER, in: HEFERMEHL, KÖHLER & BORNKAMM (eds.), *supra* note 1, at Intro., note 1.48; critical concerning "subjecting market results to norms" SCHÜNEMANN, in: HARTE & HENNING (eds.), *supra* note 1, at Sec. 3, note 163 *et seq.*: "Even if such a conflict concerning the objectives existed, it would have to be decided in favour of the freedom of competition, as prosperity not accompanied by freedom would be the democratically as well as ethically unacceptable alternative" (translation). Once a constitution or, at the European level, the EC Treaty lays down certain values, it will, however, be difficult to actually avoid ensuring that the law deriving therefrom is not directed at realising these values. This covers also competition law – as the core of the law of market behaviour – as long as this concentrates on the indispensable minimum (*cf.* also *supra* note 1) and freedom is not restricted beyond what is unavoidable. In so far, the conclusion to the deliberations of Schünemann cited here appears too simplistic.

[11] *Cf.* in this regard *infra* 5.1.

[12] *Infra* 4, in particular 4.3.

petitors are able, separately or jointly, to attain a position which severely challenges the functioning of competition.[13]
Such specific questions of antitrust law presently do not stand at the centre of the discussion. For, not only European antitrust law is comparatively very highly developed; also in the national law of EU Member States there already exists a far-reaching consensus, at least principally speaking, concerning the importance of a body of rules in the sphere of antitrust law. With a view to a European law of market behaviour as a whole this means that the component of an antitrust law essentially exists and that details related thereto need not to be discussed in the following.

It is, however, important not to loose sight of the interfaces between the various components of the law of market behaviour. In this regard, the interface between antitrust law and what is customarily termed "the law against unfair competition" is of interest in respect of the law of those states which regulate these two fields as a formal unit (e.g. Estonia[14], Hungary[15], Latvia[16] and Lithuania[17]). But also where there is a division into different enactments (or even with regard to the Common Law approach), this interface is of interest in a substantial respect in as far as it is possible to pursue coincident objectives with different components (for example, preventing market distortions).[18]

- Secondly, the component of the legal protection of consumers will not be discussed in depth at this point. Delimitation is more difficult here, however, as the national law of Member States reveals considerable structural differences with regard to the transformation of these requirements of European law. This already

---

13 *Cf.* with regard to the interrelationship and the mutual dependence in particular *e.g.* KÖHLER, in: HEFERMEHL, KÖHLER & BORNKAMM (eds.), *supra* note 1, at Intro., note 6.11 *et seq.*; BRÜNING, in: HARTE & HENNING (eds.), *supra* note 1, at Intro. F, note 125; OHLY, in: PIPER & OHLY, "Gesetz gegen den unlauteren Wettbewerb, Kommentar" Intro. note 72 *et seq.* (4th ed. 2006); *cf. also* KÖHLER, 2005 WRP 645 *et seq.*, in particular 646 and 653; FEZER, *supra* note 9, at 999; GLÖCKNER, *supra* note 9, 204 *et seq.*

14 KOITEL, "Neues im estnischen Kartellgesetz," 2002 WIRO 334 *et seq.*; as well as ENGELBREKT, in: HARTE & HENNING (eds.), *supra* note 1, at Intro. E, note 72 *et seq.*; HENNING-BODEWIG, "Unfair Competition Law" at 101 *et seq.*, with additional references, (2006).

15 VIDA, "Anpassung des ungarischen Marken- und Wettbewerbsrechts an das Europarecht," 2001 WIRO 172 *et seq.*; as well as ENGELBREKT, in: HARTE & HENNING (eds.), *supra* note 1, at Intro. E, note 709 *et seq.*; HENNING-BODEWIG, *supra* note 14, at 157 *et seq.*, with additional references.

16 In this regard *e.g.* EISFELD, "Lettisches Wettbewerbs- und Kartellrecht," 2004 WIRO 325 *et seq.*; as well as ENGELBREKT, in: HARTE & HENNING (eds), *supra* note 1, at Intro. E, note 330 *et seq.*; HENNING-BODEWIG, *supra* note 14, at 183 *et seq.*, with additional references.

17 ENGELBREKT, in: HARTE & HENNING (eds.), *supra* note 1, at Intro. E, note 351 *et seq.*; HENNING-BODEWIG, *id.*, at 187 *et seq.*, with additional references.

18 *Cf.* in this regard FEZER, in: FEZER (ed.), "Lauterkeitsrecht, Kommentar zum UWG" Intro. E, note 39 *et seq.*, in particular 41, Vol. 1 (2005); GLÖCKNER, *supra* note 9, at 216; KEßLER, "Vom Recht des unlauteren Wettbewerbs zum Recht der Marktkommunikation," 2005 WRP 1204 *et seq.*; OHLY, in: PIPER & OHLY, *supra* note 13, Intro. note 71 *et seq.*; *see also* the references in *supra* note 13.

follows from the fact that a "law against unfair competition" in the strict sense – which in itself can constitute an important source for concerns related to consumer protection – formally does not exist in certain Member States whereas special laws may govern specific sets of facts. But also in Member States which do dispose of a "law against unfair competition" in a formal sense, consumer protection law may to a greater or lesser extent be regulated as a separate field of law or may selectively be placed in a context with other legal subject matters (e.g. the general law of obligations).[19]

These formal differences in the law of Member States do not change the fact, however, that European consumer protection law, from the viewpoint of substantial law, has already experienced a far-reaching harmonisation, most recently by virtue of the Unfair Commercial Practices Directive.[20] Against this background, with a view to a European law of market behaviour as a whole, also the component of a consumer protection law will not be discussed in detail in the following. At the same time, however, the legal situation of the consumer may generally not be ignored altogether in the present case. For, the consumer plays a significant role in the context of those aspects, encompassed here by "the law against unfair competition", also beyond his immediate need for protection, as he is affected by every form of market behaviour law, at any rate potentially, even if such is directed at the behaviour among competitors.[21]

---

[19] *Cf.* in regard to the developments in particular HENNING-BODEWIG, "Das europäische Wettbewerbsrecht: Eine Zwischenbilanz," 2002 GRUR Int. 391; SCHRICKER & HENNING-BODEWIG, "Elemente einer Harmonisierung des Rechts des unlauteren Wettbewerbs in der Europäischen Union," 2001 WRP 1368; *see also* previously SCHRICKER, "Unlauterer Wettbewerb und Verbraucherschutz," 1970 GRUR Int. 32 *et seq.*; GLÖCKNER, *supra* note 9, 147 *et seq.*; in detail with regard to German law also BEATER, "Verbraucherschutz und Schutzzweckdenken im Wettbewerbsrecht" (2000).

[20] Directive 2005/29 of May 11, 2005 concerning unfair business-to-consumer commercial practices in the internal market and amending Council Directive 84/450/EEC, Directives 97/7, 98/27 and 2002/65 and Regulation No. 2006/2004 (Unfair Commercial Practices Directive), OJ L 149 from June 11, 2005, at 22 *et seq.*; *see also* in this volume SCHUHMACHER; generally with regard to harmonisation by virtue of Community law in the sphere of consumer protection law *e.g.* FEZER, 2001 WRP 989 *et seq.*, in particular 991.

[21] *See* with regard to the fact that the aims protected exist side by side and rank equally – which, in the final analysis, follows from the subject matter itself, and not only concerning cases, where all relevant interests worthy of protection are reflected in one uniform legal act – (so-called "integrated model" in the sense of a "trias of protected aims"), in particular *e.g.* KÖHLER, in: HEFERMEHL, KÖHLER & BORNKAMM (eds.), *supra* note 1, at Sec. 1, note 40; HENNING-BODEWIG & SCHRICKER, "Stellungnahme des Max-Planck-Instituts für ausländisches und internationales Patent-, Urheber und Wettbewerbsrechts zum Grünbuch zum Verbraucherschutz in der EU KOM (2002) 531 endg.," 2002 GRUR Int. 320; GAMERITH, "Neue Herausforderungen für ein europäisches Lauterkeitsrecht," 2003 WRP 162; GLÖCKNER, *supra* note 9, 447 *et seq.*; BEATER, "Europäisches Recht gegen unlauteren Wettbewerb – Ansatzpunkte, Grundlagen, Entwicklung, Erforderlichkeit," 2003 ZEuP 11 *et seq.*, in particular 48; by the same author, *supra* note 1, at Sec. 13, note 14; focusing rather more on consumer protection KEẞLER & MICKLITZ, "Die Harmonisierung des Lauterkeitsrechts in den Mitgliedstaaten der Europäischen Gemeinschaft und die Reform des UWG" 16 *et seq.* (2003).

If one attempts to define the field in which a justification is sought for statutory provisions in a positive sense, however, this concerns the body of law which deals with the competitive behaviour of "normal" (i.e. non-market-dominating) individual competitors amongst each other. In what follows, this body of law will be termed "the legal protection of the competitor" ("Recht des Wettbewerbers"; "droit du concurrent"). This theoretical approach of the legal protection of the competitor will be understood as one component of the whole of the law of market behaviour. In accordance with what has been said, the core of this component does not cover the behaviour of the individual competitor *vis-à-vis* consumers (even if the legal protection of the competitor impacts indirectly beneficially on consumers, e.g. based on intensifying effects on competition). Likewise, the particularities of antitrust law are not involved.

3. Justification of the Legal Protection of the Competitor

3.1 Overview of the National Law of EU Member States

If one proceeds from the principle mentioned at the very beginning – that the intervention of the legislator in the market forces of free competition in a constitutional state ("Rechtsstaat"), committed to liberal values, requires a specific justification – this suggests a cursory view of the objectives of those legal provisions presently existing in EU Member States, which are essentially directed at regulating behaviour in competition. Those legal provisions may be deemed to be the component defined here as the legal protection of the competitor. Admittedly, in view of the difficulty of comparing national provisions, the division into fixed categories may appear questionable in this regard, as the different fields are conceived structurally in very different ways, especially with respect to the distinction between the legal protection of the competitor on the one hand and consumer protection law on the other. Even so, one may tentatively discern about three groups:[22]

- The first group of national legal systems has developed in such a way as to emphasise the same objective of preventing unfair competition (unlauterer Wettbewerb; concurrence déloyale) as pursued by Art. 10*bis* Paris Convention, however, using varying terminology. Unfair competition is understood as an "act of competition contrary to honest practices in industrial or commercial matters" (Para. 2; "ein Zuwiderhandeln gegen die anständigen Gepflogenheiten in Ge-

[22] *Cf.* for details the country reports of HENNING-BODEWIG, *supra* note 14, at 69 *et seq.*, with additional references; GLÖCKNER, *supra* note 9, 331 *et seq.* and 341 *et seq.*; SCHRICKER & HENNING-BODEWIG, *supra* note 19, at 1367 *et seq.*, in particular 1379 *et seq.*; MICKLITZ & KEßLER, "Europäisches Lauterkeitsrecht – Dogmatische und ökonomische Aspekte einer Harmonisierung des Wettbewerbsverhaltensrechts im europäischen Binnenmarkt," 2002 GRUR Int. 885 *et seq.*, in particular 894; by the same authors, "Funktionswandel des UWG," 2003 WRP 919 *et seq.*, in particular 928 *et seq.*; KEßLER & MICKLITZ, *supra* note 21, at 36 *et seq.*; SCHÜNEMANN, "'Unlauterkeit' in den Generalklauseln und Interessenabwägung nach neuem UWG," 2004 WRP 929.

werbe oder Handel"; "act de concurrence contraire aux usages honnêtes en matière industrielle ou commerciale"). This is the case in Belgium (Loi sur les Pratiques du Commerce, 1991), Denmark (Marketing Practices Act, 2005), Finland (Unfair Trade Practices Act, 1978), France (case law based on the Code Civil), Greece (Law against Unfair Competition, 1914), Italy (case law based on the Codice Civile), Luxemburg (Act to Regulate Certain Trade Practices and to Sanction Unfair Competition, 2002), the Netherlands (case law based on the Burgerlijk Wetboek), Poland (Act on the Combating of Unfair Competition, 1993), Portugal (Law regarding Industrial Property, 2003), Spain (Act against Unfair Competition, 1991) and Sweden (Marketing Practices Act, 1995).

- The second group of Member States places alongside the safeguarding of honest practices the objective of securing the institution of free competition – at least as well, sometimes even as their primary focus. This group (using different formulations) includes Austria (Act against Unfair Competition, 1984), Czechia (Commercial Code, on the basis of law of 1991), Estonia (Competition Act, 2001), Germany (Act against Unfair Competition, 2004), Hungary (Act on the Prohibition of Unfair and Restrictive Market Practices, 1996), Latvia (Competition Act, 2001), Lithuania (Competition Act, 1999), Slovakia (Commercial Code, on the basis of law of 1991) and Slovenia (Competition Act, 1993).
- Finally, the third group of Member States cannot be associated with a specific main objective, because several different objectives are being pursued by virtue of case law or a multitude of selective enactments. This is the case in Great Britain[23], Ireland, Malta as well as Cyprus.

If one enquires against this background as to *the protected subject matter* ("Schutzobjekt") within the component of the legal protection of the competitor, one will find two different aspects. On the one hand, the national legal provisions are primarily influenced by an ethical component, which appeals to the responsibility of market participants more or less clearly and which, at times, also has links with the concept of *bona fides*. On the other hand, a number of states also treat the institution of competition as such (sometimes in a rather indirect manner by reference to the subjects in need of protection) as a subject matter deserving protection.

If one enquires as to *the subjects in need of protection* ("Schutzsubjekte"), however, one will become aware of the extent to which the different fields of the law of market behaviour, viewed as a whole, overlap. For, despite the many differences between national approaches or different sets of facts considered within the context of the law of market behaviour, it remains noticeable that the interests of all

[23] *See* with regard to the torts of "passing off" and "malicious falsehood" essentially applicable in Great Britain, but also the provisions of criminal and public law in particular CORNISH & LLEWELYN, "Intellectual Property" notes 1-15 *et seq.* and 15-19 *et seq.* (5th ed. 2003); KITCHIN, "Kerly's law of trade marks and trade names" notes 14-65 *et seq.* (13th ed. 2001). *Cf.* in this regard also the overview in OHLY, "Richterrecht und Generalklausel im Recht des unlauteren Wettbewerbs" 19 *et seq.* (1997).

participants on the market are to be protected to the one or other degree. In other words, in most instances the interests of competitors and consumers, but where appropriate also those of the general public, are being mentioned explicitly in one form or another, often cumulatively, sometimes, however, also with different intensity.[24]

Such a pluralistic approach to protection is, in fact, also highly plausible from two perspectives: On the one hand, several of the stated interests can also be protected indirectly by protecting other interests; a separation would, therefore, be artificial. On the other hand, in all national bodies of rules certain fields overlap without visible contours, i.e. what is being termed the legal protection of the competitor here, understood as a theoretical approach, cannot be viewed as a self-contained body of legal rules.

For the sake of completeness it should be mentioned that with regard to the national law of the Member States a further distinction can be drawn which adds another dimension to what has been stated so far: that according to whether a competitive relationship ("*Wettbewerbsverhältnis*") is required for the applicability of a certain norm. In this regard, the majority does not, in fact, require such a competitive relationship (anymore) to affirm unfairness as such (regardless of the issue of a right of action); this is the case, for example, in Belgium, Czechia, Denmark, Germany, the Netherlands, Slovakia, Slovenia or Sweden. A smaller group of states, however, does require such a competitive relationship (e.g. Austria, France or Greece; also the majority of commentators in Spain), whereas, in a third group of states again, a clear classification is difficult, as this depends on the question of the facts of the case (for example in Luxemburg or Portugal).[25]

3.2 The Legal Protection of the Competitor in the Law of the European Community

If already this short overview of the national legal systems of EU Member States shows how heterogeneous the approaches still are, despite certain similarities or recurring features, this is no coincidence. Although the law of the European Community harmonises national competition law, as has already been mentioned, substantially with regard to consumer protection law (so far less in a structural than in a substantial sense though) as well as antitrust law, both as separate components of the law of market behaviour, one looks in vain – at least at first sight – for a regulation of the legal protection of the competitor in the strict sense in the context of the EU.

---

[24] *Cf.* in this regard the analyses in HENNING-BODEWIG, 2002 GRUR Int. 389 *et seq.*, in particular 391; by the same author, "Richtlinienvorschlag über unlautere Geschäftpraktiken und UWG-Reform," 2004 GRUR Int. 183 *et seq.*, in particular 189; SCHRICKER & HENNING-BODEWIG, 2001 WRP 1368; HENNING-BODEWIG & SCHRICKER, 2002 GRUR Int. 319 *et seq.*; BEATER, 2003 ZEuP 11 *et seq.*, in particular 46; KEßLER & MICKLITZ, *supra* note 21, at 38 *et seq.*

[25] Details are mentioned in the country reports in HARTE & HENNING (eds.), *supra* note 1, Intro. E, and HENNING-BODEWIG, *supra* note 14, at 69 *et seq.*, with additional references; SCHRICKER & HENNING-BODEWIG, 2001 WRP 1367 *et seq.*, in particular 1368.

This lacuna has, in fact, explicitly been admitted for the first time by the most recent Unfair Commercial Practices Directive,[26] although this Directive is once again directed at consumer protection law. Recital 6 proceeds to explain that, although such unfair commercial practices may indirectly also harm "the economic interests of legitimate competitors", the Directive does not affect "the national laws on unfair commercial practices which harm only competitors' economic interests or which relate to a transaction between traders". Recital 8 then recognises: "It is understood that there are other commercial practices which, although not harming consumers, may hurt competitors and business customers. The Commission should carefully examine the need for Community action in the field of unfair competition beyond the remit of this Directive and, if necessary, make a legislative proposal to cover these other aspects of unfair competition".

On closer scrutiny already this Directive, in a sense, fills a first gap, by obliging Member States in the second sentence of Art. 11 Para. 1 to ensure that effective means exist to combat unfair commercial practices, in terms of which "persons or organisations regarded under national law as having a legitimate interest in combating unfair commercial practices, including competitors" may take legal or administrative action. Nevertheless, the reason for this extension, which admittedly is significant from a practical point of view, is, of course, not really the protection of the competitor as such, but rather the ensuing protection of consumers. To this extent the Unfair Commercial Practices Directive therefore does not, at any rate yet, genuinely open the door to a legal protection of the competitor in the strict sense, as a third component within the law of market behaviour as a whole.[27]

The fact that a legal protection of the competitors does not exist so far in EU law – or, is being discussed for the first time whatsoever – gives rise to questions. For, in terms of Art. 3 Para. 1 (g) EC, the activities of the EU also cover "a system ensuring that competition in the internal market is not distorted". The probably prevailing interpretation is that this norm is primarily aimed at the legal activity of the Community in the field of antitrust law.[28] However, if one includes the preamble, paragraph 5 of which also requires "fair competition" to be guaranteed, there is no reason why the completely open-ended wording of Art. 3 Para. 1 (g) EC should not

[26] *Supra* note 20.

[27] With regard to the discussion of the Directive, specifically of the significance of the scope of application having been limited to B2C practices, *see* HENNING-BODEWIG, "Die Richtlinie 2005/29/EG über unlautere Geschäftspraktiken," 2005 GRUR Int. 629 *et seq.*; by the same author, 2004 GRUR Int. 183 *et seq.*, in particular 189; KÖHLER, with regard to the implementation of the Unfair Commercial Practices Directive, 2005 GRUR 793 *et seq.*; GAMERITH, 2003 WRP 162; GLÖCKNER, *supra* note 9, 69 *et seq.*; *see also* in this volume SCHUHMACHER. Generally with regard to Community law against the background of the new German Law Against Unfair Competition, LETTL, "Gemeinschaftsrecht und neues UWG," 2004 WRP 1079 *et seq.*

[28] *Cf. e.g.* ZULEEG, in: VON DER GROEBEN & SCHWARZE (eds.), "Vertrag über die Europäische Union und Vertrag zur Gründung der Europäischen Gemeinschaft" EG 3, note 8 (6th ed. 2003); UKROW, in: CALLIES & RUFFERT, "Kommentar des Vertrages über die Europäische Union und des Vertrages zur Gründung der Europäischen Gemeinschaft – EUV/EG" EG 3 N 11 (2nd ed. 2002); GLÖCKNER, *supra* note 9, 16 *et seq.*

also be understood as being aimed at the law against unfair competition.[29] Especially if one considers how heterogeneous the national approaches of Member States presently are, it is – against the background that it is undisputed that competition cannot only be distorted through collusion and market power, but also through individual acts directed against specific competitors – difficult not to see that the EU has failed to adequately promote the further development of the existing primary law on the level of secondary law. As a matter of fact, it is clearly evident, for instance, with regard to the free movement of goods and services sought to be realised that different national legal conceptions as to permissible and non-permissible commercial activity substantially threaten a uniform internal market. The reasons for this lethargy are particularly worrisome in this respect: the two fields of competence existing within the Commission – the Directorate-General Consumer Protection and the Directorate-General Internal Market – which until now have not co-operated in a meaningful manner.[30]

3.3 European Harmonisation versus National Legal Protection of the Competitor

At first sight, it may appear contradictory if, on the one hand, European primary law is directed at ensuring that competition in the internal market is not distorted, but, on the other hand, a majority of all those national legal provisions which may be considered at least fragments of the legal protection of the competitor focuses on the honest practices as understood in Art. 10*bis* Paris Convention. The truth, however, rather is that this delimitation shows the way for a possible future development of European law.

In fact, a dual approach to protection is conceivable:

- The question as to whether competition is being distorted as understood in Art. 3 Para. 1 (g) EC, like the analogous question in the field of antitrust law, requires an appraisal of the market behaviour in terms of the facts of the case. The answer to this question depends on the criteria, defined as being applicable to the appraisal of the market behaviour. If one lays down uniform, objective criteria, however, to appraise the circumstances of the individual case,[31] the answer to the question of distortion of competition will ultimately not depend on national or culturally-

[29] *See also* ZULEEG (*id.*), EG 3 N 8, also referring to the preamble of the EC Treaty; SCHÜNEMANN, in: HARTE/HENNING (eds.), *supra* note 1, at Sec. 3, notes 95 and 118 *et seq.*

[30] For details, *see* HENNING-BODEWIG, 2002 GRUR Int. 395 *et seq.*; MICKLITZ & KESSLER, 2002 GRUR Int. 891 *et seq.*

[31] Article 2 (h) of the Unfair Commercial Practices Directive, *supra* note 20 does not constitute a successful attempt at laying down such criteria (*cf.* with regard to the even less successful formulation attempt in the proposal for the directive also SCHÜNEMANN, in: HARTE & HENNING (eds.), *supra* note 1, at Sec. 3, note 95; in terms thereof "professional diligence" means "the standard of special skill and care which a trader may reasonably be expected to exercise towards consumers, commensurate with honest market practice and/or the general principle of good faith in the trader's field of activity". Although this makes it clear that not only actual forms of behaviour are decisive but also normative criteria, it is not clear, however, how the reference system is to be chosen. It would not be acceptable at any rate for the addressees of the norms themselves to

specific factors, but may principally be given in a value neutral, i.e. objective, manner.

As a matter of fact, a harmonisation of national law by means of European law is primarily conceivable to the extent that the establishment of the internal market stands in the foreground, as envisaged in Art. 14 EC.[32] Viewed from this angle, an intervention in purely domestic constellations would be impermissible by virtue of the principles of subsidiarity and of proportionality (Art. 5 Para. 2 EC). This would even be the case, if the market behaviour, in fact, distorts competition on the national level; it is not for European law to intervene in this situation.

From a practical point of view, however, such distortions of competition on a strictly national level will occur exceptionally only. This is so as in the sphere of competition law the conflict of laws question as to the applicable law is based upon the so-called "effects doctrine" ("Auswirkungsprinzip"; "Marktortprinzip"),[33] which means that in a majority of cases there exists (at least potentially)

---

decide on which norms of competition law regulating market behaviour should be applicable to them, as the system of free and undistorted competition (Art. 3 Para. 1 (g) and Art. 4 Para. 1 EC) is not such that it can be at the free disposition of the market participants (SCHÜNEMANN, *ibidem*, Sec. 3, note 118 *et seq.*; critical also HENNING & BODEWIG, 2005 GRUR Int 631; less critical against the background of the objective of consumer protection KEßLER & MICKLITZ, "Die Richtlinie 2005/29/EG über unlautere Geschäftspraktiken im binnenmarktinternen Geschäftsverkehr zwischen Unternehmen und Verbrauchern," 49 Special zu BB 1 *et seq.*, in particular 14 (2005)).

32 *Cf. also* in this regard generally REICH, "Binnenmarkt als Rechtsbegriff," 1991 EuZW 203 *et seq.*

33 Otherwise than in the case of antitrust law, most Member States in the sphere of the law against unfair competition base the competition law connecting factor on the "Marktortprinzip" (the law of the country where the market is affected by the unfair competition act in question); *see e.g.* LETTL, 2004 WRP 1086; DREXL, in: REBMANN, SÄCKER & RIXECKER (eds.; editor: SONNENBERGER), "Münchener Kommentar zum Bürgerlichen Gesetzbuch," Vol. 11, "Internationales Wirtschaftsrecht, Einführungsgesetz zum Bürgerlichen Gesetzbuche (Arts. 50-245)" IntUnlWettbR, note 3 (4th ed. 2006). This has now also been laid down in Art. 6 of the planned Regulation on the Law Applicable to Non-Contractual Obligations ("ROME II" – *see* Common Position (EC) No. 22/2006, OJ C 289E/68 of November 28, 2006), which envisages to apply to non-contractual obligations arising out of an act of unfair competition the law of the country where competitive relations or the collective interests of consumers are or are likely to be directly and substantially affected.

It is disputed whether the "effects doctrine" ("Auswirkungsprinzip") internationally predominant in the sphere of antitrust law should also be applicable to the law against unfair competition; *see* in this regard *e.g.* GLÖCKNER, *supra* note 9, 294 *et seq.*, who argues that the "effects doctrine" – as a principle governing international commercial law as a whole (and also laid down in Art. 7 of the Rome II Regulation) – should also apply to the law against unfair competition, and, on the other hand, DREXL, *ibidem*, note 11 *et seq.*, who, in view of the functionality of both areas of law, prefers, as regards the outcome, to retain the separate connection to the "Marktortprinzip" and the focus on illegally causing a certain effect in the market. Both concede, however, that both approaches in practice often lead to the same results.

Cf. with regard to the conflict of laws question further SÄCKER, "Das UWG zwischen den Mühlsteinen europäischer Harmonisierung und grundrechtsgebotener Liberalisierung," 2004 WRP 1200; LEISTNER, "Comments: The Rome II Regulation Proposal and its Relation to the European Country-of-Origin Principle," in: DREXL & KUR (eds.), "Intellectual Property and

the element of transnationality, required for the applicability of European law. To such cases of a transnational character those legal rules must be applied which are directed at ensuring that competition is not distorted. Although these legal rules derive from national law, they (may) have been harmonised by European law. Consequently, this harmonisation has an influence on strictly national cases as well. In fact, it lies in the interest of the national legislator to apply corresponding rules also to purely national cases, as it would otherwise, in the case of less far-reaching rules of market behaviour, place local competitors at a disadvantage compared to foreign competitors.

- Alongside such a European harmonised legal protection of the competitor, based upon a value neutral, objective appraisal of a market distortion, Member States remain free cumulatively also to take account of culturally-specific differences and particularities. Nevertheless, this may not impair the internal market order in a non-justifiable way;[34] in particular, the application of the law may not thereby become burdened with what, in fact, are improper moral or ethical aspects, from which it is impossible to deduce a meaningful yardstick of competition law for the appraisal of commercial practices.[35]

If national regulations remain within these boundaries, however, it would not be out of place for Member States to uphold special ethical values and to integrate

---

Private International Law" 177 (2005); by the same author, "Unfair Competition Law Protection against Imitations: A Hybrid under the Future Art. 5 Rom II Regulation?," in: BASEDOW, DREXL, KUR & METZGER (eds.), "Intellectual Property in the Conflict of Laws" 129 *et seq.* (2005); GLÖCKNER, in: HARTE & HENNING (eds.), *supra* note 1, at Intro. C, note 1 *et seq.*; KÖHLER, in: HEFERMEHL, KÖHLER & BORNKAMM (eds.), *supra* note 1, at Intro., note 5.1 *et seq.*; BUCHNER, "Rom II und das Internationale Immaterialgüter- und Wettbewerbsrecht," 2005 GRUR Int. 1004 *et seq.*; MANKOWSKI, "Was soll der Anknüpfungsgegenstand des (europäischen) Internationalen Wettbewerbsrechts sein?," 2005 GRUR Int. 634 *et seq.*; PIEPENBROCK, "Die Bedeutung des Herkunftslandprinzips im europäischen Wettbewerbsrecht," 2005 GRUR Int. 997 *et seq.*

[34] In this sense also FEZER, 2001 WRP 993; more cautious STEINDORFF, "Unlauterer Wettbewerb im System des EG-Rechts," 1993 WRP 150; apparently also SÄCKER, 2004 WRP 1200, who emphasises the simplification and greater legal certainty and transparency and, therefore, the "reduction of market entry costs induced by the law", to be achieved only by virtue of a harmonisation of the European law against unfair competition; "a teleological expansive force of European law" followed therefrom, which was also reflected in the steady displacement of the statute of market success ("Markterfolgsstatut") in the law against unfair competition by the country of origin principle (translation).

[35] In this sense justifiably critical BEATER, 2003 ZEuP 45, referring to ADAM SMITH, "An Inquiry into the Nature and Causes of the Wealth of Nations" (1st ed., 1776, reprint Hackett Publishing Company 1993, at 11 (quoted from BEATER) respectively reprint The University of Chicago Press, 1976, at 18): "Competition combines two opposing factors with each other, namely behaviour guided by self-interest and the general welfare, and is based on the paradox that the strict orientation of the individual by egotistical motives may have effects which benefit all. It is not the altruism or the benevolence of the baker which makes him get up during the night and has the effect that we are able to buy fresh bread and fresh rolls every day. Consequently, ideas of morality can also not be an appropriate measure to properly assess processes in competition in legal terms" (translation).

them in their national law of market behaviour applicable within their national borders. This already follows from Art. 30 EC, in terms of which prohibitions or restrictions on imports, exports or goods in transit are permissible, if they can be justified "on grounds of public morality, public policy or public security". Also the Unfair Commercial Practices Directive thus correctly states that a European regulation should and cannot address "legal requirements related to taste and decency which vary widely among the Member States" (Recital 7). It would, as a matter of fact, also appear illusory and out of place to even think of a European harmonisation of such ethical, and often also emotional, values.[36]

The idea in Recital 13 of the Unfair Commercial Practices Directive admittedly does not fit well with this approach; in terms thereof, "in order to achieve the Community's objectives through the removal of internal market barriers, it is necessary to replace Member States' existing, divergent general clauses and legal principles". This statement can only be understood to mean that the national law of market behaviour – specifically within the context of the legal protection of the competitor, presently of interest – must (beyond the ethical approach of Art. 10*bis* Paris Convention) serve to prevent cross-border distortions of competition as understood in Art. 3 Para. 1 (g) EC, too.[37]

The dual approach to protection, therefore, does not imply that the European harmonisation of the law would absolve a competitor entering on a foreign market from becoming acquainted with the culturally-specific particularities of that market. In fact, the interest of the market participants in being able to uphold certain national ethical principles within the national market should weigh higher than synchronising such values at the European level, at least in those cases where there exist factual

---

[36] In support of drawing a clear line between the "economically founded claim to universality of the concept of unfairness and national morals" also KEẞLER & MICKLITZ, 49 Special zu BB 1 *et seq.*, in particular 13 (2005), ("The reference system for determining unfairness derives from the economic constitution of the EU, that for morals from the relevant national context" (translation)).

[37] Also against a mandatory obligation of Member States to adopt the general clause of Art. 5 of the Directive, referring to the requirements of "professional diligence", SOSNITZA, "Die Richtlinie über unlautere Geschäftspraktiken – Voll oder Teilharmonisierung?," 2006 WRP 6 *et seq.*; HENNING-BODEWIG, "Das neue UWG – von Brüsseler Gnaden?," in: OHLY, ET AL. (eds.), "FS Schricker" 710 *et seq.* (2005); HENNING-BODEWIG & GLÖCKNER, "EG-Richtlinie über unlautere Geschäftspraktiken: Was wird aus dem "neuen" UWG?," 2005 WRP 1327 *et seq.*; SEICHTER, "Der Umsetzungsbedarf der Richtlinie über unlautere Geschäftspraktiken," 2005 WRP 1090 *et seq.*; in this sense already with regard to the proposal for the directive HENNING-BODEWIG, "Richtlinienvorschlag über unlautere Geschäftspraktiken und UWG-Reform," 2004 GRUR Int. 190 *et seq.*; for Austria GAMERITH, "Der Richtlinienvorschlag über unlautere Geschäftspraktiken – Möglichkeiten einer harmonischen Umsetzung," 2005 WRP 430 *et seq.* In contrast, arguing in support of an adoption KÖHLER & LETTL, "Das geltende europäische Lauterkeitsrecht, der Vorschlag für eine EG-Richtlinie über unlautere Geschäftspraktiken und die UWG-Reform," 2003 WRP 1050 *et seq.*; also KÖHLER, "Zur Umsetzung der Richtlinie über unlautere Geschäftspraktiken," 2005 GRUR 796; LETTL, 2004 WRP 1089; VEELKEN, "Kundenfang gegenüber dem Verbraucher – Bemerkungen zum EG-Richtlinienentwurf über unlautere Geschäftspraktiken," 2004 WRP 17.

reasons for such differences. Nevertheless, in the case of this dual approach, a competitor may assume – otherwise than is the situation presently – that he will be protected in every part of the European internal market against the behaviour of another competitor distorting competition.

In summary, it may be stated that the required primary law basis for harmonising the national laws for a legal protection of the competitor exists in so far as this harmonisation aims at eliminating distortions of competition in a value neutral, objective sense. Any such harmonisation does not constitute an unjustified interference in the national law of market behaviour, seeing that national law is at most supplemented by the harmonisation in the case that the objective to prevent market distortions has not yet been realised within the national law. Beyond this, it does not constitute an interference with those national values concerning ethical market behaviour which Member States may legitimately wish to uphold.

3.4 Justifying a European Legal Protection of the Competitor

If we are concerned here with the perspectives of the European law of market behaviour, then, against the background of what has been stated above, the question arises in which circumstances a market distortion in an objective sense may be stated to exist, which, where appropriate, justifies an intervention in the market forces of free competition.

This question is of an exceptional complexity, as it has seldom been raised in this form in an abstract sense with regard to what is customarily termed the law against unfair competition (otherwise than in the case of antitrust law). It can, therefore, also not be the intention here to already provide a sophisticated answer. A number of guiding principles should rather be discussed. Proceeding from these guiding principles it appears of interest then to enquire to what extent existing European law already today accommodates the idea – if also (purportedly) not in the context of competition law – that distortions of competition (also beyond antitrust law) should be dealt with.

As to the question when undesired distortions of competition occur two narrowly related key words will be used in the following: on the one hand that of *investment* (in a wide sense, yet to be defined), on the other hand that of *amortisation* in the form of a "return on investment". For, it is evident that a participant in competition will only be willing to invest to the extent that he will in all probability be in a position to amortise the investment made – and, beyond that, to make a profit which seems worthwhile to him. Likewise, it is clear that there must be some point beyond which it is legitimate for legal norms safeguarding such an adequate amortisation to apply, to ensure that sufficient investments are made whatsoever. The question, however, is where this point lies.

This question needs to be answered with a large measure of self-restraint if – as has already been presumed in the introduction – the point of departure is a constitutional state ("Rechtsstaat"), committed to liberal ideas. This is even truer if one considers that the positive effects flowing from the preferably unrestrained functioning of the market forces of free competition are only one side of the coin of a liberal constitutional state. The other exists in the risk of the individual competitor to assess and make use of these forces wrongly. Or stated differently: It is a consequence of the liberal approach that the legal system may not be instrumentalised to absorb the consequences of individual behaviour which has not been successful – on the contrary: Functioning, dynamic and undistorted competition is actually characterised by the fact that competitors, who are unable to market their products effectively, disappear from the market. To ensure that the system of competition yields positive effects for all participants in the long term, only that participant who is able to assert himself sufficiently effectively may "survive" in the long run. If the law were to interfere with such market adjustment processes, i.e. if every investment entailed "a guarantee of amortisation", it would exceed what is justifiable in view of the objective mentioned by way of introduction: The law of market behaviour may only be aimed at preventing a (permanent) failure of the market itself – but, it may not prevent individual competitors from (necessarily) being squeezed out of the market, as only this leads to the continuous innovation desired.[38] On the other hand, competition is not free anymore if, for example, on the basis of moral considerations, it is required that there must exist equality between rivals, and the attempt of an individual competitor to secure an individual advantage for himself is held to be impermissible in terms of competition law.[39] Likewise, it would be contrary to a liberal conception of competition to consider acts of imitation as negative *per se*; for, imitations principally are an indispensable element in the market process, so as to achieve a reduction of those "special profits", which may regularly be made during the first phase in which the innovator enjoys a natural position of dominance. Only a successive increase in the volume of supply will lead to a level of "normal profits".[40]

This principle, however, is not applicable anymore – and an intervention of the law in the market forces of free competition turns out to be justifiable –,

- if an individual competitor A, in terms of value neutral, objective considerations, makes an investment in such a way as can be expected of him in the light of all the circumstances,

[38] In the same sense, defining competition as "a process of selection" *e.g.* KÖHLER, in: HEFERMEHL, KÖHLER & BORNKAMM, *supra* note 1, at Intro., notes 1.21, 1.22; KIRCHNER, "Innovationsschutz und Investitionsschutz für immaterielle Güter," 2004 GRUR Int. 604 *et seq.* (competition as "a continuous process of creative destruction"); BEATER, *supra* note 1, at Sec. 2, note 13 as well as Sec. 17, note 1, and Sec. 22, notes 3 and 38; the reference of Beater to the "adjudicator function" of consumers and commercial customers (Sec. 17, note 1) is, of course, rejected by SCHÜNEMANN, in: HARTE & HENNING (eds.), *supra* note 1, at Sec. 1, note 11 (*see supra* note 28), because competition would thereby be reduced to "a process between rivals". *See also* BEATER, *supra* note 1, at Sec. 22, note 19 as well as Sec. 1, note 76, referring to the discrepancy of case law between the constant emphasis on freedom of competition and the protection actually granted (in particular in the form of so-called "*ergänzender wettbewerbsrechtlicher Leistungsschutz*" ("supplementary protection of achievement under competition law"); *see also* in this regard OHLY, *supra* note 47.

[39] BEATER, *supra* note 1, at Sec. 2, note 14 *et seq.*, referring to a distribution of income "appropriately related to performance"; WEIHRAUCH, *supra* note 8, at 240.

[40] BEATER, *supra* note 1, at Sec. 24, note 32; WEIHRAUCH, *supra* note 8, at 170 *et seq.*; for a similar conclusion KIRCHNER, *supra* note 38, at 604 *et seq.*

- but, because of the particular market behaviour (to be defined below) of a competitor B he is unable to amortise his investment adequately.

Such a particular market behaviour may – still considered in the abstract – be assumed if competitor B by virtue of the investments made by A is able to save on his own investments, with the result that he can arrive at a comparable product as A at lower costs, which he can also offer on the market at a correspondingly lower price than A. For, in this situation, A will either attempt to enforce the (with a view to the amortisation necessarily) higher price, or he will adapt the price to that of B. In both cases – not taking into account other relevant factors, such as, for example, differences in quality – he will thus probably not be able anymore to amortise his investments; in the first case, because he will not be able to sell enough products, in the second, because the sum of the insufficient income per unit will not cover the overall expenses incurred.

From a practical point of view, not every investment is equally suited, of course, to be taken over and utilised in competition by a third party. This rather concerns specific constellations, which – as will still be shown – are also not completely unfamiliar to existing law. Typically, they exist if competitor A does not have enough time until competitor B can operate on the market[41] – consequently then, when taking over the investment can take place, for example, by simple technical means.

If such a constellation exists, the danger of a distortion of competition appears, at least, plausible. This is so as the consequence of such a taking over of another's investments within a short period of time typically will be that

- competitor A who made the investment first will withdraw from the relevant market permanently when he considers that no possibility of an amortisation exists anymore, with the result that
- the price competition, which evolved temporarily between A and competitor B, who took over the investment, disappears again (the product in question thus being sold at a higher price by B from the moment he acquires a position of dominance), whereas
- B typically will not invest in the product in question himself.[42]

At first sight, one could assume at this point – adopting a long-term perspective – that, at some stage, the demand of the market would again lead to a new competitor C recognising the opportunity of making a profit by investing in the product not developed further since. It appears questionable, however, whether such a long-term correction of a market failure (which exists here because B squeezed A out of the market without a reasonable justification[43]) by virtue of the market's own forces –

[41] BEATER, *supra* note 1, at Sec. 22, note 36, and Sec. 24, note 43; SAMBUC, in: HARTE & HENNING (eds.), *supra* note 1, at Intro. F, at note 548; in more detail in this regard WEIHRAUCH, *supra* note 8, at 192 *et seq.*

[42] *Cf.* in more depth with regard to these mechanisms and the different phases of innovation (or investment) and imitation in particular WEIHRAUCH, *supra* note 8, at 170 *et seq.*

[43] With regard to the concept of a market failure as such, *see supra* note 1.

i.e. the new appearance of C on the market – makes sense. For, on the one hand, it is questionable whether such a new competitor C can be found whatsoever, if he has knowledge of "the preceding events" (especially the prospectively insufficient period of assessment); one needs to appreciate the danger, therefore, that he will, in all likelihood – without adequate legal measures offering him protection – lack the incentive to make the investments which need to be made right from the instance.[44] On the other hand, when adopting such a long-term perspective one would – without being able to give a concrete answer here – do well to enquire as to the overall costs entailed for the economy in case of an accumulation of such unregulated processes of squeezing competitors out of the market.

The guiding principles for the legal protection of the competitor may thus – still considered in the abstract – be summarised in more or less the following way: An intervention of the law in the market forces of free competition aimed at preventing market distortions is justified when a competitor, despite objectively reasonable market behaviour, in particular meaningful own investments, is squeezed out of the market as a result of the specific behaviour of another competitor, in the sense that the investments made by the first competitor can be utilised too early or at too low a cost, and where a market failure follows from this fact in such a way that the first competitor is not willing anymore to invest in the relevant market. If these conditions are not met, competition law may not intervene in the market forces of free competition; in this case, the principle of "the advantage of the first mover" must rather be a sufficient incentive to invest in the market, in order to make a worthwhile profit by acting strategically and especially by exploiting the naturally existing time lead one has over lagging competitors.

These considerations show that the legal protection of the competitor, guided by the basic idea of protecting the institution of competition against distortions, must essentially lie in the nature of a set of legal measures directed at protecting certain investments.[45] It may well be that from a national perspective, the law of market behaviour in general – and the legal protection of the competitor in particular – is also directed at realising other (e.g. ethical) values, beyond such aspects concerning the legal protection of investments. These approaches will, however, not be discussed here, seeing that a harmonisation by virtue of European law must, in terms of what has been stated above, remain restricted to preventing objective distortions of competition from the outset.

4. The Protection of Investments in Terms of the Legal Protection of the Competitor

4.1 The Nature of the Field of the Protection of Investments

To most national competition law systems, the idea of the protection of investments as such is not completely unfamiliar. Cases of exploitation of reputation for example

---

[44] BEATER, *supra* note 1, at Sec. 22, note 38, and Sec. 24, note 43.

[45] *See also* BEATER, *supra* note 1, at Sec. 22, note 14.

typically concern constellations in which investments in a lasting positive image are required; in one way or another they are covered in every EU Member State. What differs are only the reasons advanced, by emphasising an ethical line of reasoning in most cases. In certain countries, however, the rationale of a distortion of competition through exploitation of reputation plays a role as well, at least in the light of the general purpose of the legal provisions in question. In fact, in terms of what has been stated,[46] such distortion of competition can constitute the sole justification for a harmonisation at the level of European law.

But also the investment in a more narrow sense – namely that in a product to be marketed – is in certain national legal systems or, at any rate, in terms of case law, regarded as a subject matter worthy of protection. Of course, not only do the terms used vary widely, but also the requirements. In fact, a look at the requirements unmasks quite some of the applicable national provisions on closer scrutiny as forms of intellectual property rights.[47] When it is thus required, for example – as it is in Germany for instance – that a specific product must show a special "wettbewerbliche Eigenart" ("commercial distinctiveness of the product"),[48] on the one hand, and that an imitated product be designed in a similar way (in a way which is

---

[46] *Supra* 3.4.

[47] Critically with regard to the "ergänzender wettbewerbsrechtlicher Leistungsschutz" ("supplementary protection of achievement under competition law") *e.g.* OHLY, "Gibt es einen Numerus clausus der Immaterialgüterrechte?," in: "FS Schricker", *supra* note 37, at 110 *et seq.*, with additional references, in particular in *supra* notes 37 and 38; SAMBUC, in: HARTE & HENNING (eds.), *supra* note 1, at Intro. F, note 212; BEATER, *supra* note 1, at Sec. 22, notes 16 and 18 *et seq.* and Sec. 1, note 76; *see also* WEIHRAUCH, *supra* note 8, at 240; *cf. e.g.* with regard to the question – in its answer to be denied, however – whether the Swiss Art. 5 (c) UWG has the character of a genuine right aimed at the protection of achievements, HILTY, "'Leistungsschutz' made in Switzerland?," in: AHRENS ET AL. (eds.), "FS Ullmann" (2006), at 643 *et seq.*, with additional references, also with regard to the relevant discussion in Germany (in particular notes 2, 5 and 6).

[48] With regard to the concept of "*wettbewerbliche Eigenart*" *e.g.* KUR, "Der wettbewerbliche Leistungsschutz – Gedanken zum wettbewerbsrechtlichen Schutz von Formgebungen, bekannten Marken und 'Characters'," 1990 GRUR 7 *et seq.*; SAMBUC, "Die Eigenart der 'wettbewerblichen Eigenart' – Bemerkungen zum Nachahmungsschutz von Arbeitsergebnissen durch § 1 UWG," 1986 GRUR 130 *et seq.*; by the same author in: HARTE & HENNING (eds.), *supra* note 1, Sec. 4, note 47 *et seq.*; KÖHLER, in: HEFERMEHL, KÖHLER & BORNKAMM (eds.), *supra* note 1, Sec. 4, note 9.24 *et seq.*; with regard to the (double) function and scope of this concept in German law – namely as a concept of achievement ("Leistungsbegriff") and as a distinctive feature ("Erkennungsmerkmal") – in particular also WEIHRAUCH, *supra* note 8, at 52 *et seq.* (with regard to the latter it is stated that it delimits "potential objects of imitation from so-called commodities, mass-produced articles or relevant ordinary goods. The nature of the '*wettbewerbliche Eigenart*' here is determined by the fact that it does not itself serve as a criterion of bones mores ('Sittenwidrigkeit'). A decision on bones mores is based on weighing the particular circumstances which have their basis outside the product of achievement. The '*wettbewerbliche Eigenart*', as a requirement for determining whether these particular circumstances give rise to immorality, fulfils a function of assistance and an exclusionary function." [translation]).

likely to confuse), on the other,[49] this goes to show that, in the end, what one deals with is an attempt to afford protection to the product concerned, similar to the protection granted, for instance, by design law or (based on the sign) trade mark law.

In truth, the logic of the law of market behaviour does not allow that a "genuine" protection of investments depart directly from the quality of the product which is the result of an investment.[50] It must rather be asked whether the behaviour of the competitor taking over the investment (understood as described above[51]) is likely to squeeze the original competitor out of the market and whether this leads to a market failure in the long run. If this is not the case, an intervention of the legislator in the market forces of free competition is not justified.

As against this view from a purely competition law perspective, one is prima vista inclined to raise two arguments; on closer scrutiny they are not convincing, however:

- On the one hand, it may certainly also be asked whether the behaviour of the competitor who takes over the investment is not, in fact, simply unethical and for this reason not desirable. This is reflected in the requirement, for example, in terms of which a takeover must take place in a particularly reprehensible manner, by way of a slavish imitation etc. From a European perspective, however, in terms of which the legal basis is solely directed at the market distortion (Art. 3 Para. 1 (g) EC), such criteria, at any rate to the extent that they imply value judgements,[52] are not relevant. Consequently, only national law – if at all appro-

---

[49] In terms of settled case law it is well so that alongside "*wettbewerbliche Eigenart*" there must additionally exist special circumstances which make the imitation appear unfair, whereby "an interdependency exists between the degree of '*wettbewerbliche Eigenart*', the method and the intensity of a takeover as well as their particular competition circumstances. The greater the '*wettbewerbliche Eigenart*' and the higher the degree of a takeover, the fewer are the requirements concerning the particular circumstances, establishing the unfairness in competition of the imitation" (translation); in this sense *e.g.* BGH, July 12, 2001, I~ZR 40/99, 2002 GRUR 86, 89, with additional references – *Laubhefter*; SAMBUC, in: HARTE/HENNING (eds.), *supra* note 1, at Sec. 4, note 6 *et seq.*, in particular 29, justifiably refers to the fact, however, that "not only the modalities and circumstances accompanying an imitation may contribute to a finding of unfairness, but at least also the quality of the imitated product which entailed an effort (the 'achievement')"(translation); he argues that the German Supreme Court mitigates the dogma of the purely behaviour-based conception of protection against imitations in terms of the Law Against Unfair Competition by precisely this system of interdependencies. *See also* KELLER, *supra* note 8, at 598; MÜLLER-LAUBE, "Wettbewerbsrechtlicher Schutz gegen Nachahmung und Nachbildung ge-werblicher Erzeugnisse," 1992 ZHR 480 *et seq.*, in particular 501 *et seq.* and 511.

[50] Against this background seemingly reduced too extensively to equating the protection of investments with "property" – the "genuine" (*i.e.* competition law-based) protection of investments cannot be concerned with the latter –, KIRCHNER, *supra* note 8, 2004 GRUR Int. 604 *et seq.*

[51] *Supra* 3.4.

[52] Similarly critical BEATER, *supra* note 1, at Sec. 22, note 18: "Often terms such as 'parasitism' ('*Schmarotzen*'), 'insertion' ('*Einschieben*'), 'adherence' ('*Anhängen*'), 'slavish imitation' ('sklavische Nachahmung') or 'organised acting' ('*Planmäßigkeit*') are used in this context, which may convince the impartial reader and possibly also the parties in a competition process, but which are purely suggestive and do not offer any explanation" (translation).

priate – can intervene on this level in a supplementary way, to prevent culturally-specific, ethically undesirable forms of behaviour.[53]

- On the other hand, it may, of course, be asked why the – admittedly absolutely predominant – traditional approach, which is restricted to a qualitative comparison of the (original) product with an imitation, should not be correct. This may, however, be justified by placing the question in that larger context at issue here, namely competition law in its widest sense as the core of the law of market behaviour. Competition law – and thus also the legal protection of the competitor as a component of the law of market behaviour – can never, without a particular justification, be aimed at conferring on an individual competitor a privileged position. This is so as a position in competition privileged by law is – from an economic point of view – not an end in itself (at any rate not if one does not want to resort back to natural law ideas, which would seek to justify "ownership" as such with regard to self-created – presently intellectual – property[54]). Or stated differently: The legal protection offered to the individual must entail advantages in respect of the general welfare – and, hence, in particular the whole system of competition; the offering of legal protection which benefits the individual but is detrimental to the interests of the general public must be discarded.[55]

This deliberation leads to the conclusion that a competitor can only be protected in as far as he would withdraw from the market concerned or even not invest in it at all without the protection against a takeover of his investments. Viewed from this perspective, the line of reasoning taking "a detour" via a product – which (for reasons still to be discussed[56]) as such does not enjoy protection in terms of special laws – merely constitutes a means to an end: If the manufacturing of the product by the imitator leads to a competitor being squeezed out of the market without a reasonable justification and thus to a distortion of competition in the long run, "the product" – more specifically: the investment made and accordingly the possibility of an ade-

---

53 *Cf.* in this regard also *supra* 3.3.

54 In so far justifiably cautious KIRCHNER, *supra* note 38, 2004 GRUR Int. 604 *et seq.*, where the protection of investments in terms of competition law and possible protection of investments in terms of special laws are not sufficiently distinguished, however.

55 Behind this comparison – aiming at the prevention of a potential market failure – one notices, in the final analysis, elements of the compensation criterion developed by Nicholas Kaldor and John Richard Hicks ("Kaldor-Hicks criterion") aimed at extending the scope of application of so-called Pareto welfare economics. In terms of this criterion also those economico-political measures may be seen as enhancing the general welfare which cause losses to certain groups of the population, in so far as those benefiting from that measure are in a position to fully compensate the losers, without thereby again forfeiting all welfare gains achieved. With regard to the question of the welfare effect it is not important in this regard whether actual use is, in fact, made of the possibility. What is crucial is solely that the possibility of compensation exists. For, it must be expected that the redistribution effected by an economic measure is to a certain extent politically intended, so that no compensation is desired here. *Cf.* in detail DICHTL & ISSING (eds.), "Vahlens großes Wirtschaftslexikon" A-K, Vol. 1 (2nd ed. 1987); *see also* HUNTLEY & STEPHEN, *supra* note 2, at 449.

56 *Infra* 4.2.

quate amortisation – deserves to be protected in the interest of maintaining competition free from distortions. Against this background, "the detour" via the product should not cause confusion. A court would for practical reasons have to afford protection of course to the product itself, by prohibiting its reproduction, and the order to refrain granted by the court unavoidably looks like genuine intellectual property law protection being granted to a product. Nevertheless, this perception should in consequence not mislead as to the fact that the actual goal precisely does not lie in a protection of the product as such (since this product does not enjoy protection in terms of special laws); the prohibition in question is only the consequence of the intervention in the market forces of free competition occurring in the interest of the legal protection of investments.

If the products in question, however, are able principally to coexist without this having any lasting effects upon the market concerned, the takeover does not lead to a distortion of competition, but, on the contrary, may have the – desirable – effect of intensifying competition, even if, in the long run, this may lead to the first product disappearing from the market – for example, because the quality of the second product is better. Especially against this background, however, it would not be acceptable from a competition law perspective, to prohibit a product (not enjoying protection in terms of special laws) from being imitated, and, consequently, to protect the investment made by the first competitor, as otherwise the market adjustment process, inherent in competition, would be interfered with.

In other words, the positive effect of the functioning of the market forces of free competition lies precisely in the fact that an investment may not be protected unconditionally, seeing that it is often only the possibility of resorting back to something – created by a third party – already in existence or being inspired by it that makes improvements possible at all.[57] Or once again stated differently: The fact that improvements do not occur in independent units but are of a sequential nature may not be ignored by conferring exclusive rights to competitors in a one-sided manner; otherwise it would also not be possible to maintain desirable, continuously adjusting competition based upon quality differences and price-competition.

Things seem to be different – at least at first sight – if one argues on the level of genuine intellectual property rights. This is so as in this case, viewed from the perspective of the theoretical question of the protective function, the question is not whether an investment should be protected because without such protection there would be a distortion of competition. Intellectual property law rather focuses on the quality of the result of the investment: the invention, the work, the design. The characterising element of all these investment results enjoying protection in terms of special laws is that – at least in theory – they reveal special requirements for protection, i.e. that, in a qualitative respect, they represent something extraordinary (not usual, not average). This particular background should not mislead as to the fact, however, that also intellectual property law finds its justification essentially in considerations of competition law – with various nuances in the argumentation (alongside the lines of argumentation based upon natural law ideas, not considered conclusive here, but

---

[57] *See also* the references *supra* note 38.

also alongside components pertaining to the law of personality, presently not to be discussed): Intellectual property rights too open up the prospect of attaining a special (time-limited) position in competition in the case of a special, i.e. extraordinary result of the investment.

To this extent the differences between "ordinary" competition law approaches designed to protect investments and those of intellectual property law prove to be of a gradual nature:[58]

- Where the result of the investment is not extraordinary, no special protection is afforded. In this case, the law intervenes only to the extent that the conditions required for competition in general would be negatively affected – although a justification in market terms is lacking – without protection; the protection of the individual competitor here thus rather constitutes a means to an end with a view to competition as such, and, for this reason, it would not be convincing to provide special protection to the product created by the competitor solely to safeguard the latter's individual interests. Focusing on the conditions required for competition remains correct even if – beyond the question of distortion of competition discussed presently – also ethically or culturally-specific criteria should find consideration; for, also the implementation of such values lies primarily in the general interest and not (at any rate not only) in the interest of the competitor concerned.
- If the result of the investment surpasses the hurdle of compliance with the specific requirements of intellectual property law for protection, however, the competitor concerned is accorded a special position in competition. But, even here his privileged position serves to regulate behaviour with a view to the general interest, i.e. to foster further developments. In a sense, the system of intellectual property rights may thus be viewed as a higher-level approach of protecting investments, particularly as also with regard to intellectual property rights the justification for the protection offered – as an intervention in the market forces of

[58] Similar with reference to permeability SAMBUC, in: HARTE & HENNING (eds.), *supra* note 1, at Intro. F, note 213; *see also* BEATER, *supra* note 1, at Sec. 22, note 38 and – related to criteria concerning the legal protection of innovations – also, note 62 *et seq.*; GORDON, *supra* note 2 (1994), at 328 *et seq.*, who – related to intellectual property rights – similarly argues in a competition law-oriented manner, namely by referring to an "asymmetry of market conditions" (where intellectual property rights are lacking, there must be a market failure, where intellectual property rights do exist, the market must function properly): *see also* by the same author, *supra* note 2 (1991-1992), at 853 *et seq.* To a certain extent with an apparently different approach KIRCHNER, *supra* note 38, 2004 GRUR Int. 604 *et seq.*, who in respect of the protection of investments considers the question whether there has been an innovation decisive (whereas the question of instruments of the law against unfair competition is explicitly left aside) – an approach which in the light of the arguments presented here is not conclusive, if in every case the link is made with a potential market failure.

free competition – ceases to be valid where no positive effects may be expected to derive therefrom with a view to the general welfare.[59]

4.2 The Legal Implementation of the Idea of the Protection of Investments

If the protection of investments in a wide sense thus proves to constitute the core of the legal protection of the competitor, this does not say much, of course, regarding the question of the legal implementation. In that respect one may find general clauses which are essentially directed at prohibiting such competitive behaviour which may potentially lead to a distortion of competition in the sense as it has been discussed above.

However, not only the practical application of such a generally defined norm remains highly complicated. Already in antitrust law the endeavour to define the relevant market and to assess concrete forms of behaviour of the competitors involved with a view to their effects upon this market is extremely challenging. Even more complicated is the task of distinguishing "ordinary" (i.e. not market power-based) forms of behaving which actually stimulate competition from those which distort it.[60] Furthermore, if such a general clause were formulated at the level of a European Directive, its harmonising effect would be comparatively very limited as the margin of discretion of the national legislator would naturally remain wide. Therefore, the purpose of a general clause within the framework of an EU Directive can only – but, all the same – be to present to the national legislator basic principles guided by the overarching objective of competition law for concretising norms of the legal protection of the competitor. On the national level on the other hand such general clauses may – according to the possibilities offered by the respective legal systems – constitute the basis for the development of the legal protection of the competitor by means of case law. With regard to higher-ranking aspects such as legal certainty general clauses as such do not suffice, however.

Against this background, the legal protection of the competitor can only become a practicable component of competition law as a whole, if already the legislator – firstly the European, and based upon its specifications subsequently also the national legislator – covers the relevant constellations in the form of concrete norms. These norms must define the requirements precisely and in such a way that they can

---

[59] Particularities concerning the positive effects which may ensue as a result of exclusive rights, specifically in relation to their capacity to form the subject of legal transactions (or the potential willingness to grant licenses on the basis of protective rights), but which will not necessarily ensue – *e.g.* in the case of external factors such as transaction costs which are too high or the impossibility of identifying the holder of a right – will not be dealt with in more depth at this point; for a fundamental treatment in this regard, *see* ULLRICH, "Grenzen des Rechtsschutzes: Technologieschutz zwischen Wettbewerbs- und Industriepolitik," in: SCHRICKER, DREIER & KUR, *supra* note 8, at 101 *et seq.*; *see also* in particular *e.g.* GORDON, *supra* note 2 (1994), at 347 and 360 *et seq.*; by the same author, *supra* note 2 (1991-1992), at 857.

[60] Similar with regard to the difficulty of making predictions SCHÜNEMANN, *supra* note 1, at Sec. 3, note 214 *et seq.*

be applied directly by a judge in a concrete case without further problems. Such bodies of norms – as will be shown below – are, in fact, by no means unfamiliar to existing law; what is to some extent unusual is merely the perception of placing these norms in the context of the law of market behaviour.

Seeing that this perception of a holistic approach of a law of market behaviour, i.e. of an all-embracing bracket for the various components of competition law, is non-existent at any rate at the European level, it is not surprising that European competition law appears to have a patchwork character rather than a logical structure. This reveals two weak points of the European legal system: On the one hand, in the case of many of the various pieces of legislation in existence one would have liked to have seen genuinely conclusive analyses on the question of why the relevant acts were required at all, bearing in mind the necessity identified in this article of being able to justify an intervention in the market forces of free competition. The Recitals of the Directives regularly use general and repetitive set phrases only[61] (this also referring to the general limitations deduced from the principles of subsidiarity and proportionality). This alone does not suffice, of course, to question the usefulness of such European pieces of legislation. However, the European legislator up to now, in the absence of the analyses mentioned, failed to provide a deeper insight into the essential structures of competition law. This points, at the same time, to the other, more serious, weak point: An insight into the interrelationship between the various attempts at harmonisation is lacking; but, there is also only knowledge of a fragmentary nature concerning the interfaces of the components of competition law with other legal fields (e.g. contract law).[62]

In other words, what is required is the formulation of an economically well-founded holistic approach. The latter will demonstrate to what extent certain of the components of an all-embracing law of market behaviour need, in fact, yet to be conceived and developed; possibly, such a holistic approach may, however, also reveal to what extent in certain areas the protection offered is already too extensive. Further on, it might reveal whether European law should, on the contrary, ensure that insular national approaches to protection do not interfere with the functioning of

---

[61] The reasons provided at the time as regards the Directive on Databases are, for example, characteristic in this context (Directive 96/9 of March 11, 1996 on the legal protection of databases, OJ L 077 of March 27, 1996, 20 *et seq.*; in this regard *infra* 4.3.3.1 ["Databases"]), namely Recital 12, which makes a mere unfounded assertion ("an investment in modern information storage and processing systems will not take place within the Community unless a stable and uniform legal protection regime is introduced for the protection of the rights of makers of databases"), a statement which the EU Commission in its assessment of the effects of the Directive itself exposed as being false in the meantime (*cf. infra* note 84). Comparable analyses on the effects in other fields of European legal harmonisation are lacking from the outset.

[62] In more depth in this regard KUR, 2004 IIC 1 *et seq.*, as well as by the same author, "Die Harmonisierung des Lauterkeitsrechts durch Angleichungsmaßnahmen in angrenzenden Bereichen," in: SCHRICKER & HENNING-BODEWIG (eds.), "Neuordnung des Wettbewerbsrechts" 116 *et seq.* (1998/99).

competition in the internal market.[63] In this respect, the need for clarification – as has already been explained – is the most urgent within the framework of the legal protection of the competitor, as in this regard a coherent concept of protection is lacking altogether.[64] This does not mean that we are still completely at the beginning here. If one takes into account the context of the legal protection of investments described above, one will, in fact, be able to detect quite some fragments already in current legislation, alongside certain rudimentary attempts in the case law of the ECJ at developing the field. The significance of these fragments will briefly be dealt with below.

4.3 Current Basis of the Protection of Investments in Existing Law

If one takes Art. 3 Para. 1 (g) EC or those general clauses of the national legal systems as a point of departure which regard the prevention of distortions of competition as the goal of competition law, one may, from this point onwards, perceive a scale of attempts to regulation which become all the more dense, i.e. more concrete. Admittedly, at a certain density, one looses sight of the fact that one actually still deals with the legal protection of the competitor, thus forming a component of the law of market behaviour, especially where a body of norms formally appears perhaps not to stand in a competition law context anymore.

4.3.1 General Attempts at Protecting Investments

The first level of density in some national legal systems may be found in legal attempts of an abstract, i.e. generally granted protection of investments. In the national systems in question, such protection of investments is usually placed in the context of the law against unfair competition. Even if the various approaches differ to a considerable extent, they have in common the characteristic that hardly ever the protection of undistorted competition as an institution appears to stand in the foreground,[65] but rather the protection of individual competitors with regard to a particular product. The rationale for such an individualistic approach lies in the advantage

---

63 *Cf.* in this sense also the foreword in KEßLER & MICKLITZ, *supra* note 21, where it is stated that the emphasis so far has particularly been on the protection of individual competitors "against competition" in terms of private law rather than normatively safeguarding the process of competition as such, hence, that a "micro or even macro economic perspective ... with regard to the organisation of fair competition – apart from isolated investigative approaches conducted in the 70s of the previous century – in order to obtain normative insights did not exist" (translation), this also being reflected in the fact that economists hardly addressed questions pertaining to the law against unfair competition.

64 KEßLER & MICKLITZ, *supra* note 21, ibidem; *see also* MICKLITZ & KEßLER, 2002 GRUR Int. 889. For a fundamental treatment with regard to all of the above, *see* BULTMANN, HOWELLS, KEßLER, MICKLITZ, RADEIDEH, REICH, STUYCK & VOIGT, Project Manager: MICKLITZ, "The Feasibility of a Legislative Framework on Fair Trading" November 2000 (available at <http://ec.europa.eu/comm/dgs/health_consumer/library/surveys/sur21_sum_en.pdf> status as at May 2006).

65 *See* also *supra* 3.1.

that relatively concrete requirements for the practical application of such norms exist. Thereby the legal norms become manageable for a judge, otherwise than in the case of an abstract approach relying on a general clause. Even though such an individualistic approach does not exclude applying the criteria discussed above – based on the consideration that without a market distortion protection would not be granted –, a judge will hardly deliver judgements which are restrictive in this sense. At any rate he will scarcely consider the market distortion as long as the main focus of the applicable national law is directed at ethical elements. Admittedly, arguing that the takeover of a product is not acceptable seems to be much easier where ethical elements are *per se* not met than where the stress is on competition-oriented rationales.

In European law, this first level of density of a general attempt at regulating the protection of investments is non-existent. Presently, such an attempt could, in fact, solely be directed at giving instructions to the national legislator to the effect that the crucial criterion from a European perspective can *only* be a potentially threatening market distortion.[66] In consequence, this would, however, not necessarily lead to a harmonisation by European law which extends the currently existing legal protection in the national laws. Such a harmonisation might just as well result in the formulation of general conditions, which would outline a maximum permissible protection of competitors so as not to prejudice free competition in the internal market. The objective of European legislation would thus not be to prevent certain forms of behaviour by means of concrete norms, but rather to define an economically meaningful holistic concept of the law of market behaviour to which national law – i.e. concrete rules capable of application by a judge in an individual case – would have to be subjected. Concretised legal provisions at the European level would only be conceivable in the form of (directly applicable) Community law for the prevention of unfair competition in general; currently a suitable framework for such Community law is lacking, however.[67]

4.3.2 Concretised Attempts at Protecting Investments

On the second level, the density extends beyond the general approach in that one finds here comparatively very concrete regulations. The relevant norms customarily still belong to the context of the law against unfair competition or special laws or, at any rate, have been developed by case law in a comparable context. In other words, on this level certain forms of behaviour of competitors which have been defined relatively precisely by law are rejected, thus, for example, particular forms of an exploitation of reputation. Nevertheless, the background to such norms of prohibition – to wit, that they protect investments with the aim of preventing distortions of competition – can seldom ever be identified. In the foreground rather stands the ethical approach represented up to this day by a predominance of national legal sys-

[66] With regard to the component of ethical values, to which consideration may possibly be given at the national – but not the European – level, *see supra* 3.3.

[67] *Cf.* as against that the approaches to regulation of Community law on the third and fourth level 4.3.3 and 4.3.4.

tems of EU Member States, the approach being to the effect that certain forms of behaviour are *per se* undesirable.

This second level of density may also be found at the European level, henceforth particularly in the Unfair Commercial Practices Directive,[68] as the latter – as has already been shown[69] – in Art. 11 Para. 1, 2 includes competitors among those who are entitled to bring a legal action. The aim of this Directive is, however, not directed at undistorted competition, but again is oriented at a possible violation of consumer interests. Consequently, Recital 6 emphasises only indirect harm being caused to competitors; such harm derives from a certain overlapping of the field of consumer protection on the one hand with certain concerns of competitors on the other; a specific legal protection of the competitor, however, was, as has been shown, explicitly not intended.

This restriction gives rise to a tension which yields certain dangers; with regard to the pursued holistic approach to a European law of market behaviour, these dangers must not be lost sight of: Competition – with its long-term positive effects, such as especially optimising the quality and price of a product, but also the desired continuous market adjustment processes – is not encouraged, if the boundaries of what should be permissible from the perspective of consumer protection are drawn too narrowly. For, if provisions which are too restrictive by nature have a levelling tendency, such provisions may well prejudice potentially possible market adjustment processes. In the long run this will also have negative effects on consumers. It should thus be taken into account that these two fields interact mutually: Not only does consumer protection have an indirect impact on the protection of the competitor; similarly, (too far-reaching) restrictions of the freedom of the competitor may have some influence on consumer interests. It is consequently neither in the interest of the competitor nor the consumer that the market forces of free competition are restricted beyond the degree necessary; the measure in this regard must thus primarily be guided by the question whether the legal protection sought is suited to prevent distortions of competition. Or, in the reverse: If a far-reaching protection of the consumer may be appropriate out of socio-political considerations, this does not already solely for this reason do away with the question of the consequences on the general situation of competition.

Against this background it becomes clear that, also on the second level of density, a European legal harmonisation may not simply focus on an obligation of the national legislator to provide selective legal protection in the sense of a minimum of protection. European law rather must focus on a certain margin, which clearly defines both a minimum as well as a maximum measure of protection. In both cases solely the criterion of potential distortions of the internal market may be decisive, subject to possible additional legal measures of protection by Member States to uphold requirements concerning legitimate ethical values, in as far as

---

[68] *Supra* note 20.

[69] *Supra* 3.2, note 27.

such national requirements do not stand in the way of a realisation of the internal market.[70]

4.3.3 Attempts at Protecting Investments in Special Laws

The third level of density is of a comparatively very amorphous nature, i.e. it reveals a large diversity of concrete legislative manifestations. What characterises this third level of density in particular is that the legal approaches of protection customarily do not stand in the context of norms anymore to be found in the field of the law against unfair competition or related special laws, but – from a formal perspective – are rather similar to the special legal approaches of intellectual property rights. Even so, they do not yet, as far as their character is concerned, show the phenomenon described above that, in a qualitative respect, they would cover an extraordinary subject matter of protection, to which the protection relates. This third level of density rather concerns those specific forms of investment which are especially threatened because the takeover of such investments by third parties is comparatively very easy. The provision of legal protection thus finds its principal justification in the fact that, without such protection, there would be too short a period within which the competitor making the investment could amortise the investment, wherefore competition would be distorted.

Concerning such particular investment cases European law intervenes in several constellations to achieve legal harmonisation. What is noteworthy in this regard is that the acts have primarily been prepared by the Directorate-General Internal Market and Services (DG Market), and not by the Directorate-General Competition, which up to now is considered competent only in respect of questions of antitrust law. At the same time, it would make sense to view these approaches to regulation as fragments of a legal protection of the competitor and, hence, not to place them in the context of intellectual property rights, but actually in that of a general law of market behaviour.

4.3.3.1 Categories of Cases

Presently, the aim cannot be to explain the details of these approaches to protection; it rather is shortly and by way of example to outline why in these cases of specific regulation the competition law idea of the protection of investments – such protection being intended to prevent a distortion of competition – stands in the foreground:

- *Indications of origin*: Alongside general national provisions one finds at the European level two regulations which concern the protection of geographical indications and designations of origin for agricultural products and foodstuffs and certificates of specific character for agricultural products and food-

[70] Concerning this matter, *see supra* 3.3.

stuffs.[71] It is, in fact, evident that the value of such designations or a specific character arises only if there have been sufficient investments with regard to the products involved (respectively, this depends on investments on an on-going basis), in the sense that a special appreciation develops and continues to exist on the part of customers which is associated with the specific designation in question. Those who have a share in creating such an appreciation must accordingly be protected against third parties – whose products do not satisfy the particular requirements – being able to acquire a comparable reputation. The rationale lies in the fact that specifically designated characteristics which customers are able to recognise and associate with specific quality characteristics, are capable of substantially reducing the general consumer search costs, whereas the use of any such information by third parties, who do not assure such quality characteristics with regard to their products, have the opposite effect and thus lead to a market distortion.[72] It is in the general interest, therefore, to protect those who created the special reputation against this reputation being taken over by third parties not holding a legitimate claim thereto. The justification for affording protection does not lie in the fact that those entitled to protection – as in the case of intellectual property rights – have, by virtue of their investment, produced an extraordinary result *per se* worthy of protection; rather, the individual protection granted to them is a means to an end; its justification "merely" lies in attempting to prevent a general market distortion.

- *Trade marks*: In a certain sense, trade mark law may be classified similarly, although this probably represents the densest possible form of "ordinary" competition law, as its conception customarily already markedly approximates that of intellectual property rights. If it is thus mentioned in the same breath as patent or copyright law, this hides an important difference, however: Also trade mark

[71] Regulation No. 510/2006 of March 20, 2006 on the protection of geographical indications and designations of origin for agricultural products and foodstuffs, replacing Regulation No. 2081/92 of July 14, 1992 on the protection of geographical indications and designations of origin for agricultural products and foodstuffs, and Regulation No. 2082/92 of July 14, 1992 on certificates of specific character for agricultural products and foodstuffs, OJ L 208 of July 24, 1992, at 1 *et seq.* and OJ L 93 of March 31, 2006, at 12 *et seq.*, respectively. Provisions explicitly dealing with geographical indications of origin may further be found in product-specific regulations, *e.g.* on the common organisation of the market in wine (Arts. 47 *et seq.*, 50 of Reg. No. 1493/1999 of May 17, 1999, OJ L 179 of July 14, 1999, 1 *et seq.*), on the presentation of spirit drinks (Art. 5 Para. 3 (a) and (b) read with Annex II Reg. No. 1576/89 of May 29, 1989, OJ L 160 of June 12, 1989, at 1 *et seq.*) or on mineral waters (Art. 7 *et seq.* Directive 80/777 of July 15, 1980, OJ L 229 of August 30, 1980, at 1 *et seq.*).

[72] Holding essentially the same view BEATER, *supra* note 1, at Sec. 22, note 77 *et seq.*, related *e.g.* to the public relations work of an enterprise, the discussion addressing geographical designations referring to the ECJ decision of November 10, 1992, Case C-3/91, 1993 GRUR Int. 76 *et seq.*, in particular 78 – *Exportur SA./. LOR SA et al*, and further referring to the case law of national courts.

law – as also the other rights protecting investments discussed here – is not based upon the fact that an extraordinary investment result is the subject matter of protection; for, if a graphically designed trade mark is sufficiently extraordinary, for instance, it may, in fact, be registered as an industrial design, or it even enjoys copyright protection. The trade mark is rather only kind of a symbol for the investment which its holder must make, so that customers will perceive the goods or services marketed under the trade mark in question as something special, precious, qualitatively valuable, on the one hand, and will esteem the trade mark itself in a corresponding manner, on the other. Typically, the value of the trade mark is still close to zero at the time of deposit, whereas it can increase through relevant investments; failing such investments, however – or, e.g., in the case of public scandals negatively impacting on the person or legal entity identified by the trade mark or his or its products –, it can also decrease again.[73]

It is self-evident that such investments, which may possibly be very costly and required on a continuous basis, may very easily be taken over by those who can adopt the image of a trade mark by a corresponding approximation. Consequently, also the holder of the trade mark deserves protection, however, not on the basis of the widely held view that he has, as it were, created his own "property". For, if one adopts a critical stand concerning such arguments influenced by natural law, seeing that the exclusive allocation of goods does not yet without exception and necessarily result in an economic surplus value, one can equally well explain trade mark law from the other angle: By using a suited and distinctive mark with regard to a product or service, the consumer search costs may be substantially reduced compared to the marketing of no-name products, wherefore awarding an exclusive right is economically conclusive. The trade mark is, however, again deprived of this economically useful function, if an adequate exclusive right *vis-à-vis* such third parties trying to profit from the image embodied by the trade mark does not exist. Granting such exclusive rights thus primarily lies in the general interest, to prevent distortions of competition – existing in the form that the takeover of the identity of a trade mark leads to false information and thus to disproportionally increased consumer search costs.[74] In

---

[73] KUR, "Funktionswandel von Schutzrechten", *supra* note 8, at 27 *et seq.* (in particular *supra* note 18, referring to the approach of ULLRICH, 1996 GRUR Int. 565 *et seq.*; in this regard *supra* note 8; *see* in this regard also by the same author, "Grenzen des Rechtsschutzes," *supra* note 59, at 92).

[74] *Cf.* with regard to all of the above in particular *e.g.* EGER, "Kommentar zu Helmut Köhler: Erweiterung des gewerblichen Rechtsschutzes durch UWG-Normen," in: OTT & SCHÄFER (eds.), "Ökonomische Analyse der rechtlichen Organisation von Innovationen" 271 (1994); HUNTLEY & STEPHEN, *supra* note 2, at 448 *et seq.* and 452; for a fundamental treatment, *see* LANDES & POSNER, *supra* note 4 (2003), at 166 *et seq.*; by the same authors, *supra* note 4 (Journal of Law and Economics), at 269 *et seq.*; *see also* COOTER & ULEN, *supra* note 4, 134 *et seq.*; AKERLOF, "The Market for 'Lemons': Quality Uncertainty and the Market Mechanism," 84 Quarterly Journal of Economics 488 *et seq.* (1970); BERG & LEHMANN, 1992 GRUR Int. 591.

the reverse, it follows that protection must then be denied where an interference with competition cannot be proved in an individual case.[75]

The competition law background of trade mark law is particularly clear in the case of a "mark with reputation" (e.g. Art. 9 Para. 1 (c) EC Regulation on the Community trade mark[76]); such a mark is characterised by the fact that the limitation of trade mark protection to certain categories of goods or services is transcended. It is, in fact, true that the reputation required presupposes a substantial scale of investments by the holder of the trade mark; against that background it would appear probable that the good image of such a trade mark is transferred to other categories of goods or services than those in question. Depending on the facts, this may have the effect that, in the case of "watering down" a mark with reputation, the general (and not only the product-specific) competition position of the holder of the trade mark in question is prejudiced. Even in the case of marks with reputation, however – especially with regard to the competition law core of such trade marks – the protection granted may not be extended beyond that measure truly indispensable to prevent a distortion of competition. The granting of "unconditional" protection against all forms of use of marks with reputation would, therefore, be going too far. Consequently, the question needs to be asked whether the provision of Community law, for instance, in terms of which it is not permissible "without due cause" to take "unfair advantage of ... the repute of the community trade mark", does not in certain respects threaten to "overshoot the mark".[77] For, if it is not additionally required that "the exploitation" of the mark with reputation beyond the primarily concerned categories of goods or services be accompanied by an actual (or, at least, a likely) impairment of the position of the holder of the trade mark in competition,[78] the danger arises that one leaves the context of merely preventing a distortion of competition and

75 In this context, EGER, *supra* note 74, at 271, refers to the possible negative effects of legal protection, mentioning the example of qualitatively identical products which a manufacturer offers under different trade mark names (as this sometimes occurs *e.g.* in the case of electrical appliances); in this instance, investments in the trade mark name might possibly confuse consumers, a robust protection of trade marks might thus not only create incentives for economically desirable investments in it, factually reducing the information costs of consumers, but also lead to economically undesirable excessive investments.

76 Regulation No. 40/94 of December 20, 1993 on the Community trade mark, OJ L 011 of January 14, 1994, at 1 *et seq.*

77 Also rather cautious, mentioning differentiating examples, LANDES & POSNER, *supra* note 4 (2003), at 206 *et seq.*, and by the same authors, *supra* note 4 (Journal of Law and Economics), at 306 *et seq.*

78 Art. 9 Para. 1 (c) of Regulation No. 40/94 formulates the instances of taking unfair advantage of, on the one hand, and being detrimental to, on the other, the repute of the well-known trade mark as *alternative*, not, however, as *cumulative* requirements. PIPER, "Zu den Anforderungen an den Schutz der bekannten Gemeinschaftsmarke nach der Gemeinschaftsmarkenverordnung," 1996 GRUR 657 *et seq.*; generally with regard to the Community trade mark, *see* FEZER, "Markenrecht" Intro., note 80 *et seq.* (3rd ed. 2001), with additional references.

enters the wide field of moralising judgemental decisions. It is, however, not legitimate for a European law against unfair competition to do so.[79]

- *Databases*: Almost prototypical for the third level of density appears to be the *sui generis* protection concerning databases introduced at the European level by the Directive on the Legal Protection of Databases of 1996.[80] The stated law is based upon the appreciation that "there has been qualitatively and/or quantitatively a substantial investment in either the obtaining, verification or presentation of the contents [of the database]" (Art. 7 Para. 1).[81] It is clear from the legal approach of protection of the Directive that the result of the investment in this case does not constitute something extraordinary, but may be generated by anybody applying comparable criteria who makes a corresponding investment; otherwise, the database would constitute an individual creation and therefore enjoy protection by copyright law (Art. 3). Inversely, not all kinds of a takeover of elements of a database are impermissible, but only the "extraction and/or re-utilisation of the whole or of a substantial part, evaluated qualitatively and/or quantitatively, of the contents of that database" (Art. 7 Para. 1).

  In fact, at first sight it is in a certain sense legitimate to assume that where relevant investments could unhamperedly be taken over by third parties (in the form of an extraction and/or utilisation of a relevant part of the database), distortions of competition would result.[82] Nevertheless, European database law will not be remembered as a successful attempt at regulating a phenomenon worthy of

---

[79] *Cf.* for purposes of differentiation *supra* 3.3.

[80] *Supra* note 61. For a fundamental treatment as regards this law, *see* (instead of mentioning all authors) in particular LEISTNER, "Der Rechtsschutz von Datenbanken im deutschen und europäischen Recht" (2000).

[81] The scope of this norm has, of course, now been defined more closely by the most recent case law of the ECJ, by stating that the purpose of the protection is only "to promote the establishment of storage and processing systems for existing information" and not "the creation of materials capable of being collected subsequently in a database"; ECJ, November 9, 2004, Case C-203/02, 2005 GRUR Int. 247, 250 – *British Horse-Racing* (No. 31, referring to one of the parallel cases, *ibidem*, 242, No. 40); in this regard *e.g.* SENDROWSKI, 2005 GRUR 369 *et seq.*; DERCLAYE, "Database Sui Generis Right: What is a Substantial investment? A Tentative Definition," 2005 IIC 2 *et seq.*; *see also* the case notes of LEISTNER, 2005 IIC 592 *et seq.*, HOEREN, 2005 MMR 34 *et seq.*, as well as LEHMANN, 2005 CR 15 *et seq.*

[82] *Cf. also* Recital 7 of the Directive: "Whereas the making of databases requires the investment of considerable human, technical and financial resources while such databases can be copied or accessed at a fraction of the cost needed to design them independently". *See also* in this regard LEHMANN, "The European Database Directive and Its Implementation into German Law," 1998 IIC 782, related to the motives concerning the legal protection of investments in Recitals 39 and 40. Then, generally with regard to the competition law context of the protection of databases, *see also e.g.* LEISTNER, in: BETTINGER & LEISTNER (eds.), "Werbung und Vertrieb im Internet" Part 1 B. N 57 *et seq.* (2003); THUM, in: WANDTKE & BULLINGER (eds.), "Urheberrecht", before Sec. 87(a), note 29 *et seq.* (2nd ed. 2006); VOGEL, in: SCHRICKER (ed.), "Urheberrecht, Kommentar" before German Copyright Law 87(a) *et seq.* N 36 (2nd ed. 1999); WEBER, *supra* note 8, at 589 *et seq.*; WIEBE, in: WIEBE & LEUPOLD (eds.), "Recht der elektronischen Datenbanken" Part 2 C. I. N 2 *et seq.* (as of May 2004).

investment-related protection. An assessment of the impact of the Directive, published by the EU Commission at the end of 2005,[83] rather shows that noticeable positive effects – particularly when compared to the US market where a corresponding approach to protection (amongst others with a view to possible restraints concerning the diffusion of information) has never been pursued – have failed to materialise.[84] With regard to a European law focusing on the protection of competitors against market distortions, this experience provides an important lesson: Even if a legal approach of protection seems to be plausible at first view, a merely theoretical analysis is insufficient to explain whether or not legal protection is really required. In fact, everybody potentially beneficially affected as regards his position in competition will be in a position to sketch the – theoretically – positive effects of a regulatory intervention in free competition. This may, however, not absolve us from, on the one hand, obtaining factual certainty to the effect that without legal protection a market failure actually threatens to ensue and, on the other hand, demanding proof showing that the provision of legal protection lies not only in the individual interest of the beneficiary, but in the general interest and consequently yields a positive economic benefit.[85]

The European database right sui generis is, however, also a reminder in as far as the option for action of wholly repealing the Directive, suggested by the EU Commission in its assessment, is not really viable. For, the mere repeal would inevitably lead to an uncontrolled growth of approaches to protection on the national level. This would at least be the case if a restoration of regulatory competences to Member States were deduced from a repeal of the Directive. Presently, in the light of the existence of the Directive, Member States may be said not to be competent to provide for supplementary measures of protection in the context of database investments (e.g. in the field of competition law).[86] However, if a measure of protection on the national level exceeding the current regulation by the EU (meanwhile restricted by the ECJ in its ambit[87]) were to be achieved, the prejudice to the European internal market would be clearly evident; this, it should be noted, not because of insufficient but because of (partially) excessive measures of protection.[88] The only acceptable option would thus at the most be a

[83] As a matter of fact, such an assessment should have been conducted in terms of Art. 16 Para. 3 of the Directive at the latest as on January 1, 2001.

[84] *Cf.* in this regard first evaluation of Directive 96/9/EC on the legal protection of databases of December 12, 2005, available at <http://europa.eu.int/comm/internal_market/copyright/docs/databases/evaluation_report_en.pdf> (as of May 2006). For a comparative legal perspective (instead of mentioning all authors), *see* HASAN, "Sweating in Europe: The European Database Directive," 2005 Computer Law Review and Technology Journal 479 *et seq.* (in particular in comparison to the decision of the Supreme Court, 499 U.S. 340 *et seq.* (1991) – *Feist Publications v. Rural Tel. Serv. Co.*

[85] With regard to this so-called asymmetry of market conditions *supra* note 58.

[86] *See e.g.* WIEBE, in: WIEBE & LEUPOLD (eds.), *supra* note 82, at Part 2 C. I. N 6.

[87] *Supra* note 81.

[88] *See* in this regard also KUR, HILTY, GEIGER & LEISTNER, "First Evaluation of Directive 96/9/EC on the Legal Protection of Databases – Comment by the Max Planck Institute for Intellectual Property, Competition and Tax Law," 2006 IIC 551 *et seq.*

"qualified" repeal of the Directive in the sense that a corresponding – or even more far-reaching – legal regulation on the national level would henceforth be impermissible. This would, however, not be viable in a political sense already because only recently in the context of the eastward enlargement of the EU the ten newest Member States were forced to adopt this acquis communautaire; with a view to the future enlargement of the EU this gives rise to a dilemma, namely that of either requiring all present Member States now again to repeal the legal protection afforded, or, however – even though absurd – of requiring future new Member States to adopt these sui generis measures of protection. All this could have been avoided if prior to an attempt at harmonisation sufficient genuine safeguarding measures had been taken. A possibility in this regard would in particular have been to use certain national legal systems initially as a kind of "laboratory", i.e. in a first phase to accept that in the internal market there exist different legal regulations.[89] In this way, possible positive economic effects of such a novel form of legal protection would have become discernable in that, in a country granting the relevant protection, an increase in relevant investments would have been registered, in relation to a comparable country not granting such protection. If, however, one had realised already earlier on that the sui generis right does not really yield positive results, such an economically highly complex – but, in the end, futile – process of harmonisation could have been avoided.

- *Related rights (to copyright)*: The so-called "neighbouring rights", as granted, for example, to producers of phonograms and audiovisual media as well as to broadcasting organisations, to a very large extent replicate copyright protection. The existence of these rights has its foundation not in European but in international law;[90] European law, nevertheless, presupposes their existence, as is clear already from the titles of the various Directives.[91] Obviously however, the impetus for the granting of related rights was given by national law; especially in German law,

[89] *Cf.* with regard to this laboratory function on the level of national law HILTY, "Entwicklungsperspektiven des Schutzes Geistigen Eigentums in Europa," in: BEHRENS (ed.), "Stand und Perspektiven des Schutzes Geistigen Eigentums in Europa" 160; similar KUR, 2004 IIC 5. Related to database law, for example, the "catalogue protection" of Swedish, Danish and Finnish copyright law or the Dutch "*Geschriftenbescherming*" could, in this sense, have been analysed in detail concerning the economic effects on making available data collections (*cf.* with regard to these approaches *e.g.* GASTER, "Der Rechtsschutz von Datenbanken. Kommentar zur Richtlinie 96/9/EG", Art. 7 N, 447 *et seq.* and 451 *et seq.* (Cologne 1999)).

[90] In particular the International Convention for the Protection of Performers, Producers of Phonograms and Broadcasting Organisations of October 26, 1961, so-called "Rome Convention".

[91] Thus *e.g.* in the case of Directive 93/83 "on the coordination of certain rules concerning copyright and rights related to copyright applicable to satellite broadcasting and cable retransmission" (OJ L 248 of October 6, 1993, at 15 *et seq.*), Directive 92/100 "on rental right and lending right and on certain rights related to copyright in the field of intellectual property" (OJ L 346 of November 27, 1992, at 61 *et seq.*), Directive 93/98 "harmonising the term of protection of copyright and certain related rights" (OJ L 290 of November 24, 1993, at 9 *et seq.*), or Directive 2001/29 "on the harmonisation of certain aspects of copyright and related rights in the information society" (OJ L 167 of June 22, 2001, at 10 *et seq.*).

the historical development in this regard, in fact, clearly refers to the competition law background of these rights related to copyright.[92]

Indeed, also with regard to related rights one should not allow oneself to be deceived either by the formal allusion to copyright arrangements or, in fact, by the customary treatment of these rights in conjunction with substantive copyright law. For, typically, the achievement of the person thus protected does not, of course, specifically lie in the fact that the person in question has produced something extraordinary; the person rather "only" makes the necessary investments, to either market an already existing work (e.g. a composition) by means of the production and distribution of the relevant media or to produce something capable of being broadcasted whatsoever (e.g. a talk show).[93] It is true that these investments are in part – for instance, cinematographic productions – quite substantial, while the investor inversely is at a high risk by reason of the fact that the related data carriers (such as DVDs) may be reproduced by the simplest technical means and thrown on the market in large quantities. If, against this background, the investor is granted his own related right (irrespective of the fact not to be discussed here that, in reality, the investor will take steps to be assigned the relevant copyright rights from the author to afford him the protection required), and if he therefore is in the position of preventing such – commercial – reproduction, or, if a prevention fails for factual reasons, of at least obtaining compensation (e.g. in the form of a copyright fee on empty data carriers or reproduction devices), this should not hide the fact that the legal approach of the related rights focuses on correcting a market failure. Failing correction of such market failure could lead to a distortion of competition in a way that the investments desired would not be made in the long run.

From this perspective, however, it can hardly be ignored that the duration of the protection offered, at least in many constellations, widely exceeds what, from an economic perspective with a view to a potential market failure, is necessary. Evidently and in the final analysis, when formulating the rights concerned, not criteria of competition law but, in fact, those of copyright law served as a guideline – and this has to do with the fact that a clear separation between the protection of the author – and thus of the actual creative person – by means of copyright

---

92 In detail *e.g.* KRÜGER, in: SCHRICKER (ed.), "Urheberrecht, Kommentar" Copyright Law before Sec. 73 *et seq.* N 4 (performers) (2nd ed. 1999); VOGEL, *ibidem*, Copyright Law 81 N 3 (organisers) and Copyright Law 85 N 2 (producers of phonograms); VOGEL & V. UNGERN-STERNBERG, *ibidem*, Copyright Law 87 N 3 (broadcasting organisations); KATZENBERGER, *ibidem*, Copyright Law 94 N 4 (film producers). With regard to references to competition law generally also VOGEL, *ibidem*, Copyright Law 85 N 10; SAMBUC, in: HARTE & HENNING (eds.), *supra* note 1, at Intro. F, note 225.

93 In more depth HILTY, "Gedanken zum Schutze der nachbarrechtlichen Leistung – einst, heute und morgen," 116 UFITA 35 *et seq.* (1991); by the same author, "Zum urheberrechtlichen Leistungsschutz im schweizerischen Recht am Beispiel des Tonträgerproduzenten," 1993 GRUR Int. 818 *et seq.*; SAMBUC, in: HARTE & HENNING (eds), *supra* note 1, at Intro. F, note 214; WEBER, "Datenbankrecht – Regelungsbedarf in der Schweiz?," in: WEBER & HILTY (eds.), "Daten und Datenbanken" 59 and 66 *et seq.* (Zurich 1999).

law and that of the investor within the framework of the exploitation of copyright works by means of these related rights cannot be drawn anyhow. The degree to which fairly different interests are confused with each other in this regard was shown, for example, by the heated debate on whether an extension of copyright protection from fifty to seventy years concerning works already created was meaningful a few years ago in the US.[94] It is rather ironic in this context that of all countries hence that decided in favour of the extension in question, which has accorded constitutional law status to the incentive function of copyright protection in the form of the so-called "copyright and patent clause"; ultimately, an extension of copyright protection clearly does not provide any further incentives to the author himself with regard to a work already in existence – but it does, of course, to the party exploiting the copyright. This means, in fact, that the latter is thus in a position to profit from copyright law without himself having demonstrated the creativity protected by copyright law. On the other hand, in 1998, again in the US, the protection for "works made for hire" was, however, also extended to 95 years,[95] an extension of protection which now also threatens to have an impact in Europe.[96] In reality, however, there is nothing to prove why the currently applicable period of protection – or, in fact, even a partially distinctly shorter period – should not suffice to prevent a market failure with regard to future investments concerning the exploitation of copyright protected works.[97]

---

[94] *Eldred v. Ashcroft*, 537 U.S. 186, 123 S.Ct. 769 (2003).

[95] Sonny Bono Copyright Term Extension Act of 1998 (Public Law 105-298, Oct. 27, 1998, 112 Stat. 2827). Following this adjustment, although copyright in general endures for a term of 70 years p.m.a. (17 U.S.C. Sec. 302 (a)), it now, however, in the case of pseudonymous works, anonymous works and "works made for hire", endures for a term of 95 years from the year of its first publication, or a term of 120 years from the year of its creation, whichever expires first (17 U.S.C. Sec. 302 (c)).

[96] *See* in this regard MCCREEVY, "EU-Kommissar für Binnenmarkt und Dienstleistungen, IP Policy in Europe: What Next?," 2006 GRUR Int. 363 ("We will also be looking into the difference in the length of protection given to record producers. In the USA the recording industry enjoys protection lasting 95 years, but in the EU 50 years. We are looking at whether this shorter protection is putting our music business at an economic disadvantage."). In fact, the US American concept of protecting the producer via copyright law and the European approach of granting a related right are comparable to a limited extent only; however, the European industry obviously does not face a disadvantage since its protection in the US is identical to the protection of the home industry, while the latter enjoys equal protection in Europe compared to the European industry.

[97] *See also* in this regard in particular ULLRICH, in: SCHRICKER, DREIER & KUR (eds.), *supra* note 59, at 115 *et seq.*, with the example of the term of protection in copyright law of 70 years p.m.a. for software. It should be added that the problem addressed by McCreevy, referred to in the above footnote, is already as such not conclusive: The US American as well as the European music industry enjoy identical protection in Europe – therefore, one does not deal with the issue of the own industry being disadvantaged in the own market, but at the most with that whether the general public has an interest in protection being extended. This would (only) be the case where due to a lack of adequate protection recordings which would otherwise be made are not, in fact, produced.

- *Unregistered design:* Art. 1 Para. 2 (a) read with Art. 11 of the Regulation on Designs[98] on the unregistered design introduced a provision into European Community design law, which allows for the granting of protection also without formal registration, namely for such designs which are exploited for a short period of time only (such as notably fashion concerning clothes).[99] In return, protection is limited to three years as from the date on which the design was first made available to the public within the Community.[100] Characterising the right protected is not that easy in this regard, seeing that the Regulation explicitly leaves open the relationship between the registered as well as the unregistered design right and other approaches to protection under national law – and specifically the law against unfair competition.[101] At first sight, this unregistered – just as the registered – design appears already to belong to the fourth level of density, i.e. to the "ordinary" intellectual property rights. In fact, it differs from the registered design, after all, only by reason of the lack of formal requirements as well as the clearly shorter period of protection, not, however, by reason of the general requirements of protection (Art. 4 et seqq.[102]) or with regard to the scope of protection as such (Art. 10).

  Even so, it is difficult to ignore the competition law context of the unregistered design, at any rate compared to those legal systems which know a form of protection against imitation outside the specific legal approaches[103] – be it, for instance, the legal figure of "concurrence parasitaire" of French law, developed on

---

[98] Regulation No. 6/2002 of December 12, 2001 on Community designs, OJ L 3 of January 5, 2002, at 1 *et seq.*

[99] Recital 25.

[100] A regulation which, in a certain sense, is similar, but which cannot really serve as an example, as the requirements of protection are not the same, is known in British law in which there also exists an "unregistered design": Part III of the Copyright, Designs and Patents Act 1988; *see* in this regard CORNISH & LLEWELLYN, "Intellectual Property" notes 14-37 *et seq.* (5th ed. 2003), and CORNISH, "Die Zukunft des Designschutzes in Europa aus der Sicht des britischen Rechts," 1998 GRUR Int. 368.

[101] Recital 31 and Art. 96; *see also* KUR, "Ansätze zur Harmonisierung des Lauterkeitsrechts im Bereich des wettbewerblichen Leistungsschutzes," 1998 GRUR Int. 780. This fact is not entirely trivial because in this way this restriction of the term of protection in terms of Community law to three years may, by taking "a detour" via national law – in particular in the form of instruments of competition law affording protection against imitations – again, should the occasion arise, (although not uniform in the internal market) be cancelled; *cf.* in this regard now BGH, September 9, 2005, I ZR 151/02, 2006 GRUR Int. 334 *et seq.* – *Jeans* and further *infra* note 114.

[102] There are, after all, certain differences concerning the date for purposes of determining novelty (Art. 5 Para. 1 (a) and (b)) as well as individual character (Art. 6 Para. 1 (a) and (b)).

[103] For an overview in this regard, *see* BREM, "Der ergänzende wettbewerbsrechtliche Leistungsschutz in Europa" in particular 342 *et seq.* (related to Germany, Switzerland, France, Spain and Italy) (2005).

the basis of Art. 1382 CC,[104] or also the "ergänzender Leistungsschutz" in terms of Sec. 4 No. 9 of the German UWG.[105] This is all the more so as, on the part of the party protected, no action prior to reliance on the protection provided is required, as what is essential – in contrast to registration required in the case of the registered design (Art. 1 Para. 2 (b) Regulation on Designs) – is solely making the design available to the public (Art. 1 Para. 2 (a)). In the case of relying on remedies of competition law this can be no different as a matter of principle. In particular, however, the competition law context emerges from the concrete right to restrain third parties, arising from Art. 19. For, if the registered design as an exclusive right extends to all forms of use, as they are mentioned – not exhaustively – in Art. 19 Para. 1, the "right to prevent the acts referred to in paragraph 1" in the case of the unregistered design remains restricted to acts of use which "[result] from copying the protected design" (Art. 19 Para. 2 subpara. 1). This is not the case, if the

---

[104] The legal figure of "parasitisme" has recently – despite criticism by legal commentators – been affirmed by the judgement of the French Supreme Court of January 30, 2001, Bull. Civ. IV No. 27. *See* in this regard also the note by GROßERICHTER & RAGEADE, 2002 RIW 871 *et seq.* The principle of "concurrence parasitaire" has been introduced by SAINT-GAL, "Concurrence déloyale et concurrence parasitaire (ou agissements parasitaires)" N° 25/26 RIPIA 19 *et seq.* (1956); *see* generally further *e.g.* BURST, "Concurrence déloyale et parasitisme" in particular 97 *et seq.* (1993); PASSA, "Contrefaçon et concurrence déloyale" in particular 126 *et seq.* (1997); LE TOURNEAU, "Le Parasitisme" (1998); also in German-language literature the discussions by BREM, *supra* note 103, at 293 *et seq.*, in particular 303 *et seq.*; KRAßER, "Frankreich," in: ULMER (ed.), "Das Recht des unlauteren Wettbewerbs in den Mitgliedstaaten der Europäischen Wirtschaftsgemeinschaft" 244 *et seq.* (1967); BUYDENS, "Produktpiraterie und unlauterer Wettbewerb – Die Situation in Belgien und Frankreich mit Hinweisen auf die Rechtslage in Deutschland," 1995 GRUR Int. 15 *et seq.*; SCHMIDT-SZALEWSKI, "Der Unterschied zwischen der Klage wegen Verletzung gewerblicher Schutzrechte und der Wettbewerbsklage in der französischen Rechtsprechung," 1997 GRUR Int. 1 *et seq.*

[105] The point of departure for this approach to protection was the "*Record Decision*" ("*Schallplatten-Entscheidung*") of the Supreme Court of the German Reich of April 7, 1910 (RGZ 73, 294), and – as is still the case in France today – it was based on the delictual provision of Sec. 826 BGB; generally with regard to the "*wettbewerbsrechtlicher Leistungsschutz*" ("protection of achievement under competition law"), *see e.g.* BEATER, "Nachahmen im Wettbewerb" (1995); SAMBUC, *supra* note 1; SCHULTE-BECKHAUSEN, "Das Verhältnis des § 1 UWG zu den gewerblichen Schutzrechten und zum Urheberrecht" (1994); WALCH, "Ergänzender Leistungsschutz nach § 1 UWG" (1992); WEIHRAUCH, "Der unmittelbare Leistungsschutz im UWG" (2001); *see also* FEZER, "Leistungsschutz im Wettbewerbsrecht," 1993 WRP 138 *et seq.*; VON GAMM, "Die sklavische Nachahmung," 1973 GRUR 453 *et seq.*; HUBMANN, "Die sklavische Nachahmung," 1975 GRUR 230 *et seq.*; KÖHLER, "Der ergänzende Leistungsschutz: Plädoyer für eine gesetzliche Regelung," 1999 WRP 1075 *et seq.*; KRÜGER, "Der Schutz kurzlebiger Produkte gegen Nachahmungen (Nichttechnischer Bereich)," 1986 GRUR 115 *et seq.*; KUR, 1990 GRUR 1 *et seq.*; *ibidem*, 1998 GRUR Int. 771 *et seq.*; MÜLLER-LAUBE, "Wettbewerbsrechtlicher Schutz gegen Nachahmung und Nachbildung gewerblicher Erzeugnisse," 1992 ZHR 480 *et seq.*; TILMANN, "Der wettbewerbsrechtliche Schutz vor Nachahmungen," 1987 GRUR 865 *et seq. See* most recently also WIEBE, "Unmittelbare Leistungsübernahme im neuen Wettbewerbsrecht," in: OHLY ET AL. (eds.), "FS Schricker" 773 *et seq.* (2005); RIESENHUBER, "Lego – Stein des Anstoßes," 2005 WRP 1118 *et seq.*; STIEPER, "Das Verhältnis von Immaterialgüterrechtsschutz und Nachahmungsschutz nach neuem UWG," 2006 WRP 291 *et seq.*

contested use "results from an independent work of creation by a designer who may be reasonably thought not to be familiar with the design made available to the public by the holder" (Art. 19 Para. 2 subpara. 2).[106] This restriction shows the – at least to some extent – competition law-oriented focus of the protection of the unregistered design, by aiming at preventing the imitator from saving own investments in the conception of a design and, in so doing, to distort competition in such a manner as may actually lead to a market failure.[107]

As such, there certainly do remain arguments in terms of which the unregistered design appears, in fact, as one of those "genuine" intellectual property rights which presently are assigned to the fourth level of density; it may thus be mentioned that it should be possible to formally "declare invalid" an unregistered design,[108] whereas, inversely, the fact that the unregistered design may, at least principally, be the subject of legal transactions (Art. 27 et seqq.) is, as it were, also inherent to other approaches to protection on the third level of density.[109] From such factors, which sometimes put more emphasis on the intellectual property law, at other times on the competition law component, it may, in the final analysis, however, only be deduced that the boundaries between the levels of density discussed here are porous. This realisation also does not present difficulties if one acknowledges up to the fourth and last level of density that the granting of all forms of protection at the core reflect the concern to apply legal instruments to prevent certain forms of market failure; what needs to be assured is that investments of competitors which individuals are capable of making – and which are in the general interest – are not refrained from being made because other competitors can destroy existing profit incentives by means of unhampered takeovers from the outset.

4.3.3.2 Characteristics

Typically but not without exception three particularities characterise the approaches to regulation on this third level of density. These particularities distinguish the special legislation on the third level from general competition law protecting investments on the second level of density:[110]

---

[106] *See also* Recital 21.

[107] Essentially similar Kur, 1998 GRUR Int. 780 ("for many of the cases concerned the same considerations ..., on which protection against imitation in terms of the law against unfair competition rests").

[108] Thus, at any rate, Art. 24 Para. 3 and Art. 81 (c); in actual fact it may be asked whether a right which came into existence not as a result of a formal act (such as also *e.g.* copyright) can really be formally declared invalid, or whether there is not rather a mere finding by a court that the requirements of protection in terms of Art. 4 *et seq.* never existed, and thus no protection was granted in the first place.

[109] *Cf.* in this regard *infra* 4.3.3.2.

[110] *See* in this regard – concerning rights related to copyright – Hilty, 1993 GRUR Int. 823 and by the same author, "Die Leistungsschutzrechte im schweizerischen Urheberrechtsgesetz," 124 UFITA 134 *et seq.* (1994); Weber, "Schutz von Datenbanken – Ein neues Immaterialgüterrecht?," 132 UFITA 16 *et seq.* (1996); by the same author, *supra* note 8, at 588.

- *Elements of an infringement*: The criterion for when a distortion of competition could be expected is concretised to a substantial degree. The elements of an infringement are described in such detail as is comparable to the description of the elements of an infringement in the case of intellectual property rights. Art. 13 of Regulation 2081/92 thus, for example, accurately lists the acts of takeover prohibited. The same may be said with regard to trade mark law, where one customarily finds precise provisions concerning the scope of the likelihood of confusion (e.g. Art. 9 Para. 1 (b) Regulation on the Community trade mark[111]). Typical, in particular, appears in this respect, however, especially database law, Art. 7 Para. 1 defining the extent of a permissible takeover (which must naturally be concretised by the judge). Similarly concrete are the claims for prohibition or compensation in the case of related rights – functionally approximating those under copyright law.

  By virtue of the substantial degree of concretisation of the description of such elements of an infringement, the instruments for protecting investments in question not only become much easier to apply in the courts than general competition law with its sometimes very vague definitions of the elements of an infringement. Beyond this fact, a corollary of this concretisation of cases is that, in a way, the burden of proof is reversed in that, where the elements are satisfied – e.g. if a DVD has been copied –, it is assumed without further ado that the undesired distortion of competition ensues. As dangerous as this may be where the elements of an infringement have been defined too widely (since an insignificant number of copies of the DVD e.g. do not, in fact, already lead to a distortion of competition), as clear is the advantage of not complicating the defence of the protected competitor in an absurd manner, particularly thus not to link it to evidence to be adduced by him.

  This should not, however, belie the fact that a justification for intervening in the market forces of free competition is lacking if it cannot be assumed to be highly probable that the regulated cases will effectively result in a market distortion; all possible attempts of the legislator at over-simplification (e.g. via flatrates) must always be assessed in the light of this fact. Only under these conditions is it permissible – in the general interest – to protect the individual competitor in respect of the investment he has made, not, however, to protect him, despite having made suboptimal investments, against falling prey to natural market adjustment processes.

- *Term of protection*: The second typical particularity of the approaches to regulation on this third level of density is that the investor does not have to prove that in a temporal respect he has not yet been able to achieve an adequate amortisation. Principally, the head start provided by law cannot be longer than the period required under normal conditions – i.e. when the competitor once he has made an investment behaves in an objectively correct manner in free market economy terms – to achieve a "return on investment" and an adequate profit.

---

[111] *Supra* note 76.

In reality, however, proving that such a "return on investment" has not yet been possible is a highly complex matter, seeing that many factors may be at work, which a court in the normal course of events is not in a position to assess adequately. To this extent, it may make sense if instruments for protecting investments set out in special laws provide for a flat-rate average term, after the expiry of which it may be assumed that the amortisation has taken place, or, inversely, prior to the expiry of which it is to be assumed that this could not yet be the case. Against this background, it may at least theoretically be explained why, for example, a database right *sui generis* exists for a period of 15 years or the right of producers of phonograms for 50 years.

Substantial doubt exists, however, concerning the question, how the terms applicable today have been determined. Ultimately, a term of protection may not exceed what is economically necessary, as otherwise the negative effects begin to exceed those that are positive.[112] Especially in the case of related rights it can hardly be ignored that "blind" reliance on copyright law has by far been a more influential factor in laying down the long term of protection than economic reasoning addressing the issue of an adequate amortisation period.[113] The unregistered design right is more convincing in this context, as the three years may definitely be said to cover the period of short-lived articles of design, for example, those subject to trends in fashion, without triggering prohibitive effects already because of a certain possible excessive protection for even shorter-lived articles.[114] In the case of trade mark law and indications of origin in turn, the fact that

---

[112] For a detailed discussion, *see* particularly GORDON, *supra* note 2 (1994), 358 *et seq.*, who, following LIEBOWITZ, "Copyright Law, Photocopying, and Price Discrimination," Vol. 8 Research in Law and Economics 181 *et seq.* (1986), at 183-188, shows how production incentives decrease as the term of protection is extended, whereas the "deadweight loss" factor increases, the economic goal thus being to maximise the difference between these two values.

[113] *See also* ULLRICH, in: SCHRICKER, DREIER & KUR (eds.), *supra* note 8, 115 *et seq.*; generally with regard to the different approaches to justifying the terms of protection in copyright law, *see* RICKETSON, "The Term," 1992 IIC 753 *et seq.*

[114] This restriction of the term of protection would, of course, be factually abolished or overcome where, on the basis of "the exemption" of approaches to protection of individual states in Art. 96 Community Regulation on Designs, complementary national protective rights were to be available. Legal commentators thus rightly refer to the fact that the three-year protection period is "the expression of a conscious graduation in relation to the protection of the registered design", seeing that the unregistered design, because of its lack of publicity, burdens commerce more significantly than a registered right: *See* OHLY, 2004 ZEuP 312 *et seq.*, who consistently rejects the subsequent application of the "*ergänzender Leistungsschutz*" (supplementary protection of achievement) in terms of German law; for a more open interpretation of Art. 96 (which, in its conclusions, is similarly critical, however), *see* KUR, 1998 GRUR Int. 780; the contrary view, it appears, is held (also with regard to German law) by OSTERRIETH, in: KELLER ET AL. (eds.), "FS Tilmann" 235 *et seq.* (2003). This notwithstanding, the German Supreme Court, September 9, 2005, I ZR 151/02, 2006 GRUR Int. 334 *et seq.* – *Jeans* now expressly holds that a claim based on the "*ergänzender Leistungsschutz*" on the grounds of an avoidable deception as to origin pursuant to Secs. 3 and 4, No. 9 (a) UWG is not excluded by reason of the fact that the claimants could have relied on the protection afforded unregistered designs for the jeans model manufac-

the term of protection principally is indefinite or may successively be extended without restriction at certain intervals shows that what is required are not one-time investments, but investments on a continuous basis, as the value in this regard is, as it were, not permanent and needs constantly to be acquired anew through making the investments necessary.[115]

- *Marketability*: The third particularity of such rights protecting investments set out in special laws is that the respective legal position may (as a matter of principle) be assigned, a characteristic precisely not encountered in the case of general competition law; regarding general competition law, claims for compensation which may have been granted may be assigned at the most, not, however, the rights to prevent third parties from performing the acts in question as such.

  There are limits to assignability, however, from a factual point of view. Sure enough, the results of investments in databases or phonograms or audiovisual media for example may be assigned to a third party as such without problem, as a result of which the latter naturally must be in a position to ward off a takeover of the investments concerned (as otherwise competition could be distorted unabatedly, seeing that the acquirer has in a sense redeemed the costs of the investments in the form of the price paid, and must hence now on his part be able to safeguard the – remaining – amortisation period). In contrast, it is evident that, for instance, it should not be possible to assign indications of origin in a way that would make it impossible for the market to establish a relevant correlation with typical geographical characteristics. For, this would have the result that the positive effect of reducing consumer search costs would be turned into its opposite in that, by means of relevant market confusion, there could be a downright systematic distortion of competition.

  It should be added in this context that, on the other hand, precisely this line of argumentation, which previously has also been applied to trade marks in many legal systems, has now been abandoned with regard to the latter. Trade mark rights, as a rule, may be freely traded – i.e. independently from the branch of business concerned[116] –, this not, of course, implying that they, for this reason, do not nevertheless have a basis in the legal protection of invest-

---

tured and distributed by them: "The time-limited protection for an unregistered Community design accordingly does not affect the *a priori* not time-limited claim, based on supplementary protection of achievement under competition law on the grounds of an avoidable deception as to origin pursuant to Secs. 3 and 4, No. 9 (a) UWG, Sec. 1 of the former version of the UWG". *See* in this regard also KIEHTE & GROESCHKE, "'Jeans' – Verteidigung wettbewerblicher Eigenart von Modeneuheiten," 2006 WRP 794 *et seq.*; ORTNER, "Zum gewerblichen Rechtsschutz bei Nachahmung von Modeerzeugnissen," 2006 WRP 189 *et seq.*

115 With regard to the particularities of trade mark law, *see also e.g.* HEINEMANN, *supra* note 8, at 19.

116 Thus *e.g.* Art. 17 Para. 1 Regulation on the Community trade mark *supra* note 76: "A Community trade mark may be transferred, separately from any transfer of the undertaking, in respect of some or all of the goods or services for which it is registered".

ments.[117] This new conception of trade mark rights shows, however, to what extent such rights protecting investments may, in a formal sense, be made to approximate intellectual property rights, such as copyrights or patents. As has already been observed by way of introduction, the boundaries become blurred at the latest at these points, in particular in the case of trade mark rights, where the possibility of freely assigning the rights concerned provides an additional "incentive" to invest in the quality of a trade mark image and, therefore, necessarily in that of products – and this in turn promotes the general interest by optimising competition. Irrespective of this fact, in the case of a trade mark the protected sign as such does not, in a comparable manner, constitute the extraordinary result of an investment, like a copyright-protected work or a patentable invention; rather, it only represents a specific – but likewise not necessarily extraordinary – image of the enterprise behind the trade mark or the product distributed by it.

4.3.4 Intellectual Property Law Attempts at Protecting Investments

For the sake of completeness, the fourth level of density should be mentioned at this point, which is encountered in the form of "ordinary" intellectual property rights. In terms of traditional perceptions, this level is seldom considered in the wider context of competition law; rather, references to ideas of ownership (of tangible property) dominate here.[118] This – supposedly (and especially where grounds of justification based upon natural law are relied upon for according property in the sense of an absolute right to an individual rightholder) – leads to different answers as regards the conception of a right, e.g. concerning the terms of protection. In reality, however, as has already been emphasised on a number of occasions, also traditional intellectual property rights may be justified with good grounds on the basis of aspects of competition law. They are essentially based upon the fact that the prospect of a particular (time limited) position in competition – for the purpose of amortisation and making a profit – creates a particular incentive for producing something of such an extraordinary nature that the legal protection can be linked to that result of the investment.

If one highlights the aim protected by intellectual property rights from this side, the question arises, however, whether a systematical dividing line should, in fact – in accordance with orthodox views – be drawn between the approaches to protection of competition law of the first three levels of density referred to above, on the one

[117] *Cf.* with regard to the functions of trade mark protection *e.g.* LEHMANN, "Die wettbewerbswidrige Ausnutzung und Beeinträchtigung des guten Rufs bekannter Marken, Namen und Herkunftsangaben," 1986 GRUR Int. 14 *et seq.*; HENNING-BODEWIG & KUR, "Marke und Verbraucher" 23, Vol. I (1988); KUR, "Funktionswandel von Schutzrechten," in: SCHRICKER, DREIER & KUR (eds.), *supra* note 8, at 25 *et seq.*

[118] Most recently in detail JÄNICH, "Geistiges Eigentum – eine Komplementärerscheinung zum Sacheingentum?" (2002); GÖTTING, "Der Begriff des Geistigen Eigentums," 2006 GRUR 353 *et seq.*

hand, and this fourth level containing traditional intellectual property rights, on the other. For, on closer scrutiny, one can hardly fail to conclude that it would be arbitrary to define those requirements for protection which would help in distinguishing between the extraordinary and the ordinary, so as to be able to accord a special position in competition to the one who has produced the extraordinary. Such arbitrariness can be avoided if one also on this fourth level of density defines those economic sets of facts for each sector which, in the interest of a functioning market – and in particular the production of outstanding novel products – require a special form of protection.

If one wishes to consistently think this approach through to the end also on the fourth level of density, it cannot be excluded that current intellectual property rights would acquire a clearly different – and particularly more differentiated – appearance. Following orthodox views, this fourth level of density seems to be different from the previous levels in that, in its core, it is directed at those investments which have "innovation" in the widest sense as their goal. If the goal of achieving "innovation" is not reached, the requirement for legal protection is lacking from the outset, be it for a protection of the – unsuccessful – investment as such or, however, for a protection of the result of the investment in question. In concrete terms this means that the supposed "invention" is regarded as obvious, the "work" as not creative. If the protection requirements are met, however, and the borderline suggested by intellectual property law is crossed into what may be considered "innovative", protection is granted. If protection is granted, the scope of protection on this fourth level of density – always following the orthodox view of intellectual property law – will vary, in that the scope covered stands to a certain extent in relation to the quality of "the innovation" in question. However, as against this, neither the investments actually (generally and individually) necessary to produce the innovation, nor the amortisation period (generally and individually) required are taken into account on the fourth level. Accordingly, enormous bandwidths of the most diverse constellations (from small mechanical patents to highly complex biotechnological inventions, from computer programmes to pop songs in the charts to the literary lifework of writers) are subject to uniform terms of protection – maximal 20 years in patent law, 70 years p.m.a. in copyright law.

As much as we may have got used to this concept of the protection of "intellectual property", as little can it be deduced therefrom that it is carved in stone. Nothing speaks against getting to know better the competition-based economic framework, resting as yet on very thin ice, also on this fourth level of density and, in so doing, also to subject the effectiveness of the established regime of protection to closer scrutiny. Such an examination is already mandated by the principle mentioned by way of introduction and, in the end, valid for all four levels, that in a liberal constitutional state ("Rechtsstaat") an intervention in the market forces of free competition is justifiable to the extent only that the dynamic forces of competition do not by themselves produce within an expedient period of time those results, which are intended by granting legal protection. Such restraint is imperative because an excessive intervention in free market mechanisms does not serve to correct a potential market failure anymore and, hence, also is not in the general interest anymore; it would only satisfy the special interests of those benefiting from the legal protection.[119]

4.4 Result

This cursory overview of some of the existing approaches to regulation shows that the notion of protecting investments as an instrument of avoiding distortions of competition, where possible, is by no means unknown to existing – especially also European – law. What is absent is solely the realisation that these instruments are elements of the legal protection of the competitor, and thus parts of the law of market behaviour, factually not conceived in a holistic manner. However, if one understands this law of market behaviour as a uniform legal body, i.e. directed at a sole aim, it will turn out in the end that – irrespective of all formal differences between the legal acts involved – also that question, which must constitute the basis of all further reasoning, is a uniform one: namely, whether the scope of the legal protection granted by the law of market behaviour as a whole has been determined "correctly". This question, however, relates not only to the minimum, but also to the maximum of protection. It needs, therefore, to be ascertained, on the one hand, whether the instruments presently in existence sufficiently cover those areas in which, against the background of the deliberations made, a protection of investments proves to be necessary. On the other hand, it needs similarly to be clarified whether the legal protection is limited to such interventions in free competition as may be justified in the light of considerations of competition law.

Applied to the focus in the foreground here – European legal harmonisation – a further restriction must be taken into account: the European law of market behaviour must first and foremost be directed at safeguarding the functioning of those market mechanisms aimed at realising the internal market as understood in Art. 14 EC (Art. 3 Para. 1 (h) EC). There may surely be collateral concerns such as the strengthening of the competitiveness of Community industry (Art. 3 Para. 1 (m) EC) or also consumer protection law (Art. 3 Para. 1 (t) EC), whereby these different fields of the law of market behaviour may overlap – as has been seen, not necessarily without contradiction. Irrespective of this multiplicity of grounds for regulation, the European legislator complies with its duty only, however, if it places the attempts at harmonisation in an overall context. Proceeding from the existing, overarching objectives for intervening in the market forces of free competition whatsoever, the various components of the law of market behaviour must be developed and structured in such a way that a coherent body of law is created. The European law of market behaviour can be considered coherent from the outset only, if it is capable of ensuring on the level of national law a certain bandwidth of protection entailing the grant-

[119] For a similar assessment related to copyright law, *see* GANEA, "Der Stellenwert des Urheberrechts in den Wirtschaftswissenschaften," in: GANEA ET AL. (eds.), "Festschrift für Adolf Dietz zum 65. Geburtstag" 43 *et seq.* (2001); GORDON, *supra* note 2 (1991-1992), at 857 *et seq.*; WEBER, *supra* note 8, at 593 *et seq.*; as well as with regard to "intellectual property" as a whole, GHIDINI, "Intellectual Property and Competition Law. The Innovation Nexus" 9 *et seq.* (2006).

ing of a minimum as well as a maximum of protection; for, both falling below as well as exceeding this bandwidth of protection involve the risk of prejudicing the idea of the internal market.

The question as to the correct measure of legal protection by the law of market behaviour is to a substantial extent influenced by factual and economic considerations. Jurisprudence alone will thus hardly be helpful in coherently finding the answers to the questions posed; rather, the considerable lack of understanding existing in this regard can only be dealt with meaningfully in terms of interdisciplinary research approaches. After all, jurisprudence may, however, make a decisive contribution by abandoning rigid traditional constructions. For, theoretical legal categories, as specifically reflected in the distinction between "intellectual property", said to be "absolute" in nature, on the one hand, and rights to prevent third parties from performing certain acts based on the law against unfair competition, on the other, would probably fail where the endeavour is to address the existing need for protection in an adequate but not excessive manner.[120] In particular the examples on the third level of density show that attempts at protection which are difficult to classify in a systematically meaningful manner long since exist in positive law. To force these attempts at protection into the existing doctrinal concept not yet based upon current insights into competition law would be wrong. Against this background, the sole endeavour of jurisprudence should be to examine and to advance those legal approaches to protection which, in an economic respect, prove to be indispensable to protect dynamic competition against a potential market failure in view of their nature, their effectiveness and the existing interfaces.

5. Insights

5.1 Internal Interfaces within Competition Law in a Wider Sense

The need for competition law in a wide sense is based upon the fact that potentially every market participant, by means of individual or collective behaviour, is in a position to influence the functioning of competition in such a way as to directly or indirectly positively or negatively affect other market participants. Looked at from the other side this means that all forms of legally intervening in free competition which positively or negatively affect certain market participants by nature always have an effect on other market participants not directly addressed by the concrete legal act, too.

This interdependence has factual reasons grounded in the nature of the way competition functions as such. Which system of regulating acts of intervention in free competition is chosen[121] thus, in the final analysis, remains without significance. Against the background of this appreciation it hence also turns out to be irrelevant whether individual aspects of competition law in a wider sense – e.g. consumer protection – are considered a separate body of law or are regarded as part of a compre-

---

[120] *Cf.* WEBER, *supra* note 8, at 583 *et seq.*, in particular 591 *et seq.* ("third track" ["*dritte Spur*"]).

[121] With regard to the different systems of regulation, *see supra* 4.3.

hensive body of rules (for instance an act of the law against unfair competition); in either case potential competitors will be affected indirectly. From this it follows that – irrespective of the system of regulation formally chosen – the interfaces between those fields which in their totality constitute competition law in a wider sense,[122] will always remain blurred if looked at from a functional perspective.

This means in concrete terms that the application of the law aimed at guiding the market behaviour of individual participants in competition is a highly complex matter, as it needs constantly to be observed which effect regulations in an individual field will have on all other fields. To this extent the legal protection of the competitor, focused on here, must also necessarily be seen in the context of competition law in a wider sense. This explains why the legal protection granted to an individual competitor – in the sense that forms of behaviour of third parties which may frustrate the amortisation of investments he has made are prohibited – can only at first be directed at his interests. Considered in the overall context, it is primarily in the general interest that his willingness to invest must be maintained; for, only in this way can it be assured that constantly new goods and items of value are created. Simultaneously, a view of the larger framework shows that these positive effects in the general interest depend on the actual conception and scope of the legal protection. This is so as dynamic competition from which positive effects may be expected can be promoted through legal intervention to a certain extent only. As soon as the intervention benefiting individual market participants exceeds a critical point, other potential market participants are prevented from taking part in competition; this in turn jeopardises the dynamic nature of competition. Typically, this is the case, where the investments of a market participant are not protected in the interest of functioning competition anymore, but the protection of investments, on the contrary, assists an individual market participant to escape the consequences of competition, namely a process of market adjustment.

5.2 External Interfaces in Relation to Further Bodies of Rules

The already highly complex nature of the mechanisms regulating competition law as such is enhanced further by the fact that also other bodies of rules may contain legal provisions which for their part may have an influence on the effectiveness and the dynamic nature of competition. As a typical example – not to be discussed further here, however – the way the law of contract is structured may be mentioned, as this creates an indefinite number of possibilities for guiding the behaviour of participants in competition by means of (from the perspective of competition law) external mechanisms. Excessively protective labour law provisions may thus have the effect that potentially possible investments by a competitor will not, in fact, be made, the result being that the various competition law systems of incentives directed at him fail to achieve their effect.

Depending on one's point of view one may now, in relation to competition law, consider also genuine intellectual property rights (such as, for example, copyrights

---

[122] *See* with regard to these fields *supra* 4.2.

or patents) as external bodies of rules. This will at any rate be the position of those who reject the approach proposed here, in terms of which attempts of competition law aimed at preventing a market failure gradually become more dense – from the general clause-like protection of functioning competition in general to the privileged market position by virtue of the extraordinary character of the result of an investment (e.g. an invention) in particular. However, even if intellectual property rights are regarded as an independent system of regulation (however to be justified), the conclusion that exclusive rights have a direct and far-reaching effect on the functioning of competition cannot be ignored. Irrespective of whether or not one views genuine intellectual property rights as part of competition law in its widest sense, one will hence have to accept that the granting of either more or less intellectual property protection will have different effects on the markets concerned. If these effects by their nature do not take place in an isolated but in a competition context, an interaction between competition law and intellectual property law cannot be avoided even if one were to justify the latter with regard to natural law ideas.

Considered against this background the question of the scope and the confines of the group of all those legal attempts which are regarded as part of competition law is not decisive; crucial is solely whether from a functional perspective the legal instruments in question serve to govern competition. Nevertheless, that wide a use of the term competition law fails in view of customary terminology. Even if the delimitations within competition law – as a result of the fact that the interfaces between overlapping components are unclear – may be of a highly amorphous nature, the "external limits" of the term competition law are predefined, wherefore the term is applied in a narrow sense. If one instead looks for a "more open" generic term – a term which also leaves room for those bodies of legal rules, which for their part may influence the functioning of competition, without constituting competition law norms in a technical legal sense –, the wide term of the law of market behaviour, already defined by way of introduction, is suited best. In fact, this term helps circumnavigating futile delimitation attempts; it can, for instance, hardly be ignored that legal measures of intellectual property law aimed at preventing third parties from performing certain acts in a similar way focus on undesirable behaviour of competitors in the relevant market as "proper" competition law.

5.3 Challenges for European Law

If the establishment of an internal market as envisaged in Art. 14 EC is a central objective of European law, the European legislator, in the final analysis, cannot but comprehend the market in its totality. This is true as far as the factors constituting the internal market as such are concerned, but also with regard to the legal instruments intended to guide the functioning and the existence of the internal market. Under these circumstances, what has been described here as the law of market behaviour, gains central significance. The core concern of this law of market behaviour is to influence the individual behaviour of the participants in competition in such a way that they are not in a position to manipulate the presumed favourable effects of dynamic competition – being in the general interest – in a manner that primarily benefits themselves. Admittedly, this competition-centred focus needs to be relativised to the extent that, of course, also factors not directly related to competition (such as, for example, social justice, ecological sustainability etc.) may and should have a significant influence on the conception of the law of market behaviour. However, within the framework of the liberal constitutional state ("Rechtsstaat") presumed here, legal norms aimed at safeguarding dynamic competition will, in a sense, constitute at least the nucleus of the law of market behaviour.

With a view to this competition-centred nucleus, the above discussion may be said to have shown that the approach of the law of market behaviour may under different perspectives be reduced to one idea: With regard to certain categories of investments, which are potentially threatened in that they may be taken over too easily by third parties, individual competitors are to be protected, by making available to them specific remedies, so as to ensure that the stated investments are not refrained from being made because there are no prospects of sufficient opportunities of amortisation and profit. The central element of the law of market behaviour thus is the legal protection of investments, which, depending on the circumstances, may assume a whole bandwidth of forms in positive law. The legal rules in this regard range from provisions concerning the protection of mere production investments to systems of incentives for investments aimed at actual innovation. Irrespective of this fact, however, one characteristic is always peculiar to the protection of investments: It must constantly be justifiable why there should be a protection of investments. This justification can never rest solely on the interests of the protected participant in competition; rather, his protection, in the end, seeks "only" to preserve the functioning of dynamic competition.

Such a holistic perception is lacking at the level of European law. In fact, as has been shown, numerous fragments do exist, fragments which may actually be committed to the objectives set out above. The fashioning of the various legal approaches to protection occurs to a large extent in an isolated manner, however, and without having regard to the existing interdependencies, interacting in a highly complex way. Under these circumstances, the virulent danger exists that the protection granted is not assessed in terms of its necessity for purposes of competition but in the light of arbitrary, intransparent criteria. Instead, the influence of those actors who benefit individually from legal protection appears – as in most legislative processes – to be of primary importance while the impacts of such protection on competition as a whole – and hence the general interest – remain, as experience has shown, unexplored. If the fact that the interacting interdependencies are at least partially insufficiently explored leads to approaches to protection not properly reflected on, European law runs the risk of providing excessive protection, this – contrary to the objective of the law of market behaviour – not promoting but restraining dynamic competition. This is all the more so as certain approaches to protection – primarily those on the third level of density – are preferentially "disguised" as intellectual property rights, in view of the fact that there apparently exists doubt whether the EU is competent to regulate matters pertaining to competition law.

Against this background, the demand for a holistic approach to the law of market behaviour in general – and for a focus on the legal protection of the competitor in particular – by no means implies (only) a further extension of the currently existing instruments of legal protection. It could rather be necessary to ensure the functioning of the internal market also by prohibiting the national legislator from formulating certain excessive approaches to protection. For, a harmonisation of the law of market behaviour does not necessarily entail more extensive rights being granted; where market adjustment processes are interfered with by the excessive protection of competitors, harmonisation may also lead to less extensive legal protection. One way or another, a harmonisation of the European law of market behaviour may not, however – as has been shown[123] – result in a uniform definition of ethical values; if necessary, this is the responsibility of the national legislator, in order to take account, for example, of the cultural particularities of a country. Accordingly, a European harmonisation of the law of market behaviour can only be directed at safeguarding dynamic competition in the internal market in such a way that the latter is protected against a market failure by means of an adequate but not too extensive legal approach to protection; it must be promoted in such a way that the tasks and the goals articulated in Arts. 2 and 3 EC can be fulfilled and reached.

---

[123] *Supra* 3.3.

International Unfair Competition Law

Frauke Henning-Bodewig

1. Preliminary Comment

Before discussing the harmonisation of unfair competition law within the EU we must first ask whether any international provisions exist, and if so what these are. As a rule Community law is subject to international law requirements.[1] Nor should one forget that harmonisation of unfair competition law within Europe can still only constitute the second-best solution. Competition crosses borders not only in Europe but throughout the world, as reflected in the words globalisation and internet, to take but two examples. The aim, and the desirable aim, is therefore beyond doubt a global fair-play standard in competition.

However, it is obvious that such a global harmonisation is even more difficult to achieve than European harmonisation. For this reason, the few international agreements concluded to date are all the more important. In the field of relevance here these are

- The Paris Convention on the Protection of Industrial Property (PC)
- The Agreement "Trade Related Aspects of Intellectual Property Rights" (TRIPS).

2. The Paris Convention

2.1 Unfair Competition Law as a Supplement to IP Rights

The Paris Convention dates back to 1883,[2] and is an international treaty signed by over 170 countries. The aim of the PC is to provide international protection to industrial property (the international protection of copyright is to be found in the Revised Berne Convention). Accordingly the PC primarily deals with patent, trademark and design law, as well as trade names and indications of origin. Against the background of these objectives, the provisions concerning unfair competition law are in any

---

[1] On the relationship between Community Law and TRIPS, *see* for instance the decisions of the ECJ dated June 16, 1988, Case C-53/96, 1998 ECR I-3603 – *Hèrmes* and December 14, 2000, Case C-300/98 – *Dior*, and the Havanna-decision (note 13).

[2] On the PC, *see* for instance BODENHAUSEN, "Guide to the Application of the Paris Convention of Industrial Property" (1968) and LADAS, "The International Protection of Industrial Property"(1975); WADLOW, "The International Law of Unfair Competition: the British Origins of Article 10bis of the Paris Convention for the Protection of Industrial Property," Oxford Intellectual Property Research Centre Working Paper Series No. 4 February 2003, <www.oiprc.ox.ac.uk/EJWP043.html>.

event not a priority function of the PC. The fact that they were included nevertheless is to be seen as a supplement to the hard core of IP law.

From this point of view, as a supplement to IP rights, a provision was included in the PC at a very early stage. It is today to be found in Art. 10bis of the Convention, and is of all the more importance in that it is the only comprehensive regulation of unfair competition law at international level.

2.2 The Basic Principles of the PC

As stated the PC is an international treaty, and of itself it does not create uniform substantive law. Nor does it oblige its Member States to create uniform national law. Instead, the PC "works" with two principles, namely:

- The principle of national treatment. This means that nationals of other Member States must be treated like a country's own nationals.
- The principle of minimum protection. This means that a specific minimum standard of protection is to be granted to the nationals of other Member States who are entitled to rely on the principle of national treatment.

The result of the combination of these two principles is that in any Member State the nationals of other PC states enjoy the same protection as its own nationals, and at least the minimum protection laid down in the PC. In many countries, the PC is regarded as being self executing. i.e. the nationals of other Member States can rely on it directly.[3]

Thus the PC does not include an obligation on its Member States to adopt the minimum protection into its own national law and to grant it to its own nationals. Since, however, most countries try to avoid any discrimination of their own citizen (possible according to the PC), many of them have adopted the PC minimum standard into their own national law.[4] Even if only indirectly, this led to a certain de facto harmonisation on the basis of the PC minimum standard.

2.3 The Difficulties in Creating an International Standard of Commercial Fairness

As mentioned above, the aim of the PC was the international protection of industrial property rights and not the protection against unfair competition. The fact that the latter was nevertheless included is all the more remarkable in the light of the situation at the beginning of the 20th century. At this time most states signing the Convention had at best very basic legal rules against unfair competition. Moreover, they favoured different approaches. This was due to the fact that the major industrial and

---

3 Whether this is the case is determined according to the constitutional law of each Member State.

4 In many European countries, unfair competition protection derived from Art. 10bis of the PC. An example is Belgium, where the protection was initially granted directly on the basis of this provision, then it was adopted almost word for word in the first (criminal law) regulations and subsequently extended until it led to the present very broad "Trade Practices Act" of 1991, which also serves consumer protection. *See* also the contribution of Prof Stuyck in this book.

trading nations of the time, France, Germany/Austria and Great Britain had applied very different methods in attempting to deal with the new problem of unfair competition that resulted from the introduction of the freedom of trade:

- In France, judicial practice based on Art. 1382 of the Civil Code developed a special unwritten offence of "concurrence déloyale", which provided generous tort law protection to the damaged competitor against the likelihood of confusion, imitation, disparagement, disclosure of trade secrets, parasitical competition, etc.
- In Germany and Austria, for systematic reasons separate laws were adopted to prevent unfair competitive activity, working with broadly-worded general clauses based on "bones mores" in competition and specified by means of individual offences.
- In Great Britain the special features of common law meant that the approach concentrated on the possibilities provided by this system (in particular "passing off") and for the rest relied on strong self regulation.

In the light of these differences in the legal approaches from the very start, a common solution within the framework of the PC initially appeared difficult to imagine. The fact that it ultimately happened was due to the following: All three major industrial countries of the time complained that their business enterprises were facing unfair competition when trading abroad, in particular that domestic competitors were given preference. In addition, it was realised at an early stage that IP rights did not in each case lead to fair solutions that did justice to the interests involved; thus there was a need for a more flexible supplement. Against this background, the extension of the principle of national treatment to protection against unfair competition appeared very attractive. The idea of thereby being able to provide better protection for a country's own enterprises abroad in any event proved sufficient to overcome the differences in the legal approaches.

2.4 The Compromise: A General Clause With Specific Cases

This led firstly to the still remarkable compromise between the continental European legal tradition, in particular the preference for broad prohibitions based on a general clause, and the British approach that prefers narrowly defined cases. It is not true that Art. 10bis of the PC was concluded in response to pressure by France and Germany and against the wishes of Great Britain. As more recent studies show, Great Britain was on the contrary in part the decisive force for the creation of Art. 10bis.[5]

In any event, the Brussels 1900 conference included a provision (today's Art. 10bis Para. 1 of the PC) that imposed an obligation on the Member States to extend the protection granted to nationals to members of other signatory states. The recognition of the "national principle" brought unfair competition law within the subject matter of the PC, making it a field of industrial property (according to Art. 1 Para. 2

---

[5] WADLOW, *supra* note 2.

of the PC). This is remarkable since this classification of unfair competition law under the topic of intellectual property is by no means undisputed.[6]

In subsequent revision conferences, which will not be dealt with in any further detail here, the basic provision of Art. 10bis was then extended.[7] Firstly, the obligation was included to grant effective protection against "dishonest commercial practices". At a further revision conference, agreement was reached on the definition of commercial unfairness that today can be found in Art. 10bis Para. 2 of the Convention. This defines as unfair any act that is "contrary to honest practices in industrial or commercial matters". At the 1925 revision conference of The Hague, the general clause of Para. 1 was given closer definition by means of examples; firstly through the addition of the likelihood of confusion and disparagement, and finally – but only at the 1958 revision conference – the prohibition on misleading indications. This substantive law provision was supplemented by Art. 10ter of the PC, according to which all countries of the Union are obliged to make available appropriate legal remedies to repress unfair competition, which also includes the possibility for federations and associations to take action.

2.5 Art. 10bis of the PC – Unfair Competition Law in a Nutshell

Overall, a small miracle, namely international unfair competition law in a nutshell, was created at a very early stage. The remarkable compromise between the decisive industrialised nations at the end of the 19th n century led, in brief, to the following solution:

- Protection against unfair competition is subject to national treatment, i.e. a country must grant tradesmen of another Member State the same protection as its own nationals, irrespective of their place of business.

This protection consists at least of the following:

- The Union countries grant "effective protection against unfair competition" (Para. 1).
- "Unfair competition" is defined as any act of competition "contrary to honest practices in industrial or commercial matters" (Para. 2).
- According to Para. 3, the following in particular are to be prohibited as acts of unfair competition:
- creating confusion;
- disparagement of competitors by means of false allegations;
- misleading indications about one's own products.

---

6 For instance, the ECJ does not include unfair competition law within "intellectual property", see ECJ, June 17, 1981, Case C-113/80, 1981 ECR I-01625.

7 *See* for details the literature cited *supra* note 2; in addition HENNING-BODEWIG, 30 IIC 166 (1999); HENNING-BODEWIG, "Unfair Competition Law – European Union and Member States" 17 *et seq.* (2006).

- Pursuant to Art. 10ter Para. 1 of the Convention, nationals of the other countries of the Union must be provided with appropriate legal remedies, and legal action by federations and associations must be permitted (Para. 2).

2.6 Construction of Art. 10bis of the Convention

However, how is Art. 10bis to be construed? This is difficult to answer. There is practically no recent literature on the construction of the individual terms, neither on the underlying definition of commercial fairness (infringement of "honest practices") nor on the question of how a likelihood of confusion or a likelihood of deception is to be determined and how the differentiation to IP rights (such as trademark rights) is to be made.[8] Where any position is taken up, it is emphasised that for instance the expression "honest practices" refers to actual practices in the trade in question, and that these can and must be corrected by an ethical element, since the relevant practices are only decisive if they are "honest".

The lack of a detailed analysis of the contents of Art. 10bis becomes understandable if one recalls the perspective from which the interpretation is to made. The PC is an international treaty. This means that the point of view of an individual Member State or even a group of Member States cannot be decisive for interpretation. On the contrary the PC is to be construed autonomously, i.e. from within itself.[9] Admittedly the answer to the question of what is a "trade practice" can primarily be based on the trade practices in the country in which a conflict of interest arises; however, any cross-border trade must also take into account international trade practices. It is even more difficult to answer the question of what is "honest" within the framework of these trade practices. For instance, in certain Member States the question of commercial fairness is also (or even primarily) determined by taking into account consumer interests, while in other countries it depends more on the interests of competitors, and possibly also other interests.[10] With a competitive action limited to one Member State, it can be argued that the basis must primarily be the view in this Member State; but this is not possible with multi-state competition. In this way, therefore, consumer interests can also be included in the assessment. For the rest, consumer interests, however, do not play any direct role in the provision of Art. 10bis of the PC. This provision is not a consumer protection legislation but, as its inclusion in industrial property rights and the criterion of "competitive acts" shows, a provision mainly in the interests of tradesmen.

2.7 The Harmonisation Effect of Art. 10bis of the PC

What influence does the provision in the PC have on the unfair competition laws of the individual states? In the initial stages, the effects of Art. 10bis on national legislation of the Union states were considerable. Although, as already stated, the PC did

---

[8] *See* the literature cited *supra* note 2.

[9] SCHRICKER, "Großkommentar UWG", Introduction, points F 101 et seq. (1994).

[10] On the purpose of protection of unfair competition law in the 25 EU states, *see* the country reports in HENNING-BODEWIG, *supra* note 7 (2006).

not oblige its Member States to transpose the minimum standards laid down in the Convention into their own national law, a number of Member States took Art. 10bis as the model for the adoption of national unfair competition legislation. In particular, the expression "honest trade practice" and the protection of the three special cases (the examples in Art. 10bis Para. 3) were adopted in many countries. Today, it is still obvious in many countries that European competition law has very considerable roots in Art. 10bis of the PC.

However, it is also obvious that many countries have in the meantime moved beyond Art. 10bis of the PC. This provision had its greatest effect during the stage in which the countries were attempting to develop their own national competition law and were consequently open to suggestions. By the middle of the 20th century, this development had come to a standstill, at least as far as concerned the PC. By this time, most industrial nations had developed their own unfair competition law, whose basic roots were admittedly frequently in Art. 10bis, but which had been developed in accordance with the special needs of each market and adjusted to the other elements of the respective legal system. Other Member States such as Great Britain, deliberately refused to adopt Art. 10bis into national law.

This was the limit of the effects of Art. 10bis, at least for most countries of Europe; its role as a force for further development and harmonisation was taken over by the European Union and its harmonisation efforts. In order to be able to continue to act as a pacemaker, Art. 10bis would have had to be adapted and modernised, for instance with respect to the importance of consumer protection within unfair competition law. However, there has been no such further development of the PC since the Stockholm revision conference in 1958. Nor is it probable in the light of the political constellation.

This does not mean that Art. 10bis is today without any influence. In particular in developing countries that as yet do not have a sufficient unfair competition law, there is a strong demand for a generally acceptable model for national legislation. Not least for this reason did WIPO decide in 2000 to take Art. 10bis as the basis for the "WIPO Model Provisions" which will be presented by Mr. Höpperger.

3. TRIPS

The second major international agreement in the field of intellectual property is the agreement on "Trade Related Aspects of International Property Rights" (TRIPS). TRIPS is part of the World Trade Organisation (WTO) and, like the latter, was concluded primarily at the initiative of the USA.[11]

---

[11] On the TRIPS Agreement, *cf.*, *e.g.* CHASEN ROSS, in: STEWARD (ed.), "The GATT Uruguay Round" 2245 *et seq.*, Vol. 2 (1993); BLAKENEY, "Trade-Related Aspects of Intellectual Property Rights: A Concise guide to the TRIPS Agreement" (1996); STAEHELIN, "Das TRIPs-Abkommen" (1997); GERVAIS, "The TRIPS Agreement: Drafting History and Analysis" (2nd ed. 2003); REGER, "Der internationale Schutz gegen unlauteren Wettbewerb und das TRIPS-Abkommen" (1999); MANKOWSKI, 2001 GRUR Int. 100.

3.1 Basic Features of TRIPS

TRIPS is in many respect based on the Paris Convention (often referred to as the "Paris-Plus" approad). It contains extensive and detailed provisions in all fields of intellectual property. Unlike the PC, TRIPS is not limited to a requirement for national treatment and minimum protection, but directly obliges the Member States to adjust their own national laws to the various provisions. TRIPS also includes, for the first time in intellectual property law, a most-favoured-nation clause. In addition, again unlike the PC, TRIPS devotes considerable attention to the enforcement of rights. Conflicts between Member States are to be settled by specific proceedings, the "dispute prevention and settlement procedure". Failure to comply with the TRIPS obligations can be the basis for trade sanctions and the withdrawal of trading privileges. TRIPS is directly applicable if national constitutional law permits the direct application of such international treaties.[12]

3.2 TRIPS and Unfair Competition Law

As mentioned, TRIPS' subject matter is intellectual property. According to TRIPS and unlike the PC, this does not include unfair competition law. Thus there is no provision in TRIPS that directly corresponds to Art. 10bis of the PC. Unfair competition law as such is not regulated in Part II to IV of the TRIPS Agreement, which contains the materials regulated.

On the other hand, TRIPS regulates specific cases that in certain member countries are regarded as part of unfair competition law or at least have a close relationship with it. These are the protection of business secrets and the protection of geographical indications of origin. Within these two provisions (to be found in Art. 22 Para. 2 and Art. 39 Para. 1 of TRIPS), direct reference is made to Art. 10bis of the PC. Thus according to Art. 22 Para. 2 of the TRIPS Agreement, the Member States are required to protect geographical indications of origin against misleading designations or generally anything that "constitutes an act of unfair competition within the meaning of Art. 10bis of the PC." The same applies to the protection of undisclosed information.

However, there is also a general reference to the PC. Pursuant to Art. 2 Para. 1, the PC must generally be complied with in respect of the matters regulated in TRIPS. It is not clear whether it means that TRIPS generally obliges Member States to comply with Art. 10bis of the PC (which according to the TRIPS mechanisms would imply adoption in national law). Taken literarily, the general obligation to comply with the PC only applies to the matters regulated in TRIPS and part II to IV of TRIPS do not include unfair competition law as such, but only the special aspects of geographical indications of origin and business secrets. On the other hand, the Appellate Body of the WIPO has decided that at least in respect to trade names Art. 2 must be construed widely.[13] Furthermore, in the opinion of the

---

[12] SCHRICKER, *supra* note 9.

[13] For an in-depth discussion *see* REGER, *supra* note 11 and the "Havanna Club" case, which concerned the protection of a trade name; Panel Report, US-Section 211 Omnibus Appropriations Act of 1998 of August 6, 2001 and February 22, 2002.

ECJ[14] the Member States are at liberty to construe the concept of "intellectual property", not defined in TRIPS, such that it also includes the possibility of actions under unfair competition law to prevent imitation (e.g. of a design). However, this only applies to cases such as slavish imitation, parasitic exploitation of a competitor's commercial achievements, etc., which in certain countries can lead to the same results as IP rights. Whether this means that the "Paris Plus"-effect of TRIPS can also be extended to Art. 10bis PC as such remains to be seen.

4. Conclusion

International unfair competition law is essentially to be found in Art. 10bis of the Paris Convention. This provision, almost 100 years old, contains a small unfair competition law "in a nutshell" – with a general clause, a definition of commercial fairness and three special cases. In particular during the initial stages, Art. 10bis had a great influence on the development of national unfair competition law in many countries. This pacemaker function has today, however, been considerably reduced, since it has not been possible to adapt Art. 10bis to the modern problems of unfair competition law – such as the relationship to consumer protection.

The second major international regulation in the field at issue, TRIPS, does not contain any explicit provision for unfair competition law. Whether the "Paris-Plus"-effect of TRIPS can indirectly be extended to Art. 10bis PC is doubtful. It seems that the opportunity was missed to mitigate the all-or-nothing principle of IP rights by means of a supplement to intellectual property rights through unfair competition law, and to create a uniform standard of protection of fair play in competition.

[14] ECJ, December 14, 2000, joined cases C-300/98 und C-392/98, 2000 ECR I-11307 – *Dior und Assco.*

Protection Against Unfair Competition at the International Level – The Paris Convention, the 1996 Model Provisions and the Current Work of the World Intellectual Property Organisation*

Marcus Höpperger and Martin Senftleben

1. Introduction

One of the main characteristics of a market economy is the presence of competition between various actors in the market.[1] The question where the line should be drawn between fair competition and unacceptable competitive behaviour has created abundant debate and literature. In the 90s, the World Intellectual Property Organisation (WIPO) undertook a number of activities dealing with the topic of protection against unfair competition. A study on protection against unfair competition reflecting the world situation at that time was presented in 1994.[2] WIPO Model Provisions on Protection Against Unfair Competition were published in 1996.[3] In section 2. which follows, Art. 10*bis* of the Paris Convention which anchors the protection against unfair competition in the international legal framework of industrial property rights, will be discussed. An analysis of the 1996 Model Provisions will be conducted in section 3. Section 4., the final section, contains concluding remarks and an outlook.

2. The Paris Convention

Art. 10*bis* of the Paris Convention (PC) is the basic international norm in the field of unfair competition law. By virtue of the reference in Art. 2 Para. 1 TRIPS, it creates also an obligation among WTO Members to ensure protection against unfair com-

---

* Revised and expanded version of a presentation made at the Conference on Unfair Competition Law organised by the Max Planck Institute for Intellectual Property, Competition and Tax Law, Budapest, June 16 to 18, 2005. The views expressed in the present article are those of the authors. They do not constitute an official position of the World Intellectual Property Organisation or of any of its Member States.

1 *Cf.* ULMER, "Das Recht des unlauteren Wettbewerbs in den Mitgliedstaaten der Europäischen Wirtschaftsgemeinschaft" 1-3 and 58-60, Vol. I (1965); KÖHLER, in: BAUMBACH & HEFERMEHL, "Wettbewerbsrecht" – with comments by KÖHLER & BORNKAMM 14-27 (23rd ed. 2004).

2 WIPO publication No. 725, Geneva 1994.

3 WIPO publication No. 832, Geneva 1996.

4 *Cf.* MICKLITZ (ed.), "Study of the Institut für Europäisches Wirtschafts- und Verbraucherrecht on a fair trading framework for the European Community," dated November 2000, 13 and 467, made available on the Internet at <http://www.europa.eu.int/comm/dgs/health_consumer/library/surveys/sur21_vol3_en.pdf> (date of last visit: October 25, 2005).

petition under the TRIPS Agreement.[5] In the following subsection, an overview of the historical development of Art. 10*bis* will be given. Subsequently, the contents of the provision will be discussed.

2.1 The Historical Development of Article 10*bis*

Protection against unfair competition has been recognised as an element of industrial property protection for more than a century.[6] In 1900, the Brussels Conference for the Revision of the Paris Convention agreed that "[n]ationals of the Convention [...] shall enjoy, in all States of the Union, the protection granted to nationals against unfair competition".[7] The new international norm was laid down in Art. 10*bis*. Subsequent diplomatic conferences went beyond the principle of national treatment.[8]

At the 1911 Revision Conference of Washington, agreement could be reached on an obligation among Convention countries to assure effective protection.[9] In 1925, the Revision Conference of The Hague defined this obligation in more specific terms by introducing a definition and two examples of acts of unfair competition in Art. 10*bis*. The first example clarified that all acts creating confusion with the products of a competitor must be prohibited. Pursuant to the second example, false allegations discrediting the products of a competitor constitute forbidden acts of unfair competition.[10] At the 1934 London Conference, the scope of these examples was broadened by replacing the reference to a competitor's products with the formula of "the establishment, the goods, or the industrial or commercial activities of a com-

---

5 *Cf.* FIKENTSCHER, "Historical Origins and Opportunities for Development of an International Competition Law in the TRIPs Agreement of the World Trade Organisation (WTO) and Beyond," in: BEIER & SCHRICKER (eds.), "From GATT to TRIPs – The Agreement on Trade-Related Aspects of Intellectual Property Rights" 226-238, 233-238 (1996); HEINEMANN, "Antitrust Law of Intellectual Property in the TRIPs Agreement of the World Trade Organisation," in: BEIER & SCHRICKER, *ibid.*, 239-247, 240.

6 For a brief overview of the historical development, *see* ULMER, *supra* note 1, at 21-24; BODENHAUSEN, "Guide to the Application of the Paris Convention for the Protection of Industrial Property" WIPO publication No. 611, 142-143 (1969); GLÖCKNER, in: HARTE-BAVENDAMM & HENNING-BODEWIG (eds.), "Gesetz gegen den unlauteren Wettbewerb (UWG)" 46, note 1 (2004). A detailed description is given by LADAS, "Patents, Trademarks, and Related Rights – National and International Protection" 1678-1685, Vol. 3 (1975).

7 *See "Union internationale pour la protection de la propriété industrielle," Actes de la Conférence réunie à Bruxelles du 1er au 14 décembre 1897 et du 11 au 14 décembre 1900, Berne 1901, 164 (proposal by France), 187-188, 310, 382-383 (discussion and adoption).*

8 The principle of national treatment as such does not impose an obligation on the Members of the Paris Union to afford protection against acts of unfair competition. *Cf.* LADAS, *supra* note 6, at 1678.

9 *See "Union internationale pour la protection de la propriété industrielle," Actes de la conférence réunie à Washington du 15 mai au 2 juin 1911, Berne 1911, 53 (proposal), 105, 224, 255, 305, 310 (observations and adoption).*

10 *See "Union internationale pour la protection de la propriété industrielle," Actes de la conférence réunie à La Haye du 8 octobre au 6 novembre 1925, Berne 1926, 252, 255 (proposal), 348, 351, 472, 478, 525, 546-547, 578, 581 (observations and adoption).*

petitor".[11] A proposal by Germany seeking to prohibit certain forms of comparative advertising did not meet with approval.[12] A proposal tabled by Denmark, France, Norway, Sweden and Switzerland which aimed to prohibit false allegations referring to the origin, nature, manufacture, sale of products, or the quality of the commercial establishment or to industrial awards, was also rejected.[13] At the 1958 Lisbon Conference, however, a similar proposal by Austria was adopted, which led to the incorporation of a further example of acts of unfair competition, namely acts concerning indications or allegations liable to mislead the public as to the nature, manufacturing process, characteristics, suitability for their purpose or quantity of the goods.[14]

The present text of Art. 10*bis* mirrors the outlined stages of development. The first paragraph sets forth the obligation to ensure effective protection against unfair competition. In the second paragraph, acts of unfair competition are defined as "[a]ny act of competition contrary to honest practices in industrial or commercial matters". The third paragraph contains the aforementioned examples of acts which, in particular, must be prohibited: the causing of confusion with respect to a competitor's establishment, goods or activities (item 1), the discrediting of a competitor's establishment, goods or activities (item 2), and the misleading of the public as to the nature or other characteristics of one's own goods (item 3). The provisions of Art. 10*bis* are supplemented by Art. 10*ter* which provides for appropriate legal remedies capable of effectively repressing acts of unfair competition.

2.2 The Framework for Protection Established in Art. 10*bis*

Art. 10*bis* establishes a flexible, open minimum standard of protection against unfair competition. The obligation to assure effective protection, laid down in paragraph 1, does not require the enactment of specific legislation. Its implementation into national law is allowed to reflect the different traditions and historical sources of unfair competition law.[15] General tort law provisions and, in the sphere of the Anglo-American tradition, common law actions for passing off were invoked to ensure protection, and often combined with statutes or regulations

---

[11] *See "Union internationale pour la protection de la propriété industrielle," Actes de la conférence réunie à Londres du 1er mai au 2 juin 1934,* Berne 1934, 197-198 (proposal), 418-419 (discussion and adoption).

[12] *See "Actes de Londres," supra* note 11, at 419.

[13] *See "Actes de Londres," supra* note 11, at 419.

[14] *See "Union internationale pour la protection de la propriété industrielle," Actes de la conférence réunie à Lisbonne du 6 au 31 octobre 1958*, Geneva 1963, 725, 784 (proposal by Austria), 106, 118, 725-727, 789-790, 852 (discussion and adoption).

[15] For an overview of the different traditions of unfair competition law, *see* WIPO study 1994, *supra* note 2, at 15-17; KAUFMANN, "Passing Off and Misappropriation – An Economic and Legal Analysis of the Law of Unfair Competition in the United States and Continental Europe" I.I.C. Studies, Vol. 9 (1986).

governing specific areas of fair trading. Several Members of the Paris Union, however, adopted comprehensive statutes to provide protection against unfair competition.[16]

At the core of the standard for protection against unfair competition under the Paris Convention lies the concept of "honest practices in industrial or commercial matters" on which the definition of acts of unfair competition in Art. 10*bis* Para. 2 rests. As little guidance is given at the international level, the task of tracing its conceptual contours is primarily left to national legislators and courts. Traditionally, a line is drawn between the concept of honest practices and ethical standards referring to behavioural norms of fairness and decency in a given community.[17] This ethical approach is criticised by some as being imprecise. It is argued that the determination of relevant behavioural standards strongly depends on how the trade circle is defined whose customs and habits are taken as a basis for the analysis.[18] Moreover, it is asserted that trade circles whose business practices serve as a reference point for determining honest practices *de facto* shape the legal standards, in the light of which their behaviour is to be judged.[19] Therefore, some commentators align the concept of honest practices with the objective of ensuring the efficient operation of competition as a core instrument of market economies.[20] The flexible formula of honest practices in Art. 10*bis* Para. 2 can hardly be understood to prevent national legisla-

---

16 *See* the brief overview of national approaches in the WIPO study 1994, *supra* note 2, at 20-21. As to the different approaches taken by EC Member States, *see* the overview by MICKLITZ, *supra* note 4, at 13-16 and KÖHLER, in KÖHLER & BORNKAMM, *supra* note 1, at 65-78. For a detailed description, *see* BODEWIG, HENNING-BODEWIG & BAKARDJIEVA ENGELBREKT, in: HARTE-BAVENDAMM & HENNING-BODEWIG (eds.), *supra* note 6, at 180-346.

17 *Cf.* ULMER, *supra* note 1, at 42-43; LADAS, *supra* note 6, at 1685-1686; REED, "Water from Kerry Spring and 'Honest Practices'," 26 E.I.P.R. 429-431, 430 (2004).

18 *See* SCHÜNEMANN, in: HARTE-BAVENDAMM & HENNING-BODEWIG (eds.), *supra* note 6, at 580, notes 76-78.

19 *Cf.* ULMER, *supra* note 1, at 249; MICKLITZ, *supra* note 4, at 13; SCHÜNEMANN, in: HARTE-BAVENDAMM & HENNING-BODEWIG (eds.), *supra* note 6, at 580, note 79. It seems necessary to clarify whether this critique also concerns established international trading practices which, pursuant to BODENHAUSEN, *supra* note 6, at 144, and MICKLITZ, *supra* note 4, at 467-468, may be used by national judicial and administrative authorities as a point of reference for determining honest practices in the sense of Art. 10*bis* Para. 2. *See* also WIPO Model Provisions 1996, *supra* note 3, at 6, note 1.02.

20 *Cf.* SCHÜNEMANN, in: HARTE-BAVENDAMM & HENNING-BODEWIG (eds.), *supra* note 6, at 591, notes 113-114; ULLMANN, "Das Koordinatensystem des Rechts des unlauteren Wettbewerbs im Spannungsfeld von Europa und Deutschland," 2003 GRUR 820-821; BAUDENBACHER, "Machtbedingte Wettbewerbsstörungen als Unlauterkeitstatbestände," 1981 GRUR 19-29, 21-22; LÖWENHEIM, "Suggestivwerbung, unlauterer Wettbewerb, Wettbewerbsfreiheit und Verbraucherschutz," 1975 GRUR 99-110, 103-104; NORDEMANN, "Der verständige Durchschnittsgewerbetreibende," 1975 GRUR 625-631, 629-631; SACK, "Lauterer und leistungsgerechter Wettbewerb durch Wettbewerbsregeln," 1975 GRUR 297-307, 301-302.

tors and courts from pursuing this functional approach.[21] Standards of integrity and fairness on the market would have to be derived from the requirement to meet certain conditions for safeguarding competition as an institution of a free market economy.[22] This particular view of the concept of "honest practices" may lead to the reintroduction of ethical standards, such as personal responsibility for market actions, respect for the needs of other market participants, and regard for the equality of rights in the market.[23]

A certain restriction of the scope of Art. 10*bis* seems to follow from the continuous reference to acts of competition.[24] This reference is made in paragraph 2 providing the general definition of acts of unfair competition, and reappears in the first and second example set out in paragraph 3. In both cases, the establishment, goods or activities "of a competitor" are central to the analysis. To soften the impact of that requirement on the scope of Art. 10*bis*, a competitive relationship between traders in different branches of industry or trade and even an indirect competitive relationship could be deemed sufficient.[25] The wording of Art. 10*bis* Para. 2 and Para. 3, however, does not seem to preclude a more restrictive interpretation requiring direct competition between the party committing the act of unfair competition and the party whose interests are affected.

The examples in Art. 10*bis* Para. 3 concern acts of unfair competition which, in particular, are to be prohibited at the national level. The enumeration was understood not to imply an obligation to enact specific national legislation.[26] Moreover, paragraph 3 does not limit the ambit of operation of the general definition in paragraph 2. An analysis of the three examples yields important insights into the international concept of protection. The first example, for instance, provides evidence of the particular importance the Members of the Paris Union attached to explicit recognition of an unfair competition norm concerning confusion with respect to a competitor's establishment, goods or activities, even though the Paris Convention sets

[21] *Cf.* the WIPO study 1994, *supra* note 2, at 11-13, which, on the basis of the international framework, reflects considerations of this nature. Nevertheless, SCHÜNEMANN, in: HARTE-BAVENDAMM & HENNING-BODEWIG (eds.), *supra* note 6, at 582, argues that Art. 10*bis* PC codifies dogmatic approaches of the late 19th century. This argument, however, can hardly be considered compelling. The room for interpretation offered by international norms has always been used to adapt their application to actual problems and needs. Given the flexibility and openness of the wording of Art. 10*bis*, it seems unjustified to characterise the provision as outdated. As elaborated above, the latest change to the text of Art. 10*bis*, moreover, dates back to the 1958 Lisbon Conference and not to the late 19th century.

[22] *Cf.* ULMER, *supra* note 1, at 58-59; SCHÜNEMANN, in: HARTE-BAVENDAMM & HENNING-BODEWIG (eds.), *supra* note 6, at 592, note 116.

[23] *Cf.* SCHÜNEMANN, in: HARTE-BAVENDAMM & HENNING-BODEWIG (eds.), *supra* note 6, at 608, note 165.

[24] *Cf.* GLÖCKNER, in: HARTE-BAVENDAMM & HENNING-BODEWIG (eds.), *supra* note 6, at 47, note 2.

[25] *See* BODENHAUSEN, *supra* note 6, at 144; LADAS, *supra* note 6, at 1689.

[26] *See* "Actes de La Haye", *supra* note 10, at 472.

forth specific obligations ensuring protection of typical business and product identifiers, such as trademarks, service marks and trade names.[27]

As to the second example concerning the discrediting of a competitor's establishment, goods or activities, it seems noteworthy that, as mentioned above, a proposal by Germany seeking to prohibit certain forms of comparative advertising was not accepted at the 1934 London Conference.[28] In the absence of specific rules, a national solution can be developed along the lines of the second example in Art. 10*bis* Para. 3 and the general clause of Art. 10*bis* Para. 2. In view of developments in the field,[29] such as EC harmonisation initiatives,[30] this flexible international framework seems adequate. It leaves sufficient room for future developments – including a potential trend towards strengthening the influence of constitutional guarantees, such as freedom of commercial speech.[31]

---

[27] *See* "Actes de La Haye", *supra* note 10, at 476; LADAS, *supra* note 6, at 1706-1707. *Cf.* Art. 1 Para. 2 PC. With regard to the interplay of specific intellectual property rights and supplementary protection against unfair competition, *see* SAMBUC, in: HARTE-BAVENDAMM & HENNING-BODEWIG (eds.), *supra* note 6, at 408-413. As to trademarks, *see* Ní SHÚILLEABHÁIN, "Common-Law Protection of Trade Marks – The Continuing Relevance of the Law of Passing Off," 34 IIC 722-750 (2003); BORNKAMM, "Markenrecht und wettbewerblicher Kennzeichenschutz – Zur Vorrangthese der Rechtsprechung," 2005 GRUR 97-102. Art. 10*bis* Para. 3 (1) need not necessarily lead to supplementary protection of specific industrial property rights. The international obligation to protect service marks and trade names resulting from Arts. 6*sexies* and 8 PC may be *fulfilled* through appropriate protection against unfair competition. *See* BODENHAUSEN, *supra* note 6, at 122 and 133. As to service marks, however, Art. 16 of the 1994 Trademark Law Treaty sets forth the obligation to "register service marks and apply to such marks the provisions of the Paris Convention which concern trademarks". In respect of the specific situation in the field of geographical indications, *cf.* KNAAK, "The Protection of Geographical Indications According to the TRIPs Agreement," in: BEIER & SCHRICKER, *supra* note 5, at 117-140, 119-127; VROOM-CRAMER, "Juridische aspecten van geografische aanduidingen" 22-33 (2002); INGERL & ROHNKE, "Markengesetz" 1904-1905 (2nd ed. 2003); STATEN, "Geographical Indications Protection Under the TRIPS Agreement: Uniformity Not Extension," 87 Journal of the Patent and Trademark Office Society 221-245, 233-236 (2005).

[28] *See* "Actes de Londres", *supra* note 11, at 419. As to the German approach to comparative advertising, *cf.* STECKLER & BACHMANN, "Comparative Advertising in Germany with Regard to European Community Law," 19 E.I.P.R. 578-586 (1997); KÖHLER, in: KÖHLER & BORNKAMM, *supra* note 1, at 786-788.

[29] As to recent developments and the approaches taken on the basis of the different legal traditions of unfair competition law, *cf.* WIPO study 1994, *supra* note 2, at 60-64; CORNISH & LLEWELYN, "Intellectual Property: Patents, Copyright, Trade Marks and Allied Rights" 632-635, 715-719 (5th ed. 2003).

[30] *See* Directive 84/450/EEC of September 10, 1984 on misleading and comparative advertising, as amended by Directive 97/55/EC of October 6, 1997, and the decision of the European Court of Justice, April 8, 2003, Case No. C-44/01, 34 IIC 808-814 (2003) – *Pippig v. Harlauer.*

[31] *See* WIPO study 1994, *supra* note 2, at 47-48, para. 92; ULLMANN, *supra* note 20, at 819; OHLY, "Das neue UWG – Mehr Freiheit für den Wettbewerb?," 2004 GRUR 889-900, 892-894.

The third example gives rise to the question of the objectives underlying protection against unfair competition in the Paris Convention. It can hardly be denied that Art. 10*bis*, as already indicated above, focuses on conduct between competitors.[32] Therefore, some argue that the provision is rendered incapable of reaching beyond this objective.[33] The insertion of the third example, dealing with the misleading of the public as to the nature or other characteristics of goods, however, testifies to a departure from the confinement to the interests of competitors at the 1958 Lisbon Conference.[34] It offers a gateway for lending weight to the protection of consumers.[35] As the examples in Art. 10*bis* Para. 3 concern acts which, in particular, are to be regarded as acts of unfair competition,[36] they illustrate the scope of the general clause laid down in Art. 10*bis* Para. 2. Accordingly, it appears consistent to interpret the general definition in Art. 10*bis* Para. 2 not only in the light of the objective to protect the interests of competitors (examples 1 and 2 of Art. 10*bis* Para. 3), but also with a view to ensuring consumer protection (example 3).

The catalogue of acts listed in Art. 10*bis* Para. 3 does not cover all cases which seem to be of importance. The misappropriation of trade secrets[37] and acts of free riding, such as dilution and slavish imitation, feature prominently among those cases not expressly mentioned in Art. 10*bis*.[38] With regard to the guarantee of appropriate legal remedies under Art. 10*ter* Para. 1, it appears moreover desirable to permit consumer organisations to take action against acts of unfair competition in the courts or before administrative authorities, as envisaged in Art. 10*ter* Para. 2 in respect of federations and associations of industrialists, producers or merchants.[39]

3. The 1996 WIPO Model Provisions

On the basis of the described international framework, WIPO initiated a comparative analysis of worldwide protection against unfair competition in the 90s. In 1994, the WIPO study "Protection Against Unfair Competition – Analysis of the Present World Situation" was presented.[40] The study was based on a text produced by two staff members of the Max Planck Institute for Intellectual Property, Competition and Tax Law in Munich, *Frauke Henning-Bodewig* and *Heijo Ruijsenaars*. The final version of the publication took into account the advice of twelve experts from dif-

---

32 *See* LADAS, *supra* note 6, at 1687.

33 *See* the critical comments made by SCHÜNEMANN, in: HARTE-BAVENDAMM & HENNING-BODEWIG (eds.), *supra* note 6, at 582, note 84.

34 *See* "Actes de Lisbonne", *supra* note 14, at 725, 784 (proposal by Austria), 106, 118, 725-727, 789-790, 852 (discussion and adoption). *Cf.* LADAS, *supra* note 6, at 1687.

35 *Cf.* LADAS, *supra* note 6, at 1735.

36 *See* BODENHAUSEN, *supra* note 6, at 143.

37 *See*, however, Art. 39 of the 1994 TRIPS Agreement.

38 For an overview of acts not expressly mentioned in Art. 10*bis*, *see* WIPO study 1994, *supra* note 2, at 48-68.

39 *Cf.* WIPO study 1994, *supra* note 2, at 74.

40 WIPO publication No. 725, Geneva 1994, *supra* note 2.

ferent countries.[41] The analysis yielded important reference material for law-making activities in countries seeking to modernise their domestic system of protection, and gave new impulses for further international harmonisation. Its publication was followed by the presentation of WIPO Model Provisions on Protection Against Unfair Competition in 1996.[42] In the following subsection, the Model Provisions and the preceding WIPO study will be discussed in the light of the analysis of the international framework for protection conducted in subsection 2.2. Subsequently, the legal status of the Model Provisions will be clarified.

3.1 The Contents of the Model Provisions

The 1996 WIPO Model Provisions (WMP) seek to implement Art. 10*bis* of the Paris Convention.[43] On the one hand, they define the principal acts or practices against which protection is to be granted, namely the causing of confusion with respect to another's enterprise or its activities (Art. 2), the damaging of another's goodwill or reputation (Art. 3), the misleading of the public (Art. 4), the discrediting of another's enterprise or its activities (Art. 5) and, finally, unfair competition in respect of secret information (Art. 6). On the other hand, they provide for a general clause (Art. 1 Para.1) which is intended to serve as a basis for protection against any other acts of unfair competition.[44] The system of the Model Provisions thus follows Art. 10*bis*. A general provision (Art. 10*bis* Para. 2 PC and Art. 1 Para. 1 WMP) is supplemented by the identification of certain acts which, in particular, must be prohibited (Art. 10*bis* Para. 3 and Arts. 2 to 6 WMP). The higher number of expressly listed acts of unfair competition in the Model Provisions can be seen as an indication of the objective to further concretise individual instances in which to provide protection.[45] Before revisiting the catalogue of forbidden acts, however, some horizontal conceptual considerations are addressed.

The concept of honest practices which plays a decisive role in the context of Art. 10*bis* PC was maintained in the WIPO Model Provisions. Pursuant to the general clause of Art. 1 Para. 1 (a) WMP, an act or practice "that is contrary to honest prac-

---

41 JOHN ADAMS, London; ERNESTO ARACAMA-ZORRAQUÍN, Buenos Aires; IVAN CHERPILLOD, Lausanne; GU MING, Beijing; DESMOND GUOBADIA, Lagos; FRAUKE HENNING-BODEWIG, Munich; BALDO KRESALJA, Lima; YOSHIHARU KUNOGI, Tokyo; KRISHNASWAMI PONNUSWAMI, Delhi; HEIJO RUIJSENAARS, Munich; IMRE VOROS, Budapest; GLEN WESTON, Naples, Florida.

42 WIPO publication No. 832, Geneva 1996, *supra* note 3. The Model Provisions had been prepared by the International Bureau of WIPO in the light of the 1994 WIPO study. In the preparation of the Model Provisions, BERNARD DUTOIT, Lausanne; CHARLES GIELEN, Amsterdam; WILLIAM KEEFAUVER, New Vernon; and KAZUKO MATSUO, Tokyo, gave advice.

43 *See* WIPO Model Provisions 1996, *supra* note 3, at 6, note 1.01.

44 *See* WIPO Model Provisions 1996, *supra* note 3, at 6, note 1.01. Usually, a flexible, open clause or general principle which supplements more specific regulations and allows courts considerable discretion is also a core element of national protection systems. *Cf.* WIPO study 1994, *supra* note 2, at 20-22; MICKLITZ, *supra* note 4, at 13.

45 *Cf.* GLÖCKNER, in: HARTE-BAVENDAMM & HENNING-BODEWIG (eds.), *supra* note 6, at 47.

tices" constitutes an act of unfair competition.[46] The traditional formula, however, was embedded in a broader context. Whereas, in Art. 10*bis* Para. 2, the standard of honest practices applies only to acts of competition, no such restriction is to be found in Art. 1 Para. 1 (a) WMP. By contrast, it is clarified that "omission of the requirement that the act be an act of competition makes it clear that consumers also are protected".[47] The 1994 WIPO study heralded this broader approach. As described above, the aspect of consumer protection initially entered the picture when a third example dealing with the misleading of the public was incorporated into Art. 10*bis* Para. 3 at the 1958 Lisbon Conference. The additional example suggests taking into account the interests of both competitors and consumers (see subsection 2.2.). In this vein, the 1994 WIPO study identifies as a common aspect of the examples in Art. 10*bis* Para. 3 "the attempt (by an entrepreneur) to succeed in competition without relying on his own achievements in terms of quality and price of his products and services, but rather by taking undue advantage of the work of another or by influencing consumer demand with false or misleading statements".[48] As to the purpose of protection, it states that "unfair competition law was initially designed to protect the honest businessman", and clarifies that, in the meantime, "consumer protection has been recognised as equally important".[49]

Art. 1 Para. 1 (a) WMP realises this twofold objective of protection. As the Model Provisions serve the purpose of providing guidelines for the implementation of international obligations in the field of unfair competition, it can be understood to reflect a broad approach to Art. 10*bis* PC lending weight to the interests of competitors and consumers alike. Art. 1 Para. 1 (b) WMP which concerns the entitlement to remedies was brought into line with this approach. The provision broadly refers to "any natural person or legal entity damaged or likely to be damaged by an act of unfair competition". Accordingly, remedies should be available not only to competitors and their federations, but also to consumers and consumer associations.[50] In this regard, the Model Provisions go beyond the scope of Art. 10*ter* Para. 2 PC, as proposed above (see subsection 2.2.).

---

[46] As to the difficulty of concretising the standard of honest practices in the light of the unfair acts and practices expressly listed in Arts. 2-6, *see* MICKLITZ, *supra* note 4, at 473. The view that a boundary line is to be drawn between the concept of honest practices and the specified acts considered unfair *per se* is not endorsed here. In fact, it seems more consistent to assume that the cases specified in Arts. 2-6 are examples of acts of unfair competition which, *evidently*, are contrary to honest practices. *Cf.* ULMER, *supra* note 1, at 250. For this reason, it is not necessary to give evidence of non-compliance with the standard of honest practices, as pointed out in WIPO Model Provisions 1996, *supra* note 3, at 10, note 1.07. The protection of trade secrets in Art. 6 Para. 1, requiring additionally proof of conduct contrary to honest commercial practices, is an exception to this general rule which is rooted in Art. 39 Para. 2 TRIPS.

[47] *See* WIPO Model Provisions 1996, *supra* note 3, at 10, note 1.06.

[48] *See* WIPO study 1994, *supra* note 2, at 24, para. 31.

[49] *See* WIPO study 1994, *supra* note 2, at 24, para. 33.

[50] *See* WIPO Model Provisions 1996, *supra* note 3, at 12, note 1.10. *Cf.* WIPO study 1994, *supra* note 2, at 74.

The reference to acts of competition has not only been omitted in the general clause of Art. 1 Para. 1 WMP but also throughout the catalogue of forbidden acts and practices. In consequence, Arts. 2 to 6 WMP are not restricted to relations between competitors. The requirement of a competitive relationship which, as described above, can be interpreted more or less restrictively in the context of Art. 10*bis*, was thus abandoned in the Model Provisions. They apply also in situations where there is no direct competition between the party who commits an act of unfair competition and the party whose interests are affected by the act.[51]

In Arts. 2 to 6 WMP, acts and practices against which protection is to be granted are delineated in the following way: while the first paragraph of these provisions provides a general definition of the act concerned, examples are given in the second paragraph.[52] The three cases enumerated in Art. 10*bis* Para. 3 PC reappear in the Model Provisions and are further concretised in this way. In Art. 2 WMP which, like Art. 10*bis* Para. 3 (1), concerns the causing of confusion, reference is not only made to typical business identifiers, such as marks and trade names, but also to the appearance and presentation of a product as well as marketing techniques using a celebrity or a well-known fictional character. In line with the approach taken in the 1994 WIPO study, the notes on the provision reflect a broad concept of confusion which extends to the causing of confusion as to affiliation or sponsorship. They confirm the objective to protect publicity and merchandising rights against confusing acts.[53] Art. 5 WMP corresponds to Art. 10*bis* Para. 3 (2). As to discrediting acts, the examples given in its second paragraph refer particularly to advertising and promotion, and focus on allegations concerning certain characteristics of products or services, as well as sales conditions. It is moreover clarified that relevant acts of unfair competition may also be committed by consumer associations or the media.[54] The issue of misleading the public, constituting the third example of Art. 10*bis* Para. 3, is addressed in Art. 4 WMP. Again, a broad approach is taken. The notes on the provision clarify that, besides inherently false indications, literally correct statements as well as the omission of information are to be prohibited if they give a misleading impression. Obvious exaggerations in the course of "sales talk", by contrast, need not necessarily be qualified as misleading.[55] Like in Art. 5 WMP, the examples of the second paragraph refer to advertising and promotion activities. The list of characteristics of products or services contains additionally a reference to the geograph-

---

[51] *See* WIPO Model Provisions 1996, *supra* note 3, at 10, note 1.06.

[52] For a description of the regulatory potential of the cases listed in Arts. 2-6, *see* also MICKLITZ, *supra* note 4, at 474-478.

[53] *See* WIPO Model Provisions 1996, *supra* note 3, at 16 and 20, notes 2.04 and 2.11; WIPO study 1994, *supra* note 2, at 28-29. *Cf.* RUIJSENAARS, "The WIPO Report on Character Merchandising," 25 IIC 532 (1994), and the critical comments by JAFFEY, "Merchandising and the Law of Trade Marks," I.P.Q. 240-266 (1998).

[54] *See* WIPO Model Provisions 1996, *supra* note 3, at 44, note 5.05. Due to the reference to competitors in Art. 10*bis* Para. 3 (2), it has been argued that the Paris Convention does not provide for protection against unfair press activities. *Cf.* MICKLITZ, *supra* note 4, at 468.

[55] *See* WIPO Model Provisions 1996, *supra* note 3, at 30, note 4.02.

ical origin.[56] Art. 4 WMP, however, is silent on how to determine the impression on the addressee of a misleading statement. In this respect, the 1994 WIPO study points out that the Paris Convention left this question to Member States, and provides an overview of different approaches, such as a distinction between average and gullible consumers, and the determination of a misleading effect on the basis of empirical data or through an overall estimation by the judge.[57]

Besides the cases of unfair competition listed in Art. 10*bis* Para. 3, the Model Provisions contain two additional categories of unfair acts. Pursuant to Art. 3 Para. 1 WMP, "[a]ny act or practice, in the course of industrial or commercial activities, that damages, or is likely to damage, the goodwill or reputation of another's enterprise shall constitute an act of unfair competition, regardless of whether such act or practice causes confusion". The groundwork for this additional example was laid in the 1994 WIPO study which specifically devoted attention to acts of free riding and, in particular, discussed the dilution of the "distinctive quality or advertising value" of a mark.[58] The latter formulation reappears in Art. 3 Para. 2 (b) WMP as the core element of a definition of dilution which also summarises examples of relevant acts listed in Art. 3 Para. 2 (a) WMP. According to this definition, "dilution of goodwill or reputation means the lessening of the distinctive character or advertising value of a trademark, trade name or other business identifier, the appearance of a product or the presentation of products or services or of a celebrity or well-known fictional character". Art. 3 WMP thus provides for broad protection against free riding and dilution extending to the field of publicity and merchandising.[59]

The second additional example is laid down in Art. 6 WMP and deals with unfair competition in respect of secret information. The provision is based on Art. 39 TRIPS.[60] The definition of the term "secret information" in Art. 6 Para. 3 WMP is identical to the definition of "undisclosed information" in Art. 39 Para. 2 (a), (b) and (c) TRIPS. Similarly, Art. 6 Para. 1 WMP paraphrases the general principle estab

---

[56] Information on this example and its interplay with special laws protecting geographical indications and appellations of origin is provided in WIPO Model Provisions 1996, *supra* note 3, at 38, note 4.11.

[57] *See* WIPO study 1994, *supra* note 2, at 39-40.

[58] *See* WIPO study 1994, *supra* note 2, at 54-58 and particularly para. 109.

[59] As to the dilution doctrine, *cf.* MOSTERT, "Famous and Well-Known Marks – an International Analysis" 56-68 (1997); FEZER, "Markenrecht" 840-844 (3rd ed. 2001); STRASSER, "The Rational Basis of Trademark Protection Revisited: Putting the Dilution Doctrine into Context," 10 Fordham Intell. Prop., Media & Ent. L.J. 375-432 (2000); CASPARIE-KERDEL, "Dilution Disguised: Has the Concept of Trade Mark Dilution Made its Way into the Laws of Europe?," 23 E.I.P.R. 185-195 (2001); MOSKIN, "Victoria's Big Secret: Wither Dilution Under the Federal Dilution Act," 93 Trademark Reporter 842-859 (2004); MCCARTHY, "Dilution of a Trademark: European and United States Law Compared," 94 Trademark Reporter 1163-1181 (2004). With regard to the international recognition of protection against dilution in Art. 16 Para. 3 TRIPS, *see* KUR, "TRIPs and Trademark Law," in: BEIER & SCHRICKER, *supra* note 5, at 93-116, 107-108; GERVAIS, "The TRIPS Agreement: Drafting History and Analysis" 174 (2nd ed. 2003).

[60] *Cf.* KRASSER, "The Protection of Trade Secrets in the TRIPs Agreement," in: BEIER & SCHRICKER, *supra* note 5, at 217-225; LANG, "The Protection of Commercial Trade Secrets," 25 E.I.P.R. 462-471 (2003).

lished in Art. 39 Para. 2 TRIPS: "[a]ny act or practice, in the course of industrial or commercial activities, that results in the disclosure, acquisition or use by others of secret information without the consent of the person lawfully in control of that information [...] and in a manner contrary to honest commercial practices shall constitute an act of unfair competition." The examples of relevant acts in Art. 6 Para. 2 WMP refer to industrial or commercial espionage, breach of contract, breach of confidence and related acts. The Model Provisions do not provide guidelines as to the efforts the owner of information must make in order to keep it secret. In this respect, the 1994 WIPO study suggests considering whether the information contains material that is not confidential if looked at in isolation, whether it has necessarily to be acquired by employees if they are to work efficiently, and whether it is restricted to senior management.[61] With regard to former employees, the notes on Art. 6 WMP recall that a fine line has to be walked between the legitimate use of skills, knowledge and experience acquired during employment and the unfair disclosure or use of the former employer's secret information.[62]

In sum, the Model Provisions suggest implementing the standard for protection against unfair competition on the basis of a liberal approach to Art. 10*bis* PC. Considering the questions left open in the Paris Convention, as identified in subsection 2.2., it can be concluded that they demonstrate the adaptability of international unfair competition law to actual problems and needs. The inclusion of consumer protection, the departure from the requirement of a competitive relationship, the broad approach to confusing, discrediting and misleading acts and, finally, express mention of further cases of unfair competition, concerning dilution and trade secrets, testify to the aim of updating the traditional unfair competition principle of honest practices.[63]

3.2 The Legal Status of the Model Provisions

The objective to harmonise a given area of law internationally can be pursued in different ways. An international treaty, such as the Paris Convention for the Protection of Industrial Property or the Berne Convention for the Protection of Literary and Artistic Works, has the strongest legal effect. Its adoption necessitates the convening of a diplomatic conference. States and, in certain cases,[64] also international intergovernmental organisations can formally adhere to the treaty through ratification or accession. In consequence, they become bound to the obligations it contains and

---

[61] *See* WIPO study 1994, *supra* note 2, at 51, para. 99.

[62] *See* WIPO Model Provisions 1996, *supra* note 3, at 50, note 6.08.

[63] *See* GLÖCKNER, in: HARTE-BAVENDAMM & HENNING-BODEWIG (eds.), *supra* note 6, at 47. *Cf.* earlier proposals made by ULMER, *supra* note 1, at 242-243.

[64] *See*, for instance, Art. 17 Para. 2 of the 1996 WIPO Copyright Treaty and Art. 26 Para. 2 of the 1996 WIPO Performances and Phonograms Treaty; Art. 14 Para. 1 (b) of the 1989 Protocol Relating to the Madrid Agreement Concerning the International Registration of Marks; Art. 27 Para. 1 (ii) of the 1999 Geneva Act of the Hague Agreement Concerning the International Registration of Industrial Designs.

their nationals, and persons assimilated to nationals, may avail themselves of the rights it offers.

To accelerate the development of international common principles, so-called "soft law" instruments can be applied.[65] In recent years, WIPO followed this path in areas where a fast reaction to new developments was needed to prevent emerging differences in national approaches from becoming an obstacle to the development of international harmonised principles. In the field of trademark law, three so-called joint recommendations were presented and adopted by the Assembly of the Paris Union and the General Assembly of WIPO.[66] Accordingly, they have strong persuasive authority as an expression of an international consensus.[67] States and international intergovernmental organisations cannot ratify or accede to a joint recommendation. Their domestic legislation, however, may follow its principles and provisions. Moreover, courts may align their decisions with the joint recommendations.

The 1996 Model Provisions on Protection Against Unfair Competition constitute neither an international treaty nor a "soft law" instrument. They were presented by the International Bureau of WIPO but not formally adopted by any of the aforementioned bodies. As their title indicates, they are intended to serve as a model for law-making activities and a reference point for court decisions.[68] The practical consequences of the application of the Model Provisions may therefore be similar to the influence of joint recommendations, even though their legal status is not the same. On its merits, the Model Provisions seek to provide guidance. By presenting a convincing example of how to implement international obligations in the field of the protection against unfair competition appropriately, they contribute to the harmonisation of national approaches and promote the development of further international common principles.

---

[65] As to their function and status in public international law, *see* HILGENBERG, "A Fresh Look at Soft Law," 1999 European Journal of International Law 499-516; THÜRER, "Soft Law" – eine neue Form von Völkerrecht?," 1985 Zeitschrift für Schweizerisches Recht 429-453; WENGLER, "Nichtrechtliche" Staatenverträge in der Sicht des Völkerrechts und des Verfassungsrechts," 1995 Juristenzeitung 21-26.

[66] *See* 1999 Joint Recommendation Concerning Provisions on the Protection of Well-Known Marks, WIPO publication No. 833, Geneva 2000; 2000 Joint Recommendation Concerning Trademark Licenses, WIPO publication No. 835, Geneva 2000; 2001 Joint Recommendation Concerning Provisions on the Protection of Marks, and Other Industrial Property Rights in Signs, on the Internet, WIPO publication No. 845, Geneva 2001. The joint recommendations are made available on the Internet at <http://www.wipo.int/about-ip/en/development_iplaw/>.

[67] *Cf.* WICHARD, "The Joint Recommendation Concerning Protection of Marks, and Other Industrial Property Rights in Signs, on the Internet," in: DREXL & KUR (eds.), "Intellectual Property and Private International Law" IIC Studies 257-264, 263, Vol. 24 (2005).

[68] *Cf.* MICKLITZ, *supra* note 4, at 472, who speaks of "an example for States who are obliged to provide protection against unfair competition under Art. 10*bis* of the Paris Convention or Art. 2 of the TRIPS Agreement".

4. Current Work of WIPO

Since the presentation of the WIPO study on Protection Against Unfair Competition in 1994, important developments have occurred. Considerable efforts to establish an efficient system of protection, for instance, have been made by European countries joining the European Community. Recent EC legislation on the subject, notably Directive 2005/29 of May 11, 2005, concerning unfair business-to-consumer commercial practices, aims to achieve a high level of consumer protection.[69] The recent amendment of the German law against unfair competition is an example of a shift in the general theoretical concept on which protection is based. Instead of relying on the concept of honest practices, the criterion of unfair activity for competition purposes was introduced.[70] Besides the protection of competitors and consumers, the public interest in undistorted competition is expressly recognised as one of the objectives of protection.[71]

These developments coincide with certain issues raised in the present analysis which indicate new directions in unfair competition law. Particular importance may be attached to the discussion of the core element of international protection, the concept of honest practices. It would appear necessary to explore the new connotations which the concept of honest practices receives when it is viewed from the perspective of the functional, market-based approach seeking to ensure the efficient operation of competition as a core instrument of market economies (see subsection 2.2). In particular, it would have to be clarified whether resulting principles, such as personal responsibility for market actions, respect for the needs of other market participants, and regard for the equality of rights in the market, which were already mentioned above, can serve as a basis for the development of internationally accepted common principles.[72]

As regards the objectives of protection, the market-based functional interpretation of honest practices may lead to the consideration of a threefold approach. Like

---

[69] *See* Art. 1 of Directive 2005/29/EC of May 11, 2005 ("Unfair Commercial Practices Directive"). For an overview of its provisions, *see* HANDIG, "EG-Richtlinie gegen unlautere Geschäftspraktiken," 2005 Österreichische Blätter für gewerblichen Rechtsschutz und Urheberrecht 196-203; HENNING-BODEWIG, "Die Richtlinie 2005/29/EG über unlautere Geschäftspraktiken," 2005 GRUR Int. 629-634.

[70] This shift in the theoretical approach, however, does not necessarily imply changes in the substance of protection. *Cf.* SCHÜNEMANN, in: HARTE-BAVENDAMM & HENNING-BODEWIG (eds.), *supra* note 6, at 572-573. The official draft submitted by the government, accordingly, focused on continuity rather than a change of paradigm. *See* the official document of the German federal parliament, Bundestags-Drucksache 15/1487, 16.

[71] *See* HENNING-BODEWIG, "A New Act Against Unfair Competition in Germany," 36 IIC 421-432, 425-426 (2005); OHLY, *supra* note 31, at 894-896.

[72] *Cf.* the contribution of Reto Hilty to this publication and the guidelines of ULLMANN, *supra* note 20, at 821-824. As MICKLITZ, *supra* note 4, at 467 and 473, points out, a "world standard" in the field of protection against unfair competition does not exist. It remains to be seen whether an abstract functional approach, resting on universal requirements for a functioning market economy rather than depending on specific national circumstances, could pave the way for its development.

in recent German legislation, it may appear consistent to recognise, besides the protection of competitors and consumers, the public interest in the efficient functioning of competition – in the sense of a protection of the market participants' freedom of action and decision.[73] In this vein, the 1994 WIPO study already devoted attention to national approaches including "the protection of the public at large, and especially its interest in the freedom of competition."[74]

It is beyond the scope of the present article to discuss the practical implications these conceptual considerations may have. The time seems ripe, however, to embark on an update of the 1994 WIPO study on the protection against unfair competition in the light of recent developments. The theoretical considerations outlined above may serve as a starting point for the drafting of a revised text that should also consider the approaches taken in countries whose economies are in transition from a centrally planned to a market economy. Updated material on the protection against unfair competition responds to the present need for further guidance and support in this area. The experiences made in the new EC Member States are of particular importance in this context.[75]

Recent developments may also have the potential for bridging certain conceptual differences between civil law and common law jurisdictions. Approximations in certain fields, such as comparative advertising,[76] are to be considered. The influence of constitutional guarantees, such as freedom of speech, constitutes an important issue to be addressed in this context.[77] Having expressly recognised the interests of consumers in the 1996 Model Provisions, it seems moreover desirable to follow up on the question in which way the objective of consumer protection is realised in different jurisdictions. Concepts of distinguishing between different types of consumers, such as average and gullible consumers, and different ways of determining the

---

73 *See* HENNING-BODEWIG, *supra* note 71, at 426. *Cf.* ULLMANN, *supra* note 20, at 821, who speaks of an additional safety net.

74 *See* WIPO study 1994, *supra* note 2, at 24-25.

75 *Cf.* HELM, "Intellectual Property in Transition Economies: Assessing the Latvian Experience," 14 Fordham Intell. Prop. Media & Ent. L.J. 119-215, 152-159 and 161-164 (2003); BAKARDJIEVA ENGELBREKT & HENNING-BODEWIG, in: HARTE-BAVENDAMM & HENNING-BODEWIG (eds.), *supra* note 6, at 197-200, 257-264, 290-298, 314-322, 331-344; HENNING-BODEWIG, "Unfair Competition Law – European Union and Member States" (2006).

76 However, *cf.* CORNISH & LLEWELYN, *supra* note 29, at 718-719, who emphasise the influence of different historical attitudes. For an analysis of decisions of the European Court of Justice and the German Federal Supreme Court concerning comparative advertising, *see* KÖHLER, "Was ist vergleichende Werbung?," 2005 GRUR 273-280.

77 A closer analysis of the influence of constitutional guarantees is not unlikely to trigger a much broader discussion going beyond the context of comparative advertising. *Cf.* TIMBERS & HUSTON, "The "Artistic Relevance Test" Just Became Relevant: the Increasing Strength of the First Amendment as a Defense to Trademark Infringement and Dilution," 93 Trademark Reporter 1278-1301 (2004); CANTWELL, "Confusion, Dilution and Speech: First Amendment Limitations on the Trademark Estate: An Update," 94 Trademark Reporter 547-584 (2004). In respect of the general tendency to have recourse to constitutional guarantees in order to achieve balanced results in intellectual property law, *see* GEIGER, "Fundamental Rights, a Safeguard for the Coherence of Intellectual Property Law?," 35 IIC 268-280 (2004).

effect a certain act has on the consumer could be discussed in more detail.[78] In the field of law enforcement, the role played by consumer organisations should be analysed.

These few considerations which are necessarily of an incomplete and preliminary nature already indicate that an updated study reflecting the present world situation may bring to light further principles of protection against and examples of acts of unfair competition.

---

78 *Cf.* ULLMANN, *supra* note 20, at 818-819; DAVIS, "Locating the Average Consumer: His Judicial Origins, Intellectual Influences and Current Role in European Trade Mark Law," 2005 I.P.Q. 183-203.

The Law Against Unfair Competition and the EC Treaty

Jochen Glöckner

Unlike Antitrust law, Unfair Competition law is not directly governed in the EC Treaty. The following is intended to show how European primary law nevertheless bears on the unfair commercial practices regulations of Member States.

1. Article 60 Sec. 1 of the European Coal and Steel Community Treaty

Article 60 Sec. 1 of the European Coal and Steel Community Treaty[1] prohibited unfair competitive practices in the field of prices, above all merely temporary or merely local price reductions aimed at achieving a monopoly position. The substantive effect of the regulation thus served to protect against monopolies more than to protect fair competition.[2] According to Art. 63 of the Treaty, infringements could be punished with fines, although this provision never gained any significance.[3] An extended interpretation or an application mutatis mutandis to other fields of competition outside the scope of application of the European Coal and Steel Community Treaty was always considered inadmissible.[4]

2. The Clause Laying Down the Objectives of the EC Treaty as a Unfair Competition Law General Clause?

Hints to Unfair Competition law can be found in the Preamble to the EC Treaty[5]. In the fourth paragraph, the Member States undertake to guarantee "fair competition",

---

1 Pursuant to Art. 97, this Treaty ended on July 23, 2002, the EC becoming the universal successor to the European Coal and Steel Community. *Cf.* the Protocol on the Financial Consequences of the Expiry of the European Coal and Steel Community Treaty and the Research Fund for Coal and Steel in the Treaty of Nice, OJ C 80/1, February 26, 2001.

2 FIKENTSCHER, "Das Verhältnis von Kartellrecht und Recht des unlauteren Wettbewerbs im deutschen und europäischen Recht," in: "Festschrift für Walter Hallstein" 127, 151 (1982).

3 STEINDORFF, "Unlauterer Wettbewerb im System des EG-Rechts," 1993 WRP 139.

4 FIKENTSCHER, *supra* note 2, at 152; WÄGENBAUR, "La législation de la Communauté Européenne en matière de concurrence déloyale," in: "Droit européen de la concurrence déloyale en formation" 9, 14 (1994).

5 WÄGENBAUR, *supra* note 4, at 13. The Preamble continues to be found in the Consolidated Text of the Treaty Establishing the European Community, *cf.* Consolidated Text of the Treaty for the Establishment of the European Community, OJ C 340/173, November 10, 1997. Admittedly no rights can be derived from the Preamble; nevertheless it can be used to interpret the remaining text of the Treaty, LENZ, "EU- und EG-Vertrag" note 1 to the Preamble (3rd ed. 2003); SCHWARZE, "EU-Kommentar" Preamble of the EC Treaty (2000).

and to this extent, the aim is to prevent unfair competition.[6] This is made clear by the French version, which uses the words "*loyauté de concurrence*". A further point of reference in primary law is Art. 3 Para. 1 (g) EC (ex-Art. 3 (g) of the EC Treaty), which reads:

> Art. 3
>
> (1) For the purposes set out in Article 2 the activities of the Community shall include, as provided in this Treaty and in accordance with the timetable set out therein ...
>
> g) a system ensuring that competition in the internal market is not distorted.

The system for the protection of competition required of the Community as a result covers not only measures against behaviour that falls within classical Antitrust law, but also infringements of Unfair Competition law such as the creation of a likelihood of confusion or the creation of a likelihood of deception.[7] The conceptual link to the "distortion of competition" in Art. 81 Para. 1 EC (ex-Art. 85 Para. 1 of the EC Treaty) need not be understood as a reference restricted to the Antitrust law regulations of the Treaty.[8]

Admittedly competition is primarily protected by means of the rules on competition in Art. 81 et seq. EC. Nevertheless Art. 3 Para. 1 (g) requires not only measures against classical infringements of Antitrust law but also against unfair competition if the infringement is capable of interfering with the functions of competition.[9]

At the European level the lack of symmetry in the density of primary law regulations is striking.[10] While the provision of Art. 3 Para. 1 (g) EC was included and given detailed content in the field of Antitrust law by the rules on competition in the

---

[6] ZULEEG, in: VON DER GROEBEN & SCHWARZE, "Kommentar zum Vertrag über die Europäische Union und zur Gründung der Europäischen Gemeinschaft," Art. 3 EC, note 8, Vol. 1 (6th ed. 2003). Accordingly, Arts. 81 *et seq.* EC only protect honest competition, decision of the ECJ, July 13, 1966, Case No. 32/65, 1966 ECR 458, 483 – *Italien v. Rat.*

[7] *Cf.* Recital 2 of the Misleading Advertising Directive: "misleading advertising can lead to distortion of competition within the common market", Council Directive 84/450/EEC of September 10, 1984 relating to the Approximation of the Laws, Regulations and Administrative Provisions of the Member States concerning Misleading Advertising, OJ L 250/17, September 9, 1984.

[8] In the Draft Treaty concerning a Constitution for Europe, OJ C 310/1 December 12, 2004, Art. I-3 Para. 2 uses the twin concepts of "free and undistorted" competition.

[9] *Cf.* Recital 2 of the Council Directive 84/450/EEC of September 10, 1984 relating to the Approximation of the Laws, Regulations and Administrative Provisions of the Member States concerning Misleading Advertising, OJ L 250/17, September 9, 1984 with the amendments that result from Art. 1 of Directive 97/55/EC of the European Parliament and Council of October 6, 1997 to Amend Directive 84/450 EEC concerning Misleading Advertising for the Purpose of Including Comparative Advertising OJ L 290/18, October 23, 1997; ZULEEG, *supra* note 6, Art. 3 EC, note 7.

[10] *Cf.* as example of many, VEELKEN, "Gemeinschaftsrechtliche Einwirkungen im Recht des unlauteren Wettbewerbs," 1993 EWS 377; *ibid.*, "Nationales Lauterkeitsrecht und Europäisches Gemeinschaftsrecht," in: BLOMEYER (ed.) "Europäische Union als Rechtsgemeinschaft" 141, 162 (1995).

EC Treaty itself, corresponding express regulation in the field of Unfair Competition law protection of competition in primary law still has to come. The reason given for the lack of a corresponding protection of fair competition on the basis of European law and the associated imbalance of competition protection is that firstly ensuring freedom of competition – particularly in a historical consideration – was of considerably greater importance for the integration policy objectives than ensuring fairness, while secondly the ECJ might not have been well suited to cope with the application of European Unfair Competition law.[11] To this must be added the fact that at the time when the EC Treaty was created, the convergence of the objectives of Unfair Competition and Antitrust law for the purpose of the protection of competition was by no means common grounds in every Member State.[12]

The concept of "distortion" thus comprises not only direct interventions in the freedom of activity of the market participants involved in or affected by anticompetitive practices, but also other "artificial" changes of competitive conditions.[13] The ECJ has already held that the objective set out in Art. 3 Para. 1 (g) EC is "inter alia", hence not exhaustively, pursued by the rules on competition set out in Art. 81 et seq. of the Treaty.[14] In the *Yves Rocher* decision, the ECJ also made it clear that within the limits of the *Cassis* formula the protection of fair competition served in particular to include the protection of competition against distortion.[15]

In the older literature it was suggested that a Community law general clause against unfair competition could be derived from the statement of the objectives.[16] However, even then this was subject to the restriction that this was only a general legal principle that might have had the character of legal source but not of a rule of law.[17] Either way, the Preamble and the statement of the objectives do not bring us any further: as a statement of the objectives they lack the necessary "density" of the determination of conduct, while as a general clause without the character of a rule of law and hence without sanctions, they lack "teeth".[18]

---

[11] VEELKEN, 1993 EWS 377, *supra* note 10.

[12] HUCKE, "Erforderlichkeit einer Harmonisierung des Wettbewerbsrechts in Europa" 39 *et seq.* (2001).

[13] KOOS, "Europäischer Lauterkeitsmaßstab und globale Integration" 21 *et seq.*, 24 (1996).

[14] Decision of the ECJ, January 29, 1985, Case No. 231/83, 1985 ECR 305, 10 – *Fuel prices.*

[15] Decision of the ECJ, May 18, 1993, Case No. C-126/91, 1993 ECR I-2361, 22 – *Yves Rocher.*

[16] FIKENTSCHER, *supra* note 2, at 158 *et seq.*; *ibid.*, "Wirtschaftsrecht" § 15 X.4, 668, Vol. 1 (1983). Not decided by MÜLLER-GRAFF, in: "FS-Carstens" 209, 222 (1984).

[17] FIKENTSCHER, *supra* note 2, at 160.

[18] VEELKEN, "Nationales Lauterkeitsrecht und Europäisches Gemeinschaftsrecht," 92 ZVglRWiss 241, 263 (1993); *ibid.*, 1993 EWS 377, *supra* note 10, at 378; *ibid.*, in: "Europäische Union als Rechtsgemeinschaft" *supra* note 10, at 164. Similarly, DETHLOFF, "Europäisierung des Wettbewerbsrechts" 8 (2001). VEELKEN, *loc.cit.*, at 165, would assume an unwritten Unfair Competition law at primary law level with the character of a general clause.

3. EC Antitrust Law

3.1 Agreements That Restrict Competition, Art. 81 EC

This at best covers types of competitive behaviour such as exclusionary forms of conduct practiced by cartels on the boycot.

3.2 Abuse of a Dominant Position, Art. 82 EC

The scope of application of Art. 82 is broader. In particular the individual impeding of competitors or the market in general can as a rule establish a charge of an exclusionary abuse within the meaning of Art. 82 EC. However, an infringement of this Article also requires a dominant position, which is missing in most cases.

4. Fundamental Freedoms

The fundamental freedoms are of themselves not related to Unfair Competition law. In particular, the ECJ has refused to recognise the Member States' unfair competition regulations as regulations to protect public policy – even if backed up by criminal penalties[19] – or industrial or commercial property[20] within the meaning of Art. 30 EC.

As a consequence of the failure of early efforts towards the positive harmonisation of Unfair Competition law, the ECJ, however, "discovered" at an early stage the possibility of using the fundamental freedoms to eliminate market access restrictions established by national unfair competition regulations. The free movement of goods, as generally in the development of the principles related to the fundamental freedoms, played a leading role:

4.1 Free Movements of Goods, Art. 28 EC

Article 28 (formerly Article 30) EC

Quantitative restrictions on imports and all measures having equivalent effect shall be prohibited between Member States.

4.1.1 The Creation of the Cassis Doctrine

It had always been disputed whether provisions applicable without distinction fell under the prohibition of measures having equivalent effect in the same way as dis-

---

[19] Decision of the ECJ, March 13, 1984, Case No. 16/83, 1984 ECR 1299, 33 – *Prantl.*

[20] Only the protection of geographical indications of origin in Member States is regarded as being covered by Art. 30 EC, decision of the ECJ, November 10, 1992, Case No. C-3/91, 1992 ECR I-5529, 23 *et seq.* – *Turrón de Alicante*. *Cf.* JOLIET, "Droit de la concurrence déloyale et libre circulation des merchandises," in: "Droit européen de la concurrence déloyale en formation" 29, 38 *et seq.*, 42 (1994).

criminatory provisions.[21] This question was decided by the ECJ in 1974 in the *Dassonville* ruling.[22] The case was based on a Belgian regulation that required the presentation of an official document issued by the country of export when goods bearing indications of origin were imported. The ECJ held that *any trading rules enacted by the Member States capable of directly or indirectly, actually or potentially hindering intra-Community trade* were to be regarded as a measure having equivalent effect.[23] Despite the broad wording of the *Dassonville* formula, some kept arguing that the free movement of goods merely established a prohibition on discrimination, since the *Dassonville* decision was based on an obvious discrimination by means of a Member State's regulation. The ECJ put an end to the speculations in 1979 with its decision in the *Cassis de Dijon* case:[24] According to a German regulation, fruit juice liqueurs had to contain at least 25% alcohol and for this reason the Cassis de Dijon fruit juice liqueur made in France with an alcoholic content of only 15 – 20% was excluded from the German market. The marketing regulation at issue was applied without distinction to domestic and foreign goods. Nevertheless the Court upheld the application of Art. 30 of the EEC Treaty (now Art. 28 EC), thereby confirming its extremely broad wording of the *Dassonville* formula.

The legal structure of Arts. 28 et seq. (previously Arts. 30 et seq. EC Treaty) fundamentally changed as a result of this extension of their scope of application. If any indirect and even potential restriction could be a measure of equivalent effect within the meaning of Art. 28,[25] the justification acquired a different importance.[26] Accordingly, in the *Cassis de Dijon* decision, the ECJ not only made clear the broad scope of application of the free movement of goods but also reacted to the resulting need for an extension of the justification. According to the wording in the *Cassis de Dijon* decision, obstacles to Community internal trade resulting from differences in national regulations concerning marketing are only permitted if these provisions are necessary in order to satisfy mandatory requirements relating in particular to the effectiveness of fiscal supervision, the protection of public health, the fairness of commercial transactions and the defence of the consumer.[27]

---

[21] *Cf.* PIPKORN, "Das Verbot von Maßnahmen gleicher Wirkung wie mengenmäßige Beschränkungen," in: "Beitrag des Gerichtshofes der Europäischen Gemeinschaften zur Verwirklichung des Gemeinsamen Marktes" 9, 13 *et seq.* (1981); MÜLLER-GRAFF, in: VON DER GROEBEN & SCHWARZE, "Kommentar zum Vertrag über die Europäische Union und zur Gründung der Europäischen Gemeinschaft," Art. 28 EC, note 29 with numerous references in footnote 72, Vol. 1 (6th ed. 2003).

[22] Decision of the ECJ, July 11, 1974, Case No. 8/74, 1974 ECR 837 – *Dassonville.*

[23] Decision of the ECJ, July 11, 1974, Case No. 8/74, 1974 ECR 837, 5 – *Dassonville.*

[24] Decision of the ECJ, February 20, 1979, Case No. 120/78, 1979 ECR 649 – *Cassis de Dijon.* Given the extensive literature on the scope of the Cassis judicial practice, *cf.* AHLFELD, *supra* note 5.

[25] On the development of the concept, *cf.* AHLFELD, *supra* note 5, at 26 *et seq.*

[26] NOVAK, "Ungleichbehandlung von ausländischen Produkten oder Dienstleistungen – Einheitliche Rechtfertigungstatbestände im EG-Vertrag," 1997 DB 2589, 2590.

[27] Decision of the ECJ, February 20, 1979, Case No. 120/78, 1979 ECR 649, 8 – *Cassis de Dijon.*

Doing so the ECJ paved the way to an interpretation of the free movement of goods based on the *country-of-origin principle*.[28] If there are no "mandatory requirements", there are no sound reasons for preventing alcoholic drinks lawfully manufactured and put into circulation in one Member State being imported into the other Member States. Goods that do not satisfy the requirements of the country of production need not of course be accepted by the other Member States.

4.1.2 The Relevant Objects of Protection of the Cassis Formula: Beele, Miro and Yves Rocher

In order to interpret the subject matter of protection against *unfair competition*, the ECJ, in the *Beele* case, referred to the definition in Art. 10bis of the Paris Convention, which applied to all Member States, thereby adopting the classical interpretation of Unfair Competition law.[29] The *Miro*[30] and *Yves Rocher*[31] decisions brought both an amendment and clarification. In the *Miro*[32] decision, the ECJ ascribed the likelihood of deception as to a particular alcoholic content associated with the naming of a liqueur as Genever exclusively to the field of consumer protection (para. 15). The subject matter of the protection against unfair competition only concerned the competitive advantage that was obtained by products privileged by the free movement of goods (para. 16). Similarly in *Yves Rocher*, the ECJ first examined the enticing effect of price comparisons emphasised in advertising and their tendency to mislead from the point of view of consumer protection and then addressed the question of the protection against unfair competition. On this point the ECJ held that correct comparisons of prices prohibited according to a provision of the type disputed (here Sec. 6e of the old version of the German Act against Unfair Competition) could by no means distort the conditions of competition. In contrast, a provision that prohibited such comparison was capable of restricting competition.[33] Since then the ECJ has classified the "protection against unfair competition" as being within the competition law context and has based its decision on the existence of a

---

[28] DAUSES, "Die Rechtsprechung des EuGH zum Verbraucherschutz und zur Werbefreiheit im Binnenmarkt," 1995 EuZW 425, calls this a "Copernican revolution". *Cf.* on the country-of-origin principle the Communication from the Commission concerning the Consequences of the Judgement given by the Court of Justice on February 20, 1979 in Case No. 120/78 ("Cassis de Dijon"), OJ C 256/2, October 3, 1980: "Any product imported from another Member State must in principle be admitted to the territory of the importing Member State if it has been lawfully produced, that is, conforms to rules and processes of manufacture that are customarily and traditionally accepted in the exporting country, and is marketed in the territory of the latter."

[29] Decision of the ECJ, March 2, 1982, Case No. 6/81, ECR 1982, 707, 9 – *Beele*. In the decision of the ECJ, January 22, 1981, Case No. 58/80, 1981 ECR 181, 15 – *Dansk Supermarked*, the Court had avoided an express discussion of the subject matters of protection of the *Cassis* formula and held that "the marketing of imported goods can be prohibited if the conditions on which they are sold constitutes an infringement of the marketing usages considered proper and fair in the Member State of importation".

[30] Decision of the ECJ, November 26, 1985, Case No. 182/84, 1985 ECR 3781 – *Miro*.

[31] Decision of the ECJ, May 18, 1993, Case No. C-126/91, 1993 ECR I-2361 – *Yves Rocher*.

[32] Decision of the ECJ, November 26, 1985, Case No. 182/84, 1985 ECR 3781 – *Miro*.

[33] Decision of the ECJ, May 18, 1993, Case No. C-126/91, 1993 ECR I-2361, 22 – *Yves Rocher*.

distortion of competition.[34] No considerations relating to business morality are raised in this context. In the case of regulations against infringements of competition committed by acts of *communication directed to the market* the ECJ primarily applies consumer protection as a mandatory requirement in the general interest.

4.1.3 Classification of the "Mandatory Requirement"

Depending on interpretation of the scope of the *Dassonville* formula, scholars understood the *Cassis de Dijon* decision either as an extension or as a restriction.[35] At the same time questions were raised above all by the systematic positioning of the "mandatory requirements". They were in part interpreted as restrictions on the free movement of goods that were immanent in the actus reus, and partly as an independent justification.[36] The ECJ has in any event created a flexible instrument that allows it to take greater account of the legislative objectives to justify non-discriminatory provisions than had been possible by merely interpreting the specific justifications in Art. 30 EC (previously Art. 36 EC Treaty).[37] The dual approach in certain decisions, in which the ECJ examined the justification based on reasons of the protection of health and the protection of intellectual property both as a mandatory requirement within the meaning of the *Cassis* formula and as a justification within the meaning of Art. 30 EC (previously Art. 36 EC Treaty)[38] was recognised, but the Court restricted itself to ascribing this approach to the special features of the justification used.[39]

However a *modern view* of the *Cassis* doctrine permits a different interpretation of this dual approach and of the discussion concerning the systematic position of the mandatory requirements. The possibilities for justifying interferences in the fundamental freedoms pursuant to Arts. 30, 39 Para. 3, 46 Para. 1, 55, 58 Para. 1 (b) EC (previously Arts. 36, 48 Para. 3, 56 Para. 1, 66, 73d Para. 1 (b) of the EC Treaty), together with the nationality provisos in Arts. 39 Para. 4 and 45 Para. 1 EC (previously Arts. 48 Para. 4, 55 Para. 1 EC Treaty), the *Keck* decision (see above) and the subsidiarity principle in Art. 5 Para. 2 EC (previously Art. 3b Para. 2 of the EC Treaty),[40] fit into an image of the EC Treaty that is determined above all by efforts

---

[34] KLAUER, "Die Europäisierung des Privatrechts – Der EuGH als Zivilrichter", 359 (1997). Dissenting GÜLBAY, "Vergleichende Werbung, Subsidiarität und Europa" 212 *et seq.* (1997).

[35] CAPELLI, 1981 RMC 421; BLECKMANN, "Zur Problematik der Cassis de Dijon-Rechtsprechung des Europäischen Gerichtshofs," 1986 GRUR Int. 172, 177; RABE, in: SCHWARZE (ed.) "Wirtschaftsrecht des Gemeinsamen Marktes in der aktuellen Rechtsentwicklung" 41, 43 (1983). *Cf.* the detailed discussion in KOTTHOFF, "Werbung ausländischer Unternehmen im Inland" 70 (1995); AHLFELD, *supra* note 5, at 30 *et seq.*; HÖDL, "Die Beurteilung von verkaufsbehindernden Maßnahmen im Europäischen Binnenmarkt" 88 *et seq.* (1997); WEYER, "Freier Warenverkehr und nationale Regelungsgewalt in der Europäischen Union" 49 *et seq.* (1997); DETHLOFF, *supra* note 18, at 141.

[36] *Cf.* the detailed discussion in AHLFELD, *supra* note 5, at 81 *et seq.*; BECKER, in: SCHWARZE, *supra* note 5, Art. 28 EC Treaty, 107 *et seq.*

[37] NOVAK, *supra* note 26.

[38] *E.g.* decision of the ECJ, March 12, 1987, Case No. 178/84, 1987 ECR 1227, 30 *et seq.*, 38 *et seq.* – *Reinheitsgebot.*

[39] *Cf.* NOVAK, *supra* note 26; AHLFELD, *supra* note 5, at 95 *et seq.*

[40] In this sense also HUCKE, *supra* note 12, at 57: vertical distribution of powers.

to resolve the inherent tension between the upholding of national sovereignty and the creation of conditions similar to an internal market.

In retrospect, it must be assumed that ECJ's *Cassis de Dijon* decision broke away from this polar relationship and at the same time exercised a more extensive Community mandate. By recognising them as a *mandatory requirements*, the ECJ *transposed certain general interests to the level of European law.*[41] The general interests recognised in the *Cassis* formula are not particular interests of the Members States[42] tolerated by the ECJ out of respect towards the (residual) national sovereignty.[43] On the contrary the ECJ permits certain Member State regulations if and because they protect interests whose consideration is also *"mandatory" for Community law itself.*[44]

---

[41] Correctly AHLFELD, *supra* note 5, at 237, 286. However, this approach has not been taken to the end in a number of cases. Thus AHLFELD, *supra* note 5, at 21, 98 *et seq.* still places the *Cassis* judicial practice in the context of the limits to national regulatory scope.

[42] These are protected by Art. 30 EC, *cf.* Advocate General *Trabucchi*, conclusions, 1316, 1328 in decision of the ECJ, July 14, 1976, Cases No. 3, 4, 6/76, 1976 ECR 1279 – *Kramer.*

[43] Although this view is still upheld by BLECKMANN, *supra* note 35.

[44] *Cf.* in this sense in particular the Communication from the Commission to the Council, the European Parliament and the Economic and Social Committee. The Follow-up to the Green Paper on Commercial Communication in the Internal Market, COM (98) 121 final, 5, 11. Similarly, GORMLEY, "Prohibiting Restrictions on Trade within the EEC" 52 (1985): "Thus the Court has sought to ensure that interests or values which are clearly compatible with the basic aims of the Treaty do not go unprotected in the period before their protection has been assured at the Community level." STEINDORFF, *supra* note 3, at 142; MEIER, "Die Lauterkeit des Handelsverkehrs," 1993 GRUR Int. 219, 220; MARTIN-EHLERS, "Die Irreführungsverbote des UWG im Spannungsfeld des freien europäischen Warenverkehrs" who admittedly emphasises the structural parallels to the justifications in Art. 36 of the EC Treaty (now Art. 30 EC) 29, but recognises that the ECJ helped consumer protection and the protection against unfair competition to acquire a "Community dimension" 76 (1996); PIPKORN, *supra* note 21, at 24 *et seq.*; KOOS, *supra* note 13, at 47, 74 *et seq.*; WÖHLERMANN, "Das Wirtschaftsrecht in der Europäischen Union" 142 (1998); AHLFELD, *supra* note 5, at 69, 267; BECKER, in: SCHWARZE, *supra* note 5, Art. 30 EC Treaty, note 37; mandatory requirements only related to the protection of rights protected by Community law. Dissenting SPRINGER, "Europäisches Gemeinschaftsrecht und die Auslegung des Irreführungsgebotes gemäß § 3 UWG" 35 (1995), who interprets the *Cassis* judicial practice as a means of securing the regulatory powers of the individual states. HAUSCHKA, "Lauterkeitsrecht und Verbraucherschutz zwischen nationalem Regelungsanspruch und der Rechtsprechung des Europäischen Gerichtshofs," 89 ZVglRWiss 166, 174 *et seq.* (1990), ascribes a dual function to the *Cassis* judicial practice: firstly, the ECJ regulated the powers between the Community and the Member States. Secondly, the ECJ, overcoming the absence of Community law regulations, used its own development of the law to create contents by means of which a European regulation of Unfair Competition law was established. The Micklitz Study, III, 341, draws the bold conclusion from the *Cassis* judicial practice that Art. 28 of the European Community Treaty a priori only protected the free movement of goods. This is probably incorrect if only because of the priority solution. In its decisions, the ECJ clearly weighs the mandatory requirements of fair competition against the interest of market integration.

The wording in the 2nd Heading and the 8th Consideration of the *Cassis* decision[45] is not in conflict which such an interpretation. What is "accepted" are not the national provisions but rather the resulting obstacles to the free movement of goods. This interpretation is supported by the wording in the *Miro* case: "When in order to satisfy mandatory requirements *recognised by Community law* national legislation creates obstacles to ... the free movement of goods, it must observe the limits laid down by Community law" (emphasis added by this author).[46] In this context, it is necessary to emphasise that the corresponding wording immediately follows the reference to the continuing lack of positive harmonisation,[47] which according to the principle of restricted enumerative jurisdiction[48] in turn requires a corresponding power on the part of the European legislator.

However, an interpretation of the *Cassis* doctrine in this sense is remarkable because the ECJ's *Cassis de Dijon* decision laid down the importance of consumer protection in the Common Market as early as 1979, 8 years before it was adopted by the Single European Act.[49] The same applies to environmental protection.[50]

In the final analysis the rule-and-exception relationship between positive harmonisation and negative integration was reversed by the ECJ's recruitment of the fundamental freedoms in the 1980s.[51] Following the *Cassis* decision, the negative integration by means of the fundamental freedoms acquired more than mere independent significance. The ECJ's judicature on the recognition of "mandatory requirements" has since then been ascribed the function of a pacemaker for positive harmonisation.[52] According to the Commission's White Paper on the "Completion of the Internal Market", the efforts at harmonisation should be reduced to the fields recognised by the ECJ as "mandatory requirements".[53]

---

45 Decision of the ECJ, February 20, 1979, Case No. 120/78, 1979 ECR 649 – *Cassis de Dijon.*

46 Decision of the ECJ, November 26, 1985, Case No. 182/84, 1985 ECR 3781, 14 – *Miro.*

47 The direct relationship established by the ECJ between the (still) lack of positive harmonisation and the Member States' consideration of the "mandatory requirement" is emphasised by GORMLEY, *supra* note 44, at 52; BARENTS, "New Developments in Measures Having Equivalent Effect," 18 CML Rev. 271, 286 (1981); HAUSCHKA, *supra* note 44, at 175; AHLFELD, *supra* note 5, at 70.

48 *Cf.* as example of many, OPPERMANN, "Europarecht" Sec. 6, note 62 *et seq.* (3rd ed. 2005).

49 DAUSES, *supra* note 28; AHLFELD,*supra* note 5, at 106.

50 The decision of the ECJ, February 7, 1985, Case No. 240/83, 1985 ECR 531, 13 – *Altöle II*, referred to environmental protection as an "essential objective of the Community"; *see* also expressly decision of the ECJ, September 20, 1988, Case No. 302/86, 1988 ECR 4607, 9 – *Pfandflaschen.*

51 BLECKMANN, *supra* note 35.

52 Ahlfeld, *supra* note 5, at 250.

53 Commission White Paper to the European Council, "Completing the Internal Market", COM (85) 310 final 19 notes 65 and 66.

4.1.4 Density of Controls of the "Mandatory Requirements" in the Field of Unfair Competition Law

The *Cassis de Dijon*[54] judgement, in which the ECJ gave Member States the possibility of restricting the free movements of goods by means of non-discriminatory regulations in order to satisfy mandatory requirements, in particular relating to the fairness of commercial transactions and the defence of the consumer, did not nevertheless give a clean bill of health to national unfair competition regulations of whatever kind,[55] but instead justified the need to balance the free movement of goods and the protection against unfair competition in the individual case,[56] as was made clear in the *Bocksbeutel,*[57] *Pall,*[58] *Nissan,*[59] *Clinique,*[60] *Mars,*[61] *6-Korn,*[62] *Lifting,*[63] and *Darbo*[64] decisions on the risk of deception invoked by the Member States. In these decisions the ECJ itself examined whether a description, trade mark or promotional text was misleading.[65] The development of this judicial practice is to be set out in the following contribution, which concerns the case law of the ECJ.

This is not a priority decision, but rather a balancing of the aspects that need to be taken into consideration. Where unfair competition regulations pursue the protection of the consumer or of the general public, the ECJ builds its assumptions on the concept of "an average consumer who is reasonably well-informed and reasonably observant and circumspect".[66] The model addressee is held not only to be appropriately informed but also basically capable of being informed. For this reason, unfair competition prohibitions frequently come to grief for lack of the necessity of the measure, since the desired protection of the addressee can in many instances be achieved by labelling obligations as a less restrictive means.[67]

---

54 Decision of the ECJ, February 20, 1979, Case No. 120/78, 1979 ECR 649, 8 – *Cassis de Dijon*.

55 Gormley, *supra* note 44, at 52. Dissenting still, HÖSL, "Interessenabwägung und rechtliche Erheblichkeit der Irreführung bei § 3 UWG" 325 (1986).

56 REESE, "Grenzüberschreitende Werbung in der Europäischen Gemeinschaft" 56 (1994); DAUSES, *supra* note 28. RÜFFLER, "Österreichisches und europäisches Wirtschaftsprivatrecht" 65 (1998), bezeichnet das als Optimierungsproblem.

57 Decision of the ECJ, March 13, 1984, Case No. 16/83, 1984 ECR 1299 – *Prantl*.

58 Decision of the ECJ, December 13, 1990, Case No. C-238/89, 1990 ECR I-4827 – *Pall*.

59 Decision of the ECJ, January 16, 1992, Case No. C-373/90, 1992 ECR I-131 – *Nissan*.

60 Decision of the ECJ, February 2, 1994, Case No. C-315/92, 1994 ECR I-317, 21 – *Clinique*.

61 Decision of the ECJ, July 6, 1995, Case No. C-470/93, 1995 ECR I-1923 – *Mars*.

62 Decision of the ECJ, July 16, 1998, Case No. C-210/96, 1998 ECR I-4657 – *6-Korn*.

63 Decision of the ECJ, January 1, 2000, Case No. C-220/98, 2000 ECR I-117 – *Estée Lauder v. Lancaster*.

64 Decision of the ECJ, April 4, 2000, Case No. C-465/98, 2000 ECR I-2297 – *Darbo*.

65 MEIER, *supra* note 44; DETHLOFF, *supra* note 18, at 192.

66 Decision of the ECJ, September 16, 2004, Case No. C-329/02, 2004 ECR I-8317, 24 – *SAT.1*.

67 *Cf.* TRUCHET, "Le concept du „consommateur informé" en droit européen" 31 *et seq.* (2000).

4.2 Freedom of Services, Art. 49 EC

As a consequence of the "trailblazing role" of the free movement of goods within the doctrine relating to the fundamental freedoms,[68] the control of the Member States' unfair competition regulations by means of negative integration was initially based on Arts. 30 et seq. of the EC Treaty (now Arts. 28 et seq. EC). The limit on the scope of application of the free movement of goods imposed by the *Keck* decision shifted the point of emphasis.[69] In particular the Commission now bases its efforts at harmonisation mainly on the impairment of the freedom of services. The latter is applicable if it is not goods but rather services that are marketed across borders (4.2.1).[70] The freedom of services can at the same time also indirectly cover the marketing of goods if national marketing regulations have a negative effect on the provision of services, specifically those offered by advertising enterprises (4.2.2).

4.2.1 Cross-border Marketing of Services

At the latest since the *Gebhard* decision,[71] it has been acknowledged that the freedom of services establishes a prohibition on restrictions just like the free movement of goods. This means that provisions restricting the cross-border activity of service providers are as a matter of principle covered by Art. 49 EC (previously Art. 59 EC Treaty). These include the Unfair Competition law provisions of the receiving country. The "market place rule"[72] means that as a matter of principle the domestic Unfair Competition law applies if foreign providers market their services on the domestic market.[73]

The ECJ has already decided on the relationship between the free movement of services and Member State restrictions on telephone marketing in the *Alpine Investments* case:[74] The Dutch Ministry of Finances had prohibited a Dutch company specialising in commodities futures transactions from carrying out cold calling, i.e. the practice of making telephone contact with private persons (inter alia in Belgium, France and United Kingdom) without their prior written consent in order to offer

---

68 MÜLLER-GRAFF, *supra* note 21, before Arts. 28 *et seq.* EC, note 10.

69 *Cf.* the subsequent contribution and the discussion in KUGELMANN, "Werbung als Dienstleistung," 2001 EuR 363, 374.

70 Decisions of the ECJ, October 1, 1987, Case No. 311/85, 1987 ECR 3801, 32 – *Vlaamse Reisbureaus*; March 24, 1994, Case No. C-275/92, 1994 ECR I-1039, 25 *et seq.* – *Schindler*; May 10, 1995, Case No. C-384/93, 1995 ECR I-1141 – *Alpine Investments*. On the limits, *see* Attorney General *Stix-Hackl*, conclusions, notes 34 *et seq.*, to the decision of the ECJ, January 22, 2002, Case No. C-390/99, 2002 ECR I-607 – *Canal Satélite*.

71 Decision of the ECJ, November 30, 1995, Case No. C-55/94, 1995 ECR I-4165 – *Gebhard*.

72 GLÖCKNER in: HARTE-BAVENDAMM & HENNING-BODEWIG (eds.), UWG, 2004, Introduction C note 73 *et seq.*

73 GÜNTHER, "Erwünschte Regelung unerwünschter Werbung?," 1999 CR 172, 178 comes to the conclusion that a provision that merely prohibits certain advertising measures in the domestic country does not restrict the basic freedom of the provider of the advertised services. However, this can only apply to cases in which the services are to be exported to another EEA country.

74 Decision of the ECJ, May 10, 1995, Case No. C-384/93, 1995 ECR I-1141 – Alpine Investments.

them various financial services. The company concerned objected. The preliminary reference proceedings initially concerned the question whether the *Keck* doctrine was to be extended to the free movement of services. The ECJ confirmed the application of the freedom of services because the prohibition issued by the government directly affected access to the market in services in the other Member States and was therefore capable of impeding the movement of services within the Community.[75] The ECJ's argumentation resting upon the direct restriction of market access also concerns, mutatis mutandis, providers resident within the Community[76] who have been denied access to the domestic market as a result of the objections to telephone advertising based on the market place rule.[77] This also lays down the limits to the scope of application of the free movement of services: Where the market access of service providers outside the Member State is not directly affected – and where the restrictive rule thus has a neutral effect on the market – the free movement of services does not apply.[78]

Although the Dutch measures in the *Alpine Investments* case were thus not protected by the *Keck* doctrine, they were ultimately accepted: The ECJ initially adopted the submission by the Dutch government that the private person generally surprised by cold calling was not able to obtain information about the risks that resulted from the type of transactions proposed or to compare the quality and price of the caller's services with those offered by the competition. Since the futures market was extremely speculative and difficult to understand for capital investors with little experience, the ECJ held that it was necessary to protect them from the most aggressive methods of customer advertising.[79]

---

[75] Decision of the ECJ, May 10, 1995, Case No. C-384/93, 1995 ECR I-1141, 32 *et seq.* – *Alpine Investments.*

[76] Art. 36 of the Treaty on the European Economic Area, OJ L 1/3, January 3, 1994, extends the territorial scope of application of the fundamental freedoms to the European Economic Area. For linguistic reasons, the following will nevertheless only refer to the "Community" and the "Union".

[77] GLÖCKNER, "'Cold Calling' und europäische Richtlinie zum Fernabsatz," 2000 GRUR Int. 29, 35. RÜFFLER, *supra* note 56, at 94; SACK, "Staatliche Werbebeschränkungen und die Art. 30 und 59 EG-Vertrag," 1998 WRP 103, 113, are of the view that *Alpine Investments* does not show whether the *Keck* doctrine was applicable to the free movement of services since it did not concern a restriction on imports but on exports. WEINAND, "Europarecht und Recht gegen den unlauteren Wettbewerb" 64 *et seq.* (1998), would transfer the principles of the *Alpine Investments* decision to restrictions on imports, but regards it as a restriction of the *Keck* doctrine. BURCKHARDT, "Die lauterkeitsrechtliche Beurteilung des modernen Direktmarketings" 175 (2000); DETHLOFF, *supra* note 18, at 236, derives e contrario from the decision that the *Keck* doctrine is to be applied to restrictions on imports. This is also suggested by the ECJ decision of January 22, 2002, Case No. C-390/99, 2002 ECR I-607, 29, 30 – *Canal Satélite*, but without any express comment. HOLOUBEK, in: SCHWARZE, *supra* note 5, Art. 49 EC Treaty, note 61 would not apply the *Keck* doctrine to restrictions by the receiving country because the free movement of services is based on the country-of-origin principle.

[78] HÖDL, *supra* note 35, at 187, also assumes that the decision confirms the intention of the *Keck* decision

[79] Decision of the ECJ, May 10, 1995, Case No. C-384/93, 1995 ECR I-1141, 46 – *Alpine Investments.*

4.2.2 Impairment of Advertising and Marketing Service Providers

National marketing regulations – including those relating to unfair competition – in particular restrict the providers of advertising media such as the publishers of magazines or television broadcasters and marketing agencies. This is particularly obvious in the field of telemarketing, which is subject to a relatively strict regulatory framework in Germany, Austria and Switzerland. Agencies that have specialized in the conduct of telephone, fax or email advertising broadly permitted in the Member State of their registered office are generally prohibited, for instance, from accessing the German market.[80] The same applies to classical advertising services if they can be provided across borders, such as the drafting and designing of print media advertisements.

Advertising and marketing activities by self-employed third parties (this affects not only advertising agencies and indirect marketing providers but also for instance the publishers or TV broadcasters that provide advertising space) must be measured according to the criteria of Arts. 49 et seq. EC.[81] Admittedly, in the case of independent services for third parties the distinction according to the market neutrality of the regulation restricting imports as developed by the ECJ by its *Keck* decision[82] need not be applied by analogy simply because the case concerns a measure for the promotion of the sale of *goods.*[83] An unjustified differentiation of the European law requirements depending on whether the measure is a party's own advertising or advertising for a third party is excluded by the fact that the point of reference for the fundamental freedom is no longer the import of *goods* but rather the cross-border provision of *services.*

However, the principles developed in the *Keck* decision are applicable mutatis mutandis to cross-border advertising services, i.e. all that is covered is advertising regulations that make access to the market more difficult for foreign providers of

---

[80] GÜNTHER, *supra* note 73.

[81] Decisions of the ECJ, April 26, 1988, Case No. 352/85, 1988 ECR 2085, 13 *et seq. – Bond van Adverteerders et al.*; July 9, 1997, Case No. C-34-36/95, 1997 ECR I-3843, 48 – *De Agostini*; October 28, 1999, Case No. C-6/98, 1999 ECR I-7599, 49 – *ARD v. PRO Sieben Media AG*; October 5, 2000, Case No. C-376/98, 2000 ECR I-8419, 99 – *Bundesrepublik Deutschland v. Parlament und Rat*; March 8, 2001, Case No. C-405/98, 2001 ECR I-1795, 37 – *Konsumentombudsmannen (KO) v. Gourmet International Products AB (GIP).* On this there is a clear shift of accent particularly in the efforts at harmonisation by the Commission.

[82] Decision of the ECJ, October 28, 1999, Case No. C-6/98, 1999 ECR I-7599, 49 – *ARD v. PRO Sieben Media AG*, concerned provisions restricting exports. The stricter regulations of the country of domicile for calculating the permissible duration of advertising interruptions in television programmes only disadvantages the television providers based in this country against their competitors in other Member States. However, the resulting discrimination of nationals is covered neither by the basic freedom nor by general equal treatment requirements. *Cf.* Attorney General Jacobs, final pleadings note 83 *et seq.*, to decision of the ECJ, October 28, 1999, Case No. C-6/98, 1999 ECR I-7599 – *ARD v. PRO Sieben Media AG*; decision of the ECJ, October 28, 1999, Case No. C-6/98, 1999 ECR I-7599, 53 – *ARD v. PRO Sieben Media AG.*

[83] Decisions of the ECJ, July 9, 1997, Cases No. C-34-36/95, 1997 ECR I-3843, 50 – *De Agostini*; March 8, 2001, Case No. C-405/98, 2001 ECR I-1795, 37 *et seq.* – *Konsumentombudsmannen (KO) v. Gourmet International Products AB (GIP).*

advertising services than for domestic providers.[84] Such an interpretation is confirmed by the decision of the ECJ in the *Alpine Investments* case and in its arguments concerning the restriction of market access. Restrictive advertising regulations of the country of import regularly have a neutral effect on the market for advertising services.[85] Conversely, permitting the specific form of advertising on the basis of the freedom of services would put to foreign agencies in a better position.

Moreover, interferences in the free movement of services can be justified in accordance with the *Cassis* doctrine applicable to the movement of goods.[86] In the *Gebhard*[87] decision, the ECJ made it clear that national measures that hinder or make less attractive the exercise of the fundamental freedoms guaranteed by the Treaty must fulfil four conditions: they must be applied in a non-discriminatory manner, they must be justified by imperative requirements in the general interest, they must be suitable for securing the attainment of the objectives they pursue and they must not go beyond what is necessary to attain it.[88] These conditions were confirmed in the *De Agostini* case.[89]

5. European Fundamental Rights as Parallel and Conflicting Forces

5.1 The Development of European Fundamental Rights

Originally, the EC Treaty was drawn up without fundamental rights. This is not surprising if account is taken of the fact that Community law is implemented essentially by means of the authorities and courts in the Member States. That nevertheless spaces void of fundamental rights were created as a result of the ECJ's case law developing the principles of direct effect and primacy of EC law, led to the first constitutional crisis in the EEC. The German[90] and the Italian[91] constitutional courts saw themselves obliged to provide the protection of their national constituencies against burdensome Community law measures.

---

[84] KUGELMANN, 2001 EuR 363, 369.

[85] PERAU, "Werbeverbote im Gemeinschaftsrecht" 171 (1997). There is a difference to the effects of advertising regulations on the cross-border marketing of products. *Cf.* the particular justification of the lack of market neutrality in decision of the ECJ, March 8, 2001, Case No. C-405/98, 2001 ECR I-1795, 21 *et seq.* – *Konsumentombudsmannen (KO) v. Gourmet International Products AB (GIP)*, and previously the reference in EFTA-GH, June 27, 1997, Case No. E-6/96, 1997 EFTA Ct. Rep. 56, 73 – *Wilhelmsen.* This went unnoticed by the ECJ in its justification of the Gourmet decision, March 8, 2001, Case No. C-405/98, 2001 ECR I-1795, 39 – *Konsumentombudsmannen (KO) v. Gourmet International Products AB (GIP).*

[86] Decisions of the ECJ, July 9, 1997, Cases No. C-34-36/95, 1997 ECR I-3843, 51 *et seq.* – *De Agostini*; October 28, 1999, Case No. C-6/98, 1999 ECR I-7599, 50 – *ARD v. PRO Sieben Media AG.*

[87] Decision of the ECJ, November 30, 1995, Case No. C-55/94, 1995 ECR I-4165 – *Gebhard.*

[88] Decision of the ECJ, November 30, 1995, Case No. C-55/94, 1995 ECR I-4165, 37 – *Gebhard.*

[89] Decision of the ECJ, July 9, 1997, Cases No. C-34 - 36/95, 1997 ECR I-384, 52 – *De Agostini.*

[90] BVerfGE 37, 271 (1974) – *So lange I.*

[91] Corte Costituzionale, December 18, 1973, published in part in 1974 EuR 255.

As a consequence, the ECJ found itself obliged to confirm the commitment of the Communities to the fundamental rights at every occasion. Such a particular occasion was given within the framework of the legal protection against burdensome measures of the European Commission in antitrust proceedings.[92] The fundamental rights are still[93] protected on the basis of the development of judge made law, a development that can rely on the general legal principles specified in Art. 228 EC as source of law, and on the documentation of these principles in Art. 6 Para. 2 and 3 of the EU Treaty, their content being based on the European Human Rights Convention as a source of legal principles. Art. 6 Para. 2 of the EU Treaty, however, does not adopt these sources as direct law, but instead words them as separate concretisation under Union law with effect throughout the entire system of basic laws within the Union.[94]

The importance of fundamental rights for Unfair Competition law will increase should the European Constitution ever be adopted or if the fundamental rights charter be ratified in isolation if the Constitution finally fails to be adopted. The Charter of Fundamental Rights will establish both the freedom to conduct a business (Art. II-76) and the right to the free expression of opinion and information (Art. II-71).

5.2 The Function of the Fundamental Rights in Conflict With the Fundamental Freedoms

The constitutional dispute was focused above all on the assumed insufficient protection of the fundamental rights against the assertion of the fundamental freedoms.[95] In the *Schmidberger* case, the ECJ nevertheless justified the restriction on the free movement of goods (blockade of the Brenner Motorway by Austrian protestors) on the grounds that European law itself is committed to comprehensive protection of the fundamental rights.[96]

5.3 Making Use of the Function of the Fundamental Rights in Parallel to the Fundamental Freedoms

In the contrary direction, the fundamental rights had limited importance until recently. The fundamental rights of the participants in competition, mostly the free-

[92] Decision of the ECJ, September 21, 1989, Cases Nos. 46/87 and 227/88, 1989 ECR 2859 – *Hoechst*.

[93] The EU Constitution Part II is intended to contain a separate list of fundamental rights, Treaty for a European Constitution, OJ C 310/1, December 16, 2004.

[94] Beutler, in: von der Groeben & Schwarze, "Kommentar zum Vertrag über die Europäische Union und zur Gründung der Europäischen Gemeinschaft" Art. 6 EU, note 44, Vol. 1 (6th ed. 2003).

[95] *Cf.* in particular decision of the ECJ, December 9, 1997, Case No. C-265/95, 1997 ECR I-6959 – *Importblockade*.

[96] Decision of the ECJ, June 12, 2003, Case No. C-112/00, 2003 ECR I-565, 74 – *Schmidberger*. On possible conflicts, *cf.* decision of the ECJ, October 14, 2004, Case No. C-36/02, 2004 ECR I-9609 – *Omega*.

dom of opinion (Art. 10 European Human Rights Conventions) which also includes commercial speech[97], and possibly the freedom of art, and at least, however, the freedom of profession and business,[98] all of which are restricted by unfair competition regulations, took second place in European law as against their fundamental freedoms (c.f. above).

The ECJ decision in the *Karner* case of March 25, 2004[99] will prove to be pioneering from a qualitative point of view. This case concerned an advertising prohibition under Austrian law (Sec. 30 Para. 1 of the Austrian Act against Unfair Competition, reference to goods from an insolvency). This prohibition on advertising was compatible with Art. 28 EC since on the basis of the *Keck* doctrine it had a neutral effect on the market.[100] However, the ECJ did not restrict itself to this finding, but continued its examination with the question whether the Austrian regulation might infringe fundamental European rights. This approach is remarkable in two respects. Firstly, as far as can be seen it was the first time the ECJ measured national legal regulations that were not issued as an implementation of Community law against the criteria of European fundamental rights, and secondly, it did this independently of the fundamental freedoms since the scope of application of the free movements of goods was not even available.

6. Definition of Objectives and Jurisdiction: Resolution of an Apparent Conflict

The points of reference for unfair competition regulations can be found in particular in the definitions of objectives and the legislative powers of the EC Treaty.

6.1 Internal Market: Art. 3 Para. 1 (h) in Conjunction With Arts. 94 et seq. EC

The activity of the Community according to Art. 3 Para. 1 (h) EC comprises the approximation of the laws of the Member States to the extent required for the functioning of the common market. On this basis the Community has the power to adopt regulations endowed with direct effect on the establishment or the function of the common market or that have the latter as their subject matter, Arts. 94 and 95 EC. In historic terms, too, the internal market competence to harmonise the law was primarily used for Unfair Competition law. Different unfair competition regulations in the Member States constitute a prime obstacle to market access.

---

97 References in BUSCHLE, "Kommunikationsfreiheit in den Grundrechten und Grundfreiheiten des EG-Vertrages" 113, 137 *et seq.* (2004).

98 Neither the freedom of profession nor of business are guaranteed as such in the EHRC. In order to justify the freedom of profession the ECJ relies on the constitutions of the Member States. The freedom of commerce and business is specified as a concretisation of the freedom of profession, decision of the ECJ, May 14, 1974, Case No. 4/73, 1974 ECR 491, 14 – *Nold.*

99 Decision of the ECJ, March 25, 2004, Case No. C-71/02, 2004 ECR I-3025 – *Karner.*

100 Decision of the ECJ, March 25, 2004, Case No. C-71/02, 2004 ECR I-3025, 43 – *Karner.*

6.2 Consumer Protection: Art. 3 Para. 1 (t) in Conjunction With Arts. 153 et seq.

The Community's activity also includes a contribution to the strenghthening of consumer protection, Art. 3 Para. 1 (t) EC. This is reflected firstly in the fact that a high level of consumer protection is to be taken as a base for legislation based on the internal market power pursuant to Art. 95 Para. 3. Secondly, Art. 153 Para. 3 (a) makes it clear that an element of consumer policies in the Community should be the adoption of measures pursuant to Art. 95 at a high level of protection. However, both show that consumer protection does not establish an independent legislative competence – for instance to adopt a general prohibition on tobacco advertising based on the protection of health. Nevertheless, the Consumer Protection Office became an independent Directorate General for Health and Consumer Protection at the European Commission and has in recent years been the stimulus for the relevant legislative proceedings of the Community.

6.3 Competing Jurisdictions in the Truest Sense of the Word?

In the 1990s, the Internal Market Directorate General was working on a communication on commercial communications in order to reduce the market access obstacles identified in the differences in the Member States' unfair competition regulations. In doing so it relied widely on the country-of-origin principle.

Since 1999 the Consumer Protection Directorate General has, in contrast, recognised the consumer protection effect of Unfair Competition law. The competing involvement of two directorates general within the European Commission led in 2001 to a reciprocal blockade of a variety of legislative proceedings within the European Commission lasting several months.

6.3.1 Unfair Competition Law and Consumer Protection in the Internal Market

Unfair Competition law and consumer protection are not a basic obstacle to market integration. Following the failure of the early attempts at overall harmonisation of Unfair Competition law and – more generally – after establishing the "New Strategy" to implement the internal market,[101] Unfair Competition law and Consumer law as parts of the national legal systems nevertheless often appeared as an obstacle to integration, as the *Cassis* formula showed. This fact, in combination with the institutional separation within the European Commission discussed above, also seemed to prevent the insight that if total harmonisation at the required high level of protection was achieved, the interests in market integration and the interests in consumer protection would coincide.

---

[101] *Cf.* the Commission White Paper to the European Council, "Completing the Internal Market", COM (85) 310 final, 6 note 13; and Council Resolution dated May 7, 1985 on a New Concept in the Field of Technical Harmonisation and Standardisation, OJ C 136/1, June 4, 1985.

6.3.2 Purposes of Protection Under Unfair Competition Law

The same discussion arose again within Unfair Competition law: According to the general view in Germany, Austria and Switzerland, and not least also due to the Directive on Misleading and Comparative Advertising in the version in force up to June 11, 2005, Unfair Competition law protects competitors, purchasers, in particular consumers, and the general public against impairments of competition (the triple purpose of protection).

Here, too, attempts are repeatedly made to play off the different objects of protection against each other. As a classical example, mention is made of the sale below cost. This practice is allegedly in the interests of consumers while damaging competitors. Such a presentation is however truncated. Consumers, too, have no longer-term interest in sales at below cost if such sales can eliminate competitors from the market and provide a monopoly rent to the surviving monopolist.

There should therefore be no dispute about the purposes of protection but rather about the economic plausibility of the underlying story: Does every sale below cost really mean that competitors are eliminated from the market without being replaced by other competitors? Even if this is the case, are the purchasers willing to pay the monopoly surcharge?

6.3.3 Inherent Link Between Competition Protection and Consumer Protection

Competition and private autonomy are two sides of the same coin. They are in an insoluble relationship of interaction: competition initially requires freedom of contract because it alone ensures the elementary choice necessary for competition, i.e. the substitutability of supply. On the other hand, freedom of contract requires competition, since only a functioning competition is able to neutralise even the largest differences in power. Thus competition protection is always also the protection of the weaker contracting party. This justifies the special protection granted to competition by the legal system as ensured by Antitrust law and Unfair Competition law.

However, competition occasionally fails for structural reasons in the light of the objectives it is pursuing, which justifies the necessity for special consumer protection. If this consumer protection is provided, either by measures making up for the consumer's inferiority in information terms (e.g. a duty to inform and explain, known as *complementary consumer protection*), or by measures that eliminate the consumer's inferiority by granting him particular private law remedies (such as the right of revocation, the invalidity of unfair clauses or binding regulations known as *compensatory consumer protection*), this also protects competition by means of the protection of substantive freedom of contract.

Despite this link, it seems appropriate in the light of the different modes of operation to separate Unfair Competition law as an element of competition protection law from Consumer law in a stricter sense. The former only considers collective consumer interests, and logically does not provide individual remedies. This perspective is one of the bases for the Directive on Unfair Commercial Practices.

6.3.4 Protection of Competitors and Consumers Merge in Competition Protection

An examination of the Community law *acquis communautaire* confirms the primacy of competition protection over the protection of competitors and consumers. With respect to the protection of competitors under Unfair Competition law, European law and the international law that must be taken account of has above all a tendency to intensify protection in the field of intellectual property law.[102] This is reflected not least in the most recent Directive on the Enforcement of Intellectual Property Rights.[103] The requirements of Community law are aimed at ensuring a minimum standard of protection.

This tendency towards protection finds its limits where Unfair Competition law is either used as an artificial means of partitioning markets (preventing parallel imports) or to create barriers to market access. In the latter case, the ECJ does not include in its considerations according to the *Cassis* doctrine the interests of the competitors affected by a reverse discrimination.

However, it can be seen that European law restricts the Unfair Competition law protection of competitors based on Member States' unfair competition legislation – above all in the field of intellectual property protection – only if this is necessary in order to pursue the objective of the internal market or to eliminate barriers to market access. Both market integration and the prevention of artificial barriers to market access are essential elements of European competition protection.

A closer look at the European legal basis and requirements for the protection of the demand side of the market reveals a similar picture to that for the protection of competitors. The Consumer Law Directives contain only very restricted market behaviour rules, which essentially concern specific forms of competitive behaviour in distance sales. In contrast, the Directive on Unfair Commercial Practices has a broad scope of application. The positive harmonisation measures have a tendency to intensify protection as a consequence of the minimum clauses they contain. The Directive on Unfair Commercial Practices admittedly does not permit any more extensive protection, but the objective of total harmonisation that limits the extent of protection results precisely from the intended reduction of obstacles to market access that follow from the different requirements of the Member States' legal systems.

The requirements resulting from the guarantee of the fundamental freedoms bring about, on the other hand, a reduction of protection afforded to consumers. Of particular importance is the ECJ's reliance on "an average consumer who is reasonably well-informed and reasonably observant and cirumspect". The model consumer of the ECJ cuts off Unfair Competition law protection at precisely the point were it is needed most.

---

[102] *Cf.* KUR, in: SCHRICKER & HENNING-BODEWIG (eds.), "Neuordnung des Wettbewerbsrechts" 116, 137 (1998/99).

[103] Directive 2004/48/EC of the European Parliament and Council of April 29, 2004 on the Enforcement of Intellectual Property Rights, OJ L 157/45, April 30, 2004.

However, this limitation of protection of the demand side of the market and of the consumer is tied to the pursuit of the objective of the internal market and hence derived from a leitmotif of European competition protection.

7. Conclusion

If the various aspects are brought together, the conclusion is that European Unfair Competition law actually already exists on a primary law basis. Its foundation is the definition of objectives in Art. 3 Para. 1 (g) EC and it is given body by the established case law of the ECJ on the basis of the *Cassis* doctrine. It reveals that the Court has adopted the protection against unfair competition and of consumers into European law. European Unfair Competition law, on the basis of Art. 3 Para. 1 (g) EC pursues the aim of protecting competition against distortion. Protection of competitors and protection of consumers are subsumed within this protection of competition. Fields of tension are resolved by means of the primacy of competition protection.

7.1 Competition Protection as a Community Objective

Article 3 Para. 1 (g) EC requires the Community to create a system to protect competition against distortion. Admittedly, the protection of competition is afforded primarily by means of the competition rules in Arts. 81 et seq. EC. Nevertheless, Art. 3 Para. 1 (g) requires not only measures against classical Antitrust law infringements but also against unfair competition if such infringement is capable of impairing the functions of competition.[104] The concept of "distortion" covers not only direct interventions in the freedom of action of market participants involved in or affected by an antitrust practice, but also other "artificial" changes of competition conditions.[105] The primary law asymmetry between Antitrust and Unfair Competition law regulations (see above) does not affect the powers of the Community legislature to adopt directives to harmonise Unfair Competition law on the basis of Art. 3 Para. 1 (g) in conjunction with Arts. 94 and 95 EC (previously Art. 100 and 100a of the EC Treaty).[106] In this context, special mention must be made of the Directive on Misleading and Comparative Advertising, which expressly includes the protection of

---

[104] *Cf.* as example Recital 2 of the Council Directive 84/450/EEC of September 10, 1984 relating to the Approximation of the Laws, Regulations and Administrative Provisions of the Member States concerning Misleading Advertising, OJ 1984 No. L 250/17, with the amendments that result from Art. 1 of Directive 97/55/EC of the European Parliament and Council of October 6, 1997 to Amend Directive 84/450/EEC concerning Misleading Advertising for the Purpose of Including Comparative Advertising OJ L 290/18, October 23, 1997; ZULEEG, *supra* note 6, Art. 3 EC, note 7.

[105] KOOS, *supra* note 13.

[106] WÄGENBAUR, *supra* note 4, at 9, 15, 25; Koos, *supra* note 13, at 84.

competition against distortion in its Recitals.[107] The subsidiarity principle of Art. 5 Para. 2 EC (previously Art. 3b Para. 2 of the EC Treaty) has not affected this situation.[108] The judgement of the ECJ[109] on the Tobacco Advertising Directive however shows that a specific nexus to the internal market is necessary.

7.2 Body Given by the Cassis Case Law

The existence of a European framework,[110] standard[111] or criterion[112] of fair trading based on the *Cassis* decision is an indication of a "developing European Unfair Competition law".[113] This is all the more the case if this judicial practice is interpreted as the adoption by the judges of specific general interests into European law. On the basis of such an assumption, there cannot be a "European fair competition criterion" without a European Unfair Competition law in the proper sense as a source of law.[114]

The Community mandate defined in the definition of objectives goes further than its concretisation in written primary and secondary law.[115] To this extent the *Cassis* decision seems merely to be a development of the law by the judges with respect to the acknowledgement of the protection of consumers and the fairness of commercial transactions,[116] taking up and giving concrete content to the objective

---

[107] Recital 2 of the Council Directive 84/450/EEC of September 10, 1984 relating to the Approximation of the Laws, Regulations and Administrative Provisions of the Member States concerning Misleading Advertising, OJ L 250/17, September 19, 1984, with the amendments that result from Art. 1 of Directive 97/55/EC of the European Parliament and Council of October 6, 1997 to Amend Directive 84/450/EEC concerning Misleading Advertising for the Purpose of Including Comparative Advertising OJ L 290/18, October 23, 1997.

[108] STEINDORFF, "Unvollkommener Binnenmarkt," 158 ZHR 149, 168 (1994); KOOS, *supra* note 13, at 88 *et seq.*, 126.

[109] Decision of the ECJ, October 5, 2000, Case No. C-376/98, 2000 ECR I-8419, 83 *et seq.* – *Bundesrepublik Deutschland v. Parlament und Rat.*

[110] MEIER, *supra* note 44, at 220.

[111] VEELKEN, 1993 EWS 377, 385, *supra* note 10.

[112] KOOS, *supra* note 13, at 77 *et seq.*

[113] VEELKEN, 1993 EWS 377, 385, *supra* note 10. Similarly SCHLUEP, "Die Europaverträglichkeit des schweizerischen Lauterkeitsrechts," in: "Un droit européen de la concurrence déloyale en formation?" 67, 72 (1994) sees "modules for a superordinate fair competition system" in the judicial practice on the mandatory requirements.

[114] This was already pointed out by the early criticism by MASCLET, 1980 RTDE 611, 625, of the *Cassis* decision. DERINGER, "Zum Spannungsverhältnis zwischen den Freiheiten des Gemeinsamen Marktes und den nationalen Interessen der Mitgliedsstaaten," in: "FS-Kutscher" 95, 100 (1981) also raised the question of the power to recognise "mandatory requirements".

[115] AHLFELD, *supra* note 5, at 248 *et seq.*

[116] *Cf.* STEIN, "Richterrecht wie anderswo auch?," in: "FS-Heidelberg" 619 *et seq.* (1986); EVERLING, "Wirtschaftsverfassung und Richterrecht in der Europäischen Gemeinschaft," in: "FS-Mestmäcker" 365 *et seq.* (1996); LADEUR, "Richterrecht und Dogmatik – eine verfehlte Konfrontation?," 1996 KritV 77, 89 *et seq.* On the status of judge-made law, *cf.* OHLY, "Generalklausel und Richterrecht," 201 AcP 1 *et seq.* (2001).

provisions of the EC Treaty[117] and hence the written legal principles.[118] Such a development of the law is legitimate[119] and even required as part of systematic and objective interpretation as understood in continental Europe.[120] In this context, it is worth noting that the European legislature has approved the ECJ's approach in connection with the *Cassis* decision and for its part reacted with a "New Strategy" concerning the necessity of positive harmonisation measures. The de-facto harmonisation of the law by the ECJ by means of negative integration in the field of the definitions of objectives in the Treaty is thus part of the acquis communautaire.

Accordingly, there is no reason why the *definition of the objectives of competition protection*[121] as hammered out the secondary Community law[122] and the ECJ's case law on the protection against unfair competition as a mandatory requirement in the general interest should not be used as a source of law or point of reference for a European fair competition standard.[123] The comments by the ECJ in the Albako judgment are to be viewed as a confirmation of the existence of Community Unfair Competition law principles. This case concerned the decision of the Commission to provide consumers on the market of Berlin (West) with 900 tonnes of butter from public stocks free of charge (known as Berlin butter). According to the opinion of the Frankfurt District Court, such a measure was an infringement of Sec. 1 of the old version of the German Act against unfair competition from the point of view of an interference with the market. In its decision, the ECJ first of all justified the priority given to Community law.[124] Remarkably, it supported its decision with the additional comment:

> "In that regard, it must also be pointed out that the validity of measures adopted by the community institutions may be affected by their incompatibility with the *principles laid down by community law in the field of competition.* The community institutions must take into account, in particular, *the requirement of fair trade*. However, under the common organization of the agricultural markets, they must reconcile that requirement with the aims set out in Article 39 of the EEC Treaty. In this case the competent community institutions would not appear to have exceeded the discretion which they

---

[117] The subject of protection against unfair competition can be based directly on Art. 3 Para. 1 (g) EC in the light of its interpretation by decision of the ECJ dated May 18, 1993, Case No. C-126/91, 1993 ECR I-2361, 22 – *Yves Rocher.* For consumer protection, recourse can be had to Art. 3 Para. 1 (t) EC.

[118] The *Cassis* decision's function as a gap-filler has already been pointed out by BARENTS, *supra* note 47; GORMLEY, *supra* note 44, at 52; HAUSCHKA, *supra* note 44, at 175. *Cf.* on the law-creating element of the *Cassis* decision, MEIER, *supra* note 44, at 220; MARTIN-EHLERS, *supra* note 44, at 21; WÖHLERMANN, *supra* note 44, at 144; AHLFELD, *supra* note 5, at 253, 279.

[119] On considerations based on jurisdiction aspects, *cf.* AHLFELD, *supra* note 5, at 247 *et seq.*

[120] *Cf.* as example of many, decision of the German Federal Constitutional Court 75, 223, 241 *et seq.*, 243 (1987) – *Richtlinienbeschluss*: Development of judge-made law corresponds with "centuries of common European legal tradition and legal culture".

[121] *Cf.* SCHERER, "Die Wirtschaftsverfassung der EWG" 136 *et seq.*, 137 (1970).

[122] In the Micklitz Study, III, 339, the Unfair Competition law provisions in secondary law are referred to as the "blossoms" of a principle rooted in primary law.

[123] Similarly, SCHLUEP, *supra* note 113.

[124] Decision of the ECJ, May 21, 1987, Case No. 249/85, 1987 ECR 2345, 12 *et seq.* – *Albako.*

must have in order to reconcile that requirement with the aims in question." (emphasis added by this author).[125]

7.3 Relationship to the Protection of Competitors and Consumers

The examination of the European legal requirements based on the purpose of protection has shown that European law basically adopts a positive attitude towards the Unfair Competition law protection of competitors and consumers, encouraging it in part by means of separate legal measures. This positive attitude finds its limits at the point were the protection of competitors and consumers is instrumentalised in order to partition the internal market (in particular to prevent parallel imports) or otherwise has a non-neutral effect on the market and unreasonably acts as an obstacle to the import of goods. A decisive aspect appears to be the interest in market integration which is also an essential element of European competition protection. Consumer and competitor protection are to this extent limited by the protection of competition. In the final analysis, a *primacy of the protection of competition* over the protection of competitors and consumers can be derived at the level of European law. Neither consumers not competitors can demand more than what the protection of competition is capable of bearing.

[125] Decision of the ECJ, May 21, 1987, Case No. 249/85, 1987 ECR 2345, 16 – *Albako*.

The ECJ's Case Law on Unfair Competition

Jochen Glöckner

As was already shown in the presentation of the primary law basis for Unfair Competition law, an extensive case law of the European Court of Justice has evolved since the beginning of the 1980s and is of indirect or direct importance for the national unfair competition legislation in the Member States. The following is intended less to be an attempt of an overall presentation of this case law – which would go beyond the limits available[1] – but instead will emphasise the special features of its development. A list of the ECJ's leading cases on Unfair Competition law (1.) is followed by an examination of the special features of European judicial practice on Unfair Competition law (2.).

1. Case Law in the Field of Unfair Competition

1.1 Primary Law

1.1.1 Article 28 EC

1.1.1.1 Scope of Application

On the question of *discrimination* by means of an assumption of deception in the case of intellectual property rights in another Member State: decisions of the ECJ, Case No. 177/83, 1984 ECR 3651 – *Kohl*; Case No. C-238/89, 1990 ECR I-4827 – *Pall*.

On *restriction* as a result of restrictive regulations: decisions of the ECJ, Case No. 8/74, 1974 ECR 837 – *Dassonville*; Case No. 120/78, 1979 ECR 649 – *Cassis de Dijon*; Cases No. C-267, 268/91, 1993 ECR I-6097 – *Keck and Mithouard*; Case No. C-315/92, 1994 ECR I-317 – *Clinique*; Case No. C-254/98, 2000 ECR I-151 – *TK-Heimdienst*; Case No. C-405/98, 2001 ECR I-1795 – *Gourmet.*

1.1.1.2 Justification

Protection of industrial and commercial property pursuant to Art. 30 of the EC: decisions of the ECJ, Case No. 177/83, 1984 ECR 3651 – *Kohl*; Case No. C-3/91, 1992 ECR I-5529 – Turròn de Alicante.

[1] On the free movement of goods, *see*, for a comprehensive discussion, HEERMANN, "Warenverkehrsfreiheit und deutsches Unlauterkeitsrecht" (2004).

Cassis exception:

On the model consumer: decisions of the ECJ, Case No. 16/83, 1984 ECR 1299 – *Prantl*; Case No. C-238/89, 1990 ECR I-4827 – *Pall*; Case No. C-373/90, 1992 ECR I-131 – *Nissan*; Case No. C-315/92, 1994 ECR I-317 – *Clinique*; Case No. C-470/93, 1995 ECR I-1923 – *Mars*; Case No. C-210/96, 1998 ECR I-4657 – *6-Korn*; Case No. C-220/98, 2000 ECR I-117 – *Lifting*; Case No. C-465/98, 2000 ECR I 2297 – *Darbo*.

Sales promotions: decisions of the ECJ, Case No. 286/81, 1982 ECR 4575 – *Oosthoek* (prohibition on free gifts); Case No. C-368/95, 1997 ECR I-3689 – *Familiapress* (advertising prize competitions).

Marketing rules: decisions of the ECJ, Case No. 382/87, 1989 ECR 1235 – *Buet* (doorstep sales); Case No. C-384/93, 1995 ECR I-1141 – *Alpine Investments* (telephone advertising).

Advertising prohibitions: decisions of the ECJ, Case No. C-362/88, 1990 ECR I-667 – *GB-Inno* (own-price comparisons); Case No. C-126/91, 1993 ECR I-2361 – *Yves Rocher* (own-price comparisons); Case No. C-405/98, 2001 ECR I-1795 – *Gourmet* (alcohol advertising); Case No. C-71/02, 2004 ECR I-3025 – *Karner* (use of the term "bankruptcy goods").

Competitor protection: decisions of the ECJ, Case No. C-6/81, 1982 ECR 707 – *Beele* (slavish imitation); Case No. C-100/02, 2004 ECR I-691 – *Gerolsteiner* (trademark protection against exploitation without a likelihood of confusion within the field of similarity); Case No. C-58/80, 1981 ECR 181 – *Dansk Supermarket* (incursion into a marketing system).

Advantage achieved through breach of the law: decision of the ECJ, Case No. C-254/98, 2000 ECR I-151 – *TK-Heimdienst* (infringement of trading law regulations).

1.1.2 Freedom of Services, Art. 49 EC

Decisions of the ECJ, Case No. C-384/93, 1995 ECR I-1141 – *Alpine Investments* (telephone marketing); Cases No. C-34-36/95, 1997 ECR I-3843 – *De Agostini* (television advertising); Case No. C-405/98, 2001 ECR I-1795 – *Gourmet*.

1.2 Secondary Law

Uniform standard for deception maintaining the basic freedoms and secondary law prohibitions on deception: decisions of the ECJ, Case No. C-373/90, 1992 ECR I-131 – *Nissan*; Case No. C-315/92, 1994 ECR I-317 – *Clinique*; Case No. C-470/93, 1995 ECR I-1923 – *Mars*; Case No. C-220/98, 2000 ECR I-117 – *Lifting*.

Directive on Comparative Advertising: decisions of the ECJ, Case No. C-112/99, 2001 ECR I-7945 – *Toshiba*; Case No. C-44/01, 2003 ECR I-3095 – *Pippig*.

2. Special Features of European Case Law

2.1 The Evolution of Case Law in Respect of the Model Consumer

The Italian national Prantl operated a wine and beverages trade in Germany. He was charged with a breach of Sec. 17 of the German Wine Regulation for selling wine from South Tyrol in what are known as bocksbeutel bottles. This bottle shape has been used in Italy in normal practice for over 100 years. The German Wine Regulation, however, reserved this bottle shape to quality wines from specific areas of cultivation in Franken and Baden. The ECJ[2] held that the application of Sec. 17 of the Wine Regulation to the case in question constituted an infringement of Art. 30 of the EC Treaty (now Art. 28 EC). Admittedly, the protection of consumers against possible confusion with respect to the products they bought was a protectable objective of the German regulation. However, the ECJ assumed that the Community law regulations on the labelling of wines contained particularly detailed provisions that could be used to avoid the risk of deception (para. 29).

There is little to argue against the result reached by the ECJ in the *Bocksbeutel* decision. It appears plausible that wine purchasers generally check what they are buying, since the qualitative differences in the products available are large and the purchasers typically have considerable interest in the product. Wine purchasers pay attention not only to the grape variety and the vintage but above all to the place of origin. Country of origin, area of cultivation and location are of importance and are examined when buying wine. Under these circumstances, the explanatory notice "South Tyrolia, Italy" was capable of excluding a possible likelihood of deception that might result from the shape of the bottle and the labelling that might be in German.

The attentive and informed average purchaser, whose existence is the starting point for the *Bocksbeutel* decision, must also have been in the ECJ's mind in the *Nissan* decision[3] on this issue, since the facts of the case suggested a certain likelihood of deception. A car dealer in Bergerac had published advertisements in the press with the statement "Buy your new vehicle cheaper" followed by the claim "1 year manufacturer's guarantee". The advertisement concerned vehicles imported from Belgium that had been registered for the purpose of importation but had never been driven. They were sold more cheaply in France than the prices charged by the local authorised dealers, because the basic Belgian models had a lower standard of equipment than the basic models sold in France. Although, therefore, there was a tendency in the advertisements towards deception from a number of points of view (are vehicles already registered in fact still new cars? Does it matter that a part of the one-year manufacturer's warranty has expired since first registration? Should the lower standard of equipment of the European imports have been mentioned?), the

---

2 Decision of the ECJ, March 13, 1984, Case No. 16/83, 1984 ECR 1299 – *Prantl.*

3 Decision of the ECJ, January 16, 1992, Case No. C-373/90, 1992 ECR I-131 – *Nissan.*

ECJ denied a relevant risk of deception within the meaning of the Misleading Advertising Directive. The decision no doubt holds a special position, concerning the possibility of parallel imports in the motor vehicle sector. It was with this in mind that the ECJ preceded its justification by stating that parallel imports enjoyed a certain degree of protection under Community law, since they encouraged the development of trade and the strengthening of competition.

The question of the model consumer arose again in a dispute between the Verband Sozialer Wettbewerb e.V. on the one side, and *Clinique Laboratories SNC* and *Estée Lauder* on the other side concerning the use of the designation "Clinique" for the marketing of cosmetics in the Federal Republic of Germany.[4] In the view of the Berlin District Court that was hearing the case it would have been necessary to determine by means of an opinion poll whether the label "Clinique" in fact led to deception amongst a not insubstantial percentage of consumers based on the similarity with the German term "Klinik" (= hospital) possibly implying a pharmaceutical effect. The Court, however, held that this kind of evidence would be superfluous if the prohibition of the designation in question constituted an unlawful restriction of intra-Community trade, and referred the case to the ECJ for a preliminary ruling.

Although the ECJ primarily applied the Misleading Advertising Directive to the designation "Clinique", it interpreted the concept of misleading advertising in the Directive in the light of the provisions of the EC Treaty concerning the free movement of goods. There was therefore a need for a balancing of interests. The ECJ held that it was itself able to determine whether the German prohibition of this designation for the marketing of cosmetics could be justified by the objective of consumer protection or of human health. Because the company range of cosmetic products was marketed in Germany exclusively by perfume shops and the cosmetics departments of department stores, hence none of the products being available in pharmacies, and because the products were presented as cosmetics and not as pharmaceuticals, and finally because the products were lawfully sold in other Member States under the name "Clinique", apparently without consumers being mislead by the use of this name, the ECJ did not regard a prohibition of the use of the name "Clinique as necessary in order to achieve the objective of consumer protection or consumer health. The clinical or medical connotation of the term was not sufficient to ascribe a misleading effect to the name that might justify its prohibition for the products sold under the said conditions.

The *Mars* decision[5] dealt with the sale of ice cream bars in a packaging bearing the imprint "plus 10 %" on a part of the ice cream bar in a contrasting colour, such part being substantially larger than 10 % of the size of the bar. The ECJ assumed that the reasonably circumspect consumer could be deemed to know that there was not necessarily a link between the size of publicity markings relating to an increase in the size of the product and the extent of such increase.

---

4 Decision of the ECJ, February 2, 1994, Case No. C-315/92, 1994 ECR I-317 – *Clinique*.

5 Decision of the ECJ, July 6, 1995, Case No. C-470/93, 1995 ECR I-1923 – *Mars*.

It was above all the latter decision that caused scholars to assume that the question of whether there was a relevant likelihood of deception was based only on normative considerations. This was supported in particular by the German wording. In the light of the resulting uncertainty, the German Federal Administrative Court referred questions to the ECJ in the 6-Korn case, the aim being to force the ECJ[6] to adopt a position on methodological issues as well. However, the ECJ avoided answering these methodological questions. On the question of the likelihood of deception, it had always reached a decision itself if the contents of the file were sufficient. It had based its decisions on the "presumed expectations of an average consumer who is reasonably well-informed and reasonably observant and circumspect" without ordering an expert's report or commissioning a consumer poll. The same could also be done by the national courts. If the national courts, however, had particular difficulties in determining whether the details in question could be misleading, they were not prevented by Community law from investigating this in accordance with national law by means of an expert opinion or a consumer poll.

The solution of the ECJ decision in the *Darbo* case lies between the *Clinique* and *6-Korn* decisions. This case concerned the use of the adjective "naturrein" (naturally pure) for jam that was to a significant extent contaminated with the usual pollutants. The ECJ, in formal terms, maintained the position it had adopted in the *6-Korn* case. It was a matter for the national courts to determine whether a designation, a trademark or advertising could be misleading. However, in contrast to the *6-Korn* decision, the ECJ believed that it had sufficient indications to be able to make findings about the pollutants contained in the jam.

The development of this line of cases makes three things clear. Firstly, it shows the dynamic character of European judge-made law – the case by case development of European Unfair Competition law is a process and not a status, and the content of European unfair competition principles changes with practically every new decision.

Secondly, European judge-made law is subject to a certain and at times considerable degree of uncertainty. The reasons for this are known: unlike national legal systems, European law can by its very nature not be built upon a specific dogmatic acquis. Instead, the development of the law must be worked out, a process that is affected by the different methodological and specialist prior knowledge of the now 27 judges. The consequence is that even comparatively clear questions that need to be answered for a homogenous development of the law are not infrequently left without final clarification, as is shown by the *6-Korn* decision and the subsequent to-ing and fro-ing on the determination of a likelihood of deception. Even comparatively simple questions, such as whether the adjective "average" in the German version of the judgements relates only to the standard of intelligence and awareness of the consumer or also lays down the degree of attention applied in perception, often give rise to years of discussions in European law. It is only as a result of

6 Decision of the ECJ, July 16, 1998, Case No. C-210/96, 1998 ECR I-4657 – *6-Korn*.

more recent alternative translations (the German wording now used is that of the "normally informed and appropriately attentive and circumspect average consumer"[7]) that the last question has been clarified such that only an attentiveness appropriate to the situation is to be required.

Finally, the development described has shown that the development of European law is also controllable to a greater extent than it usually appears to be. The responsibility for this lies with the courts of the Member States, which are in a position to pick suitable cases, to word the questions and where appropriate to submit well-reasoned proposals for their decision, thereby influencing the further development of European law in a judicial dialogue. A negative example of this is the decision in the *Clinique* case: the submitting court should have carried out an opinion poll that might have been necessary and then submit to the ECJ the question whether the percentage of consumers misled found by the poll constituted a "substantial number" within the meaning of the *Nissan* decision. However, the German court did not proceed in this way, but conversely submitted the question of the relevance of the likelihood of deception under European law to the ECJ. For its part, the ECJ did not apply judicial self-straint and instruct the German court to adopt findings of fact and provide it with general indications as to how these should be assessed in law, but instead de facto decided the dispute.

2.2 The Reading of European Decisions

Taking the example of the development of what is known as the Keck doctrine, it is also possible to show that the special features of European case law must at the same time influence the reading of the decisions. In the case of *Keck and Mithouard,*[8] the managers of two supermarkets were accused in criminal proceedings of having sold beer and coffee below purchase price in breach of the general French prohibition on resale at a loss. The defendants argued that the prohibition infringed the provisions concerning the free movement of goods. The French court hearing the case then submitted the matter to the ECJ for a preliminary ruling. In fact, the prohibition of sales at a loss was covered by Art. 30 of the EC Treaty (now Art. 28 EC) when applying the *Dassonville* formula, because the prohibition of sales at a loss denied the participants in business a means of promoting sales and could thus restrict the sales volumes of goods from other Member States. For this reason, the ECJ saw itself obliged to review and clarify its previous case law. The Court held that the application of national provisions that restricted or prohibited *certain selling arrangements* was not capable of restricting trade between the Member States. It made clear that this was only the case if the provision in question applied to all relevant traders operating within the national territory and so long as they affect in the same manner, in law and

---

7 Decision of the ECJ, September 16, 2004, Case No. C-329/02 P, 2004 ECR I-8317, para. 24 – *SAT.1*; *cf.* SACK, "Die neue deutsche Formel des europäischen Verbraucherleitbilds," 2005 WRP 462.

8 Decision of the ECJ, November 24, 1993, Cases No. C-267, 268/91, 1993 ECR I–6097 – *Keck and Mithouard.*

in fact, the marketing of domestic products and of those from other Member States. The *Keck* decision was followed by a flood of publications in which the scope of this new privilege was examined. Only eighteen months after the decision, the ECJ adopted a further decision clarifying most of the questions raised. In the *Alpine Investments* case,[9] the governments of the Netherlands and the United Kingdom argued that a national prohibition of unsolicited advertising telephone calls was exempt from the scope of application of the freedom of services on the basis of the *Keck* doctrine. This was not endorsed by the ECJ. The ground for the exemption of the selling arrangements lay in the fact that the application of such provisions *were not capable of blocking or considerably restricting market access for these products in the importing Member State more* than was the case for domestic products. It is no doubt because the decision concerned the freedom of services that it was only rarely considered with respect to the scope of application of the *Keck* doctrine. As a result, it was not until January 2000 that the ECJ, when determining whether a specific marketing provision fell under the *Keck* doctrine, had direct recourse to the examination of whether the market access for goods from other Member States was impeded more strongly than for domestic goods[10]. It expressly cited the *Alpine Investments* decision on the freedom of services. In 2001, in the decision on the *Gourmet* case,[11] the ECJ then inverted the *Keck* formula entirely: although it cited the relevant grounds for the *Keck* decision, it focused on the question of a restriction of market access.

Hiding the critical test in the subsumption would not be considered good style for a German court. Nevertheless, the *Keck* decision leaves little to be desired in terms of clarity. What is necessary, however, is a willingness on the part of the users of the law to consider the factual context and the problems peculiar to European law when dealing with the decisions of the European courts.

2.3 The ECJ as Supreme Competition Court

The following thesis is put forward in a certain contradiction to the above, and can be derived from the *Toshiba* and *Pippig* line of cases. A catalogue intended by the defendant Katun for trade dealers, advertising parts and consumption materials it marketed for photocopiers, including photocopiers manufactured by the plaintiff Toshiba, contained a list in which the article name of the "original manufacturer" was listed under the heading "OEM Art. No." (OEM = Original Equipment Manufacturer) followed by the Katun article name, followed by a description of the product and finally the list of devices for which the accessories were intended. Secondly, the catalogue contained notices such as "You can reduce your costs without losing performance or quality. Thanks to the lower service and operating costs, these quality products overall represent a more profitable alternative for dealers or the ideal solution for many high-performance Toshiba photocopiers". On the basis of the Ger-

[9] Decision of the ECJ, May 10, 1995, Case No. C-384/93, 1995 ECR I-1141 – *Alpine Investments*.
[10] Decision of the ECJ, January 13, 2000, Case No. C 254/98, 2000 ECR I–151 – *TK-Heimdienst*.
[11] Decision of the ECJ, March 8, 2001, Case No. C 405/98, 2001 ECR I–1795 – *Gourmet*.

man Federal Court's leading case, *Verbrauchsmaterialien*[12], the submitting court assumed that the use of Toshiba's article numbers was not necessary in order to inform the customers about the usability of the rival products. It misled consumers by claiming the equivalent quality of the products and unlawfully exploited Toshiba's reputation. However, in the light of Directive 97/55/EEC on Comparative Advertising, the court doubted whether these principles continued to apply and submitted the following questions to the ECJ for a preliminary ruling: Is it to be regarded as comparative advertising within the meaning of the Directive if a supplier of spare parts and consumable items indicates the original article numbers in its catalogue? The ECJ[13] answered this question in the affirmative. The submitting court had put the further question whether such was a permissible comparative advertising. This question was answered by the ECJ in the affirmative. The subsequent question whether the original article numbers were distinguishing marks within the meaning of Art. 3a Para. 1 (g) of the Directive on Comparative Advertising was answered by the ECJ in the negative, as was the question whether their use in the competitor's catalogue unfairly exploited *Toshiba's* reputation.

All the questions raised are specific unfair competition questions. In none of the cases did the ECJ return the matter to the Member State's court, and instead answered all of them itself. The ECJ applied a similar approach in the 2003 *Pippig* decision,[14] again answering all the questions. The case was returned only with respect to the factual preconditions for image transfer within the meaning of Art. 3a Para. 1 (a) of the Directive. Both decisions make it clear that the ECJ is indeed capable of deciding like a specialized court outside the field of application of the fundamental freedoms, specifically in the interpretation of secondary Community law.

In fact, the ECJ will in the future be challenged to a greater extent than ever before as a supreme competition court in order to give concrete meaning to the vague legal terms and general clauses, thereby contributing to the essential homogenous development of the law within a Union of 27 Member States.

2.4 The ECJ as Supreme Competition Court under the Application of the Unfair Commercial Practices Directive

The above discussion has already examined the interaction between Member States' courts and the ECJ. One consequence of the European assignment of judicial competence is that it is in the first place the Member States' courts that are required to hammer out the various general clauses in European law. However, constructive primacy is enjoyed by the ECJ. It has the opportunity to exercise this primacy through preliminary rulings pursuant to Art. 234 EC. However, the role of the Member States' courts in the judicial dialogue should not be underestimated. As already set out above, they make a considerable contribution to the development of European

[12] Decision of the German Federal Supreme Court, March 28, 1996, I ZR 39/94, 1996 GRUR 781 – *Verbrauchsmaterialien.*

[13] Decision of the ECJ, October 25, 2001, Case No. C-112/99, 2001 ECR I-7945 – *Toshiba.*

[14] Decision of the ECJ, April 8, 2003, Case No. C-44/01, 2003 ECR I-3095 – *Pippig*.

law by picking the cases that are submitted for preliminary rulings, by wording the questions and by justifying these questions. The possibility of submitting preliminary questions was created when the Directive entered into effect, i.e. on June 12, 2005. References before the expiry of the implementation period can be justified in accordance with the anticipated interpretation of the Unfair Competition Acts in the light of the Comparative Advertising Directive by the German and Austrian courts[15] with the competition-focused approach that the courts should not today prohibit an a priori desirable competitive conduct that tomorrow will be a permissible competitive conduct. The considerable litigation especially in Germany and Austria in the field of Unfair Competition law will also provide plenty of opportunities for the selection of appropriate questions for the preliminary proceedings. In the field of Trademark law, the ECJ has already shown its willingness to adopt good arguments from the submitting courts – even against the conclusion of the Advocate General.[16]

The submitting courts will have to comply with a number of general principles: European competition regulations are primarily a set of liberal rules as follows in particular from Art. 4 EC. Cases on which preliminary rulings are based should for this reason involve serious infringements of protectable interests.

The European rules on unfair competition are above all an autonomous set of rules. Justifications that are based only on well-established legal principles in national Unfair Competition laws are not convincing in this form.

Finally, European unfair competition rules are a set of rules that is still in development. In its first decisions, the ECJ is hardly likely to adopt systematic basic findings but will instead, as the past has shown, proceed step by step.

---

[15] Decision of the German Federal Supreme Court, February 5, 1998, I ZR 211/95, 1998 GRUR 824, 827 – *Testpreis-Angebot*; Decision of the Austrian Supreme Court, September 29, 1998, 4 Ob 235/98, 1999 GRUR Int. 794 – *AMC / ATC*.

[16] Decisions of the ECJ, January 9, 2003, Case No. C-292/00, 2003 ECR I-389 – *Davidoff*; Cases No. C-53-55/01, 2003 ECR I-3161 – *Linde*; Case No. C-100/02, 2004 ECR I-691 – *Gerolsteiner*.

Secondary Unfair Competition Law

Frauke Henning-Bodewig

1. The Start of Harmonization

Despite the judicial practice of the ECJ in the field of unfair competition law as presented to us by Prof. Glöckner, this judicial practice is unable to achieve genuine harmonisation. The ECJ can only identify infringements by national regulations (or their interpretation) against the fundamental freedoms of the EC Treaty. Even if this frequently leads indirectly to the contested regulation being adjusted to the standards of other Member States, this is only a de facto effect and cannot achieve a uniform standard of protection, in particular by raising the level of protection. This can only be achieved by means of Community Directives or Regulations.

Immediately after conclusion of the Treaties of Rome, a start was made on the harmonisation of unfair competition law within the then EEC.[1] The chances were initially good. This was due firstly to the fact that the EEC at that time consisted of only six countries (France, Italy, Germany and the Benelux States). Secondly, these countries were at least able to agree on the basic preconditions of unfair competition law. In all of them unfair competition law had developed from general tort law; the aim was to protect the "honest tradesman" against dishonest practices by his competitors; all six countries granted protection on the basis of a general clause; the common background of Art. 10bis of the Paris Convention was unmistakable. And finally the penalties for infringements imposed by all six countries were primarily, or at least also, civil law penalties.

The harmonisation work was prepared by means of a comparative law expertise by the Max Planck Institute under Eugen Ulmer.[2] The Ulmer expertise proposed a harmonisation of unfair competition law in the broad sense – thus including trade names, famous trademarks and indications of geographical origin – under a general clause based on Art. 10bis of the Paris Convention.

Ultimately, however, these plans for a comprehensive harmonisation were not implemented. The decisive factor was time. Although there was basic agreement on the Ulmer proposal, almost 20 years were spent working out details. During this time not only did the political power relationships change within the EU, there was also a change in the basic consensus that had prevailed until then.

---

[1] *Cf., e.g.* SCHRICKER, "Twenty-Five Years of Protection Against Unfair Competition," 26 IIC 782 (1991); BAKARDJIEVA ENGELBREKT, "Unfair Competition in flux? National legencies, Institutional Choice and the Process of Europeanization" 1, note 3 (2003).

[2] ULMER (ed.), "Das Recht des unlauteren Wettbewerbs in den Mitgliedstaaten der Europäischen Wirtschaftsgemeinschaft" 8 volumes (1965-2005); some volumes are translated into French, Italian, Spanish, Dutch.

In particular, the political changes included the membership of Great Britain and Ireland, both of whom had reservations against the continental approach of a broad general clause and enforcement primarily by means of civil law. On the basis of the common law principles, and convinced of the advantages of strong self-monitoring, they regarded the approach applied in the Ulmer expertise to be unacceptable.

Another obstacle was the shifting of weight that unfair competition law underwent as a result of notions of consumer protection. There was, admittedly, agreement that the consumer needed better protection against unfair competition and that the original approach of unfair competition law, which focused on the protection of the "decent businessman" did not do justice to the modern concept of equal market partners. However, there were differences in the way in which the Member States approached these consumer interests. In the countries in which there were separate laws to prevent unfair competition (such as Germany, Austria, Belgium and Luxemburg), the purpose of protection was relatively easily extended by means of case law, which culminated in a triple-purpose of protection, the aim of unfair competition law being to protect competitors, consumers and the general public. In countries (like France and Italy) in which protection of the tradesman against unfair competition was provided on the basis of tort-law provisions, it proved impossible to expand the protection conceived as a purely individual right. The result was supplementary protective legislation for consumers, not infrequently within administrative law or criminal law. In Great Britain, finally, consumer protection was mainly provided by means of a strong self-regulation in conjunction with a number of administrative provisions, while the protection of competitors continued to be dealt with by narrowly-defined common law offences, in particular passing off.[3]

These differences in legal tradition made the harmonisation work considerably more difficult. In addition, within the Commission, the Internal Market Directorate was joined by the newly founded Consumer Protection Department, which became also responsible for unfair competition law. This led to a split in powers and not infrequently to disagreement on substantive issues.

In the light of these difficulties, it is hardly surprising that the subsequent work led to an increasing reduction of the harmonisation plans as originally conceived.[4] What began as a comprehensive project to harmonise the entire field of unfair competition law was cut back to what was just about capable of achieving a consensus. This consensus was possible in particular with respect to advertising, and yet a draft Directive on misleading and unfair advertising published in 1979 failed because the British considered the concept of unfairness to be too vague. Directive 84/450/EEC adopted in 1984 was thus limited to misleading advertising, with unfair advertising left for "later" regulation. However, this never happened, and instead the Directive was extended in 1997 through the inclusion of comparative advertising while a

[3] Of course there are now numerous mixed forms. The unfair competition law of the 25 Member States is set out in detail HENNING-BODEWIG, "Unfair Competition Law – European Union and Member States" (2006).

[4] For details *see* OHLY, in: SCHRICKER & HENNING-BODEWIG (eds.), "Neuordnung des Wettbewerbsrechts" (1998/1999).

number of media and product-specific Directives were adopted that also applied to advertising. Only in 2005, a Directive on Unfair Commercial Practices with a broader approach was adopted; it is, however, restricted to "B2C"-relationships as Prof. Schuhmacher will later explain in detail.

2. Directive 84/450/EEC on Misleading Advertising

2.1 The Basic Features of the Directive

Directive 84/450/EEC[5] was thus above all a compromise. Since it laid down a comparatively low minimum standard that was already exceeded in most Member States, and left out disputed issues concerning the definition of "misleading" and the question of enforcement, almost all Member States could retain the approach they were already familiar with.

It is only looking back that it becomes apparent that the Directive on Misleading Advertising nevertheless made a considerable contribution to the harmonisation of unfair competition law. From today's point of view, it is remarkable that Art. 1 decidedly adopted a triple purpose of protection i.e. the approach of integrated competitor and consumer protection.[6] The definition of advertising in Art. 2 No. 1 has also proved to be pioneering. According to this, advertising is "the making of a representation in any form in connection with a trade, business, craft or profession in order to promote the supply of goods or services" This shows that it is the aim of promoting sales that matters (with the result that as a rule the activity of the media is not covered), and that, as the term "representation" shows, only verifiable details fall within the provision and not, for instance what is known as suggestive advertising.

Although the fundamental prohibition on misleading advertising in Art. 2 Nos. 1 and 3 is broadly worded in the manner of a general clause – the Directive uses the terms "deception" and "misleading" synonymously – it follows that there is a further criterion, namely that the assessment must be based on the point of view of the target group. In addition, it is sufficient for the advertising to be capable of misleading; there is thus no need for proof of actual deception.[7] And finally, the deception must be capable of influencing the conduct of the addressees of the advertising or of damaging competitors, i.e. it is only relevant deception that is covered.

Art. 3 of the Directive provides further indications about the definition of deception. It primarily deals with the subject matter of deception, with three groups being mentioned as examples: the characteristics of the goods, the price and the character-

5 Council Directive 84/450/EEC of September 10, 1984, relating to the approximation of the laws, regulations and administrative provisions of the Member States concerning misleading advertising. OJ L 250/17, September 19, 1984; *see* also HENNING-BODEWIG *supra* note 3.

6 This modern integrated approach has been reversed by Directive 2005/29/EC; *see* the decisions below and the paper by Prof. Schuhmacher in this book.

7 The ECJ *Nissan* decision (Case C-379/90, 1992 ECR I-00131) is not entirely clear on this point; *see* also Case C-220/98, 2000 ECR I-00117 – *Estée Lauder and Lancaster.*

istics of the advertiser. In the introductory sentence, finally, it is emphasised that the advertising is to be assessed in all its features.

On the other hand there are no details about the model consumer on whom the definition of deception is based, or about any percentage of misled addressees. This highly-criticised gap, however, has been filled by the ECJ, which – as Prof. Glöckner has explained in detail – has developed the benchmark of the "reasonable average consumer" in a series of decisions on the prohibition of deception.[8]

2.2 The Enforcement of the Law

The Directive also allows the Member States considerable leeway in enforcing the law. According to Art. 4, all that is required is, as already laid down by Art. 10bis of the Paris Convention, that "adequate and effective means ... for the control of misleading advertising" must be available. Persons or organisations regarded under national law as having a legitimate interest in prohibiting misleading advertising must be granted a right to take legal action. The enforcement of the law must be possible either by a court or an administrative authority. Self-regulation alone is not sufficient (Art. 5). Pursuant to Art. 4 Para. 2, the penalties must include the prohibition order (including with interim effect), and must be independent of evidence of fault or damage. It must be possible to enforce rights by means of interlocutory injunction proceedings. In addition, the courts or administrative authorities must be able to reverse the burden of proof in suitable cases (Art. 6).

2.3 The Harmonisation Effect

As stated at the beginning, the harmonisation effect of the Directive was initially regarded negatively. This was due partly to the fact that the Directive only contains a minimum protection regulation (Art. 7), permitting Member States to maintain stricter rules. At the same time, thanks to the very broadly worded enforcement regulations, even Member States such as Great Britain were able to maintain the basic principles of their own systems.[9]

The originally rather negative view of things must, however, today be qualified, as already mentioned. The judicial practice of the ECJ, in particular the development of the benchmark of the reasonable average consumer, has filled the gaps in the Directive and ultimately led to considerable harmonisation after all. Admittedly, it has not been possible to eliminate all differences in interpretation.[10] Looking back, however, it can be said that at least the largest differences have been smoothed out. As an example we can mention Germany and Italy. Thus the originally very strict

---

[8] *See* the contribution by Glöckner in this book and HENNING BODEWIG, *supra* note 3.

[9] The Directive's obligation to allow legal remedies either before the courts or before the administrative authorities was solved in Great Britain such that the Director of the Office of Unfair Competition can file an action in cases where he deems it appropriate. As a rule this is only the case if self-regulation has failed, which so far has been held rarely to be the case.

[10] Which is small wonder since the legal assessment of advertising etc. always also reflects a nation's cultural value.

protection against deception in Germany has been increasingly relaxed, while in Italy, where there were originally considerable deficits in the protection, it is now very efficiently enforced by the Autorità Garante.[11] Above all it has been possible to give the countries that joined the EU in 2004 a certain guidance to help them gradually adjust their national law.

2.4 The Changes Resulting From the Unfair Commercial Practices Directive

However, in the meantime there have been changes that might reduce the importance of Directive 84/450/EEC. As we will hear from Prof. Schuhmacher,[12] the 2005 Directive on Unfair Commercial Practices also contains provisions on misleading advertising. However, unlike the Directive 84/450/EEC, which starts from a triple purpose of protection, the new Directive is limited to actions towards consumer.

The resulting overlap has been solved in such a way that the original Directive 84/450/EEC now only applies to advertising to businesses, while misleading details in the B2C relationship are to be assessed according to the new Unfair Commercial Practices Directive. It is doubtful whether this involves a change in terms of content. The latter Directive admittedly provides more extensive and more detailed regulations of the offence of deception. However, this is essentially a codification of the ECJ's judicial practice on the Misleading Advertising Directive. The same applies to the provision concerning the enforcement of the law, which essentially conforms with the previous Directive. Against this background, significant changes are not to be expected, and it is all the more regrettable that the result is a further (unnecessary) fragmentation of Community law.

3. Directive 97/55/EC Concerning Comparative Advertising

3.1 Overview of the Rules Concerning Comparative Advertising

In 1997, Directive 97/55/EC[13] introduced into Directive 84/450/EEC a further set of rules, namely those concerning comparative advertising. However, from a regulatory point of view, there was a difference from the very start. While the provisions concerning misleading advertising merely created a Community-wide minimum standard (Art. 7), the conditions for permissible comparative advertising are laid down exhaustively in Art. 3a. Consequently, the Member States are not permitted to prohibit comparative advertising that satisfies the conditions of Art. 3a. Nor, however, are they allowed to permit advertising that does not satisfy these requirements. This applies to all three parts of a comparison – the details about the advertiser's own products, the details about the rival product and the details about the relationship

---

[11] *See* the overviews of German and Italian law in: HENNING-BODEWIG, *supra* note 3.

[12] *See* the contribution by Prof. Schuhmacher in this volume.

[13] Directive 97/55/EC of the European Parliament and of the Council of October 6, 1997 amending Directive 84/450/EEC concerning misleading advertising so as to include comparative advertising. OJ L 290/10, October 23, 1997.

between the two. It also applies to the question of whether the comparison is misleading.[14]

As far as comparative advertising is concerned, the Directive 2005/29/EC does not involve any restriction on the protection of the businessman.[15] Accordingly in the field of comparative advertising, the original triple purpose of protection of Directive 84/450/EEC continues to apply, i.e. consumers and businesses are equally protected.

The Directive refers to "comparative advertising". According to Article 2 No. 2a 'comparative advertising' means any advertising "... which explicitly or by implication identifies a competitor or goods or services offered by a competitor".

According to Recital 6 of Directive 97/55/EC, the concept of comparative advertising has deliberately been worded broadly in order to cover all models of comparative advertising. This is also assumed by the ECJ.[16] Accordingly, it beyond doubt covers critical comparative advertising ("X is better than Y") and derivative advertising ("X is just as good as Y"). On the other hand, it is not entirely clear whether it also applies to personal advertising and unilateral criticism.

Nor is clear whether a comparison is always necessary. This requirement is missing in the legal definition in Art. 2 No. 2a. It might be concluded from the overall context, the frequent use of the term "comparative advertising" and the reference to "competitors" that there must be a comparison between competing enterprises, goods or services. This would, however, remove unilateral criticism, in particular disparagement ("X charges excessive prices") from the field of regulation.

The ECJ's Toshiba decision[17] – in which a manufacturer of spare parts had named the trademark and the article numbers of the original Toshiba appliances as a reference – is not entirely unambiguous: On the one hand, the ECJ, referring to the intended broad wording, states that any reference to competitors is sufficient, while at the same time it emphasises the existence of a "comparison" in the specific case, since the advertising implied that the spare part had the same characteristics as the original. In practice, this problem thus loses importance, since most indications, references etc. which appear unilateral at first sight, include indirect allegations of equivalence. According to the meaning and purpose of the provision, the decisive factor will be whether the addressee of the advertising is shown alternative purchase possibilities. According to Recital 2 of the objectives of the Directive, comparative advertising must help demonstrating objectively the merits of the various comparable products. This is not the case if a famous product is primarily used as an attention getter (but is satisfied in the case of a "demand" to

---

14 This was confirmed by the ECJ in the decisions Case C-112/99, 2001 ECR I-7945 – *Toshiba Europe* and Case C-440/01, 2003 ECR I-03095 – *Pippig*.

15 Directive 2005/29/EC on Unfair Commercial Practices has made some minor changes concerning misleading and confusing comparative advertising; for the rest, only the numbers have changed.

16 Cases C-112/99, 2001 ECR I-7945 – *Toshiba Europe* and C-44/01, 2003 ECR I-03095 – *Pippig*.

17 *See supra* note 16.

compare or a reference to the suitability of one's own product as a spare part, accessory etc.[18]).

A vital element of comparative advertising according to Art. 2 No. 2a is the direct or indirect reference to one or more competitors or their products or services. A direct reference is if mention is made of a competitor, his products, services or trademark. An indirect reference can occur if the reference to a specific competitor is obvious in the light of the circumstances (from the point of view of the target group). The overall arrangement of the advertising (e.g. a more or less clear reference to the trademark or famous advertising of the competitor) plays just as much a role as market conditions.

A mere comparison between systems or types of products in which the individual supplier can not be identified (e.g. a comparison of packaging made of glass and of plastic) is not regarded as comparative advertising within the meaning of Directive 97/55/EC according to the prevalent opinion.[19] However, there has still to be a decision by the ECJ on this question.

3.2 The Limits of Comparative Advertising

Although the aim of Directive 97/55/EC was to establish the admissibility of comparative advertising, this type of advertising is subject to considerably stricter regulations than other advertising.

3.2.1 Pursuant to Art. 3a Para. 1 (a), the comparison must not be misleading. In the relationship between business and consumers, the question of misleading has now to be determined on the basis of Arts. 6 and 7 of the Directive 2005/29/EC (while in the B2B relationship, it is still determined on the basis of Art. 2 No. 2 of Directive 84/450/EEC). It remains to be seen whether and what differences in interpretation might result.

The prohibition on misleading advertising is at first glance self evident, since it applies in any event to all types of advertising. However, there may be specific problems with comparative advertising. In particular, the question arises whether a comparison that does not list all the relevant points is necessarily misleading. This must as a matter of principle be answered in the negative. There is no obligation to be complete. This follows inter alia e contrario from Art. 3a Para. 1 (c), according to which the characteristics compared must be "representative" etc. It is only in exceptional cases that the selection of individual characteristics can be so arbitrary that the result is a misleading overall impression. Although the advertiser is at liberty to decide whether he wishes to name the rival product, the failure to do so can also be misleading in specific constellations.[20] On the other hand, it is not dishonest for comparative prices to be determined by test purchases and for the advertiser only to

[18] *See* for instance the decision of the German Federal Supreme Court, October 15, 1998, I ZR 69/96, 1999 GRUR Int. 453 – *Vergleichen Sie,* (implied claim of equivalence in terms of price and/or quality); a different result was reached in the decision of the German Federal Court, July 15, 2004, I ZR 37/01, 2005 GRUR 163 – *Aluminiumräder.*

[19] *See* the country reports in HENNING-BODEWIG, *supra* note 3.

[20] ECJ, Case C-444/01, 2003 ECR I-03095 – *Pippig.*

include certain products in his range as a result of test purchases. Nor can any objection be raised to the fact that the comparison uses a product where the price (or quality) difference is particularly large.

3.2.2 According to Article 3a Para. 1 (b) a comparison shall (only) be permitted if "it compares goods or services meeting the same needs or intended for the same purpose". It must therefore (from the point of view from the target group) at least be a substitute product. Accordingly the comparison need not necessarily concern identical products.[21]

3.2.3 According to Article 3a Para. 1 (c) comparative advertising shall (only) be permitted if "it objectively compares one or more material, relevant, verifiable and representative features of those goods or services, which may include price". "Objectivity" does not necessarily mean completeness.[22] What is not clear, on the other hand, is whether a comparison of purely subjective preferences ("I prefer X to Y") is prohibited. Strictly speaking such comparison is neither objective nor verifiable. A prohibition, however, would lead to the strange result that the Directive aimed at liberalising comparative advertising would be stricter than the previous national laws of almost all Member States, which had at least tolerated such subjective preference comparisons.[23]

3.2.4 The comparison must also refer to goods or services or their price. Accordingly, personal comparative advertising ("X is a foreigner, I am not") is no doubt always prohibited. In a literal construction, business-related details such as sales figures, the product's fame or the circulation of media, do not fall under the term "characteristics".

The requirement of "verifiability" is closely connected with the requirement of objectivity. Verifiability first of all means that the allegations must concern facts, since it is only these that can be checked for objective justification. What matters is that they can be verified by the addressees, i.e. the recipient of the advertising must himself, with reasonable effort, be able to verify the characteristics compared.

3.2.5 The characteristics compared must also be "material, relevant and representative". All of these features ultimately amount to the same thing: the aim is to prevent a distorted overall image by selecting immaterial, irrelevant characteristics that are as a rule of no relationship to the purchase. What is decisive for the purchase and hence "material" etc. depends on the type of product.

3.2.6 Article 3a Para. 1 (d) prohibits any comparison that "creates confusion in the market place between the advertiser and a competitor or between the advertiser's trademarks, trade names, other distinguishing marks, ..., goods or services and those of a competitor". Frequently trademark law claims would also be possible here. As the ECJ made clear in its Toshiba decision,[24] the regulation of comparative advertising is to be construed such that it takes into account the intention of Direc-

---

[21] For this reason, the provision in France restricting price comparisons to identical products had to be repealed.

[22] *See* the *Pippig* decision of the ECJ, *supra* note 20.

[23] Thus for instance the German Federal Supreme Court, May 22, 1986, I ZR 11/85, 1987 GRUR 49 – *Cola-Test* with comment by SACK.

[24] *See supra* note 16.

tive 89/104/EC (and vice versa). It is mainly agued that the terms that are used identically in both provisions (for instance likelihood of confusion) are to be construed on the basis of the same principles (such that in subparagraph d, as in trademark law, the abstract likelihood of confusion is sufficient and there is no need for the showing of actual confusion). In addition, the underlying model consumer, that of the reasonably attentive and reasonably circumspect average consumer, is identical in both cases.

3.2.7 One of the practically most important limits on comparative advertising is found in Article 3a Para. 1 (e), according to which comparative advertising "shall not discredit or denigrate the trade marks, trade names, other distinguishing marks, goods, services, activities or circumstances of a competitor". It is here that one can find the largest differences in the interpretation by the Member States.[25]

In principle, it is agreed that what is known as system-immanent criticism does not amount to "discrediting" – the milder form of "denigration". Any critical comparative advertising comprises a certain negative presentation of the competitor or his products. If this were prohibited, the intended liberalisation of comparative advertising would not be achieved. What is therefore meant is only "unnecessarily" discrediting comparative advertising. This occurs if the comparative advertising is primarily aimed at attacking or denigrating the competitor or his product. The latter can in particular be concluded from an unreasonably aggressive tone, an irrelevant representation or evaluation or a "global disqualification". In contrast, neither the selection of one of several of the competitor's products (for instance the one with the greatest price or quality difference) nor the pictorial representation of the rival's logo is of itself discrediting.[26] The decisive factor is always the addressee's interest in information. The exact interpretation of this interest (and the aspects named above) still leaves much room for different interpretations.

3.2.8 Differences in the interpretation by Member States also occur in another important limit, that of exploitation of reputation. According to Article 3a Para. 1 (f) comparative advertising shall not "take unfair advantage of the reputation of a trademark, trade name or other distinguishing marks of a competitor or of the designation of origin of competing products". Here, too, the "attachment" to another's reputation ("X is just as good as Y") that is necessary involved in comparative advertising is permitted, since otherwise derivative comparative advertising would be forbidden per se. Such conduct is at least not "unfair". There must in addition be particular circumstances for the transfer of the reputation of a sign to another to be regarded as unfair, for instance an excessive emphasis of the well-known rival product. It is not sufficient, however, to claim expressly or implicitly that an inexpensive product is equivalent to a prestigious brand product,[27] nor to use a competitor's ordering number system to show the purpose of one's own compatible product.[28]

---

[25] For the different points of view, *see* for instance the country reports France and Belgium on the one hand and Great Britain on the other hand, in: HENNING-BODEWIG, *supra* note 3.

[26] *See supra* note 20.

[27] As held by the ECJ in the *Pippig* decision, *supra* note 20.

[28] *See* the *Toshiba* decision, *supra* note 16.

3.2.9 Article 3a Para. 1 (f) restricts comparisons for products with designation of origin to products with the same designation. According to this "champagne clause", included at France's request, products bearing designations of origin cannot be compared with products without a designation of origin (thus champagne cannot be compared with sparkling wine, and instead comparisons can only be made between various champagne brands). According to Article 3a Para. 1 (h) comparative advertising shall not "present goods or services as imitations or replicas of goods or services bearing a protected trademark or trade name". This provision provides a certain degree of protection against comparison for the manufacturers of original goods (e.g. pharmaceuticals and perfumes) who, often after expiry of industrial property rights, cannot take actions against imitations as such.

3.2.10 According to Article 3a Para. 2 "any comparison referring to a special offer shall indicate in a clear and unequivocal way the date on which the offering ends or, where appropriate, that the special offer is subject to the availability of the goods and services, and where the special offer has not yet begun, the date of the start of the period during which the special price or other specific conditions shall apply". The information about any restrictions on a special offer, in particular a reference to any restricted stocks, is also to be regarded from the point of view of deception (see the Directive on Unfair Commercial Practices)[29] and is additionally regulated in the field of the internet (Directive on E-Commerce).[30] Accordingly these requirements apply irrespective of whether the advertising in question is a comparison or not.

3.3 The Harmonisation Effect

The harmonisation effect of Directive 97/55/EC has been considerable. Almost all Member States have implemented the Directive – in most cases word-for-word. Thus the unhappy situation of some Member States strictly prohibiting comparative advertising and others permitting it has been eliminated. Problems still result from the interpretation of a number of vague terms such as "discrediting" and "exploitation of reputation", but these differences can be expected to be settled in future decisions by the ECJ.

4. Directive 89/552/EEC on Television Broadcasting Activities

4.1 Overview of the Directive

Council Directive 89/552/EEC of October 3, 1989 as amended by Directive 97/36/EC of June 30, 1997 ("Television-Directive")[31] was adopted word-for-word in practically all Member States. It includes provisions on television advertising, sponsoring, teleshopping – i.e. fields that in the opinion of most Member States also concern

[29] *See* the contribution by Prof. Schuhmacher in this book.
[30] For details, *see* 5.
[31] OJ L 298/23, October 17, 1989.

unfair competition law. The Directive applies to all aspects of television (but not radio) originating in the EU.

Like the Misleading Advertising Directive, the Television Directive lays down a minimum level of protection, i.e. the Member States can adopt stricter and more detailed regulations for the broadcasters within their territory (Art 3 Para. 1), but combines this with the country-of-origin principle. The provisions of the Television Directive take priority over those of Directive 2005/29/EC on Unfair Commercial Practices.

4.2 The Regulation of Television Advertising

Television advertising is defined in Article 1 (c) of the Directive as

> "... any form of announcement broadcast (...) in order to promote the supply of goods or services, including immovable property, or rights and obligations, in return for payment."

The definition corresponds to that of the Directive on Misleading Advertising, but with the additional requirement that the advertising is in return for payment. According to a more recent decision of the ECJ,[32] this does not cover indirect television advertising, for instance resulting from the fact that advertising hoardings are broadcast during the transmission of a sports event.

Article 10 contains the general principles for distinguishing between advertising and programme. Television advertising shall be "readily recognisable as such and kept quite separate from other parts of the programme service by optical and/or acoustic means". Subliminal techniques and surreptitious advertising are expressly forbidden. Surreptitious advertising is defined in Article 1 (d) as: "... the representation in words or pictures of goods, services ... in programmes when such representation is intended by the broadcaster to serve advertising and might mislead the public as to its nature. Such representation is considered to be intentional in particular if it is done in return for payment or for similar consideration."

To date, this includes methods such as product placement, in which television broadcasters demand or receive payment for the placing of branded products, etc. However, a recent proposal for an amendment of the TV Directive is aiming for considerable liberalisation precisely in this point.[33] According to this amendment, it should be sufficient for the product placement to be disclosed at the beginning and end of the programme.

In order to avoid the impression of an unlawful combination with the programme, Article 10 Para. 2 also lays down that "isolated spots shall remain the exception". With respect to the placing of advertising generally, Art. 11 contains the

---

[32] Case C-429/92, 2004 ECR I-0000 – *Baccardi*.

[33] Proposal of December 13, 2005 for a Directive of the European Parliament and of the Council Directive 89/552/EEC on the coordination of certain provisions laid down by law, regulation or administrative action in Member States concerning the pursuit of television broadcasting activities, COM (2005) 646 final.

basic rule that advertisements shall be inserted between programmes. Under certain conditions, however, interruptions in programmes are also permitted. Art. 18 lays down the maximum advertising time per day (a maximum of 15 % of daily broadcasting time for advertising spots and a maximum of 20 % in any one hour).

The Television Directive also contains prohibitions and restrictions on advertising for specific products. There is a complete prohibition on television advertising for cigarettes and other tobacco products (Art. 13) and for pharmaceuticals and medical treatment only available on prescription (Art. 14). Art. 15 imposes restrictions on advertising for alcoholic beverages that largely correspond with the codes of conduct of the International Chamber of Commerce. Article 16 deals with the protection of minors against television advertising. Television advertising "shall not cause moral or physical detriment to minors" and shall therefore "not directly extort minors to buy a product or a service by exploiting their inexperience or credulity," nor directly encourage minors to persuade their parents to buy the goods being advertised, exploit the special trust in parents, teachers or unreasonably show minors in dangerous situations.

Finally, Art. 12 contains general requirements applicable to the content of all television advertising. According to this, television advertising shall not

- prejudice respect for human dignity;
- discriminate on grounds of race, sex, nationality;
- be offensive to religious or political beliefs;
- encourage behaviour prejudicial to the protection of the environment.

The Directive also regulates sponsoring, i.e. according to Art. 1 (c) any contribution to the financing of television programmes with a view to promoting sales.[34] According to Article 17 Para. (b) sponsored programmes must be clearly identified as such by the name and/or logo of the sponsor at the beginning and/or the end of the programme. The reference to the sponsor can also be repeated during the programme if the public is not "encouraged to buy" by the sponsored programme.

4.3 The Country-of-Origin Principle

Unlike Directive 84/450/EEC on Misleading and Comparative Advertising, the Television Directive lays down a country-of-origin principle. Art. 3 Para. 2 provides that

> "Member States shall, by appropriate means, ensure, within the framework for their legislation, that television broadcasters under their jurisdiction comply with the provisions of this Directive."

According to Art. 3 Para. 3, all Member States are obliged to make available "appropriate means" to ensure that third parties directly affected, including the nationals of other Member States, can address the judicial authorities or other agencies in order to obtain the actual application of the national provisions to the broadcast.

[34] For instance, the event sponsor can be identical with the programme sponsor.

In compensation, Art. 3 lays down the principle of reciprocal recognition

> "Member States shall ensure freedom of reception and shall not restrict retransmission on their territory of television broadcasts from other Member States, which fall with the field coordinated by this Directive."

The receiving Member States no longer have as a matter of principle any powers of examination in the areas coordinated by the Directive. The only exceptions are subject to very close limits, namely if the broadcast received obviously, seriously and grievously infringes Arts. 22 and 22a (protection of minors).

The country-of-origin principle, however, only applies within the "coordinated field" of the Directive. According to the 1997 "de Agostini" decision of the ECJ,[35] this only covers the areas directly harmonised by the Directive. The de Agostini decision concerned television advertising broadcast from Great Britain to Sweden in Swedish[36]. It was contested by the Swedish Consumer Ombudsman as being an infringement of the deception provisions of the Marketing Act and the Broadcasting Act (prohibition of television advertising directed at children under 12). The ECJ emphasised that the Television Directive only achieved partial coordination with respect to television advertising and sponsoring, for instance on advertising directed at children, which for this reason cannot be reviewed again by the receiving country. In contrast, misleading advertising is not coordinated by the Television Directive, with the result that the receiving country remains entitled to apply controls, according to the prevailing place-of-market principle of international private law.[37]

5. Directive 2000/31/EC on Electronic Commerce

5.1 Overview of the Directive

Directive 2000/31/EC of June 8, 2000 (Directive on E-Commerce)[38] deals with three topics – contracts concluded by electronic means, liability of intermediary service providers and regulation of "commercial communication". According to Article 1 Para. 1 the Directive "seeks to contribute to the proper functioning of the internal market by ensuring the free movement of information society services between the Member States". Although it aims at increasing consumer confidence, it is not restricted to the protection of consumers but aims at ensuring legal certainty for competitors and business as well. The provisions of the E-Commerce Directive take priority over those of Directive 2005/29/EC on Unfair Commercial Practices.

---

[35] ECJ, July 9, 1997, joined cases C-34/95, C-35/95 and C-36/95, 1997 ECR I-03843 – *De Agostini.*

[36] It was undisputed that the advertising was directed to the Swedish market.

[37] For details of the country-of-origin principle and the place-of-market principle, *see* HENNING-BODEWIG, *supra* note 3.

[38] Directive 2000/31/EC on Certain Legal Aspects of Information Society Services, in particular Electronic Commerce; in the Internal Market of June 8, 2000 (E-Commerce Directive); OJ L 178/1, July 17, 2000.

5.2 The Regulation of Commercial Communications

The Directive applies to all "commercial communications" in electronic commerce. The concept of commercial communication, first launched in the Green Paper on Consumer Protection,[39] is broader than that of advertising. According to Art. 2 (f), it covers "... any form of communication designed to promote, directly or indirectly, the goods, services or image of a company, organisation or person pursuing a commercial, industrial or craft activity or exercising a regulated profession." It does not apply to "information allowing direct access to the activity of the company" etc. or to "communications relating to the goods, services or image of the company, organisation or person compiled in an independent manner, particularly when this is without financial consideration".

Pursuant to Article 7 Para. 1 all commercial communication must at least be clearly identifiable as such. Furthermore, the natural or legal person on whose behalf the commercial communication is made shall be clearly identifiable; promotional offers and promotional competition or games must be clearly identifiable as such and the condition for participation etc. must be presented clearly and unambiguously.

Article 7 deals with unsolicited commercial communications by electronic mail. Commercial e-mails shall be clearly and unambiguously identifiable as such, and without prejudice to Directive 97/7/EC and Directive 97/66/EC – which allow Member States to set up an "opt-in" system for e-mail advertising and certain forms of telephone advertising – opt-out registers in which natural persons not wishing to receive such commercial communications can register themselves, must be consulted regularly and respected.

According to Article 8 Member States shall ensure that commercial communications by "regulated professions" (called liberal professions in other Directives) are permitted "subject to compliance with the professional rules regarding, in particular, the independence, dignity and honour of the profession ...".

5.3 Country-of-Origin Principle

With some exceptions, the E-Commerce Directive subjects the regulation of commercial communications to the country-of-origin principle. According to Article 3 Para. 1 each Member State "... shall ensure that the information society services provided by a service provider established on its territory comply with the national provisions applicable in the Member State in question which fall within the coordinated field". Furthermore Article 3 Para. 2 states that Member States "... may not, for reasons falling within the coordinated field, restrict the freedom to provide information society services from another Member State".

According to Art. 3 Para. 3, exceptions to this principle apply to unsolicited e-mails and to the fields specified in the annex, including copyright, neighbouring rights, rights referred to in Directive 87/54/EC and Directive 96/9/EC as well as

[39] COM (2001) 531 final.

industrial property rights; the freedom of the parties to choose the law applicable to their contract, contractual obligations concerning consumer contents; the permissibility of unsolicited commercial communication by electronic mail. Furthermore, Member States may derogate from Paragraph 2 under certain conditions, especially where public policy, public health or security or the protection of consumers are involved.

The country-of-origin principle laid down in Art. 3 is very broad, much broader than that in the Television Directive.[40] This is due to the different definition of the coordinated field in Art. 2, which encompasses all "requirements laid down in Member State's legal system applicable to information society service provides or information society services".

This covers the whole area of advertising, marketing, sponsoring, sales promotions etc. However, pursuant to Article 2 (h) (ii) the coordinated field does not cover requirements such as requirements applicable to goods as such, to the delivery of goods or to services not provided by electronic means.

6. Directive 2002/58/EC on Privacy and Electronic Communications

Directive 2002/58/EC of July 12, 2002 concerning the processing of personal data and the protection of privacy in the electronic communication sector[41] primarily deals with aspects of data protection. However, Article 13 Para. 1 also (again) regulates advertising by fax or telephone.

> "The use of automated calling systems without human intervention (automatic calling machine), fax simile machines (fax) or electronic mail for the purposes of direct marketing may only be allowed in respect of subscribers who have given their prior consent."

As a result, the protection already granted by the Distance Selling Directive (opt-in for voice mail systems and fax) is extended to email advertising and SMS advertising. According to Art. 13 Para. 2, there is an exception for specific cases in connection with previous contracts.

For all other cases, either the Distance Selling Directive applies directly or the Member States are free to choose between opt-in and opt-out. In any event, account must be taken of transparency requirements, and an address must be given in order to terminate future e-mails (Art. 13 Para. 4).

These provisions take priority over those of Directive 2005/29/EC concerning Unfair Commercial Practices.

---

[40] In detail HENNING-BODEWIG, *supra* note 3.

[41] OJ L 201/37, July 31, 2002.

The Unfair Commercial Practices Directive

Wolfgang Schuhmacher

Directive 2005/29/EC concerning Unfair Business-to-Consumer Commercial Practices in the Internal Market was adopted on May 11, 2005. This contribution sets out the main contents of the Directive in brief, and then analyses the problem of the partial harmonisation of competition law, the extensive list of "per-se prohibitions" in the Annex to the Directive (the "blacklist") and the Directive's model consumer. Finally, the question of the implementation obligation (in particular of the "blacklist") will be discussed.

1. Background and Purpose of the Directive

Directive 2005/29/EC of the European Parliament and of the Council concerning Unfair Business-to-Consumer Commercial Practices in the Internal Market and amending Council Directive 84/850/EEC, Directives 97/7/EC, 98/27/EC and 2002/65/EC of the European Parliament and of the Council and Regulation (EC) No. 2006/2004 of the European Parliament and of the Council was adopted on May 11, 2005. The work began with the Green Paper on Consumer Protection in the European Union dated October 2, 2001 COM (2001) 531[1]. The Directive has had an eventful legislative history.[2] Political agreement having been achieved in the Council on May 18, 2004 and the Joint Position having been adopted on November 15, 2004, the European Parliament in its recommendation for the second reading on February 7, 2005, put forward 19 proposals for amendments, which were accepted by the Commission in its Statement dated March 15, 2005, thereby clearing the way to the adoption of the Directive.[3]

The Directive harmonises the legal regulations of the Member States concerning unfair commercial practices, including unfair advertising, that directly harm consumers' economic interests and as a result indirectly harm the economic interests of legitimate competitors. In this way, it is intended to eliminate the uncertainty as to which national regulations apply to unfair commercial practices that damage the consumers' commercial interests and create obstacles to both enterprises and con-

---

1 Follow-up document COM (2002) 346 final.

2 *See* the list of all intermediate documents in GAMERITH, "Richtlinienvorschlag über unlautere Geschäftspraktiken – Möglichkeiten einer harmonischen Umsetzung in die nationale Rechtsordnung" 116 *et seq.* (2004) = GAMERITH, "Der Richtlinienvorschlag über unlautere Geschäftspraktiken – Möglichkeiten einer harmonischen Umsetzung," 2005 WRP 391, 433 *et seq.*

3 OJ L 149/22, June 11, 2005. The proposed Directive has already been discussed in detail in numerous contributions; *cf.* GAMERITH *supra* note 2 and the references in this study; on the Directive itself, *see* HENNING-BODEWIG, 2005 GRUR Int. 629 *et seq.* and HANDIG, 2005 ÖBl 196 *et seq.*

sumers.[4] Since it is a purely consumer protection directive, it does not affect the national laws on unfair commercial practices which harm only competitors' economic interests or which relate to a transaction between traders; nor does it cover accepted advertising and marketing practices such as legitimate product placement, brand differentiation or the offering of incentives which may legitimately affect consumers' perceptions of products and influence their behaviour without impairing their ability to make an informed decision.[5]

Nor does the Directive concern individual actions lodged by those who have been harmed by an unfair commercial practice, nor the Community and national rules on contract law, intellectual property rights, health and safety aspects of products, the conditions of establishment and authorisation regimes, in including those rules which, in conformity with Community law, relate to gambling activities.[6]

2. The Contents of the Directive

2.1 General

In accordance with what was said above, Art. 1 describes the purpose of the Directive as

> "to contribute to the proper functioning of the internal market and achieve a high level of consumer protection by approximating the laws, regulations and administrative provisions of the Member States on unfair commercial practices harming consumers' economic interests".

Pursuant to Art. 3, the Directive applies

> "to unfair business-to-consumer commercial practices, as laid down in Art. 5, before, during and after a commercial transaction in relation to a product".

Of particular importance is also the fact that the Directive, while basically aiming at complete harmonisation, since according to Art. 4 the Member States

> "shall not restrict the freedom to provide services nor restrict the free movement of goods for reasons falling within the field approximated by this Directive,[7]"

will not achieve this objective soon, since according to Art. 3 Para. 5, the Member States are permitted for a period of 6 years from the date of implementation

> "to continue to apply national provisions within the field approximated by this Directive which are more restrictive or prescriptive than this Direc-

---

[4] *Cf.* Recitals 4 and 6 of the Directive.

[5] Recital 6.

[6] Recital 9.

[7] The importance and scope of this vaguely worded regulation are disputed, *cf.* most recently GAMERITH, 2005 WRP 391, *supra* note 2, at 411 with notes = GAMERITH, *supra* note 2, at 54.

tive and which implement directives containing minimum harmonisation clauses."

2.2 General Clause: "Unfair Commercial Practices"

In terms of content, the Directive is based on a general clause that consists of a general prohibition of unfair commercial practices (Art. 5 Para. 1). A commercial practice is then defined as unfair if

> "a) it is contrary to the requirements of professional diligence, and
>
> b) it materially distorts or is likely to materially distort the economic behaviour with regard to the product of the average consumer who it reaches or to whom it is addressed or of the average member of the group when a commercial practice is directed to a particular group of consumers" (Art. 5 Para. 2).

Thus in its scope of application, the Directive replaces the vague legal concept of "honest practices" of the Act against Unfair Competition by the equally vague concept of "professional diligence". Art. 5 Para. 4 then states that commercial practices shall in particular be unfair if they are misleading or aggressive.

2.3 Misleading and Aggressive Business Practices

These two variations of unfairness are defined in detail; thus Arts. 6 and 7 define misleading acts and misleading omissions. The former is the case if a commercial practice

> "contains false information and is therefore untruthful or in any way, including overall presentation, deceives or is likely to deceive the average consumer, even if the information is factually correct, in relation to one or more of the following elements, and in either case causes or is likely to cause him to take a transactional decision that he would not have taken otherwise".

This is followed by a comprehensive list. Misleading by omission is the case if a commercial practice

> "in its factual context, taking account of all its features and circumstances and the limitations of the communication medium, omits material information that the average consumer needs, according to the context, to take an informed rational decision and thereby causes or is likely to cause the average consumer to take a transactional decision that he would not have taken otherwise" (Art. 7 Para. 1).

Again, this is followed by a list of various examples.

Art. 8, finally, defines a business practice as aggressive

> "if, in its factual context, taking account of all its features and circumstances, by harassment, coercion including the use of physical force or undue influence, it significantly impairs or is likely to significantly impair the average consumer's freedom of choice or conduct with regards to the product and

thereby causes him or is likely to cause him to take a transaction decision that he would not have taken otherwise".

2.4 Annex 1: Per-se Prohibitions (the "Blacklist")

A central element of the Directive is finally the list in Annex 1 to the Directive of the "commercial practices which are in all circumstances considered unfair". This Annex contains no fewer than 31 per-se prohibitions, of which 23 can be ascribed to the field of misleading commercial practices.

Various points must be emphasized:

2.4.1 This Annex grew in the course of the legislative history; while the Commission's proposal dated June 18, 2003 contained only 19 per-se prohibitions, the text on which the Competitiveness Council reached political agreement at its session on May 18, 2004 already contained 29; the European Parliament added two and amended parts of the list in its recommendation for the second reading dated February 7, 2005. This Annex will therefore have central importance for the application of the law, if only because of its quantitative extent.

2.4.2 The importance of this Annex is established in Art. 5 Para. 5 of the Directive. According to sentence 2 (which was only introduced by the European Parliament in the said recommendation), this list applies

> "uniformly in all Member States and may only be modified by revision of this Directive".

This is intended to create absolute legal certainty to the extent that a "concealed" amendment of the Annex cannot be achieved by means of another Directive, while at the same time the Annex is also intended to ensure that the law is absolutely identical in all Member States.

2.4.3 What this means for the individual Member State is something I cannot assess. From an Austrian point of view, however, it must be pointed out that most of the prohibitions contained in the Annex are either already the subject matter of special offences or have been or could be covered by judicial practice on the basis of Secs. 1 and 2 of the Act against Unfair Competition.

For the application of the law, the regulatory method of the Directive described above in any event means the following:

It will first be necessary to examine whether a commercial practice falls within the blacklist of Annex 1; if it does not, it must be examined whether it is a misleading or aggressive practice. If this is not the case, recourse must be had to the general clause of Art. 5 Para. 1 and Para. 2.

I shall discuss later the question of the implementation of the Annex.

3. Theories About the Directive in the Competition Law Context

3.1 The Directive continues the partial harmonisation of competition law for consumer protection purposes and maintains the fragmentation of consumer protection with respect to unfair commercial practices.

According to Recital 6, the present Directive harmonises the laws of the Members States on unfair commercial practices including unfair advertising, which directly harm consumers' economic interests and thereby indirectly harm the economic interests of legitimate competitors. This statement creates the impression that the result is the complete harmonisation at least of consumer-related unfairness. This is anything other than true; Recital 9 of the Directive for instance states that the Member States will be able to retain or introduce restrictions and prohibitions of commercial practices on grounds of the protection of the health and safety consumers in their territory wherever the trader is based, for example in relation to alcohol, tobacco or pharmaceuticals. In addition, the Directive is without prejudice to the rights of Member States to go beyond its provisions to protect the economic interests of consumers in the field of financial services and immovable property (likewise Recital 9).

Above all, however, the entire field of sales promotion is excluded, which is known to be intended to be reserved for a separate regulation.[8] Accordingly, the Directive is far from being a general harmonisation of even only (consumer-related) unfair competition law.[9]

3.2 This waiver of the harmonisation of "related" fields – which above all concern the protection of competitors – leads to a further fragmentation of competition law.

On this point, Recital 6 lays down that the Directive does not cover the national rules with respect to unfair commercial practices

> "which harm only competitors' economic interest or which relate to a transaction between traders".

At the same time, Recital 8 acknowledges the close connection between the protection of competitors and the protection of consumers, by stating:

> "This Directive directly protects consumers' economic interests from unfair business-to-consumer commercial practices. Thereby, it also indirectly protects legitimate businesses from their competitors who do not play by the rules in this Directive and thus guarantees fair competition in fields coordinated by it. It is understood that there are other commercial practices which, although not harming consumers, may hurt competitors and business customers. The Commission should carefully examine the need for Community

---

[8] The last relevant documents dates from September 18, 2004 (Interinstitutional file 2001/0227 (COD)), Document No. 12498/04 – Amended Proposal for a Regulation by the European Parliament and Council Concerning Sales Promotion in the Internal Market – Political Agreement (Public Consultation); September 24, 2004 – Discussion in the Council leading to a Draft Comment on the Proposal for a Regulation by the European Parliament and Council concerning Sales Promotion in the Internal Market dated November 11, 2004, Document No. 14402/04; in the meantime, however, the proposal has been withdrawn by the Commission (*cf.* Communication by the Commission dated September 27, 2005, COM (2005) 462 final).

[9] Hence the appropriate criticism in VEELKEN, "Kundenfang gegenüber dem Verbraucher," 2004 WRP 1, 9; in agreement, GAMERITH, 2005 WRP 391, *supra* note 2, at 407 = GAMERITH, *supra* note 2, 42 *et seq.*

action in the field of unfair competition going beyond the remit of this Directive and, if necessary, make a legislative proposal to cover these other aspects of unfair competition."

Admittedly, it is self-evident that legal reforms can in the great majority of cases only pursue a policy of small steps and that "radical changes" tend to be rare; nevertheless it must be clearly stated on the other hand that this procedure in practice conflicts with the programmatic statement of Recital 3 ("the laws of the Members States related to unfair commercial practices make differences which can generate appreciable distortions of competition and obstacles to the smooth functioning of the internal market."). Seen in this light, the Directive on Unfair Commercial Practices may be a step in the right direction, but is merely a small step that must be followed by others as soon as possible. Moreover, mention must also made of the fact that the case group of "slavish imitation" (which constitutes a classical example of a factual constellation that affects both competitor and consumer interests) has been included at least indirectly in the blacklist in the Annex. According to item 13,

"Promoting a product similar to a product made by a particular manufacturer in such a manner as deliberately to mislead the consumer into believing the product is made by the same manufacturer when it is not"

is unfair per se.

This clearly shows that there are certain competition law constellations in which competitor and consumer protection cannot be separated.[10]

3.3 The Directive leads to a return of the per-se prohibitions, which in national law the ECJ has mainly viewed negatively.

As already mentioned, the Annex to the Directive contains no fewer than 31 commercial practices that are considered unfair in all circumstances. The specific ability to mislead or (in the case of aggressive business practices) an ability of the aggressive business practices to interfere with the freedom of decision of the consumers affected is irrelevant.

In contrast, in its judicial practice to date, the ECJ has overwhelmingly qualified per-se prohibitions in national law as unreasonable and required national judges to provide evidence of a specific risk to the object of protection at issue. Examples from judicial practice concern the prohibition of "instead-of price advertising" in Luxemburg and Germany[11] and the Austrian prohibition on any accessory competitions in the marketing of periodicals.[12]

---

[10] This fragmentation of competition law has been criticised strongly above all in Austrian and German literature; *cf.* for instance GAMERITH, 2005 WRP 391, *supra* note 2, at 413 *et seq.* = GAMERITH, *supra* note 2, at 56 *et seq.*; GLÖCKNER, in: HARTE- BAVENDAMM & HENNING-BODEWIG (eds.), "UWG" Introduction B, notes 176 *et seq.*, both with further references (2004).

[11] Decisions of the ECJ, March 7, 1990, Case No. C-362/88, 1990 ECR 667 – *GB-INNO-BM* = 1991 ZfRV 37; May 18, 1993, Case No. C-126/91, 1993 ECR I-2361 – *Yves Rocher* = 1994 ZER 68 = 1993 GRUR 747 with comment by BORNKAMM.

[12] Decision of the ECJ, June 26, 1997, Case No. C-368/95, 1997 ECR I-3689 – *Familiapress* = 1997 wbl 333 = 1997 MR 158 = 1997 ZER 118 = 1997 ÖBl 229 = 1997 ecolex 586.

However, this approach only contains an apparent contradiction. National per-se prohibitions are an obstacle to the free movement of goods and services, while Europe-wide uniform per-se prohibitions promote the exercise of these freedoms by creating an absolutely identical law in the areas they cover. The regulatory method as such is thus not to be contested and has already been applied in the Contract Clause Directive,[13] although to a considerably smaller regulatory content; I shall return to this point when discussing the question of implementation.

A very different question is whether such a large number of per-se prohibitions was necessary and whether these have all been worded appropriately. This question must be left aside in full.

3.4 The Directive represents a partial abandonment of the model of the "averagely informed, attentive and reasonable average consumer" within the meaning of the ECJ judicial practice,[14] and leads to a return to the gullible consumer in competition law. At the same time, it includes a contradiction.

The theory set out above is based on Art. 5 Para. 2 (b) and Para. 3 of the Directive. Pursuant to Art. 5 Para. 2 (b), a commercial practice is unfair

> "if it materially distorts or is likely to materially distort the economic behaviour with regard to the product of the average consumer whom it reaches or to whom it is addressed, or of the average member of the group when a commercial practice is directed to a particular group of consumers".

This corresponded essentially with the contents of the Commission Proposal dated June 18, 2003. However, the final legislative text also contains a paragraph 3 (introduced in the 2004 draft) that brings back the vulnerable consumer. This provision states:

---

[13] Directive 93/13/EEC of the Council dated April 5, 1993 concerning Abusive Clauses in Consumer Contracts. On the harmonisation of the legal situation in Austria after the implementation of this Directive, *see* SCHUHMACHER & HAYBÄCK, 1999 Zeitschrift für Schweizerisches Recht 361 *et seq.*

[14] HELM, "Das Verbraucherleitbild des Europäischen Gerichtshofs und des Bundesgerichtshofs im Vergleich," in: "FS Tilmann" 135, 140 *et seq.* (2003), pointed out in a detailed analysis that the German wording stands by itself in the context of the versions of the decision in other languages. The requirement that the modern consumer must be reasonable is not found in the decisions in other languages in this form. Thus in the English version of the "Gut Springenheide" decision, it states that the decisive factor is "the presumed expectations of an average consumer who is reasonably well-informed and reasonably observant and circumspect" and in the French version *"l'attente présumée d'un consommateur moyen, normalement informé et raisonnablement attentif avisé"*. He concluded that the German wording was based on an inaccurate translation (*loc.cit.*, 141). For this reason, minorities will be also protected against being misled, it being a matter for the national judge according to ECJ judicial practice to determine, according to his own law, the minimum percentage of consumers that must be misled by a statement (*loc.cit.*, 142).

> "Commercial practices which are likely to materially distort the economic behaviour only of a clearly identifiable[15] group of consumers who are particularly vulnerable to the practice or the underlying product by virtue of their mental or physical infirmity, age or credulity in a way which the trader could reasonably be expected to foresee, shall be assessed from the perspective of the average member of that group. This is without prejudice to the common and legitimate advertising practice of making exaggerated statements or statements which are not meant to be taken literally".

The following must be stated:

In the literature it has admittedly been rightly pointed out that the less-than-averagely informed, attentive and reasonable consumer has not been completely abandoned by the judicial practice of the ECJ;[16] nevertheless these are only individual cases.[17] The Directive is thus clearly intended to increase the level of protection and to consolidate and enforce these approaches in the ECJ's judicial practice.

At the same time, it frustrates this objective through the last sentence of Art. 5 Para. 3, according to which the common and legitimate advertising practice of making exaggerated statements or statements not meant to be taken literally (hence what is known as "blatant advertising") remains unaffected. The resolution of this conflict is thus left to judicial practice and in reality constitutes the squaring of the circle.[18]

A further corrective is the requirement that consumers' economic conduct must be "materially influenced". In the legal definition of Art. 2 (e), the criterion of the "material influencing of the consumer's economic behaviour" is defined such that it concerns the application of a commercial practice that perceptibly impairs the consumer's ability to make an informed decision, thereby causing the consumer to take a transactional decision that he would not have taken otherwise. Overall, it thus creates a considerable field of tension.

4. On the Implementation of the Directive (in particular Annex I) in National Law

4.1 According to the Judicial Practice of the ECJ

> "the implementation of a Directive does not necessarily require the legislature to become active in each Member State; nevertheless it is vital that the national law at issue in fact ensures the complete application of the Directive by the national authorities, that the legal situation resulting from this law is

15 The last two words were only inserted by the European Parliament's fifth amendment proposal.

16 KÖHLER, in: BAUMBACH & HEFERMEHL, "Wettbewerbsrecht" Sec. 1 Act against Unfair Competition, note 20 (2004); likewise HELM, *supra* note 14, at 142.

17 *Cf.* decisions of the ECJ, July 9, 1997, joined Cases No. C-34/95, C-36/95 – *De Agostini* = 1997 wbl 423 = 1997 ZER 141 = 1997 MR 242 = 1997 ÖBl 306; and 1989 ECR 1235 – *Buet* = 1990 EuZW 69.

18 For more details on the model consumer of the Directive, *see* HELM, "Der Abschied vom „verständigen" Verbraucher," 2005 WRP 931 *et seq*.

> sufficiently certain and clear and that the beneficiaries are put into a position of acquiring knowledge of all their rights and if necessary asserting them before the national courts."[19]

This last requirement is regarded by the Court as being particularly important if the Directive is intended to allow claims to nationals of other Member States.[20]

4.2 What this means for the present case, in particular the implementation of Annex I (the per-se prohibitions/blacklist), will be the subject matter of intense debate, and is disputed both in Austria and in Germany. Thus *Gamerith* argues that the list of commercial practices in Annex I of the Directive should not be implemented. He claims that most cases in this list are covered by Austrian judicial practice on the Act against Unfair Competition, some even by special legislation (e.g. pyramid sales systems, Sec. 27 of the Act against Unfair Competition; prohibition on certain advertising to bereaved families, Sec. 57 (1) of the Trade Regulation 1994; misleading editorial advertising, Sec. 26 of the Media Act). The failure to comply with information obligations can be subject to the penalties proposed in Sec. 2 (1a) of the Act against Unfair Competition; the infringement of statutory information obligations can also be effectively pursued as a breach of the law pursuant to Sec. 1 of the Act. In addition, *Gamerith* points out that most cases could easily be included within Arts. 6-8 of the Directive.[21] In contrast, other authors argue that implementation should be done at least by means of a precise reference to the Annex.[22]

In Germany, *Glöckner*[23] refers to the ECJ decision in the case of Com v. Sweden and argues that it is not necessary

> "for all the elements of the Directive to be included in the implementation legislation".

This decision concerned the implementation of the Contract Clause Directive 93/13/ EEC, the Annex to the Directive not having been included in the legislative text. The

[19] Decision of the ECJ, May 10, 2001, Case No. C-144/99, note 17 – *Com v. NL* = 2001 wbl 215 = 2001 EuZW 437 with comment by LEIBLE = 2001 EWS 484 with comment by MICKLITZ; *cf.* also the final pleadings by Attorney General Geelhoed in Case No. C-478/99, note 34; HERRMANN, "Richtlinienumsetzung durch die Rechtsprechung" 210 *et seq.*, 244 (2003); Case No. C-162/99 – *Com v. I*, note 22 = 2001 wbl 78 = 2001 ZER 17 = 2001 ZASB 15; Case No. C-478/ 99, note 21 = 2002 wbl 215 = 2002 ZER 148; final pleadings by Attorney General Geelhoed in Case No. C-58/02, note 35; final pleadings by Attorney General Tizzano in Case No. C-144/99, notes 9 und 36.

[20] Decision of the ECJ, May 10, 2001, Case No. C-144/99, note 17, 18 – *Com v. NL* = 2001 wbl 215 = 2001 EuZW 437 = 2001 ZER 113. *Cf.* recently Decision of the ECJ, January 7, 2004, C-58/02 – *Com v. Spain* = 2004 ZER 5.

[21] GAMERITH, *supra* note 2, at 112 = GAMERITH, 2005 WRP 391, *supra* note 2, at 432.

[22] KLAMERT, "Zur Umsetzung der Richtlinie gegen unlautere Geschäftspraktiken," 2005 ecolex 95 *et seq.*; likewise KUCSKO, "Memo: Wider die Harmonisierungsresistenz," 2005 ecolex 96 *et seq.*

[23] GLÖCKNER, "Richtlinienvorschlag über unlautere Geschäftspraktiken, deutsches UWG oder die schwierige Umsetzung von europarechtlichen Generalklauseln," 2004 WRP 936, 941 *et seq.*

ECJ did not regard this as an insufficient implementation of the Directive because the Annex was taken up completely in the materials to the Act. This was justified on the grounds that the list of clauses in standard terms of business that could be declared unfair contained in the Annex is not exhaustive pursuant to Art. 3 Para. 3 of the Directive and was only of indicative or exemplary character[24] (Note 22 of the decision). For this reason, it was also the case that a clause included in the list was not necessarily to be regarded as unfair and, conversely, a clause not included in the list could nevertheless be held to be unfair (note 20).

Glöckner regards this legal situation as comparable to the Directive concerning Unfair Commercial Practices:

> "Here too, the special factual constellations do not provide any more rights than the general clause; they merely state irrevocably when a commercial practice is unfair. Against this background, ... even if the Directive on Unfair Commercial Practices enters into effect, it should be sufficient for national law to contain an approximate wording of the individual factual constellations as long as it is certain that firstly the substantive standard of protection required by the Directive (per-se unlawfulness of the competitive conduct described in the special factual constellations of the Directive) is created and, secondly, the protected consumer can acquire knowledge of the rights granted to him without difficulty."

4.3 The following objections can be raised to the arguments set out above:

In contrast to the Contract Clause Directive, Annex I of the Directive on Unfair Commercial Practices is not only of indicative character but contains binding law in the interests of legal certainty and legal uniformity in all Member States. This follows beyond doubt from Art. 5 Para. 5, recalled once again here, according to which

> "Annex 1 contains the list of those commercial practices which shall in all circumstances be regarded as unfair. The same single list shall apply in all Member States and may only be modified by revision of this Directive".

Accordingly, the aim intended does not correspond to a merely "approximate" wording of individual factual constellations, and even less so to an entire waiver of its implementation. In addition, reference is made to the decision in Com v. Kingdom of the Netherlands,[25] in which the ECJ dismissed the argument put forward by the Dutch government that the objectives pursued by the Directive could be achieved by means of a systematic interpretation of Dutch regulations, and above all referred to the publicity requirement. It emphasized that this condition was particularly important

> "if the Directive is intended to allow claims to nationals of other Member States. Precisely that is the case here, since the Directive aims ... to protect

[24] Art. 3 Para. 3 of the Contract Clause Directive reads as follows: "The Annex shall contain an indicative and non-exhaustive list of the terms which may be regarded as unfair."

[25] *Cf. supra* note 19.

> the citizen in his role as consumer when buying goods and services on the basis of contracts to which the legal regulations of other Members States apply".

In summary, it can therefore be stated that in the present case neither an "approximate" implementation nor an inclusion of the Annex in the materials of the law is sufficient. The aim of the Annex of ensuring absolute legal certainty and legal uniformity can therefore only be achieved by including the Annex in the legislative text or by declaring the Annex to be binding (by means of a reference in the law).[26]

---

[26] This view is also supported by SEICHTER, "Der Umsetzungsbedarf der RL über unlautere Geschäftspraktiken," 2005 WRP 1087, 1094 *et seq* and GLÖCKNER & HENNING-BODEWIG, "EG-Richtlinie über unlautere Geschäftspraktiken: Was wird aus dem "neuen" UWG?," 2005 WRP 1311, 1323; for a more detailed analysis of the implementation requirements *see* SCHUHMACHER, "Zur Umsetzung der Richtlinie über unlautere Geschäftspraktiken," in: GRUBER & RÜFFLER (eds.), "Gesellschaftsrecht, Wettbewerbsrecht, Europarecht. Hans-Georg Kappensteiner zum 70. Geburtstag" 139 *et seq.* (2007).

Belgian Report: Example of an Integrated Approach

Jules Stuyck

1. Belgian Law Against Unfair Competition and Trade Practices: a General Introduction

The historic basis of the law against unfair competition in Belgium is Article 1382 Civil Code (the Code Napoléon) on tort liability. A merchant who violated, on purpose or by negligence, with a competitive aim, a right that a competitor derived from an industrial or commercial organisation committed an act of unfair competition.[1] The law of "concurrence déloyale" was seen as a tool to protect the "business" ("fonds de commerce") as the sum of the different elements used by a merchant to operate on the market: his trade name and trade marks, the design of his products, his goodwill, his contracts with suppliers and clients, his manufacturing processes and so on. The law against unfair competition was hardly distinct from the law of industrial property that was its inspiration.

Actions for tort liability are basically claims for damages. The plaintiff has to prove a prejudice caused by the act of unfair competition. The Royal Decree n° 55 of December 23, 1934 (equivalent to an Act of Parliament) introduced a special action for a cease and desist order before the president of the commercial court (in Belgium this is a professional judge) against every act which was contrary to honest business practices ("acte contraire aux usages honnêtes en matière commerciale") and by which a merchant or a craftsman harmed or tried to harm the goodwill, credit or competitive capacity of a competitor. Thus, a preventive action became possible against acts of unfair competition. The R.D. was the implementation in Belgium of Article 10bis Para. 2 of the Paris Union Convention on Protection of Industrial Property.[2] R.D. n° 55 also gave a non-exhaustive list of acts of unfair competition[3], facilitating the emergence of a rich case law on unfair competition.[4]

During the economic crisis of the 1930s other laws regulating market behaviour saw the light of day: laws on auctions, end of season and clearance sales, doorstep selling, sales on markets and other off-premise sales, premium offers and so on (called "la police du commerce"). All these laws were enforced by criminal sanctions.

Criminal prosecution as a means for enforcing laws on trade practices was not a success. On the other hand, the availability of the efficient action for a cease and desist order was limited: the case law of the Cour de Cassation excluded this action in case of infringements of intellectual property rights and some case law even

---

1 *See* MOREAU, "Traité de la concurrence illicite" (1904).

2 *See* GOTZEN, "Vrijheid van Beroep en Bedrijf & Onrechtmatige Mededinging" (1963).

3 As in Art. 10bis Paris Convention inserted in 1900 and amended in 1925 (in brief: causing confusion with or denigrating a competitor or taking advantage by misleading the public).

4 *See* in particular SCHRICKER & FRANCQ, "La répression de la concurrence déloyale" tome II/1 (Belgique) (1974).

excluded the "action en cessation" in cases of criminal infringements (like infringements of the "police du commerce" laws).

The Act of July 14, 1971 on Trade Practices ("loi sur les pratiques du commerce", "wet betreffende de handelspraktijken") integrated R.D. n° 55 (the law against unfair competition in the strict sense) with the "police du commerce" laws, added new per se rules (regulations and prohibitions) concerning sales methods which until that day had not been specifically regulated (sales in rented private premises and sales at a loss), sharpened existing prohibitions (the prohibition of premium offers was extended to joint offers) and, finally, added provisions on the information and protection of consumers against certain forms of advertising (misleading advertising) and certain sales methods (like inertia selling). The "action en cessation" became possible for most of the infringements of the Act, including a new general clause which prohibited every act which was contrary to honest business practices ("usages honnêtes en matière commerciale") by which a merchant harmed or tried to harm the professional interests of one or more other merchants.

Compared to R.D. n° 55 the notion of "concurrence déloyale" was broadened by the deletion of a reference to the goodwill or competitive capacity in the notion of prejudice; every professional interest was henceforth protected, i.e. plaintiff and defendant do not necessarily have to be direct competitors (a manufacturer can e.g. act against a retailer).

If consumer protection was one of the objectives of the 1971 Act, it remained secondary. The scope of the substantive provisions in the consumers' interest was limited. Consumer organisations could bring a collective action for a cease and desist order against certain infringements of the Act only.

The last important reform so far was the adoption of the Act of July 14, 1991 on Trade Practices and the Information and Protection of Consumers (TPCA) ("loi sur les pratiques du commerce et l'information et la protection du consommateur", "wet betreffende de handelspraktijken en de voorlichting en bescherming van de consument"). This Act has primarily introduced new regulations in the field of consumer protection including a new general clause prohibiting acts contrary to honest business practices by which a "seller" harms or is likely to harm the interests of one or more consumers (Article 94), the old general clause of the 1971 Act now being rephrased as a prohibition of acts contrary to honest business practices by which a "seller" harms or is likely to harm the professional interests of one or more other "sellers". "Seller" is defined in an absurd complicated manner. It amounts to excluding from the application of (most of the provisions of) the Act the liberal professions as well as certain other economic activities (sickness funds,[5] private schools, certain aspects in the field of the sale of real estate).

[5] The exclusion of these private bodies (most of them linked to a political family) from the application of the TPCA was one of the reasons why the definition of "seller" was made so complicated. However in a judgment of May 23, 2003, 2003 Revue de droit commercial belge / Tijdschrift voor Belgisch Handelsrecht (R.D.C.) 787 the Court of Appeal of Brussels decided that the offer of (hospitalisation) insurances by the sickness funds on the market, in competition with the insurance companies, constitutes a commercial act. For such an offer the sickness funds are therefore to be qualified as "sellers" within the meaning of the TPCA.

The original TPCA of 1991 already incorporated the implementation of the Misleading Advertising Directive of 1984 and the Directive on Off-Premise Sales of 1985. Several EC Directives in the field of consumer protection, adopted after the TPCA (comparative advertising, unfair contract terms, distant selling) have led to amendments of the TPCA and to the adoption of specific legislation concerning unfair contract terms, misleading and comparative advertising and distant selling for the professions (now coordinated in the Act of August 2, 2002 with similar provisions as those of the TPCA and an action for a cease and desist order before the civil court of first instance). The recent Consumer Sales Directive however has been implemented by inserting a new section in the Civil Code.

2. Does the Law Against Unfair Competition Form a Separate Branch of the Law in Belgium?

Traditionally the law against unfair competition is considered as a separate branch of the law, distinct from the law of intellectual property and from antitrust law. The relationship with these other branches of the law is discussed hereinafter. It will appear that the relationship with antitrust law is growing tighter.

Since the adoption of the TPA of 1971 the law against unfair competition has lost some of its specificity. The law against unfair competition as it existed then, i.e. a general clause translating into Belgian law Article 10bis of the Paris Convention and concretising Article 1382 C.c. (tort liability), enforced by the special action for a cease and desist order, was integrated in one law together with a certain number of per se rules which on the one hand were the codification of the existing case law on misleading, denigrating and comparative advertising and on the other hand extended the existing protection of small shop keepers against unusual sales methods and methods of sales promotion. Thus the TPA of 1971 introduced a prohibition of joint offers (a law of 1935 only prohibited sales with free premiums) and (following the French example) a prohibition of sales at a loss. Consecutive amendments introduced even stricter rules on the announcement of discounts (especially during the periods preceding the periods of the summer and winter end of season sales).

In 1991 with the adoption of the TPCA one law integrated the existing law against unfair competition – which at that time had already become a broader branch of the law, i.e. the law on trade practices – with new provisions on consumer protection. As it has already been mentioned, the TPCA also became the law in which the implementation of the EC consumer directives in the field of advertising, unfair contract terms and distant selling were integrated.

Neither the TPA of 1971 nor the TPCA of 1991 formally define their objectives. In reality they contain a mixture of rules devoted to "protect" competitors and consumers. Marcel Gotzen who defended a thesis devoted to the law against unfair competition in 1963[6] identified a "kampprijsnorm": the law against unfair competi-

[6] *See supra* note 2.

tion protected the competitor who had won a battle. Existing positions are protected. The law against unfair competition protected existing positions and usages and (later) weaker parties. The effect of the intervention of the courts on the functioning of the market was not questioned. A good example was the strict prohibition of comparative advertising. But the awareness that the traditional standards of fair competition could form entry barriers led to a progressive change in the case law. The Court of Appeal of Brussels allowed, in 1983, an advertising campaign of Pepsi Cola with the results of a blindfold test with an implicit reference to Coca Cola (the absolute market leader in Belgium) creating thus a (new) exception to the prohibition "for imperative competition reasons".[7] Other judgments accepted derogations from the ban on comparative advertising in the interest of correctly informing consumers.[8]

But 1991 was also the year that, under pressure of developments at the EC level, Belgium adopted a Competition Act, containing the domestic equivalent of Articles 81 and 82 EC (antitrust law) and of the Merger Regulation. This act has a clear objective, i.e. to promote effective competition. Naturally questions arose about the consistency of many provisions of the TPCA with the competition rules.[9] A crucial question was that about the relationship between the prohibition of restrictive practices (Article 2 of the Competition Act, very similar to Article 81 EC) and the general clause on unfair competition (Article 93 TPCA). The problem was that in the past the courts had often condemned restrictive practices, e.g. selective distribution systems and refusals to deal (ensuing from these systems) as acts of unfair competition. The Competition Act and the EC competition rules however allow for certain restrictive practices because they are "de minimis", comply with the conditions for a declaration of inapplicability (cf. Article 81 Para. 3), or are considered to be compatible with the requirements of workable competition (e.g. selective distribution systems). In 2000 the Cour de cassation decided that a restrictive practice which, like a refusal by a non-dominant undertaking to supply a prospective client, is not contrary to the competition rules, cannot be qualified as an act of unfair competition, except, so it would seem, where that practice constitutes an abuse of right.[10]

It would however be too farfetched to consider that in Belgium competition law consists of two branches: competition law proper (antitrust and merger control) and the law against unfair competition. The law against unfair competition, or better: the law on trade practices, contains too many provisions which do not deal with com-

---

7 Court of Appeal, Brussels, June 7, 1983, 1983 Journal des Tribunaux (J.T.) 717 – *Pepsi-Cola v. Coca-Cola*; The Cour de Cassation (Cass.) confirmed this judgment: Cass., March 21, 1985, 1985 Arresten van het Hof van Cassatie 1001.

8 STUYCK, "Handelspraktijken" 228 (2nd ed. 2004).

9 *See* e.g. VAN DEN BERGH, "Discriminatie van een onafhankelijke afnemer," 1993 Jaarboek Handelspraktijken 682.

10 Cass., January 7, 2000, 2001 Revue Critique de Jurisprudence belge (R.C.J.B.) 249, note STUYCK.

petition, but which aim at protecting individual and collective interests (of small shop keepers and consumers).[11]

This brings me to a last complex relationship, i.e. of unfair competition law with consumer law. The TPCA indeed does not only contain rules on advertising and sales promotions (being the clearest expression of the way in which undertakings compete on consumer markets) but also rules on the pre-contractual and contractual protection of the consumer (distant selling, off-premise sales, unfair contract terms).

The uniting factor of consumer law and unfair competition law is the action for a cease and desist order before the president of the commercial court pursuant to the TPCA. Indeed the Cour de Cassation has confirmed in 1985 that the infringement of any legal or regulatory provision in the course of business constitutes an act which is contrary to honest business practices.[12] This means that where a seller infringes a provision of consumer law (e.g. labelling requirements for food stuffs, the Consumer Safety Act, etc.) this will automatically constitute an act which is contrary to honest business practices. If one or more consumers are harmed or can be harmed by such an infringement there is a violation of Article 94 TPCA against which the individual consumer as well as a (recognised) consumer organisation can bring an action for a cease and desist order (Art. 98 TPCA). It should be noted that more and more specific consumer laws (Consumer Credit Act, the provisions on consumer sales in the Civil Code, ...) provide expressly that consumers or their organisations can bring an action for a cease and desist order.

The action for a cease and desist order under the TPCA is also often used in case of violations of EC or Belgian antitrust law. This has also to do with the (so far) relative ineffectiveness of the action of the competition authorities (limited, but now growing resources, which, in the past, have been devoted almost exclusively to merger control).

3. The Legal Bases of the Integrated Approach

As explained above Belgium has one Act of Parliament, the TPCA, which deals with unfair competition law, the protection of small shop keepers and consumer protection in the field of advertising, sales promotions, sales methods, consumer information and certain aspects of consumer contract law (like unfair contract terms). Case law has recognised the interaction between antitrust law and trade practices law. There is also an integration process between these two branches of the law as a result of two important currents in case law: (i) the possibility to bring violations of

---

[11] The author actually defends the view that antitrust law is the core of consumer law (*see* STUYCK, "EC Competition Law After Modernization: More than ever in the interest of Consumers," 2005 Journal of Consumer Policy (J.C.P.) 1-30). The TPCA is definitely an example of overregulation. Some of its provisions (sales at a loss, joint offers, announcement of discounts, end of season sales...) have also been questioned in the light of the EC Treaty provisions on free movement of goods and services (*see* more in WYTINCK, "De verenigbaarheid van de wet handelspraktijken met het EEG-recht," in: STUYCK & WYTINCK, "De nieuwe wet handelspraktijken" 176 *et seq.* (1992).

[12] Cass., May 2, 1985, 1985 R.D.C. 631, note I.V.

antitrust law before the judge of the trade practices and the broad scope of the general clauses of Articles 93 and 94 TPCA, since violations of any legal provision in the course of business which harm competitors or consumers are an act of unfair competition and (ii) the exclusion of the applicability of the doctrine of unfair competition to restrictive practices that are not contrary to antitrust rules.

Formally speaking the integrated approach to unfair competition and consumer protection in the field of trade practices is not absolute. There are indeed two general clauses, one on unfair practices vis-à-vis consumers (Article 94 TPCA) and another on unfair competition (Article 93 TPCA). However both clauses are based on the same notion of fault, i.e. the violation of honest business practices. The split between the two general clauses was only meant to make a distinction as to locus standi with regard to the cease and desist order: the cessation of violations of Article 93 TPCA (which also requires harm or potential harm to professional interests) can only be sought by "interested parties" (generally competitors) and professional organisations; the cessation of violations of Article 94 TPCA (which also requires harm or potential harm to consumers) can only be sought by "interested parties" (consumers), consumer organisations and the Minister of Economic Affairs. Nevertheless the split between the two general clauses has laid the basis for an autonomous interpretation of the notion of acts contrary to honest business practices harming consumers in Article 94 TPCA (as distinct from the traditional notion of acts of unfair competition, as now enshrined in Article 93 TPCA). In its "Movitex" judgment of 1997 the Cour de Cassation[13] has ruled that Article 94 TPCA prohibits all acts by which a seller "manipulates" a consumer. The notion of "manipulation" is very close to the notion of "misleading" the consumer. In the same judgment the Court found it superfluous to examine a plea based on one of the per se rules on advertising (Article 23, 10°: a ban on advertising that raises the hope or the certainty of the consumer that he has won a prize by chance). The Court has thus recognised the "catchall" character of Article 94 TPCA. It remains now to be seen whether the general clause of Article 94 as it is will be a sufficient basis for an interpretation which is consistent with the new general clause on unfair commercial practices of the Unfair Commercial Practices Directive[14] (Article 5: requirement of professional diligence as defined there) and with the "small general clause" of that Directive on aggressive commercial practices (Article 8).

4. The Fields Covered by the Integrated Approach

The TPCA as such relates to marketing practices (price indication, labelling, advertising, sales methods, consumer information, unfair competition, unfair commercial practices in general) but, as a result of the possibility to bring a cease and desist order under this Act in case of any infringement of a legal provision in the course of business, violations of various laws, such as antitrust law, consumer law, the law on

[13] Cass., October 17, 1997, 1998 R.C.J.B. 411, note STUYCK.

[14] Directive 2005/29 of May 11, 2005, OJ L149/22, June 11, 2005.

lotteries and games of hazard, the Price Regulation Act and even of town planning regulations and so on have led to applications of the general clauses of the Act.

Two areas are expressly excluded from this scope. The first exclusion is a statutory one: Article 96 TPCA excludes infringements of intellectual property rights. As a result of a recent judgment of the Cour d'Arbitrage (Belgian's quasi-constitutional court) trade mark infringements can now be brought before the judge of the trade practices.[15] The second area is excluded by case law: an action for a cease and desist order under Article 93 or 94 TPCA cannot be brought against violations of contractual obligations (concurrence between an action *ex delicto* and an action *ex contractu* is only possible where the act is at the same time the violation of a contractual obligation and of a general obligation which would also exist in the absence of a contract)[16] (see more under 6).

5. Which Interests are Protected?

It has been indicated above (see 2.) that the TPCA does not clearly define its objectives. It can however be inferred from the preparatory works of the TPCA that it aims at protecting the interests of competitors and consumers. In reality many of its provisions have been adopted with the aim to protect small shop keepers. The prohibitions of sales at a loss, of joint offers and of the announcement of discounts six weeks before the periods for summer and winter end of season sales are good examples of that aim. The general clauses of Articles 93 and 94 (honest business practices) clearly relate respectively to the protection of the professional interests of other sellers (generally competitors) and those of one or more consumers.

Since the law has given professional associations and consumer organisations the right to bring an action for a cease and desist order against infringements of the Act which are likely to harm the collective interests of their members,[17] it is obvious that the TPCA does not only protect individual interests of competitors and consumers, but also their collective interest.

The Act however does not pursue as such the protection of any "general interest". However in case of a cease and desist order based on Article 93 or 94, where the violation of honest business practices consists in the violation of antitrust rules or other rules of general interest (product safety, law on games of chance, and lotteries...) the Act actually serves the protection of a general interest, albeit at the request of parties seeking the protection of an individual or collective interest only.

---

15 Judgment of January 9, 2002, case 2/2002, Moniteur belge (Belgian Official Gazette, M.B.), March 19, 2002; *see* PUTTEMANS, "Action en cessation, Cour d'Arbitrage et droits intellectuals: d'oł venons-nous, oł en sommes-nous, oł allons-nous?," 2002 R.D.C. 812.

16 Cass. June 4, 1993, 1994 R.D.C. 610, note STUYCK & PAUWELS, "Oever coëxistentie en samenloop tussen de vordering tot staken en de vordering ex contractu".

17 They have locus standi whenever they act in defence of the collective interests as defined in their articles of association (Article 98, § 1 (2)).

6. Relationship with Antitrust Law, IP Rights, Contract Law and Tort Law

6.1 Antitrust Law

The relation with antitrust law has been described in section 2. The action for a cease and desist order against acts of unfair competition (violations of honest business practices) is also available in case of antitrust infringements. On the other hand the Cour de Cassation has ruled that restrictive practices which are compatible with the antitrust rules cannot be declared contrary to Article 93 or 94 TPCA (acts contrary to honest business practices), except where the conduct in question constitutes an abuse of right (e.g. a purely arbitrary refusal to sell by a non-dominant undertaking).[18]

6.2 IP Rights

6.2.1 IP Rights in General

The relation with IP rights is complex. Article 96 TPCA excludes the action for a cease and desist order under the Act in case of acts of counterfeiting which fall within the scope of application of the laws on patents, trade marks, designs or models and copyright and neighbouring rights. Article 96 is a rule excluding concurrence between the action for a cease and desist order under the TPCA and the specific actions in case of infringements of the IP laws mentioned in Article 96 TPCA. There is concurrence when two different actions based on the same facts are possible between the same two parties.

With regard to concurrence between an action for a cease and desist order under the TPCA and specific actions based on infringements of IP laws, it must first be observed that Article 96 TPCA does not mention all IP laws. Since Article 96 TPCA does not mention data base protection, infringements of the Data Base Protection Act[19] can be brought before the judge of the TPCA (by qualifying violations of this Act as unfair competition). Likewise Article 96 TPCA mentions neither plant breeder's rights nor chips protection. However the TPCA action for a cease and desist order is also excluded for these IP rights, since the Plant Breeder's Rights Act[20] and the Chips Act[21] confer exclusive competence in case of violations of these Acts to the (civil) court of first instance.

The court of first instance is also exclusively competent for infringements of the Patents Act and the Copyright Act (which also addresses neighbouring rights) and provides for an action for a cease and desist order before the president of that court which is very similar to the action for a cease and desist order under the TPCA.

In view of the exclusive competence of the court of first instance for copyright, patent, plant breeder's rights, chips and design and models infringements, the prob-

[18] See *supra* note 11.

[19] Act of March 11, 1996 implementing the Data Base Protection Directive.

[20] Act of May 20, 1975, M.B. September 5, 1975.

[21] Act of January 10, 1990, M.B. January 26, 1990.

lem of concurrence between actions based on these laws and the TPCA does not even occur.

However two other questions – not dealt with by Article 96 TPCA – can arise.

The first one is co-existence between the action of the TPCA and the specific action under the relevant IP law. There is co-existence where the same facts give rise to two different actions by two different persons. Case law has e.g. accepted that the exclusive competence of the court of first instance in case of copyright infringements does not exclude the possibility of an action for a cease and desist order by a competitor who is not the copyright holder.[22]

The second and last question is that of so-called accompanying acts, e.g. where the person infringing another person's IP right also denigrates him or makes misleading statements about his products. Accompanying acts which can be distinguished from an IP infringement and which constitute a violation of honest business practices (e.g. misleading the public; but not the fact of creating confusion with a competitor's products where that confusion is already created by the IP infringement)[23] can form the object of an action for a cease and desist order under Article 93 TPCA.

6.2.2 Trade Marks

The rule of Article 96 TPCA excluding concurrence between the action for a cease and desist order under that Act and the specific IP law infringement also applies to trade marks. This exclusion has given rise to a lot of controversy and hesitations in case law and legal literature. Some have even advocated the abrogation of Article 96 TPCA.[24] The basic problem is that there is no action for a cease and desist order pursuant to the law which implemented the Benelux Trade Mark Law (the Copyright Act provides for an action for a cease and desist order before the president of the court of first instance) although trade mark disputes are quite similar to unfair competition disputes and are very often intertwined with unfair competition in the strict sense, e.g. conduct consisting in taking advantage of the reputation and the creative efforts of a competitor by causing confusion with his trade marks, other signs than trade marks and declarations which are denigrating, misleading and so on. Finally it is argued that the rationale for the anti-concurrence rule (i.e. avoiding to thwart competence rules or to provoke a "negative reflex effect", i.e. that acts which are legal in the light of the relevant IP law would be qualified as unfair competition) would not be convincing (any more) at least not with respect to trade marks.

---

[22] Court of Appeal, Brussels, October 2, 1996, 1997 R.D.C. 434 (the plaintiff alleged that his advertising campaign had been imitated by his competitor, who thus unfairly benefited from his investment, while the advertising agency held the copyright in that campaign).

[23] In this last example there is indeed "concurrence", i.e. the same facts form the object of two different actions. Article 14 (1) Benelux Design and Models Act expressly excludes the action for unfair competition for facts which only infringe a design or model (*see* also Benelux Gerechtshof (Benelux Court, BenGH) December 21, 1990, 1990-1991 Rechtskundig Weekblad (R.W.) 905).

[24] *See* in particular PUTTEMANS, "Droits intellectuals et concurrence déloyale" (2000).

According to the Cour de Cassation Article 96, which refers to "acts of counterfeiting", only excludes the TPCA action for a cease and desist order with respect to "hard core" trade mark infringements ("counterfeiting"), i.e. the use of a trade mark or a corresponding sign as a trade mark for the identical or similar goods), now Article 13A (1) (a) and (b) Benelux Trade Mark Law. This led to a situation in which actions for a cease and desist order against trade mark infringements were possible where these trade mark infringements were not acts of "counterfeiting". Cases of "counterfeiting" were those referred to in Article 13A (1) (a) and (b) Benelux Trade Mark Law, i.e. the use, in the course of business, of a sign which is identical to or corresponds with the trade mark for goods which are identical or similar to the goods for which the trade mark is registered. The action for a cease and desist order remained possible for infringements referred to in Article 13A (1) (c) and (d) Benelux Trade Mark Law, i.e. (c) the use of a sign, in economic life, which is identical to or corresponds with a trade mark for goods which are not similar, where the trade mark is known in the Benelux territory and by this use, without valid reason, an unjustified benefit is drawn from the reputation of the trade mark or its distinctive character is harmed, respectively (d) the use, otherwise than to distinguish the goods (e.g. as a reference in comparative advertising), of the trade mark where, without valid reason, an unjustified benefit is drawn from that use or the distinctive character of the trade mark is harmed.

However – surprisingly[25] – in a judgment of January 9, 2002 the Cour d'Arbitrage decided that this distinction is contrary to the equality principle of the Constitution.[26] As a result of this judgment the courts now very generally accept actions for a cease and desist order in case of trade mark infringements whatever their nature. However, it is debatable whether the judge of the trade practices can order anything else than the cessation of the use of the sign which infringes the trade mark (e.g. the annulment of the trade mark).

6.3 Contract Law

The Cour de Cassation decided already in 1943 that an action for unfair competition was excluded with regard to conduct which can only be considered unfair because one of the parties violates a contractual obligation, e.g. the non-performance of a non-compete clause by the vendor of a business.[27]

More recently the Court has expressly accepted the possibility of an action for a cease and desist order pursuant to the TPCA in case of co-existence (a situation not covered by the 1943 case law) i.e. where an action for a cease and desist order is brought by a plaintiff who claims that the defendant commits an act of unfair competition while the conduct in question is at the same time the violation of a contract

---

[25] The author fails to see why a different treatment (the availability/non-availabilty of an efficient action for a cease and desist order) in two different types of situations constitutes discrimination.

[26] M.B., March 19, 2002, (2nd ed.); this is a preliminary judgment, hence Article 96 is not annuled. The legislator will have to adapt the TPCA.

[27] Cass., November 25, 1943 (two judgments), 1944 Pasicrisie belge (Pas.) I, 70 and 72.

to which the plaintiff is not a party (e.g. the violation by the defendant of the terms of a concession granted, by contract, by the public authorities, and by doing so abusing its dominant position). Where the conduct of the defendant is only the violation of a contractual obligation, i.e. in the absence of a contract (with another person than the plaintiff) his conduct would not be illegal or unfair, the action under the TPCA will fail.[28]

In case of concurrence (i.e. of two different actions between the same two parties) the situation is less clear. According to a well established case law of the Cour de Cassation concurrence between the actio ex delicto and the actio ex contractu in general is excluded, but there is controversy as to what this exactly means. According to one (restrictive) school the action in tort is excluded as soon as the conduct which is reproached is also the violation of a contractual obligation; according to another school (whose adherents seem to be in the majority) the action in tort is only excluded where the conduct reproached is only the violation of a contractual obligation (i.e. it is not contrary to the general duty of care resting on every person, even in the absence of a contract). In practice the two interpretations do not lead to a different result in the majority of the cases. To give an example: according to the restrictive school an action for a cease and desist order would e.g. be excluded where the parties have entered into an agreement in which one of them has undertaken to refrain from a certain conduct, e.g. the use of a confusingly similar trade name, which is already contrary to Article 93 TPCA. The majority opinion leads to a result which is the same as in the case of co-existence (see above)[29] i.e. the action in tort or the action for a cease and desist order is possible, notwithstanding the existence of a contractual obligation; according to the minority opinion this is not possible.

6.4 Tort Law

The relationship between Articles 93 and 94 of the TPCA (the general clauses) and tort law is simple: the former are an application in the sphere of trade of Article 1382 Civil Code (see 1.).

Contrary to Articles 93 and 94 TPCA the per se rules of the TPCA do not require the proof of harm or potential harm, but violations of these provisions are nevertheless, in principle, of an extra-contractual nature.

The situation has become more complicated with the introduction of provisions on unfair contract terms in the TPCA. Violations of these provisions can also be tackled with a cease and desist order. Only the ordinary judge can declare these clauses null and void, but a consumer organisation can e.g. obtain an order addressed to a seller or even a professional association recommending the use of standard clauses to cease to apply unfair clauses.

A violation of a provision of the TPCA is a fault within the meaning of Article 1382 C.c. Every person suffering a prejudice as a result of such a violation can claim damages. Claims for damages for violations of the TPCA (not so frequent) will gen-

---

[28] Cass., June 4, 1993, 1994 R.D.C. 610, note STUYCK & PAUWELS.

[29] *See* further STUYCK, *op.cit.*, 67-71.

erally follow a judgment by the president of the commercial court finding a violation of the TPCA. Such a finding (when definitive) binds the (ordinary) judge who has to decide on a claim for damages.

7. Sanctions

The central sanction in the Act, and also the most popular one, is the action for a cease and desist order before the president of the commercial court. The judge can attach a periodic penalty payment to the observance of his judgment. The judgment can be executed notwithstanding an appeal.

In addition the president can order the publication (in the press, on the radio and on TV and so on) of the judgment or a summary of it where that publication contributes to the cessation (e.g. correcting a misleading advertisement).

Claims for damages can be brought before the ordinary courts (see 6.4 above).

Many violations of the TPCA are also criminal offences (especially in the field of consumer protection, but also e.g. the announcement of discounts during six weeks before the end of season periods!) in their own right (Article 102). All violations in bad faith, of any provision of the Act, with the exception of violations of Article 30, the general obligation to inform consumers properly and Article 93, the general clause on unfair competition, are also criminal offences (Article 103). Criminal sanctions for violations of the TPCA are seldom applied.

Infringements of the prohibition of pyramid selling and of sales making falsely reference to a charitable or humanitarian action (Articles 84 and 85 TPCA) are sanctioned with severe criminal sanctions (up to 5 years prison), rightly so.

It is also a criminal offence to violate a definitive cease and desist order, but in practice parties prefer to bring a claim for the payment of the periodic penalty which is generally imposed on the losing defendant.

8. Involvement of an Agency

Belgium has no Consumer Ombudsman, or agency charged with the enforcement of the Act. Consumers can however lodge a complaint with the Disputes and Mediation Service of the Federal Service for Economy, SME and Energy (the former Ministry of Economic Affairs). The civil servants of the Federal Service have powers to make a procès-verbal, to transfer a file to the Public prosecutor (in case of a criminal infringement of the TPCA) or to propose an administrative fine to the seller concerned (paying this fine will bar the possibility of a criminal prosecution).

The Minister of Economic Affairs can bring an action for a cease and desist order before the president of the commercial court, except in case of violation of Article 93 (unfair competition). He can also give a warning to the seller concerned. The warning has no formal legal consequences except that during the period given to the seller to cease the contested conduct neither the Minister of Economic affairs nor the Public Prosecutor can bring an action in court (in case of the Minister: an action for a cease and desist order).

Brief Report on Italian Unfair Competition Law

Paolo Auteri

1. Historical Origin and Legal Basis of Unfair Competition Law

As in France, the law against unfair competition in Italy was originally developed by case law within the limits of the general tort clause in the 1865 Civil Code, according to which "*any act by a person that causes harm to another renders the person whose fault has caused the harm liable for damages*". Unfair competition was regarded as a special actus reus under tort and was sanctioned essentially in the form of liability for damages.

In 1928, the Italian legislature fulfilled its obligations imposed by the Hague version of the Paris Convention by introducing Art. 10bis of the Paris Convention into domestic law to the benefit of both foreigners and nationals. As a result, "*from 1928 until the new Civil Code was adopted in 1942*", writes Schricker,[1] "*Art. 10bis in conjunction with general tort law acted as the Italian provision on unfair competition*".

However, unfair competition law retained its close relationships to general tort law even after the 1942 Civil Code made it the subject matter of separate regulation in Arts. 2598 et seq., which, following the model of Art. 10bis of the Paris Convention, contain both a general clause and a number of individual factual constellations, together with the penalties. Admittedly, the entire regime is shaped in view of the legal remedy of an injunction, which can be issued irrespective of fault and harm on the basis of an objective finding of dishonesty. However, according to the general clause in Art. 2598 No. 3 of the Civil Code, unfair competition is characterised not only by the contradiction between the action and the principles of professional correctness but also by its ability "*to harm another's business*".[2] The remedy of an injunction (together with elimination) has the purpose of preventing the commission, continuation or repetition of a tort which is in any event characterised by a capacity to cause harm. Art. 2601 of the Civil Code grants a right of action for competition law litigation to professional associations "*if the unfair competition infringes the interests of a professional group*", but this action is intended to prevent activities that have the unfair features covered by the general clause and that there-

[1] "Einleitung: Internationalrechtliche Fragen," in: JACOBS, LINDACHER & TEPLITZKY (eds.), "UWG Großkommentar" note F 46 (1994); *see* also ULMER & SCHRICKER, "Das Recht des unlauteren Wettbewerbs in den Mitgliedstaaten der EWG" V, Italien, 4 *et seq.* (1965).

[2] According to the general clause, unfair competition is committed not only by anyone who commits one of the specific actions described, but also by anyone who "*directly or indirectly uses any other means that is not consistent with the principles of professional correctness and is capable of harming another's enterprise*".

fore are not only in conflict with professional correctness but also capable of harming competitors.[3]

2. Unfair Competition Law and General Tort Law

Nevertheless, unfair competition law is today regarded as an autonomous legal institution that can be distinguished both from general tort law and from intellectual property law.

The law against unfair competition can be distinguished from general tort law both in terms of the criterion for determining unlawfulness and by the penalties or remedies which, as already stated, are primarily an injunction and an order to eliminate, while an award of damages is made easier by the fact that negligence is assumed once it has been held that an unfair competitive activity has been committed. It is therefore regarded as necessary to limit the scope of application of unfair competition law as against general tort law. According to the prevailing opinion, unfair competition law only applies to competitive activities that are committed by one entrepreneur to harm another competitor. The preconditions for the application of the prohibition on unfair competition are, according to case law and the prevailing opinion, the status of the plaintiff and defendant as entrepreneurs and the existence of a close competitive relationship between them. Logically, the right to file a competition law action is restricted to the entrepreneur who has suffered harm or who is exposed to the risk of harm. In addition, the professional associations are entitled to file an action concerning activities that not only satisfy the unfairness criteria of the general clause but also impair the general interests of the professional group.

3. Subject Matter of Unfair Competition Law and Its Distinction From Provisions Which Regulate the Activity of Enterprises on the Market Through Administrative and Criminal Measures

Accordingly, unfair competition law is based on the provisions of the Civil Code that prohibit unfair competition in a general clause, lay down the remedies and penalties and extend the right to file an action to professional associations. Art. 2598 of the Civil Code defines a number of factual constellations that are automatically regarded as unfair. However, other special constellations of unfair competition are also provided for as part of legislation outside the Civil Code. According to current opinion, unfair competition covers any conduct that has been prohibited for the purpose of protecting competitors (amongst others) and allows the latter, expressly or implicitly, to take judicial steps to request the application of the remedies and penalties laid down in Arts. 2599 et seq. of the Civil Code. Thus, for instance, unfair competition law includes the regulation that governs the protection of business and

---

3 This traditional view of the law against unfair competition, set out in summary by AUTERI, "La concorrenza sleale," in: RESCIGNO (ed.), "Trattato di diritto privato" 341 *et seq.*, Vol. 18 (1983), is also shared by the prevailing theory: *see* for instance ABRIANI & COTTINO, "La concorrenza sleale," in: COTTINO (ed.), "Diritto industriale" 271 *et seq.*, Vol. 2 (2001) and VANZETTI, in: VANZETTI & DI CATALDO, "Diritto industriale" 3 *et seq.* (4th ed. 2003).

trade secrets originally introduced into the Patent Act to implement Art. 39 of the TRIPS Agreement and now inserted into the Industrial Property Code (adopted by Regulation No. 30 dated February 10, 2005); the same is true of the provision in the Copyright Act that protects press reports by press agencies and prohibits the "*systematic reproduction of published or broadcast information or news for the purpose of profit by newspapers or other periodicals and by broadcasting companies*". The same applies, in my view, to the prohibition on misleading advertising and the regulation of comparative advertising contained in Regulation No. 74/92 which now became a part of the "Codice del consumo" adopted by Regulation No. 206 dated September 6, 2005. In contrast, according to the prevailing opinion, the law against unfair competition does not include the regulations that use administrative or penal measures to regulate the activity of enterprises on the market in the interest of the general public, such as special sales events and sales at below cost. However, the prevailing opinion is that the infringement of public-law regulations is an infringement of the principles of professional correctness if such regulations also pursue the purpose of regulating competition.[4] Thus in practical terms, the scope of unfair competition law is considerably extended, for instance by the numerous regulations which, primarily on the basis of EC Directives, regulate advertising disseminated with respect to particular goods or services or by particular media.[5] The same no doubt applies to the regulations of the newly adopted Directive on Unfair Commercial Practices once it is implemented in domestic law.

4. The Relationship of Unfair Competition Law to Antitrust Law, the Law of Contracts and Intellectual Property Law

A similar criterion is used to distinguish unfair competition law from antitrust law. Although the two legal institutions pursue complimentary purposes in the regulation of competition, the purpose of antitrust law is to protect the freedom of competition in the general interest and only indirectly the interests of the (individual) entrepreneur (or consumer) who is affected by anticompetitive conduct, while the purpose of unfair competition law is to directly protect the interests of competitors in the honest pursuit of competition. However, it has always been assumed that conduct that infringes the competition rules of the EC Treaty is as a matter of principle also in conflict with professional correctness and constitutes unfair competition if it is capa-

---

4 Thus MARCHETTI, "Boicottaggio e rifiuto di contrattare" 203 *et seq.* (1969); AUTERI, *supra* note 3, at 415 *et seq.* and no doubt also MANSANI, "Ribassi di prezzo, offerte promozionali e concorrenza sleale" 131 *et seq.* (1990); *cf.* also VANZETTI, *supra* note 3, at 96 *et seq.* and FLORIDIA, "Concorrenza sleale e pubblicità," in: AUTERI, FLORIDIA, MANGINI, OLIVIERI, RICOLFI & SPADA, "Diritto industriale. Proprietà intellettuale e concorrenza" 308 *et seq.* (2nd ed. 2005); in case law, Corte di Cassazione (Cass.), December 17, 1994, No. 10863, 1995 Giur.ann.dir.ind. 62 and Cass., March 25, 1988, Nr. 2579, 1988 Giur.ann.dir.ind. 76.

5 For an overview, *see* BASTIAN, "Werberecht in Italien" 10 *et seq.* (1996). The view that the infringement of such regulations fundamentally infringes professional correctness is upheld by the present author, "La disciplina della pubblicità" in: AUTERI, FLORIDIA, MANGINI, OLIVIERI, RICOLFI & SPADA, *supra* note 4, at 334 *et seq.*

ble of injuring one or more competitors.[6] This applies in particular with respect to a number of forms of conduct that traditionally fall within the case groups of unfair competition developed within the framework of the general clause. These include the boycott, the refusal to deal and sales below cost. According to the Decree on the Antitrust Act No. 287 dated October 10, 1990, however, the opinion seems to be prevailing that the application of the Antitrust Act excludes the application of unfair competition law, since jurisdiction for the application of domestic antitrust law is reserved to the Autorità garante della concorrenza e del mercato and to the appeal courts, acting as courts of first instance.[7] What is unclear is the extent to which unfair competition law can also prohibit conduct that is not objected to under antitrust law because it does not have any perceptible effect on the market.[8] In any case it is generally agreed that the purposes of antitrust law are superordinate to those of unfair competition law, and that antitrust law is expected to exercise a considerable influence on the application of unfair competition law.

Since, as already stated, unfair competition law is a part of tort law and relates to competitive activities, i.e. to conduct between businesses that are in competition with each other, it is basically assumed that conduct within the framework of a contractual relationship and in particular conduct that infringes contractual obligations can of itself not constitute unfair competition as against the other party to the contract.[9] This of course does not mean that conduct regulated by contract cannot constitute unfair competition as against third parties (such as a boycott).

Unfair competition law can also be distinguished from intellectual property law. Forms of conduct that constitute infringements of exclusive rights are per se unlawful irrespective of how they are evaluated in the light of professional correctness. However, there are close relationships between competition law and intellectual property law, since the latter also performs the function of regulating aspects of competition. Thus on the one hand it is claimed that the prohibition on unfair competition in part plays a supplementary role to the exclusive rights in that it protects similar interests with respect to conduct that does not constitute an infringement of rights – which applies in particular to the prohibition on the causing of a likelihood of confusion and on the claiming of performances belonging to other competitors in relation to the right to a trademark and other distinctive signs – while it is also argued that unfair competition law should not be used to establish or extend exclusive rights, a principle that above all serves to apply limits to the unfairness of slav-

---

6 Above all MARCHETTI, *supra* note 4, and LIBERTINI, "I principi della correttezza professionale nella disciplina della concorrenza sleale," 1999 Eur. Dir. Priv. 533 *et seq.*

7 On the same lines LIBERTINI, "Il ruolo del giudice nell'applicazione delle norme antitrust," 1999 I Giur. comm. 670, and *ibid.*, *supra* note 6, at 553 *et seq.* and Trib. Roma, March 31, 2000, 2001 Giur.ann.dir.ind. 178.

8 Assenting, LIBERTINI, *supra* note 6; Foggia District Court, April 11, 2000, 2001 Giur.ann.dir.ind. 804 and Bari District Court, July 15, 1993, 1993 Giur.ann.dir.ind. 664. Concerning sales at below cost, *cf.* MANSANI, *supra* note 4, at 51 *et seq.*

9 *E.g.* Cass., March 21, 1972, No. 1023, 1972 Giur.ann.dir.ind. 28 and Corte di Appello di Milano (App. Milano), May 14, 1996, 1996 Giur.ann.dir.ind 811.

ish imitation. Nevertheless, judicial practice tends to regard the infringement of trademark and patent rights as being unfair of itself.

5. The Interests Protected by Unfair Competition Law: Meaning and Scope of "the Principles of Professional Correctness"

The view according to which unfair competition law only pursues the purpose of solving conflicts between competitors and protecting the interests of entrepreneurs as individuals or as a group with respect to economic competition was subject to considerable criticism from many sides in legal theory, particularly during the 1970s. An attempt was made to extend the scope of application of the provision in two directions. Firstly, by granting consumers or at least consumer associations the right to file an action and hence to enjoy direct protection in analogous application of Art. 2601of the Civil Code, and secondly by applying the provision to activities committed by non-entrepreneurs or non-competitors to harm enterprises if such activities have an effect on the competitive situation of the party affected, causing it harm in competition. According to this view, unfair competition law regulates economic competition with the aim of ensuring that it is conducted correctly, i.e. in accordance with the rules regarded as being necessary or useful for the optimum function of the market, such being in the general interests of everyone involved, above all consumers.[10]

However, the view referred to was unable to convince the courts and prevailing theory to recognise a right of action under competition law for consumer associations and to extend the scope of application of the legal institution beyond the competitive relationship. The final word in this debate was spoken by the Constitutional Court in 1988. In a ruling dated February 7, 1980,[11] the Milan District Court had submitted the question of the constitutionality of Art. 2601, the provision that grants professional associations but not consumer associations the right to file competition law actions, to the Constitutional Court on the grounds that the discrimination of consumer associations was unjustified and infringed the principle of equal treatment. By ruling dated January 21, 1988, No. 59,[12] the Constitutional Court dismissed the question as inadmissible. It was "*the function of the legislature and not the Constitutional Court to create suitable protection for consumers*".

However, there has been a fundamental review of the importance of the scope of the general clause and the "principles of professional correctness" in legal theory, and in part no doubt also in judicial practice.[13] Today, there is a broad consensus that

---

[10] Above all GHIDINI, "Slealtà della concorrenza e costituzione economica" (1978) and SANTAGATA, "Concorrenza sleale e interessi protetti" (1975). For a critical analysis of these opinions, *see* JAEGER, "Valutazione comparativa di interessi e concorrenza sleale," 1970 I Riv.dir.ind. 5 *et seq.* and AUTERI, *supra* note 3, at 346 *et seq.*

[11] 1980 Giur.ann.dir.ind. 204.

[12] 1988 I Foro it. 2159 and in 1990 GRUR Int. 326.

[13] *Cf.* as example of many MARCHETTI, *supra* note 4, at 237 *et seq.*; JAEGER, *supra* note 10; AUTERI, *supra* note 3, 360 *et seq.*; LIBERTINI, *supra* note 6. For a detailed exposition, *see* SCHALTENBERG, "Die Bekämpfung irreführender und unlauterer Werbung in Italien" 17 *et seq.* (1987).

unfair competition law protects not only the interests of entrepreneurs but also those of the general public, and hence also the interests of consumers, in the correct and effective operation of the mechanisms of competition. It is acknowledged that the principles of professional correctness – no matter how they are interpreted, either as ethical, commercial or legal rules – are based on the interest of the general public and that these interests are in the foreground in the evaluation of certain competitive activities.

Nevertheless, case law and prevailing theory insist that unfair competition law only directly protects the interests of entrepreneurs in their relationship to competitors in that only the latter are given the right to demand compliance with the principles of professional correctness and to file the corresponding actions. This is irrespective of the nature and the protective purpose of the rules that competitors are obliged to comply with as a result of professional correctness.

In fact, the difficulty of using unfair competition law to protect consumers is due less to the protective purpose of the substantive provisions of competition law and more to the traditional reluctance of the Italian legislature to refuse consumer associations the right to file an action for an injunction on the grounds of an infringement of the regulations that govern the market behaviour of enterprises and competition, even if such provisions also have the purpose of protecting consumers. The development of the rules on misleading advertising is indicative in this respect.

6. The Influence Exerted on Unfair Competition Law by the Law Prohibiting Misleading Advertising and the Powers of the "Autorità garante della concorrenza e del mercato"

The legal situation that I have presented above has in part changed over the last few years as a consequence of a number of laws adopted to implement EC Directives.

Regulation No. 74 dated January 25, 1992 implemented EC Directive No. 84/450/EEC on Misleading Advertising.[14] The Regulation adopted the substantive provisions of the Directive word for word, including that of Art. 1, which explains the three-fold purpose of the regime. The function of preventing misleading advertising has been entrusted to the Autorità garante della concorrenza e del mercato, the autonomous administrative authority that had already been set up by the Antitrust Act. The authority acts upon application by competitors, consumers and their associations, checks advertising within the framework of proceedings and, if it regards the advertising to be misleading, issues a justified decision prohibiting (further) dissemination and if necessary orders the publication of the decision or a corrective advertisement. The decisions of the authority can be contested before the administrative courts. According to the judicial practice of these courts, the authority does not act in the interests of the party that has filed a complaint against the advertising

[14] For a detailed exposition and analysis, *see* BASTIAN, *supra* note 5, at 95 *et seq.*; in Italian literature, as an example of many MELI, "La repressione della pubblicità ingannevole" (1994); FUSI, TESTA & COTTAFAVI, "La pubblicità ingannevole" (1993); and, for a summary, AUTERI, *supra* note 5, at 341 *et seq.*

but rather in the general interest, with the result that the proceedings are conducted ex-officio even if the applicant withdraws the complaint (for instance as a consequence of a settlement).[15] A decision that holds the contested advertising not to be misleading can only be contested before the administrative courts by the applicant and any other party if they can prove a specific interest in the advertising being prohibited,[16] i.e. as a rule by competitors and their associations and consumer associations which, as will be discussed below, have been granted the right to file actions to protect certain general consumer interests by the Law dated July 30, 1998, No. 281; however, this right is under no circumstances held by consumers, who will never have an interest of their own in prohibiting advertising whose misleading character is known to them.

However, as stated above, the Regulation also has the purpose of directly protecting competitors and consumers. The former can, directly or through their associations, file a competition law action with the ordinary courts as provided for expressly by the Regulation. The judge assesses the advertising on the basis of the substantive provisions of the Regulation. For the latter provides for misleading advertising as a special constellation of unfair competition.[17]

The original wording of Regulation No. 74/92 did not provide for any right of consumers and their associations to file an action against entrepreneurs before the ordinary courts. The protection of consumer interests was entrusted entirely to the Autorità garante. However, Law No. 281 dated July 30, 1998 allows consumer associations that satisfy certain requirements to file an action to protect particular interests not only before the administrative courts but also before the ordinary courts, requesting an injunction, elimination and the publication of the decision. This Act also mentions the right "*to reasonable information and correct advertising*". Accordingly, consumer associations can take measures before the ordinary courts against entrepreneurs that disseminate misleading advertising. Subsequently, Law No. 281/1998 was amended by Regulation dated April 23, 2001, No. 224, implementing Directive No. 98/27/EC, with the result that consumer associations are entitled to bring an action in any case of an "*infringement of the collective interests of consumers mentioned in the EC Directives listed in the Annex*", the same Directives as listed in the Annex to Directive No. 98/27/EC, which also includes the Directive on Misleading Advertising. All these provisions, as in general those concerning mis-

15 *See inter alia* the decisions of the Autorità Garante della Concorrenza e del Mercato dated January 29, 2004, No. 12866 and May 27, 2004, 2004 Giur.ann.dir.ind. 1249.

16 The Lazio Tribunale regionale amministrativo, the first instance administrative court, had denied the right of petitioners, competitors or consumer associations to contest decisions of the authority (*see* for instance the decision dated August 27, 1999, 1999 Giur.ann.dir.ind. 1429). Most recently, however, the Consiglio di Stato, the second and final instance administrative court, upheld in particular the right of action of consumer associations in its decision dated February 3, 2005, 2005 III Foro it. 403.

17 *See inter alia* decisions of the Trib. Roma, March 31, 2003, 2003 Giur.ann.dir.ind. 867; February 2, 1999, 2000 Giust.civ. 1189, and February 25, 1998, 1999 Giur.it. 335; in the literatures: VANZETTI in: VANZETTI & DI CATALDO, *supra* note 3, at 88 *et seq.* and AUTERI, *supra* note 5, at 343 *et seq.*

leading and comparative advertising, have been inserted in the "Codice del consumo", adopted by Regulation No. 206 dated September 6, 2005, which in Article 139 grants a general right of action to consumer associations in any case of violation of the provisions of the "Codice".

Following the adoption of Law No. 281/98, the three-fold purpose of the regulation of misleading advertising is pursued by providing for different measures to protect each of the protected entities and interests – the power of the Autorità garante to adopt decisions for the protection of the general interests, the competition law action to protect the interests of competitors and the action by consumer associations to protect specific consumer interests. One might say that, in implementing the EC Directive, the Italian legislature has remained true to the system of the separation of protective purposes despite the wording of Art. 1 of the Regulation. However, this symmetry in the protection of the three groups of interests is only of a formal nature. While competitors can file an action not only for an injunction and elimination but also for damages, the right of action of consumer associations is limited to actions for an injunction and elimination. Only individual consumers are empowered to file an action for damages, but they will rarely do so. Leaving aside the fact that to my knowledge consumer associations have not exercised their right to file an action in the field of advertising, since it is more advantageous to address the Autorità garante.

7. The Provisions on Comparative Advertising

As is well known, Directive No. 97/55/EC regulates comparative advertising within the framework of the old Directive on Misleading Advertising which it amended. The Italian legislature implemented Directive No. 97/55/EC by amending Regulation No. 74/92, introducing into the Regulation the substantive law provisions of the Directive laying down the conditions for the lawfulness of comparative advertising and requiring the Autorità garante to prevent unlawful comparative advertising.[18] It would therefore seem appropriate to assume that what I have said with respect to misleading advertising also applies to comparative advertising.

Nevertheless, some of the conditions for the lawfulness of comparative advertising have been adopted primarily or exclusively for the protection of the competitors to whom the comparative advertising refers, with the result that it can apply not only to advertising that can negatively affect consumers' economic conduct but also to such advertising that only injures competitors. It is probably not without significance that Art. 1 of the amended Directive does not extend the three-fold protective purpose to comparative advertising. In such cases, there is not even an interest on the part of the general public that might justify the involvement of an administrative

---

[18] On Directive 97/55/EC and then Regulation No. 67 of February 25, 2000, *see* as example of many MELI, "La pubblicità comparativa fra vecchia e nuova disciplina," 1998 I Giur. comm. 267 *et seq.*; FLORIDIA, "Il controllo della pubblicità comparativa in Italia," 1998 Dir.ind. 165 *et seq.*; AUTERI, "La pubblicità comparativa secondo la Direttiva 97/55/CE," 1998 Contratto e impresa/Europa 601 *et seq.*; FUSI, TESTA & COTTAFAVI, "Le nuove regole per la pubblicità comparativa" (2000) and AUTERI, *supra* note 5, at 352 *et seq.*

authority such as the Autorità garante whose function is apparently to safeguard the interests of the general public. There is therefore good reason for disputing the authority's power to take action against comparative advertising that does not impair consumer interests.[19] At least it should be assumed that in such cases the Autorità can only act upon application by the competitor harmed.[20] Moreover, competitors who feel threatened by comparative advertising can file a competition law action against the originator of the advertising before the ordinary courts, as provided for by Art. 7 Para. 13 of Regulation No. 74/92 (and now by Art. 26 Para. 14 of the Codice del consumo). For, by laying down the conditions for the lawfulness of comparative advertising, Regulation No. 74/92 (and now the Codice del consumo) provides for a special unfair competition constellation to supplement Art. 2598 of the Civil Code and at the same time limits the prohibition of disparagement contained in this provision.

Consumers and their associations can only urge the authority to act with respect to comparative advertising that is misleading, and consumer associations can only file an action before the ordinary courts based on Law No. 281/98 with respect to comparative advertising that infringes the consumers' collective interests "*in reasonable information and correct advertising*".

8. The Principles Which Characterise Italian Competition Law and Its Development Trends

The provisions on comparative advertising show very well both the principles that characterise Italian competition law and its development trends.

The provisions regulating economic competition such as those concerning advertising as a rule pursue a number of purposes: the regulation of the market in the interests of the general public, the protection of competitors and the protection of the consumers or users of goods or services offered on the market. When the public interest is in the foreground, the market and competition is frequently regulated by means of administrative or even penal regulations or, as is increasingly frequently the case with respect to advertising, by transferring the duty to ensure compliance with regulations in the interests of all market participants to an independent administrative authority. However, the interests of competitors and/or those of consumers may be in the foreground. In Italian law, unfair competition law directly protects competitors' interests in other competitors complying with the regulations that prohibit or require certain conduct, and with the rules of a variety of kinds to which the paradigm of professional correctness refers, protecting these interests by allowing

[19] I upheld this view in the publications cited *supra* note 18 and in the essay "I poteri dell'Autorità garante in materia di pubblicità ingannevole e comparativa," 2002 I Riv.dir.ind. 266 *et seq.*, 281 *et seq.* Meli and Floridia also argued in favour of a limitation of the Authority's powers concerning comparative advertising that was (also) misleading. However, the Authority has also held itself competent in cases in which no consumer interests were involved. Characteristic is decision No. 9989 dated September 27, 2001 in the case of *Telenorba v. Telerama.*

[20] Details in FUSI, TESTA & COTTAFAVI, *loc.cit.*, 345 *et seq.* The Authority appears to be tending in this direction.

competitors who are injured by the infringement of such rules to file an action for an injunction, elimination and damages. The interests of the individual consumers are also protected. If they are injured by unlawful market behaviour, they can claim damages on the basis of contract law or general tort law. The right to file an action for an injunction and elimination is, however, reserved to consumer associations that satisfy certain requirements, but only in the event of an infringement of certain interests or rights. The trend, partly determined by European law, is towards extending the right of action of consumer associations. However, even if they were to be granted the right of action generally to protect consumer interests, and in particular in the event of unlawful or unfair competition, they would nevertheless not be empowered to file an action to terminate all and any unfair competitive activities. Their action would depend on a specific interest in terminating an activity that harms consumers, while not every unfair competitive activity is capable of harming consumers. This requirement is not necessarily satisfied by unlawful comparative advertising or in particular by advertising that unfairly exploits the reputation of another's trademark. Moreover, an interest of the consumers which could justify the right of action of consumer associations would not be present in case of infringement of secrecy, slavish imitation, poaching employees, enticement to breach of contract and many other typical constellations of unfair competition.

9. Conclusion: No Significant Difference Between Italian Competition Law and That of Other Legal Systems

Finally, I think it is possible to state that this difference between Italian competition law, which is characterised by the separation of protective purpose, and that of other legal systems which protect the interests of entrepreneurs, consumers and the general public within the framework of a single field of law, is probably not so great if account is taken not only of the law against unfair competition in the narrow sense but also of all the provisions that regulate competition in the interests of consumers and the general public. For, on the one hand one can discern in Italian law a tendency towards protecting consumers not only by administrative law instruments but also within the framework of private law by granting consumer associations the right to file an action for an injunction against specific anticompetitive conduct if it is capable of injuring the collective interests of consumers. Secondly, it appears to me that other legal systems also restrict the right of action of consumer associations with respect to anticompetitive conduct that might directly injure consumer interests. The difference will become even smaller if consumer associations' right of action in Italy is extended to the infringement of an increasing number of competition rules. And this development will be encouraged by the new Directive on Unfair Commercial Practices.

The Scandinavian Model of Unfair Competition Law

Antonina Bakardjieva Engelbrekt

This contribution aims to give a brief introduction into the law against unfair competition of the Scandinavian countries, namely Denmark, Finland, Norway and Sweden.[1] Presenting the Scandinavian approach is highly relevant for a discussion on the future of unfair competition law in Europe for at least two reasons:

First, as is well known, the Scandinavian countries, with the pioneering role of Sweden, developed in the early 1970s their very distinctive approach to the regulation of marketing practices, which was strongly influenced by the consumerist ideas of the time. This approach, with the paradigmatic institution of the Consumer Ombudsman, evolved as an alternative to the then dominant competitor-oriented approach and continues to provoke interest and attention also internationally.

The second and more pragmatic reason to study the Scandinavian experience stems from the fact that the two most recent and important Community acts in the field of commercial practices, namely the Unfair Commercial Practices Directive[2] and the Regulation on Consumer Protection Cooperation[3], are clearly influenced by Scandinavian law and practice.[4] Given the ongoing process of transposition of these instruments into national law, gaining better insights into the Scandinavian approach can be useful.

1. Background and General Approach

Unfair competition law in the Nordic countries, the way it evolved in the 1970s, exhibits many similar characteristics.[5] It has therefore become customary to speak

---

[1] Although Norway is not a member of the European Union, as an EEA country it participates indirectly in the legislative process at the EU level and is bound by Community law.

[2] Directive 2005/29/EC of the European Parliament and of the Council of May 11, 2005 concerning unfair business-to-consumer commercial practices in the internal market ("Unfair Commercial Practices Directive").

[3] Regulation (EC) No 2006/2004 of the European Parliament and of the Council of October 27, 2004 on cooperation between national authorities responsible for the enforcement of consumer protection laws (the Regulation on Consumer Protection Cooperation).

[4] Micklitz and Keßler discern a "Scandinavian imprint on recent Community proposals in the field of fair trading law", MICKLITZ & KEßLER, "Europäisches Lauterkeitsrecht. Dogmatische und ökonomische Aspekte einer Harmonisierung des Wettbewerbsverhaltens im europäischen Binnenmarkt," 2002 GRUR Int. 885 *et seq.*, 891. Jim Murry, Director of BEUC, speaks of a 'swedisation' of Community consumer policy, *see* interview in 2 KonsumentMakt 4 (April 2003).

[5] KUR, "Neuere Entwicklungen im Verbraucherschutzrecht der skandinavischen Länder," 1979 GRUR Int. 510 *et seq.*

of a Scandinavian model of unfair competition law (or rather marketing practices law). As a first and important distinctive feature of that model, one should mention the central place awarded to consumer interests in legislation, in administrative practice and in case law. Related to this, is further the strong commitment on the part of the state to the protection of consumer interests. This commitment is institutionalised in the office of the Consumer Ombudsman (CO), which has become the "trade mark" of the Nordic approach. The Consumer Ombudsmen play a prominent role in the enforcement and thus in the shaping of the Marketing Practices Acts. As the name of the institution suggests, however, it is in many respects a question of a mediating body, relying primarily on negotiations, guidance, reprimand and voluntary compliance. Formal judicial proceedings before specialised courts[6] occur more rarely. Finally, the approach is characteristic with its broad conception of marketing practices and is consequently not centred on the notion of competitive relationship.

Historically, Sweden was the engine behind the legislative and political developments that led to present-day Nordic marketing practices law. Back in the 1960s all Scandinavian countries had their pre-World War II laws on unfair competition, largely following the 1909 German UWG prototype. With time a need for modernisation and regional harmonisation of these laws was commonly perceived. In all countries legislative committees were created, which worked closely together within the framework of Nordic legal cooperation. In 1966 these legislative committees submitted to their respective governments nearly identical proposals for national unfair competition laws that were expected to lead to a high degree of uniformity.[7] The drafts demonstrated an increased awareness of the importance of consumer interests, but were as a whole shaped traditionally with a focus on competitors' interests. This approach did not prove bold enough to satisfy the political ambition of the Swedish lawmaker for a more unequivocal engagement of the state with the cause of consumers. Therefore Sweden, in a rather unprecedented manner, disrupted negotiations and proceeded individually with the innovatory concept of a Marketing Practices Act.[8] The other Nordic countries gradually followed suit.

The new developments fitted well into the concept "market law" (marknadsrätt) advanced in 1969 by Ulf Bernitz in his doctoral dissertation.[9] According to this conceptualisation market law is this part of the legal order, which by way of framework rules governs the carrying on of business or trade and the conduct of entrepreneurs in the marketplace. Rules on establishment, marketing and competition, as well as

---

6 Swedish Market Court (MD), Finnish Market Court (MT), Norwegian Market Council (MC) and the Danish Maritime and Commercial Court (SH).

7 *See* Betænkning 416/1966 angående en ny Konkurrencelov (Denmark); KM 1967:A9 (Finland); Innstillning fra konkurranselovkomitéen, 1966 (Norway); SOU 1966:71, Otillbörlig konkurrens (Sweden); *cf.* KAULAMO, "Finnland," in: SCHRICKER (ed.), "Recht der Werbung in Europa" 9 (2002).

8 *See* the *travaux préparatoires* to the Swedish 1970 MFL Prop. 1970:57, 57; *cf.* KOKTVEDGAARD & HEIDE-JØRGENSEN, "Lærebog i konkurrenceret" 41 (6th ed. 2005); KAULAMO, *supra* note 7, at 9.

9 BERNITZ, "Marknadsrätt" (1969).

consumer protection belong here.[10] Market law consequently defines, but also limits, the fundamental freedoms in a market economy, namely freedom of establishment, of competition, of contract, of consumption and of association. In a broader sense, the discipline thus encompasses a wide range of rules from price regulation to environmental law and consumer protection. However, the most important constituent elements of market law are, according to Bernitz, the law on marketing practices and antitrust law. The concept "market law" won legislative and academic recognition in the other Nordic countries as well.[11]

Given the active involvement of the state and of public institutions in the enforcement of marketing practices law, the area came to be perceived predominantly as having public law character, or in any case as a legal area of a mixed nature.[12] This has become particularly visible in the course of implementing relevant Community Directives like the Injunctions Directive and the E-Commerce Directive. To take one example, the question of the relation of the country-of-origin principle to the private international law against unfair competition, a very controversial issue in Germany subject to lively academic and legislative debate[13], has not caused dogmatic difficulties in the Nordic countries. Cross border advertising and marketing are here regarded to raise predominantly questions of defining the territorial scope of regulatory competences of the EU Member States rather than questions of conflict-of-laws.[14]

It should be noted, however, that despite the many similarities in the law and practice of the Scandinavian countries, there are not insignificant differences between the individual legal systems in view of structure and scope of the legislation, balance of the protected interests, regulated factual situations, sanctions and

---

[10] BERNITZ, *supra* note 9, at 63.

[11] *See* MADSEN, "Markedsret" Part 2 (4th ed. 2000); GUNDERSEN & BERNITZ, "Norsk og internasjonal markedsrett" (1977). Occasionally market law is used as synonymous with marketing practices law. One speaks of market law in a narrow sense.

[12] *See* BERNITZ, *supra* note 9, at 77; *cf.* KOKTVEDGAARD & HEIDE-JØRGENSEN, *supra* note 8, at 54.

[13] *See* for instance DETHLOFF, "Europäisches Kollissionsrecht des unlauteren Wettbewerbs," 2000 JZ 179 *et seq.*; DETHLOFF, "Europäisierung des Wettbewerbsrechts" (2001); OHLY, "Das Herkunftslandprinzip und Kollisionsrecht," 2001 GRUR Int. 899 *et seq.*; MANKOWSKI, "Das Herkunftslandprinzip als Internationales Privatrecht der E Commerce-Richtlinie," 100 ZvglRWiss 137 *et seq.* (2001).

[14] For a summary of the Swedish view *see* BOGDAN, "EU Direktivet om förbudsföreläggande för att skydda konsumenternas intressen," 1998 SvJT 532 *et seq.* A similar view seems to be taken in Denmark. *See* the Government Bill concerning the transposition of the E-Commerce Directive into Danish law, where a distinctive characteristic of public law rules is said to be that the sanction for infringement is a prohibitive injunction, positive injunction or criminal sanction ("förbud, påbud eller straff") Lovforslag nr. L 61, 15. For Norway, a discussion on the public/private law character of marketing practices law is to be found in Chapter 4.2.4.3 of the Governmental Bill on amending the Market Conduct Act so as to transpose the Injunctions Directive, Ot.prp.nr. 91 (2000-2001). For a detailed analysis *see* BAKARDJIEVA ENGELBREKT, "Fair Trading Law in Flux? National Legacies, Institutional Choice and the Process of Europeanisation" 506 *et seq.* (2003).

procedure.[15] Importantly, in the 1970s the rupture with the previous competitor-oriented unfair competition law approach was less marked in Denmark and Norway than in Sweden and Finland.[16] In Denmark and Norway for instance, the scholarly tradition of treating marketing practices law (similarly as earlier unfair competition law) as part of competition law in a broad sense, together with antitrust law, has been kept alive.[17] Likewise the Marketing Practices Acts in these countries cover expressly (or have been interpreted by the courts to cover) a rich variety of factual situations that concern mainly competitors' interests.

2. Legal Basis

The legal basis of unfair competition law is in Denmark the Marketing Practices Act No. 428 of June 1, 1994, which substituted the Marketing Practices Act of 1975, and which has since then been consolidated in LBK 699/17.7.2000 and revised in 2003 and 2004 (DanMFL).[18] In Finland the central provisions concerning business-to-business relations are to be found in the Unfair Trade Practices Act (UMCA) No. 1091/1978 and those concerning business-to-consumer relations – in Chapter 2 of the Consumer Protection Act (CPA) No. 38/1978, both acts revised on many occasions. In Sweden a new Marketing Practices Act (SweMFL) was adopted in 1995 (SFS 450:1995), replacing the Marketing Act of 1975. Finally, in Norway the Marketing Control Act (MCA) of June 16, 1972 is still in force with many subsequent amendments.[19] Needless to say, these legislative acts are in the process of being revised with a view to transposing the Unfair Commercial Practices Directive into national law.[20] In all countries there is a plethora of media-specific and product-specific provisions on marketing dispersed in numerous legislative acts, which will not be discussed here.[21]

Already when presenting the legislative basis of marketing practices law a first evidence of the existing differences in approach and legislative technique can be discerned. Whereas in Denmark, Sweden and Norway we have to do with marketing practices acts that treat consumer and competitor interests in a joint manner, the

---

[15] KUR, *supra* note 5, at 510 *et seq.*; KUR, "Das Recht des unlauteren Wettbewerbs in Finnland, Norwegen und Schweden," 1996 GRUR Int. 38 *et seq.*

[16] *See* BULL & LØCHEN, "Lov om kontroll med markedsføring og avtalevilkår av 16. juni 1972: praktisk håndbok" 13 *et seq.* (1982); KOKTVEDGAARD, *supra* note 8, at 41 *et seq.*

[17] *See* KOKTVEDGAARD & HEIDE-JØRGENSEN, *supra* note 8, at 17 *et seq.*

[18] At the time of writing, a draft for a new Marketing Practice Act is being discussed in Denmark, which, if adopted, is expected to enter into force in 2006.

[19] Despite their different names, the legislative acts will in the following be occasionally addressed as the Marketing Practices Acts.

[20] *See* BAKARDJIEVA ENGELBREKT, "EU and Marketing Practices Law in the Nordic Countries. Consequences of a Directive on Unfair Business-to-Consumer Commercial Practices," Nordiska Ministerrådet 2005:424, available at <http://www.norden.org/pub/sk/showpub.asp?pubnr=2005:424>.

[21] For a detailed overview of such provisions *see* KUR & SCHOVSBO, "Dänemark," (1998); KUR, "Schweden," (1998); KAULAMO, "Finnland," (2002), in: SCHRICKER (ed.), "Recht der Werbung in Europa" (1995).

Finnish lawmaker has opted for splitting the regulation of marketing practices into two separate legislative acts: the UMCA dealing with business-to-business relations, and the CPA dealing with business-to-consumer relations. In this respect Finland occupies a unique position among the Nordic countries. The choice for a divided approach was influenced by the for the time very radical political decision to have a comprehensive Consumer Protection Act seeking to cover all aspects of consumer protection, including at present consumer purchase contracts, consumer services contracts, distance selling, consumer credit, time-share, etc.[22] The UMCA, and in particular its general clause, is however largely similar in terminology to Chapter 2 CPA (Regulation of Marketing Practices).[23]

3. Scope of the Legislation and Protected Interests

3.1 Marketing Practices

As is evident from the title of the legislative acts, the accepted name of the discipline in the Scandinavian countries since the 1970s is not unfair competition law, but marketing practices law. This is not just a technical detail, but reflects the different legal policy objectives pursued by the new legislation and the broader view advocated, emphasising not competitors' interests, but rather consumers' collective interests and the interests of society at large. Marketing is regarded as a socially relevant and important activity and not just a matter for tradesmen. The presence of a competitive relationship is therefore not a condition for applying the law.

The concept "marketing practice" is defined very broadly as any act undertaken in the course of business activity (cf. Art. 1 DanMFL, Art. 1 MCA). It is in most countries seen to extend not only to pre-contractual relations, but also to acts during or after performing a transaction.[24] Both business-to-consumer and business-to-business relations are covered with the already mentioned exception of the Finnish dual-track marketing practices law.

3.2 Protected Interests

At the centre of attention are the interests of consumers. Yet, it should be emphasised that marketing practices law is viewed as an integrated area, where the legitimate interests of traders in fair marketing are equally protected. In academic and preparatory works it is acknowledged that the interests of competitors in fair competition are largely in conformity with the interests of consumers in true and correct information and in good marketing.[25] This view is also reflected in the system of

---

[22] Product liability and product safety have, however, remained outside the scope of the CPA. *See* KAULAMO, *supra* note 7, at 11.

[23] KAULAMO, *supra* note 7, 7 *et seq.*

[24] A more restrictive approach is taken under the Swedish MFL where marketing is defined as "advertising and other measures in business activity likely to promote the sale of and the access to products". (Art. 3 (2) SweMFL).

[25] *See* for instance already the Government Bill to the 1970 SweMFL, Prop. 1970:59.

enforcement, which gives a right of action not only to the competent Consumer Ombudsmen and to consumer associations, but also to individual tradesmen and business associations. The interest of society at large in fair and workable competition forms a background to the legislation, but does not find expression in the texts of the respective legal acts.

Historically, an overemphasis of the interests of consumers and a neglect of competitors' interests could be observed in Sweden during the 1970s and 1980s. The 1970 and 1975 SweMFL consciously left outside their scope a number of situations that had traditionally been subsumed under unfair competition law, such as product imitations, protection of trade secrets, libel and discrediting of competitors, interference with contractual relations, etc.[26] Furthermore, the competent Market Court adopted a rather restrictive position when interpreting the general clause of good marketing. In a 1984 article Bernitz called unfair competition law "a legal area that has fallen into oblivion".[27] The situation changed considerably, however, with the 1995 SweMFL. A special provision on confusing product imitations was introduced in the Act (cf. Art. 8 SweMFL). Moreover, the general clause has been increasingly interpreted by the Market Court in a generous manner to cover a more diverse category of acts of unfair competition, for instance misappropriation of goodwill without proof of consumer confusion, abuse of intellectual property rights, etc. (see below).[28]

The protected consumer and competitor interests are primarily of an economic nature. Preparatory works stress the consumer interest in true and adequate information for rational consumer choice.[29] Competitors' interests in fair competition are likewise mentioned. Yet there are also other, broader ethical and social interests that are taken into consideration when determining the standard of good marketing, such as the protection of children, environmental protection, consumer privacy and protection against the detrimental effects of excessive alcohol consumption. In case law and practice it is often underlined that traders have a general duty to conduct socially responsible marketing.[30] This attitude finds expression in cases filed by the CO, where marketing is challenged because it is directed to children,[31] because it shows children in precarious situations (e.g. skateboard-racing without the necessary pro-

---

[26] Some of these factual situations, and importantly trade secrets, remained in the law against unfair competition of 1931 (SFS 1931:152), which however was repealed in 1990 when the Trade Secrets Act (SFS 1990:409) entered into force.

[27] BERNITZ, "Otillbörlig konkurrens: det glömda rättsområdet," in: "Festskrift Jan Hellner" 115 *et seq.* (1984); *cf.* BERNITZ, "Otillbörlig konkurrens mellan näringsidkare" (1993).

[28] *See* NORDELL, "Marknadsrättens goodwillskydd" (2003).

[29] *See* for instance the Government Bill to the first SweMFL, Prop. 1970:59.

[30] *See* KAULAMO, *supra* note 7, 75 *et seq.*

[31] From Finnish case law *see*: MT 1987:13 – *CO v. McDonald's Oy*; MT 1990:16; MT 2001:016 – *CO v. DNA Finland Oy*. From Swedish case law *see* MD 1983:16 – *Skandinavisk Press Svenska Försäljnings AB*; MD 1999:26 – *Svensk-norsk Idéköp. Cf.* Guidelines on the Norwegian Consumer Ombudsman's Practices, Marketing in Relation to Children and Young People, of March 1999, available at: <http://www.forbrukerombudet.no/asset/864/1/864_1.pdf>.

tective equipment)[32], it prompts toleration of violence[33], or contains 'green claims' for products, which are in principle detrimental to the environment.[34]

In Denmark, Norway and Finland the general clause of good marketing practice is interpreted to also extend to sexually discriminatory advertising.[35] In Norway sexually discriminatory advertising is explicitly prohibited in Art. 1 (2) MCA.[36] By contrast, in Sweden the objective of the MFL is seen to be to protect the interests of consumers in their capacity as purchasers of goods and services and not in terms of their sexual belonging.[37] That is why the control of sexually obtrusive and discriminatory marketing is left to industry self-regulation.

Also in other important respects the scope of Swedish marketing practices law is more narrowly defined when compared with the other Nordic counterparts.[38] The reason for this is the strong constitutional status traditionally granted to freedom of the press and to freedom of expression in this country.[39] Following a line of seminal cases of the Swedish Supreme Court, a statement or representation in the printed media can be controlled by means of the Marketing Practices Act only if it is of a purely commercial nature, i.e. if it has been made in the course of commercial activity, pursues the promotion of goods and services and has purely commercial matters as its subject.[40] Conversely, if in commercial marketing broader social and political

---

32 MD 1979:24 – *DonGeorge AB*.

33 MD 1996:7 – *Unit* concerning prohibition of an advert depicting a shoe tramping on a human face.

34 MD 1990:20 *Hydro: eco friendly petrol*; MD 1991:11 *Opel Omega: eco friendly car*; MD 1992:23 – *Lever* and MD 1994:10 – *Ariel: eco-friendly washing powder*.

35 *See* BRUUN NIELSEN, "Harmonisation of EU Marketing Law," 509 TemaNord 40 *et seq.* (2002); KAULAMO, *supra* note 7, 76 *et seq.* with references to case law.

36 *See* BRUUN NIELSEN, *supra* note 35, at 49.

37 MD 1976:8 – *CRC-Lafo AB*.

38 For instance the ethically controversial Benetton marketing campaigns using shocking photos on themes associated with human solidarity, social responsibility, compassion (H.I.V. positive person; Soldier's bloody clothes) or environmental consciousness (Petrol Duck), were in Finland and Norway scrutinised under the general clause of good marketing, whereas in Sweden such matters were directed to the self-regulatory Board of Ethical Marketing. Interestingly, the result in substance was different in Finland and Norway. The conclusion reached by the Finnish Market Court was that in particular the photograph with the bloody clothes of a Bosnian soldier did not trigger fear of war and violence (as claimed by the Consumer Ombudsman) and was therefore not against good market behaviour. In Norway the same advert was considered a cynical means of attracting attention to one's own products, offensive and unfair to consumers, and consequently falling foul of the general clause of good marketing conduct of the MCA. *See* the decisions of the different bodies with comment by KUR, 1996 GRUR Int., 251 *et seq.*

39 With the Freedom of the Press Act of 1766 Sweden was the first country in the world to constitutionally guarantee freedom of the press. The relevant legislation nowadays is the Freedom of the Press Act (Tryckfrihetsförordningen, TF, SFS 1949:105) for the printed media and the Freedom of Expression Act (Yttrandefrihetsgrundlag, YGL, SFS 1991:1469) for other media. On the relations with the Marketing Practices Act *see* Prop. 1970:57, 67; *cf.* LEVIN, "Werbung und Informationsfreiheit," 1987 GRUR Int. 207.

40 1975 NJA 589 – *Helg-Extra*; 1977 NJA 751 – *Vivo-Favör*. Specific exceptions exist in TF and YGL for the control over the marketing of tobacco, alcohol and other products, which follow however the same principle. *See* Chapter 1 Art. 9 TF, *cf.* 2001 NJA 319 – *KO v. Swedish Match* on the marketing of snuff tobacco; *cf.* Chapter 1 Art. 12 YGL.

issues are addressed, indirectly taking a stand in the public debate, the marketing cannot be stopped by means of marketing practices law.[41]

4. Relations to Neighbouring Areas

4.1 Antitrust Law

As far as the interface with antitrust law is concerned, it is generally recognised that the two areas are closely related as they both aim at regulating competition. This close interrelationship is reflected institutionally in the setting up of specialised courts (Market Courts in Finland and Sweden and a Market Council in Norway) that decide both in cases of infringements of marketing practices law and of antitrust law. The original idea has been to achieve a certain degree of coordination between competition law and marketing practices law by charging the same judicial body with enforcement.

Yet, while acknowledging the link between marketing practices and antitrust law, there has been an express legislative intent to keep a clear functional distinction between the two areas. In particular, it is underlined in preparatory works to the SweMFL that marketing practices law should not be used as a disguised means for protecting competitors against hard competition in situations that remain outside the scope of antitrust law. In other words marketing practices law should not be applied in a manner restricting competition.[42] In Norway the relationship between the general clause of the MCA, on the one hand, and the Competition Act and the Price Regulation Act, on the other, is regulated expressly in Art. 20 MCA. According to this provision, the general clause of Art. 1 MCA "shall not apply to the substance of offers, demands or agreements concerning prices and business terms and conditions of members of the business community. Nor does the provision apply to the establishment or implementation of agreements to restrain competition or to a refusal to maintain business connections". Consequently, it appears that the group of cases known under the German UWG as *Behinderungswettbewerb* (obstructive competition), i.e. boycotts, price-cutting with the purpose of eliminating a competitor, inducing breach of contract, etc. should as a matter of principle be addressed under the respective Antitrust (Competition) Acts.[43] In Denmark, however, the dominant view in doctrine and practice seems to be that there may nevertheless arise situations where it would be possible and indeed desirable to enjoin such acts of obstructive competition on the basis of the general clause of the Marketing Practices Act rather than by means of antitrust law (e.g. boycotts, price wars and the like).[44]

Corresponding to the understanding of the functional distinction between marketing practices law and antitrust law, there are separate agencies entrusted with law enforcement in the two areas, namely a Consumer Protection Agency (with CO) and

---

[41] *See* MD 1994:1 – *Botkyrka kommun*; MD 1997:4 – *Egmont Serieförlag*.

[42] *See* already prop. 1970:57, 57; for the 1995 SweMFL *see* SOU 1993:59, 198.

[43] *See* BULL & LØCHEN, *supra* note 16, at 164 *et seq.*

[44] *See* KOKTVEDGAARD & HEIDE-JØRGENSEN, *supra* note 8, 334-335 with references to case law.

a Competition Authority. Occasionally the question has been raised of merging the two enforcement authorities.[45] So far such proposals have not found approval and the "loose coordination" approach through a Market Court is preferred.

4.2 Intellectual Property (IP) Law

The close connections between marketing practices law and intellectual property (IP) law are generally acknowledged in legal doctrine and in legislative material. As a matter of principle, it is agreed that marketing practices law should not serve to extend exclusive IP rights beyond their scope and term of protection.[46] What is not protected by exclusive IP rights should be free for others to use. At the same time, it is accepted that under specific circumstances products of intellectual creativity (or successful investment) that are not covered by IP rights, either because they cannot pass the threshold for protection or because protection has expired, may need "incidental" protection against unfair uses leading for instance to misappropriation of goodwill or creating a risk of confusion as to the commercial origin of a product.[47]

The links between marketing practices law and industrial property law have been kept tighter in Danish and Norwegian law than in Swedish and Finnish law. Thus, the Marketing Practices Acts in Denmark and Norway regulate trade secrets, geographical indications of origin, product and commercial sign imitations, either by special provisions[48] or through the general clause of good marketing.[49] In Sweden a split between the two fields has been more consistently pursued. Trade secrets were left outside the scope of the 1970 MFL and a provision on misleading product imitations was not included until the 1995 MFL. Moreover, the courts were rather restrictive in applying the general clause of the earlier MFL to situations bordering IP protection. Meanwhile the principle of strict separation has been significantly relaxed, though (see below).[50]

Institutionally, in countries having specialised Market Courts the exclusive jurisdiction of these courts in matters of marketing practices law has rendered difficult the joinder of claims under the Marketing Practices Acts with claims based in exclusive IP rights, the latter being as a rule within the competence of ordinary courts.

---

[45] *See* in Sweden, Statement of Government Policy, September 18, 2001.

[46] KOKTVEDGAARD & HEIDE-JØRGENSEN, *supra* note 8, at 354 *et seq.*

[47] KOKTVEDGAARD & HEIDE-JØRGENSEN, *supra* note 8, at 352 *et seq.*; BULL & LØCHEN, *supra* note 16, 47 *et seq.* with reference to KNOPH, "Åndsretten" 555 (1936).

[48] *See* for instance Art. 5 DanMFL on the use of confusingly similar commercial signs and Art. 8 a MCA on product imitations; Art. 10 DanMFL and Arts. 7 and 8 MCA on trade secrets; Art. 9 MCA on geographical indications.

[49] For the use of the general clause as a complement to IP law in Denmark *see* KOKTVEDGAARD & HEIDE-JØRGENSEN, *supra* note 8, at 336. Concerning in particular protection against slavish imitation, it is argued that the protection under marketing practices law is compatible with IP law, because it is of a different kind than IP protection. It arises in a different way and has a different content. Thus it requires a product that is marketed, often a product which is well established on the market, and has certain market value, the protection is narrower since it only addresses narrow imitations, and it lasts only while the market value is preserved. *Ibid.*, 353.

[50] NORDELL, *supra* note 28.

Parallel application of IP law (notably trade mark law) and marketing practices law is possible but in separate proceedings.[51] In Denmark, the Copenhagen Maritime and Commercial Court which has the main jurisdiction over marketing practices claims is also competent to hear cases of trade mark infringements. Hence, cumulative application of the Danish Trade Mark Act and the DanMFL is possible and also occurs frequently. More difficult is the bringing of joint claims under DanMFL and copyright law and patent law.[52]

4.3 Tort Law

In Sweden and Finland there has been a traditional reluctance against opening tort law to claims for compensation of pure economic loss.[53] Therefore attempts to rely on general tort law in order to remedy some situations of unfair competition, for instance boycotts and predatory pricing, have remained unsuccessful. Also under the 1975 SweMFL the possibilities for compensation of damages caused by acts of unfair marketing were limited. Today, damages can be claimed for infringement of the specific (catalogue) provisions of the 1995 SweMFL, but not on the basis of the general clause (cf. Art. 22 SweMFL). In Denmark and Norway, compensation for damages can be sought for any infringement of the provisions of the Marketing Practices Acts, even for violation of the general standard of good marketing, whereby the general rules of tort law apply.[54]

4.4 Contract Law

Marketing practices law in the Nordic countries has a number of intersections with contract law as well. Thus the Swedish and Finnish Consumer Contract Acts contain provisions according to which claims in advertisements are viewed as part of the contract or can be used to interpret the conditions of a consumer contract. The general clause of the Danish MFL has moreover been seen to provide the basis for regulation of unfair terms of consumer contracts.[55] Concerning situations involving the interests of business operators, as mentioned above, the general clauses of the Marketing Practices Acts have occasionally been interpreted to prohibit interference with contractual relations or predatory pricing, thus prescribing certain contractual conduct or allowing for termination of contract.

---

[51] For Finland *see* KAULAMO, *supra* note 7, 89 with reference to MT 1999:15 – *Viagra v. Viagrene*. For examples of the parallel application of the Swedish Trade Mark Act and SweMFL *see* 1995 NJA 635 – *Galliano/Gaetano* and MD 1996:3 – *Galliano/Galanto*; MD 1985:11 – *Philip Morris* and the similar trade mark case.

[52] *See* KUR & SCHOVSBO, *supra* note 21, at 113 *et seq. See*, however, the "Newsbooster" case on a search service for newspapers through deep-linking, where an infringement of database rights was considered at the same time an act contrary to good marketing practice, U 2003.1063 SH, KOKTVEDGAARD & HEIDE-JØRGENSEN, *supra* note 8, at 288.

[53] *See* KLEINEMAN, "Ren förmögenhetsskada" 206 *et seq.* (1987), with references to early case law.

[54] *See* Art. 13 (2) DanMFL, *cf.* KUR & SCHOVSBO, *supra* note 21, at 116.

[55] *See* KOKTVEDGAARD & HEIDE-JØRGENSEN, *supra* note 8, at 46, 53.

5. Main Substantive Provisions

5.1 General Clauses of Good Marketing

All of the above mentioned Marketing Practices Acts build on broad general clauses requiring business conduct to be in conformity with good marketing practice[56], alternatively prohibiting conduct in contradiction with such standard.[57] The terminology used differs slightly from country to country: good marketing practices (Sweden, Denmark), good business practice (Norway), *bonos mores* (Finland). There is, however, no significant difference in content or interpretation. Important is the understanding that the standard of good marketing shall not only be set in view of the dominant perceptions and practices of business operators in the respective industry sector, but should also take into account the interests of consumers and of society at large.[58] In Finland the CPA and the UMCA have each its general clause, whereby the general clause in the CPA is centred on the interests of consumers and the one in the UMCA – on the interests of tradesmen. The harmonious interpretation of the two clauses is ensured by the common jurisdiction of the Market Court.[59]

In the concretisation of the general clause the guidelines, issued by the CO and the Consumer Agencies, play an important role. The guidelines are as a rule elaborated in consultation with the affected business and consumer circles, often in Nordic cooperation.[60] The guidelines are not formally binding but enjoy a high level of compliance, partly due to the involvement of the affected industry in their drafting. The ICC Code of advertising practice is likewise a traditional source for ascertaining the standard of good marketing and is often invoked in the decisions of the respective courts.[61]

The illegality principle (lagstridighetsprincipen) is widely accepted and means that a breach of statutory duties, set out in legislation outside the scope of marketing practices law, constitutes simultaneously a violation of the requirement of good marketing. This "spring-board" function of the legality principle is illustrated by cases where the marketing of illegal decoder equipment for satellite TV[62] or using the symbols of the Red Cross[63] is enjoined as being against good marketing standards. As a specific application of the illegality principle can also be seen those provisions in the Marketing Practices Acts which authorise the CO to take action

---

[56] *See* Art. 4 (2) SweMFL.

[57] *See* Art. 1 DanMFL, Art. 1 MCA (Norway); Chapter 2 Art. 1 CPA and Art. 1 UMCA (Finland).

[58] *See* the general clause in the Finnish CPA: In the course of marketing no measure shall be used that is against *boni mori* or that is in any other way *unfair to consumers* (Chapter 2 Art. 1 CPA).

[59] KAULAMO, *supra* note 7, 10.

[60] *See* for instance The Nordic Consumer Ombudsmen's position paper to trading and marketing on the Internet and in similar communication systems, <http://www.forbrukerombudet.no/index.gan?id=505&subid=0>.

[61] *See* BAKARDJIEVA ENGELBREKT (2003), *supra* note 14, at 144, 278, 456; KOKTVEDGAARD & HEIDE-JØRGENSEN, *supra* note 8, at 47.

[62] *See* MD 2002:15 – *STOP* on decoding equipment, *cf.* the similar cases MD 2002:16; MD 2004:17.

[63] MD 2000:8 – *Bodion.*

against marketing in violation of restrictions set out in so-called "annex" (adjacent) legislation (for instance restrictions on the marketing of alcohol and tobacco products, of prescription medicines and drugs, prohibitions of TV advertising addressing children, etc.).[64]

The situations that have been subsumed under the general clause in the individual countries vary depending on the comprehensiveness of the specific provisions and the approach as to the interface with antitrust law, IP law and constitutional law. For instance in Sweden, where no express provision on disparagement and discrediting of competitors exists, such acts can be scrutinised and enjoined under the general clause of good marketing.[65] Another area of intense application of the general clause is in situations of so-called "goodwill appropriation" (renommésnyltning).[66] In Denmark the general clause has been used as a basis for developing rich case law on confusing and slavish product imitations as well as for addressing some situations of unfair price competition.[67]

5.2. Information Disclosure Duties

The consumer oriented approach to marketing practices has brought to early recognition of the importance of all-sided information for consumer choice. All Nordic Marketing Practices Acts contain specific rules on information disclosure in marketing.[68] Thus, the Swedish Marketing Practices Act in Article 4 (2) stipulates a positive information disclosure duty, stating:

> In their marketing traders shall provide information which is of particular importance from a consumer point of view.

This clause is remarkable in that it is not (expressly) confined to "invitations to purchase" and sets no (express) limitations in regard to the advertising medium. In practice, however, a number of limitations have been acknowledged.[69] A positive duty to disclose is also to be found in Art. 3 DanMFL, but it applies only to situations of making an offer and conclusion of a contract and is also subject to other conditions. The Danish and Norwegian marketing laws stipulate information requirements also in a negative way as part of the rules on misleading advertising and marketing.[70] A negative duty not to mislead or act unfairly by omission is enshrined in Chapter 2

---

64 *See* Art. 22 SweMFL; Art. 12 MCA (Norway).

65 MD 1987:11 – *Arma ni.*

66 *See infra* section 5.3.3.

67 KOKTVEDGAARD & HEIDE-JØRGENSEN, *supra* note 8, at 351 *et seq.*

68 For an account of the information disclosure provisions in the Nordic marketing practices laws *see* BRUUN NIELSEN, 509 TemaNord (2002).

69 For instance information on the price is considered mandatory under this provision only in case of marketing a specific product and not in the general advertisement of a business activity (*See* MD 1981:5 – *McDonald's*).

70 *See* Art. 3 Norwegian MCA; Art. 2 (1) DanMFL; *cf.* SCHULZE & SCHULTE-NÖLKE (eds.), "Analysis of National Fairness Laws, Comparative Part" 33 *et seq.*, available at: <http://europa.eu.int/comm/consumers/cons_int/safe_shop/fair_bus_pract/green_pap_comm/studies/index_en.htm>.

Art. 1 (2) CPA (Finland). The rule is, however, confined to information in respect of the health or the economic security of consumers.

The information clauses find further concretisation in legal requirements that all marketing shall be identifiable as such (cf. Art. 5 SweMFL, Art. 2 DanMFL, Art. 3 CPA) and in more specific information requirements concerning labelling, price, special offers or specific products.[71]

5.3 Specific Provisions

Besides the general clause and the information duty, all acts contain more or less detailed catalogues of specific prohibitions and requirements.

5.3.1 Misleading Advertising

Among the specific provisions in the Marketing Practices Acts the prohibitions of misleading advertising occupy a central place. These have often the character of "small general clauses" (cf. Art. 2 DanMFL; Chapter 2, Art. 2 CPA; Art. 6 SweMFL; Art. 2 MCA) and are among the most frequently applied provisions of the Marketing Practices Acts. The Swedish provision is fleshed out with more details as to the specific aspects in which an advert should not be misleading, mentioning in particular health-related claims and environmental claims (cf. Art. 6 SweMFL).

In judging whether an advert is misleading, decisive importance is attached to the perceptions of the targeted customer group. For advertisements addressing the general public it is the presumed average consumer with 'normal' comprehension, experience and expertise that is taken as a benchmark.[72] The average consumer is, however, not seen as a rational '*homo economicus*' fully detached from reality. This consumer is considered not to have particular experience of the product in question and is presumed to read adverts casually. Therefore it is the aggregate overall impression by casual contact that is important.[73] In case of doubt, the Market Courts tend to follow a strict line of reasoning proceeding from the general consumer protection objective of the Marketing Practices Acts. If the advert is directed to a particular customer group, the perceptions of the average customer in this particular

71 *See* for instance, Art. 11 DanMFL on labelling and packaging; Art. 13 SweMFL on special offers.

72 *See* already the traveaux préparatoires to the 1970 Swedish MFL SOU 1966:71; Prop. 1970:59. *Cf.* the more recent cases MD 2001:26 – *Stora Kopparbergs Bergslags AB mot Alcro-Beckers AB*; MD 2003:31 – *KO mot FörsäkringsRådet K. J. AB.*

73 The average consumer is for instance not expected to carefully read small print or to pay attention to quotation marks and question marks used to reverse or place a statement in a larger context. BERNITZ, "Svensk Marknadsrätt" 116 (1991); SVENSSON, STENLUND, BRINK & STRÖM, "Praktisk marknadsrätt" 68 (7th ed. 1996). *See* MD 1975:20 – *Philips* on the discrepancy between the impression from the casual reading of an ad and the text in small print (Sweden); *cf.* on similar line of reasoning in the case law of the Finnish Market Court MAURI, "Finland," in: SCHÜLZE & SCHULT-NOLKE, "Analysis of National Fairness Laws Aimed at Protecting Consumers in Relation to Commercial Practices" available at: <http://europa.eu.int/comm/consumers/cons_int/safe_shop/fair_bus_pract/green_pap_comm/studies/unfair_practices_en.pdf> (visited October 30, 2005).

group are decisive. Thus, a professional audience is normally associated with relaxing the standard of deception. Conversely, advertising targeting consumer groups less capable of critical and informed judgment (for instance children, the elderly, and the sick) is subject to stricter scrutiny.

The standard of protection is as a whole high, chiefly due to the fact that the burden of proof lies with the party who makes verifiable claims, i.e. the advertising trader. The principle of a reversed burden of proof is expressly stipulated in the DanMFL (Art. 2 DanMFL) and firmly established in case law in Sweden and Norway.[74] Exaggerations are not tolerated. Claims of the sort "the best", "the cheapest" are taken as verifiable claims and often lead to injunctions.[75]

5.3.2 Comparative Advertising

The emphasis on consumer interests in the Marketing Practices Acts of the 1970s brought with it a more liberal attitude to comparative advertising in all Nordic countries. Preparatory works and legal doctrine explicitly note the value of truthful comparative advertising, and in particular comparative price advertising, for improved consumer information and intensified competition.[76] Also in case law price comparisons have been treated relatively generously. On the whole, the standard has been rigorous, though. Strict requirements of objectivity, relevance, representativeness and truthfulness have applied.[77] Partly due to the reversed burden of proof it has not been easy for traders to demonstrate that their comparative claims meet such stringent requirements.[78] Nowadays all countries have implemented almost literally the provisions on comparative advertising of the Misleading and Comparative Advertising Directive.[79] Paradoxically, the implementation of this directive, which, at least in theory, is oriented towards liberalisation, may have led to a tightening of the legal regime of comparative advertising in the Nordic countries.[80]

5.3.3 Parasitic Competition

As mentioned above, the functioning of marketing practices law as a complement to intellectual property rights has been readily acknowledged in Denmark and Norway, and more reluctantly so in Sweden and Finland. The Danish and Norwegian Mar-

---

[74] In Finnish marketing practices law, the burden of proof is reversed only when applying the general clause and not in connection with the special provision on misleading advertising, where the CO carries the burden to prove that advertising statements are misleading. *Cf.* KAULAMO, *supra* note 7, 31 *et seq.*; *cf.* WILHELMSSON, "Konsumentskyddet i Finland: allmän del" 127 (1989).

[75] *See* MD 2005:8 ("Scan") concerning among others the claim "the best pork in the world".

[76] *See* Prop. 1970:59, 63; KOKTVEDGAARD & HEIDE-JØRGENSEN, *supra* note 8, at 285.

[77] *See e.g.* MD 1987:10 – *Preglandin/Maxglandin.*

[78] *See* more recently MD 2005:32 – *Cobolt Specialisterna* on the incorrect price comparison of dental products.

[79] *See* Art. 8 a SweMFL, Art. 2 a DanMFL, Art. 4 a CPA and Art. 2 (3) UMCA (Finland).

[80] *See* BERNITZ, "The EC Directive on Comparative Advertising and its Implementation in the Nordic Countries: Especially in Relation to Intellectual Property," 42 Scandinavian Studies in Law 11 *et seq.* (2002).

keting Practices Acts included provisions on confusingly similar commercial signs and products already in their original version from the 1970s and these provisions are often invoked by affected business operators. According to Art. 5 DanMFL the use of marks and signs to which one is not entitled and of confusingly similar trade marks and other distinctive commercial signs is prohibited. The concept of commercial sign has been interpreted broadly to encompass words, combinations of words, trade and business names, domain names, musical and smell signs, and also packaging, dress-up, decorations, and the very form of the product, if distinctive.[81] In Norway, Art. 8 a (formerly Art. 9) MCA bans the use of imitations not only of distinctive commercial signs but more generally of products, if the use constitutes unfair exploitation of the efforts or results of another person and creates a risk of confusion as to the origin of the product. By the term "product" a large category of goods and services are covered, including advertising brochures and concepts, databases, the appearance of business premises and company façade, company uniforms, etc.[82] With the 1995 SweMFL the Swedish lawmaker introduced a similar prohibition on the use of distinctive products and commercial signs likely to create confusion as to the origin of the product (Art. 8 SweMFL). In Finland a specific provision is still missing from the UMCA and CPA, but the general clause of the UMCA has been invoked to enjoin the marketing of confusingly similar commercial signs and products.[83]

A common prerequisite for the application of the above mentioned provisions is the distinctiveness of the sign/product, which can also be acquired through use.[84] Decisive is also the risk of confusion as to the origin of the product or sign. In establishing such risk the courts apply an all-sided assessment similar to that applied in trade mark cases and proceed from the perceptions of the average consumer of normal comprehension and intelligence, taking into account the specifics of the relevant consumer circles. A consensus exists that prohibitions on imitations of commercial signs and products under the Marketing Practices Acts cannot extend to the functional elements of a product (cf. Art. 8 SweMFL, Art. 8 a MCA). In all countries these provisions have given rise to abundant case law and to the application of the Marketing Practices Acts often concurrently with or instead of trade mark and other IP law.[85]

---

81 *See* KOKTVEDGAARD & HEIDE-JØRGENSEN, *supra* note 8, at 346 *et seq.*

82 *See* BULL & LØCHEN, *supra* note 16, at 113 *et seq.*

83 *See* KAULAMO, *supra* note 7, 88 *et seq.*

84 *See* KOKTVEDGAARD & HEIDE-JØRGENSEN, *supra* note 8, at 348.

85 For Sweden *see* 2003:7 – *Digestive* and MD 2003:22 – *Fazer* concerning imitation of product packaging, and MD 2001:12 – *Elflugan* concerning the imitation of the design of the product itself (a distinctively shaped lamp). *See* also the recent MD 2005:33 – *Puma* on the confusing imitation of PUMA's sport shoes Repli Cat and MD 2005:26 – *Taxi Göteborg* on similar dress-up of taxi-cabs able to mislead as to the commercial origin of taxi services. Particularly interesting is the Lego case, where the copying of Lego bricks was found to go beyond the functional aspects needed to ensure compatibility and to give rise to confusion, *see* MD 2004:23 – *Lego*. A similar result was reached in a different LEGO case in the Danish Maritime and Commercial Court but on the basis of the general clause DanMFL, U 95/92 SH, *cf.* KOKTVEDGAARD & HEIDE-JØRGENSEN, *supra* note 8, at 366.

In addition to the specific provisions, the general clauses of the Danish, Norwegian and more recently also of the Swedish Marketing Practices Acts have been used to prohibit other forms of parasitic competition even in the absence of confusion. The contours of this case law are far from clear, since the decisions are to a large extent situation-specific. The general clause of Art. 1 DanMFL has been used to enjoin product imitation, whereby the courts in Denmark seem to have attached decisive importance to elements like the closeness of imitation, the systematic character of the imitation and the absence of objective reasons for copying as a means of entering the market.[86] Also under the general clause, the products that have been granted protection have been of a very wide variety: not only physical products such as fashion, furniture, household and design articles, but also TV shows (formats), databases, the specific shaping of business premises, etc.[87]

In Sweden under the general clause a special category of infringements gradually took shape, the so-called goodwill appropriation or free-riding (*renommésnyltning*).[88] According to the case law the following elements are necessary in order to establish goodwill appropriation: (i) a tradesman (free-rider) triggers unauthorised association with the product, activity, symbols, etc. of another trader; (ii) the "free-rider" uses to his economic advantage the positive perceptions of consumers established through the efforts of the other tradesman; (iii) the free-riding is potentially harmful to the affected tradesman and is likely to distort consumers' overview over the market.[89]

Still hesitant remains the attitude in Finland, where the general clause has been restrictively interpreted and confusion is almost always required.[90]

5.3.4 Sales Promotions

Sales promotions are addressed in all Marketing Practices Acts albeit in a different way. In Denmark and Norway certain types of sales promotions are subject to restrictions or outright prohibitions.[91] For instance collateral gifts are prohibited in Denmark unless the value is negligible (Art. 6 DanMFL). Prohibited is further the setting of a quantitative ceiling on the number of goods that may be purchased (Art. 7 DanMFL), whereas the use of trade stamps, coupons, commercial lotteries and prize competitions is subject to a number of restrictive requirements (Arts. 8 and 9 DanMFL). In Norway collateral gifts and lotteries are likewise severely

---

86 KOKTVEDGAARD & HEIDE-JØRGENSEN, *supra* note 8, at 351 *et seq.*

87 *See* KOKTVEDGAARD & HEIDE-JØRGENSEN, *supra* note 8, at 359 *et seq.*

88 *See* the leading case MD 1999:21 – *Robinson,* where the Market Court laid down the criteria, which have been subsequently followed in other decisions, *e.g.* MD 2000:25 – *Hästens/Skeidar* and MD 2001:16 – *Hästens/Lagans* concerning close imitations of the popular chequered white-blue appearance of *Hästens* bed mattresses. An earlier case is MD 1993:9 – *Hugo Boss.*

89 *See* for instance MD 1999:21 – *Robinson* concerning the use of the word "Robinson" on the packaging of potato chips and in a TV advertising campaign shortly after a successful TV show with the same name and trying to free-ride on the public interest provoked by the show.

90 KAULAMO, *supra* note 7, 92.

91 *See* KOKTVEDGAARD & HEIDE-JØRGENSEN, *supra* note 8, at 294 *et seq.*; BRUUN NIELSEN, *supra* note 35, at 52-53.

restricted (cf. Arts. 4 and 5 MCA). A more liberal attitude is taken in Sweden and Finland, where in the 1990s the existing prohibitions on combined offers and other types of sales promotions were replaced by detailed information disclosure requirements. Thus in Sweden, Art. 13 MFL allows special offers provided that the conditions and nature of the offer and possible time and other limitations are clearly stated.[92] Similar is the provision of Chapter 2 Art. 4 CPA in Finland.

5.3.5 Aggressive Marketing

The standard of good marketing practice has often been interpreted to also require respect for consumers' integrity and private sphere.[93] Art. 1 of the Norwegian MCA stipulates that in the interpretation of the standard of good marketing emphasis can be placed "on whether the advertising due to its design, format, extent or other measures, appears particularly intrusive". More recently, the implementation of the Community Directives on Door-to-Door Selling, Distant Selling and E-Commerce have led to the detailed regulation of high pressure selling methods such as direct marketing, sales outside business premises, unsolicited delivery of goods, unsolicited e-mail, invoice fraud etc. These rules largely correspond to Community requirements.[94]

5.3.6 Obstructive Competition

Disparagement and discrediting of competitors is specifically addressed in Art. 2 (2) DanMFL and Art. 2 UMCA, which prohibit the use of improper and derogatory statements in relation to another tradesman.[95] Otherwise, discrediting competitors by dissemination of incorrect statements is subsumed under the prohibition of misleading advertising and the disparagement of competitors by recourse to true information is tackled under the general clause of good marketing if it is considered unfair. In Sweden, case law under the general clause has initially been scarce,[96] but recently discrediting is more frequently invoked as constituting allegedly improper

[92] *See* also Arts. 9-11 SweMFL setting certain conditions applicable to the use of the terms: "bankruptcy sale", "clearance sale" and "sale"; *cf.* Art. 2 (4) MCA.

[93] *See* the case law in Norway and Denmark, BRUUN NIELSEN, *supra* note 35, 42, 48.

[94] *See* for instance Art. 6 a DanMFL on unsolicited calls, Art. 2 a CPA on unsolicited delivery of goods and false invoices, Arts. 2 a, 2 b and 2 c MCA on unsolicited delivery of goods, unsolicited marketing via e-mail and other communication means, Arts. 13 b, 13 c and 1 d SweMFL on unsolicited delivery of goods and unsolicited marketing, respectively. In addition there is in all countries special legislation on, among others, information society services.

[95] KOKTVEDGAARD & HEIDE-JØRGENSEN, *supra* note 8, at 280 *et seq.*

[96] *See* the case MD 1987:11 – *Arma ni* where a pun of words was used transforming the well-known mark "Armani" into the Swedish expression "arma ni" (in English "poor you"), implying that the prices charged by Armani for their garments were excessively high and indirectly claiming that the advertising Swedish company, Kapp Ahl offers clothes as good for much lower prices. The advert was considered against good marketing because it unnecessarily discredited the reputed Armani company. A parallel claim that the advertisement constituted also goodwill exploitation was dismissed.

marketing.[97] The special provisions on comparative advertising apply to discrediting comparisons.

As mentioned above other forms of obstructive competition, such as boycotts, price-cutting aimed at eliminating competitors and interference with contractual relations (e.g. enticing employees of a competitor to terminate or otherwise act in breach of their contract) have occasionally been enjoined on the basis of the general clause in Denmark.

In Denmark, Norway but also in Finland the protection of trade secrets is partly regulated by the Marketing Practices Acts (cf. Art. 10 DanMFL; Arts. 7 and 8 MCA; Art. 4 UMCA). In Sweden a separate legislative act on trade secrets applies (SFS 1990:409).

6. Enforcement

The Scandinavian model is probably best known for its institutional framework and the particularities of procedure and enforcement.

6.1 Consumer Ombudsman and Consumer Agency

In all countries a pride of place is given to the Consumer Ombudsman, a higher public official of high repute and legal competence, who together with an Agency (alternatively a team of expert employees as in Norway) is responsible for monitoring the market and for ensuring compliance with the marketing practices law. Institutionally the CO is linked to a Consumer Protection Agency or Office: the Swedish National Board for Consumer Protection (Konsumentverket); the Finnish Consumer Agency (Konsumentverket); the Danish National Consumer Agency (Forbrugerstyret), which differ slightly in structure and competencies. The Consumer Ombudsman and the Consumer Agency conduct negotiations with industry and with individual traders, and elaborate guidelines for market behaviour in particular industry sectors or for types of practices in cooperation with the affected industry. In most countries the Ombudsman is also authorised to issue injunctive orders against traders who are purportedly in breach of the respective acts. To be effective such orders must usually be approved or accepted by the addressees.[98] The model thus rests in many respects on an assumption of voluntary compliance and a well-minded business community.

6.2 Specialised (Market) Courts

In case voluntary settlement is not achieved, the dispute can be brought before a court of law. The organisation of judicial enforcement in such a way that specialised

[97] *See* MD 2005:17 – *Tele2* claiming that a promotional character used by a competitor ("lille Bill") has been lying and should be ashamed; MD 2005:11 – *Spannmålsodlarna* on discrediting traditional agricultural production in an advert on ecological products; MD 2005:8 – *Scan* concerning false statements that import meat can contain residues of medicines.

[98] These powers are often limited to cases of minor importance. If the order is opposed by the addressee, moreover, the CO must bring a case before the competent court (*see* Art. 19 DanMFL, *cf.* Art. 21 SweMFL).

courts are charged with this task is certainly one additional distinctive feature of the Scandinavian model. In Sweden and Finland the so-called Market Courts and in Norway the Market Council were founded particularly for dealing with marketing practices and antitrust law, but also with some other matters of protection of collective consumer interests such as unfair contract terms and product safety. In Denmark already from the beginning the adjudicative functions under the Marketing Practices Act were assigned to the existing Copenhagen Maritime and Commercial Court (Sø-och Handelsretten).

The specialised courts differ in their composition and nomination procedures from ordinary courts. Apart from qualified judges there are experts sitting on the panels or representatives of the affected interest groups, e.g. industry representatives, or representatives of consumer and trade unions.[99] The Market Courts decide most cases as courts of first and last instance. This secures expediency and efficiency. In Sweden, cases involving administrative penalty or in which damage compensation is claimed are referred in first instance to the Stockholm City Court, whereas the Market Court decides as an Appellate Court. The decisions of the Market Court can be challenged on grounds of constitutionality before the Supreme Court by extraordinary means of judicial control. The decisions of the Copenhagen Maritime and Commercial Court can be appealed before the Danish Supreme Court.

6.3 Remedies

The central remedy in Scandinavian marketing practices law is the prohibition order (injunction), which is issued subject to the penalty of a fine upon further violation (förbud). There is also a possibility to seek a positive injunction prescribing certain conduct or information disclosure (påbud). In cases of urgency an interlocutory injunction may be sought.

Damage compensation exists as a possible remedy in all countries. In Sweden, however, such claims are limited only to infringements of the catalogue provisions and not of the general clauses (cf. Art. 29 (1) SweMFL). The compensation claims can extend to material and non-material losses (e.g. goodwill loss), whereby circumstances of a non-economic nature can also play a role in determining the scale of compensation.[100] Due to the well-known difficulties of producing convincing evidence regarding the extent of the damages incurred and causality, such claims are rarely successful. The courts have a certain leeway to determine the amount of damage compensation but have been rather restrictive in their estimation.[101]

The action for damages is in Denmark and Sweden open not only to business operators but also to individual consumers (cf. Arts. 29-30 SweMFL; Art. 13 (2)

[99] In Finland the Market Court is composed of representatives of industry and consumers. The situation was similar in Sweden, but with the 1995 SweMFL the principle of representation was abandoned. Industry representatives were replaced by experts. For an analysis of these changes *see* BAKARDJIEVA ENGELBREKT, *supra* note 14, at 570 *et seq.*

[100] *See* Art. 29 (2) SweMFL; *cf.* KUR & SCHOVSBO, *supra* note 21, at 116.

[101] A reversal of this tendency can arguably be discerned in Denmark and Sweden. *See* KUR & SCHOVSBO, *supra* note 21, at 116; BAKARDJIEVA ENGELBREKT, *supra* note 14, at 580.

DanMFL). The practical relevance of this possibility has so far been limited. More significance could be attached to the recently acquired powers of the Danish and Swedish CO to file action for damages in the name of groups of consumers (see Art. 20 DanMFL, cf. Swedish Group Proceedings Act 2002, SFS 2002:599).[102] Under the Swedish Group Proceedings Act lawsuits on behalf of harmed consumer groups can likewise be filed by consumer organisations and individual consumers belonging to the group.

In Finland the Market Court can prescribe different corrective measures subject to penalty of a fine (Art. 7 UMCA). The publication of the court decision at the expenses of the defendant can also be ordered (Art. 8 UMCA).

Administrative penalties in different forms are also applied. Thus in Sweden, the 1995 MFL introduced the so-called "market disturbance fee" largely with the intention to emulate the system of sanctions under the Competition Act. However, the sanction has been imposed only very rarely and the amount of the penalties has been relatively modest, especially when compared with penalties in antitrust cases. A similar sanction was introduced also in Finland (cf. Art. CPA; Art. 9 UMCA). Penal sanctions are envisaged in the Danish, Norwegian and Finnish Marketing Practices Acts, but recourse to such sanctions is extremely rare.[103]

An often underestimated aspect when discussing enforcement and procedure in unfair competition law is the question of litigation costs. In Sweden, until the changes of 1995 the procedure was based on the main principles of administrative law. Litigation costs were then carried by the parties as incurred. The 1995 act brought the procedure more in line with classical civil procedure with a possibility for the winning party of getting compensation for litigation costs from the losing party. Arguably this change, as well as some other changes in the rules on composition of the Market Court and in substantive law, resulted in more legal actions being brought by competitors. At the same time the CO has become more hesitant in his enforcement tactics.[104]

6.4 Locus Standi

The Consumer Ombudsmen have a right to file a lawsuit in the respective court. A right of action is also granted to individual competitors, to business, consumer and wage-earners associations and, in some countries, at least in theory, also to individual consumers.[105] In Norway the right of action of competitors, consumers and business and consumer organisations is subsidiary to that of the CO (cf. Art. 13 MCA). In other words, traders, consumers or their associations must always file their complaint with the CO and can institute proceedings before the Market Court only when the CO has stated that s/he is not interested in pursuing the case. In Finland the *locus*

---

[102] *Cf.* Lindblom, "Lagen om grupprättegång – bakgrund och framtid", 2005 Svensk Juristtidning, 129 *et seq.* for review of recent case law.

[103] *See* Art. 22 (1) DanMFL; Chapter 11 Arts. 1 and 2 CPA.

[104] BAKARDJIEVA ENGELBREKT, *supra* note 14, at 585 *et seq.*

[105] In Sweden individual consumers have only a right of action for damages, but cannot bring an action for an injunction. *See* for Denmark KUR & SCHOVSBO, *supra* note 21, at 113.

standi of consumer associations alone is designed as subsidiary to that of the CO. In Sweden the CO enjoyed a similar privileged position in terms of litigation powers under the 1975 MFL. With the reform of 1995, however, competitors were granted a full-fledged independent right of action and are nowadays zealous litigants, who, particularly recently, have come forward as the main actors, shaping the interpretation of the MFL.

7. Conclusion

In concluding, several more general observations should be made. The admittedly cursory presentation above, hopefully demonstrates that the Scandinavian model is not cast in stone. While preserving its distinctive features, the model is continuously being subjected to refinement and readjustment. Changes are certainly experienced under the influence of European integration, but are also a result of endogenous processes of "learning from experience", of seeking better substantive outcomes and better cohesion with the rest of the national legal system. Whereas the reforms of the 1970s may have resulted in an overemphasis of the interests of consumers at the expense of those of competitors, this bias in legislation and enforcement has gradually been overcome. Nowadays there is a recognition of the co-existence of the interests of consumers and those of honest competitors in fair competition and proper marketing. This lesson may be important in light of the ongoing process of transposing the Unfair Commercial Practices Directive into national law.

Refinement and readjustment affect not only the substantive rules of marketing law but also the institutional design of enforcement and the rules of procedure. These institutional and procedural changes have often an important impact on the frequency with which certain interests will be heard before the relevant decision-making bodies and respectively on the shape and interpretation of the substantive rules and the level of protection. Arguably, some of the above mentioned procedural changes in the 1995 SweMFL (direct *locus standi* for competitors, more market oriented composition of the Market Court, possibility of having litigation costs compensated) have turned marketing practices law into a more attractive litigation area for both businessmen and their lawyers. The effect has been that competitors' claims are increasingly brought before the courts, making the latter in turn more responsive to such claims.

Finally, the differences that remain in the detail of substantive law, law enforcement and doctrinal interpretation between the individual Nordic countries, even after years of consciously pursued alignment and harmonisation, probably warn against all too optimistic forecasts for harmonisation at the European level. Unfair competition law has been and remains a disparate area where a whole array of public policy objectives are involved. The discipline is moreover intertwined in a complex way with other branches of law such as intellectual property, antitrust, tort law, consumer law, contract law, playing often a complementary function. Last but not least, constitutional law and fundamental rights set important limitations. Therefore the specific shaping of national unfair competition law is influenced by the national idiosyncrasies of these other adjacent legal areas, which accounts for the many faces of unfair competition law and for the elusive enterprise of its harmonisation.

Unfair Competition Law in the United Kingdom

Jennifer Davis

It is a generally accepted truth that the United Kingdom has neither a general statute protecting traders against unfair competition nor has it developed a general tort of unfair competition.[1] However, if one examines judicial dicta this conclusion appears less certain. For example, recently in *Arsenal v. Reed* (2003)[2], the ECJ set out important principles as to when use of a registered trade mark is infringing use.[3] However, in the United Kingdom where the case originated, *Arsenal v. Reed* has also been widely touted as the case in which the Court of Appeal finally recognised that domestic law does indeed encompass a general tort of unfair competition. In the case, the claimants were a football club who had a number of registered trade marks, including the word "Arsenal" and a shield logo, registered against a range of goods, including clothing; the defendant Mr. Reed was a trader who had sold clothing carrying the Arsenal trade marks outside the Club's ground for many years. The claimant brought an action against Mr. Reed for registered trade mark infringement, which raised the questions subsequently addressed by the ECJ. The Club also sued Mr. Reed in the tort of passing off. In his judgement, Lord Justice Aldous noted obiter that the "cause of action traditionally called passing off, [is] perhaps best referred to as unfair competition".[4] In making this observation, Lord Justice Aldous took as his authority a statement made by Mr. Justice Cross as long ago as 1969[5] referring to another passing off case, *Bollinger and Costa Brava Wine*[6], decided in 1960. According to Mr. Justice Cross: "In truth the decision [in *Bollinger*] went beyond the well-trodden paths of passing-off into the unmapped area of 'unfair trading' or 'unlawful competition'."

Nonetheless, those who adhere to the majority view regarding the UK and unfair competition might also find judicial dicta during this same period which points the other way. For example, in *Cadbury-Schweppes v. The Pub Squash* (1981),[7] again

---

1 *See* for example, CORNISH & LLEWELYN, "Intellectual Property: Patents, Copyright, Trade Marks and Allied Rights" 13 (5th ed. 2003); SANDERS, "Unfair Competition Law: The Protection of Intellectual and Industrial Property" 23 (1997); ROBERTSON & HORTON, "Does the United Kingdom Need an Unfair Competition Law?," 12 E.I.P.R. 568 (1995).

2 ECJ, November 12, 2002, Case C-206/01, 2003 ETMR 19 – *Arsenal v. Reed.*

3 For an account *see* SUMROY & BADGER, "Infringing 'Use in the Course of Trade': Trade Mark Use and the Essential Function of a Trade Mark," in: PHILLIPS & SIMON (eds.), "Trade Mark Use" 163-180 (2005).

4 2003 ETMR 73 CA at Para. 70 – *Arsenal v. Reed.*

5 High Court of Justice, 1969 R.P.C. 1 at 23, 28 – *Vine Products Ltd. v. MacKenzie & Co Ltd.*

6 High Court of Justice, 1960 R.P.C. 16 and 1961 R.P.C. 116 – *Bollinger, J. v. Costa Brava Wine Coy. Ltd.*

7 Supreme Court of New South Wales, 1981 R.P.C. 429, at 463 – *Cadbury-Schweppes Pty. Ltd. v. The Pub Squash Co. Ltd.*

concerning passing off, Mr. Justice Powell concluded that the judgement in the Bollinger case had not brought into being "a new species of tort", unfair competition, "independent of the tort of passing off". And this was a conclusion which Lord Scarman chose not to challenge when the case subsequently came before the Privy Council.[8] As recently as 1994, Mr. Justice Jacob in *Hodgkinson Corby v. Wards Mobility Services* (1995) stated plainly that in the UK, "There is no tort of competition".[9] This essay will look at the law related to unfair competition in the UK. It will suggest that much of the confusion, which is to be found both in judicial dicta and academic comment, as to whether and to what extent domestic law protects against unfair competition, might be overcome by identifying exactly what is meant by "unfair competition" in these contexts. It will suggest that what constitutes "unfair competition" in the UK has historically been narrowly defined by judges, successive governments and indeed by academics and that, at least in relation to the courts, this continues to be the case.[10] The first part of this essay will look at how statute law in general protects against anti-competitive practices and provides consumer protection against unfair trade practices. It will suggest that these two aims are to be distinguished from the protection against unfair competition, which is afforded to traders through the torts of passing off and malicious falsehood. The second part of this essay will look at both passing off and malicious falsehood. It will be argued that it is these two torts which offer the primary defence for traders against what, in the UK, is generally understood as unfair competition. Finally, this essay will consider the possibility that the UK courts might in the future develop a general tort of unfair competition, either through the extension of the tort of passing off or through the development of a sui generis tort. It will suggest that the historical reasons underlying the unwillingness of the courts to develop a general tort of unfair competition, in particular their belief that the public interest is best served through a minimum of judicial intrusion into the market, still obtains. This point will be illustrated by an examination of how the courts have interpreted the comparative advertising provisions of the 1994 Trade Marks Act. The essay will conclude that the evidence points away from the emergence of a general tort of unfair competition any time soon.

---

[8] In turn, Lord Scarman was endorsing the opinion stated a year earlier by Lord Diplock that although the judgement in Bollinger went "rather further" than previous passing actions, it still fell clearly within that tort. 1979 F.S.R. 397 – *Erven Warnink Besloten Vennootschap and Another Appellants v. J. Townend & Sons (Hull) Ltd. and Another Respondents*. In making his statement, Lord Diplock explicitly disagreed with the statement of Lord Cross in *Vine v MacKenzie*.

[9] Court of Justice, 1995 F.S.R. 169 at 175 – *Hodgkinson Corby Ltd. and Another v. Wards Mobility Services Ltd.*

[10] Art. 10*bis* of the Paris Convention provides a definition of unfair competition. However, in the UK the law affecting unfair competition has developed without reference to Art. 10*bis*. DWORKIN, "Unfair Competition: Is the Common Law Developing a New Tort?," 1 E.I.P.R. 242 (1979). On Art. 10*bis see* also WADLOW, "The Law of Passing Off" 52-93 (3rd ed. 2004).

1. Anti-competitive Practices and Consumer Protection

We have suggested that in the UK the concept of unfair competition is a narrow one. Before turning to look at how its remit has been circumscribed in case law, it is worth noting that there are, of course, a range of legal rules which address competition more generally in the UK, including aspects of competition which in other jurisdictions might fall to be dealt with by general unfair competition laws. What these latter measures have in common is that they are generally creatures of statute, that they are more likely to address competition in the context of the relationship between business and consumers, rather than between businesses, although not exclusively so, and finally that more often than not they carry criminal rather than civil penalties.[11] Thus, the 1998 Competition Act and the 2002 Enterprise Act are modelled on Arts. 81 and 82, Treaty of Rome. Generally, the Competition Act outlaws agreements which restrict competition and forbids the abuse of a dominant position.[12] The Competition Act also established the Competition Commission whose role is to investigate mergers and acquisitions as well as general trade practices which may distort the market.[13] The Commission can adopt remedies to deal with the problems identified by its investigations. The Enterprise Act most notably established the Office of Fair Trading (OFT). The OFT's stated goal is "to make markets work well for consumers".[14] It is charged with enforcing competition and consumer protection rules.[15] It may also bring actions on behalf of consumers. Given that their primary focus is the functioning of the markets, it is possible to categorise both these Acts as being concerned with anti-competitive practices rather than with unfair competition.[16]

The Trade Descriptions Act and the Control of Misleading Advertising Regulations are perhaps the two most important pieces of legislation regulating the relationship between businesses and consumers, rather than between businesses. As such, it is submitted that they are more accurately described as consumer protection laws rather than laws addressing unfair competition. The Trade Descriptions Act imposes criminal remedies for, inter alia, applying false or misleading descriptions of goods. The Act defines which descriptions of goods are deemed to be trade descriptions, including descriptions relating to quantity or size, composition, methods of manufacture, fitness for purpose, other physical characteristics, claims that the goods have been tested or approved and claims about the history of the goods

---

[11] Where the Acts introduce an action carrying civil penalties, it is most likely such actions will not be initiated by individual consumers but rather by representative bodies, such as the Office of Fair Trading (OFT).

[12] WHISH, "Competition Law" 70 (5th ed. 2003).

[13] For example, the Commission is presently investigating store credit cards which they believe are supplied in such a way that distorts the market.

[14] WHISH, *supra* note 12, at 67.

[15] Including the Control of Misleading Advertising Regulations 1998, the Consumer Credit (Advertisements) Regulations 1989, the Unfair Terms in Consumer Regulations 1999.

[16] CORNISH & CLARK make this distinction in their book "Law and Society in England 1750-1950" 267 (1989).

including previous ownership or use. Interestingly, the Act also covers false descriptions as to origin, and thus offers remedies for the use by a trader of a "false" trade mark or brand name. As a result the Act is often used to address the problem of counterfeit goods. The Trade Descriptions Act thus covers types of behaviour which are also dealt with by the common law tort of passing off and the 1994 Trade Marks Act (TMA 1994).[17] The Control of Misleading Advertising Regulations[18] outlaws advertising which, inter alia, contains false statements of fact or conceals or omits important facts. Complaints, in the first instance, are handled by the Advertising Standards Authority (ASA) but, following a referral from the ASA, complaints may be investigated by the OFT which can seek an injunction to stop the advertisement. In addition, the Control of Misleading Advertising Regulations covers comparative advertising which may be misleading. The regulation of comparative advertising is also now covered by the TMA 1994; while misleading advertising more generally may be the subject of an action in passing off.[19] Thus, like the Trade Descriptions Act, the Regulations trespass on ground which is already occupied by laws relating to unfair competition. However, both the Regulations and the Act differ from the latter, not least because of their emphasis on the relationship between the trader and consumer and the fact that they prescribe action to be taken by state agencies rather than by individuals.

Another perspective on the divide between consumer protection laws and unfair competition in the UK is offered by the Government's approach to the implementation of the Unfair Commercial Practices Directive.[20] The Government describes the Directive as having its effect on "unfair trading practices" rather than unfair competition.[21] As such, the government makes it clear that the Directive affects the relationship between the consumer and the trader, and is, indeed, primarily concerned with consumer protection not with business relationships. Thus, according to the

---

[17] The 1994 Trade Marks Act introduces criminal penalties for trade mark infringement. It is an offence for a person who with a view to gain for himself or another, or with intent to cause loss to another, and without the consent of the proprietor, *inter alia* applies to goods or their packaging a sign identical to, or likely to be mistaken for a registered trade mark. (Section 92 (a)). This section of the Act was designed to address the problem of counterfeit goods operations.

[18] The control of Misleading Advertisements Regulations 1998 (SI 1998/915) is amended to implement the EU Directives on misleading and comparative advertising. There is also a British Code of Advertising, Sales Promotion and Direct Marketing, which is voluntary and requires advertising to "accept the principles of fair competition generally accepted in business" and "to be prepared with a sense of responsibility to consumers and society" <www.asa.org.uk>.

[19] Section 10 (6) TMA 1994. The approach of the UK courts to comparative advertising is addressed in Part 3 below.

[20] (2005/29/EC). It is expected that the Directive will be fully implemented in the UK by June 2007 and come into force in December 2007.

[21] DTI, "Operation of General Rules and the Notion of Fairness in English Law". According to this report, "English law tends to prioritise different values to those favoured by other European legal systems. First, as a matter of doctrinal form, English contract law prefers specific provisions to general clauses; and, secondly, a matter of doctrinal substance, the default values of English contract law are those of self-reliance and individualism rather than mutuality and cooperation". Report, Para. 6 <www.dti.gov.uk/ccp/topics1/unfair.htm>.

government[22] the Directive "covers all unfair business-to-consumer commercial practices that harm consumers' economic behaviour before and after a commercial transaction". It sees the Directive's primary application against commercial practices which are either misleading or "aggressive". Generally, for a practice to be judged "unfair", it must, according to the Department of Trade and Industry (DTI), "impair the average consumer's judgement so that he takes (or is likely to take) a transactional decision he would not have taken otherwise". The major change that the government therefore foresees as being necessary for existing consumer legislation is that it be amended to incorporate this test of unfairness.[23] The government lists 26 Acts, which it believes will need to be amended, including the Trade Descriptions Act.[24] By contrast, there is no mention of the effect of the Directive on common law rules which have been developed to address unfair competition, and in particular misrepresentation.[25] Nor is there any intimation that new legislation will be necessary to address aspects of unfair competition which are not now covered by various common law remedies. It may of course be argued that the distinction between unfair trading practices and unfair competition is a narrow one. Unfair trading practices adopted by one trader, while impacting on the consumer, will almost certainly also disadvantage all other competing traders who do not adopt the same practices. However, it is submitted here that the law which addresses unfair competition as it is properly understood in the UK is concerned primarily with the direct relationship between competing traders. It is to the law relating to unfair competition that this essay now turns.

2. Unfair Competition and the Economic Torts: Passing off and Malicious Falsehood

We have noted that the prevailing view is that the UK does not have a general tort dealing with unfair competition. Instead, the courts have developed a number of specific torts which deal with different aspects of unfair competition.[26] There is rather less agreement as to how one identifies those torts which should be viewed as primarily addressing issues of unfair competition. For example, Carty in her book,

---

[22] "Report of DTI Workshop on the Effectiveness of Criminal Sanctions Following Transposition of the Unfair Commercial Practices (UCP) Directive" 18 (June 2005) <www.dti.gov.uk/ccp/topics1/unfair.htm>.

[23] *Supra* note 22, at 3.

[24] "The Executive Summary of the DTI's formal consultation paper on implementing the EU Directive on Unfair Commercial Practices and amending Consumer legislation" 7 (December 2005) <http://www.dti.gov.uk/ccp/consultpdf/ucpukcondoc.pdf>.

[25] The Report commissioned by the Government to examine the implementation of the Directive, discusses misrepresentation only in the context of breach of contract between the trader and the consumer, 49. It explicitly states that it will not consider misrepresentation in the context of common law or equity. TWIGG-FLESNER, PARRY, HOWELLS, NORDHAUSEN, MICKLITZ, STUYCK, WILHELMSSON, "An Analysis of the application and scope of the Unfair Commercial Practices Directive: a report for the Department of Trade and Industry," May 18, 2005, <www.dti.gov.uk/ccp/topics1/unfair.htm>.

[26] SANDERS, *supra* note 1, at 24; *see* also CARTY, "An Analysis of the Economic Torts" 11 (2001).

An Analysis of the Economic Torts, identifies six different torts, including conspiracy, inducing breach of contract, passing off and malicious falsehood which "attack excessive competition or economic endeavour through diversion of custom or attacks on commercial links".[27] By contrast, Robertson and Horton suggest that there are three key torts which address aspects of unfair competition: passing off, inducing breach of contract and injurious (or malicious) falsehood.[28] Cornish and Llewelyn note that certain aspects of the law of confidence also protect against acts of unfair competition.[29] This section will focus on the torts of malicious falsehood and passing off, for three reasons. First, it would be fair to say that, in general, it is these two torts which address most closely those acts which are accepted both domestically and internationally as constituting unfair competition. Secondly, in recent decades, it has been the tort of passing off that has been viewed by both the judiciary and academic observers as most likely to provide the basis for the development of a general tort of unfair competition. Thirdly, when the judiciary now addresses unfair competition, it does so, with perhaps one key exception, in the context of passing off actions. The exception is comparative advertising, which is now covered by Section 10 (6) of the 1994 Trade Marks Act.[30] Finally, it is worth noting that in contrast to actions relating to unfair trade practices which, as we have seen, are generally initiated by the state, an action for passing off or malicious falsehood will be brought by a trader against a competitor. Furthermore, the remedies for both passing off and malicious falsehood, characteristically an injunction, damages or an account of profits, are all designed to be of direct benefit to the claimant, rather than to the consumer at large.

The tort of malicious falsehood, sometimes called injurious falsehood or trade libel, has three basic components. There must be a falsehood, which must be "malicious" in that it is calculated to cause damage.[31] The falsehood must have some connection with the claimant, rather than be a general falsehood which might affect all the traders in the same class.[32] The element of malice is subjective. In other words, the defendant must either know his statement is untrue or be reckless as to whether it were false or not.[33] Finally, the claimant must show that the words of the defendant caused him special damage. Alternatively, if the words were calculated to cause pecuniary damage in respect of the claimant's trade or business, then damage will be

---

[27] CARTY, *supra* note 26, at 2. The other torts she identifies are unlawful conspiracy, intimidation, unlawful interference with trade, deceit and the tort of negligence. *See* also DWORKIN, *supra* note 10, at 241.

[28] ROBERTSON & HORTON, *supra* note 1, at 569.

[29] CORNISH & LLEWELYN, *supra* note 1, at 13. Most obviously by protecting ideas which are communicated under an obligation of confidence, provided they are identifiable, original, of potential commercial attractiveness and capable of reaching fruition. 1984 QB 44 – *Fraser v. Thames Television Ltd.*

[30] The approach of the UK courts to comparative advertising is considered in section 3 below.

[31] Court of Appeal, 1991 F.S.R. 62 as per Glidewell LJ at 66 – *Kaye v. Robertson.*

[32] 1985 A.C.154 as per Lord Watson at 166 – *White v. Mellin. See* also High Court of Justice, 1999 F.S.R. 161 at 165 – *Schulke & Mayr U.K. Ltd. and Another v. Alkapharm U.K. Ltd.*

[33] *Supra* note 31, as per Glidewell LJ at 66.

assumed.[34] It is a defence against malicious falsehood to show that the alleged misrepresentation is true. The type of misrepresentations covered by malicious falsehood includes allegations that the goods of the claimant are counterfeit or inferior. Malicious falsehood might also cover false statements that the claimant has ceased trading or that its goods are hazardous.[35]

Despite the breadth of the misrepresentations which might fall to be described as a malicious falsehood, the tort has not been widely used. There are a number of reasons for this. One common use for malicious falsehood had been in cases of comparative advertising. Comparative advertising is now covered by the Trade Marks Act 1994.[36] Secondly, there is a considerable overlap between the situations which might be covered by an action for passing off and one for malicious falsehood. However, with passing off, it is not necessary for the claimant to prove malice on the part of the defendant. Thirdly, the courts have generally been reluctant to find malice unless the defendant's behaviour is particularly reprehensible and the claimant is "deserving", for fear of interfering with legitimate competition.[37] In particular, the courts have consistently held that mere "puffing" – that is claiming that one's goods are better than those of a competitor either explicitly or implicity – would not be actionable under this tort. The test is: "whether a reasonable man would take the claim being made as being a serious claim or not".[38] In general, the courts have taken the view that the public is assumed to expect a degree of hyperbole in advertising and thus only infrequently will the "reasonable man" test lead to a finding of malicious falsehood.[39] It has been suggested that behind this test lies the courts' reluctance to become involved in judging the merits of rival brands in the context of comparative advertising.[40] Indeed, it has been further asserted that the courts' continuing insistence upon a malicious statement about the claimant or his goods ensures that the tort of malicious falsehood is "one of the chief barriers to the adoption of any broad conception of unfair competition".[41]

Malicious falsehood is concerned with the defendant's making false representations about the claimant's goods. By contrast, passing off is primarily concerned with the defendant's making false representations about its own. It is worth noting that, despite the dicta of Lord Justice Aldous in *Arsenal v. Reed*, passing off is not conterminous with unfair competition. Passing off is concerned with a misrepre-

---

34 Section 3 (1) Defamation Act 1952.

35 For a full list, *see* WADLOW, *supra* note 10, at 386-390.

36 And the Trade Descriptions Act. *See* above.

37 CARTY, *supra* note 26, at 172.

38 High Court of Justice, 1975 F.S.R. 323 – *De Beers Abrasive Products Ltd. v. International General Electric Co. of New York Ltd.*

39 *See* for example the comparative advertising cases, High Court of Justice, 1996 R.P.C. 307 – *Barclays Bank plc v. RBS Advanta* and High Court of Justice, 1997 F.S.R. 34 – *Vodafone Group plc v. Orange Personal Communications Services Ltd.*

40 WADLOW, *supra* note 10, at 401. The courts have developed a similar test in relation to comparative advertising under the Trade Marks Act 1994.

41 CORNISH & LLEWELYN, *supra* note 1, at 629. *See* also *Schulke & Maryr v. Alkapharm* as per Jacob J., *supra* note 32, at 164.

sentation by a trader which causes or is likely to cause damage to the claimant's goodwill. As Adams points out, such misrepresentations fall within the definition of unfair competition offered by Art. 10*bis* of the Paris Convention, but there are other types of misrepresentation identified under Art. 10*bis* which will not be addressed by passing off. [42] For example, in *Schulke & Mayr v. Alkapharm* (1997), the defendant made misleading claims about the quality of his own goods which suggested they were of the same quality as the claimant's goods. However, the defendant did not refer to the claimant's goods in so doing. This was held not to constitute passing off by Mr. Justice Jacob, who noted that, "Passing off involves not only a false representation but a false representation related to the plaintiff's product or goodwill, not a false representation in the air".[43] Nor, it is submitted, does passing off offer a general remedy for "misappropriation". Passing off will not protect against "slavish" copying of a product were there is no customer confusion. According to Mr. Justice Jacob in *Hodgkinson Corby v. Wards Mobility*: "There is no tort of copying. There is no tort of taking a man's market or customers... There is no tort of making use of another's goodwill as such."[44] Nor does passing off provide a general remedy against brand "look-a-like" products which do not give rise to customer confusion.[45]

At the centre of the tort of passing off is deception. Furthermore, in the "classic" formulation of passing off, this deception must damage the claimant's goodwill.[46] Goodwill has been defined as the "attractive force which brings in custom".[47] It is distinct from the get up or indicia under which the claimant may trade and which may have become distinctive of his goodwill. Goodwill is understood by the courts to be a form of property, and in its traditional form, passing off will protect damage to goodwill rather than to the claimant's get-up or insignia as such.[48] Passing off has its roots in the tort of deception. However, unlike the tort of malicious falsehood, passing off does not now depend upon any fraudulent intent by the defendant. Nonetheless, at the centre of the tort of passing off is the necessity for

---

[42] ADAMS, "Unfair Competition: Why a Need is Unmet," 8 E.I.P.R. 259, 260 (1992).

[43] *Schulke & Mayr v. Alkapharm, supra* note 32, at 166.

[44] *Hodgkinson Corby v. Wards Mobility Services, supra* note 9, at 174-175.

[45] MILLS, "Own Label Products and the "Lookalike" Phenomenon: A Lack of Trade Dress and Unfair Competition Protection," 17 E.I.P.R. 116 (1995). Although, in 1997 R.P.C. 513 – *United Biscuits (UK) Ltd. v. Asda Stores Ltd.*, the court found deception in part because the defendant, a supermarket chain selling "own brand" products, had chosen to "live dangerously" by appropriating aspects of the claimant's packaging.

[46] The "classic trinity" of goodwill, misrepresentation and damage was identified in 1990 R.P.C. 341 HL – *Reckitt & Colman Products Ltd. v. Borden Inc.* If goodwill and a misrepresentation are present the court is likely to assume damage or its likelihood. WADLOW, *supra* note 10, at 254-255.

[47] 1901 AC 271 as per Lord Macnaghten – *IRC v. Muller & Cos. Margarine Ltd.*

[48] Judicial Committee of the Privy Council, 1976 F.S.R. 256 – *Star Industrial Co. Ltd. v. Yap Keww Kor (trading as New Star Industrial Co.)* as per Lord Diplock. *See* WADLOW, *supra* note 10, at 107-114. The question of whether passing off now protects the get-up or indicia apart from goodwill will be considered below.

the claimant to show that customers or prospective customers of its product or services have been deceived. Customers are to be taken as they are found.[49] They are not "morons in a hurry"[50], but are assumed to be "normally observant"[51]. In fact, the customer in passing off bears a close resemblance to the "average consumer", who has been identified in European unfair competition law and now finds a place in the Unfair Commercial Practices Directive.[52] It is not necessary for a majority of customers to be deceived, but only a "significant" or a "substantial" number.[53] Nor, to succeed in passing off, is it necessary to prove damage to the claimant's goodwill. It is enough to show that there is a likelihood of damage. Indeed, the courts are ready to assume a likelihood of damage, if the claimant can show that the other two elements of a passing off action, goodwill and a misrepresentation, are present.[54]

Passing off encompasses a growing array of practices which might fall under the rubric of unfair competition in other jurisdictions. When passing off first developed in the nineteenth-century, its basic principle was stated to be: "A man is not to sell his goods under the pretence that they are the goods of another man...."[55] At its heart, passing off continues to protect a claimant against false claims that the defendant's goods are those of the claimant. However, since the nineteenth century the tort has expanded to cover a range of other misrepresentations as to origin. Thus, passing off will also protect a trader against a defendant who sells the claimant's goods but claims they are of a superior quality when they are of an inferior quality and as a result harms the claimant's goodwill.[56] It will protect against a defendant who adopts the claimant's style of advertising and so misleads the public as to the origin of his own goods.[57] Passing off may protect against supermarket "look-alikes", where the defendant has adopted the claimant's get-up and the public is deceived as to the origin of the goods.[58] Passing off will protect a claimant when a rival trader advertises his goods and services to the public by falsely representing that the claimant's goods are his own (rather than, in the traditional form of passing off, that his goods are the

---

49 *Reckitt & Colman v. Borden* as per Lord Oliver, *supra* note 46.

50 High Court of Justice, 1979 F.S.R. 113 as per Foster J. – *Morning Star Cooperative Society Ltd. v. Express Newspapers Ltd.*

51 2001 IP & T 787 – *BP Amaco plc v. John Kelly Ltd.*

52 For the Directive, *see* Para. 18. The leading ECJ case on unfair competition is 1 CMLR 1383 (1999) – *Gut Springenheide and Tusky v. Oberkreisdirektor des Kreises Steinfurt – Amt für Lebensmittelüberwachung.* He has since been imported into European trade mark law. *See* DAVIS, "Locating the average consumer: His judicial origins, intellectual influences and current role in European trade mark law," 2 Intellectual Property Quarterly 183-204 (2005).

53 High Court of Justice, 1998 R.P.C. 117 HC – *Chocosuisse Union des Fabricants Suisses de Chocolat v. Cadbury Ltd.*

54 WADLOW, *supra* note 10, at 244. *See* 1984 F.S.R. 175 – *Stringfellow v. McCain Foods (GB)*; Court of Appeal, 1996 R.P.C. 697 CA – *Harrods Ltd. v. Harrodian School Ltd.*

55 6 Beav 66 (1842) – *Perry v. Truefitt.*

56 84 LJ Ch. 449 (1915) – *Spalding AG & Bros. v. A.W. Gamage Ltd. and Benetfink & Col Ltd.*

57 *Cadbury-Schweppes Pty. Ltd. v. Pub Squash Co. Pty. Ltd.*, *supra* note 7.

58 *United Biscuits v. Asda, supra* note 45.

claimant's).[59] Passing off will protect a trader against misrepresentations that the defendant's goods are licensed by the claimant or have been endorsed by him. Passing off is thus a useful tool for protecting the goodwill of those involved in character and personality merchandising.[60] Passing off will protect a claimant when the defendant misrepresents that there is a trade connection between his goods or services and those of the claimant.[61] The courts may find passing off in all these circumstances even if there is no common field of activity between the claimant and the defendant.[62] In the leading case, *Lego Systems A/S v. Lego M. Lemelstrich* (1983)[63], the claimant made the well-known plastic bricks and the defendant made plastic garden furniture. The court held that the defendant was misrepresenting its goods as those of the claimant. The court found that the claimant would be likely to suffer damage through loss of the potential to licence or franchise its mark for similar goods in the future and through loss of the ability to control its reputation.

The tort of passing off will protect a claimant in a variety of situations where the defendant makes false representations as the origin of its goods. Through the "extended" form of passing off, the tort has also developed to protect a claimant against misrepresentations by the defendant as to the quality of its goods. In the first case, *Bollinger v. Costa Brava Wine* (1960), the defendant sold a Spanish sparkling wine as "Spanish champagne". The claimants were French champagne producers. The court found passing off, in that the defendant was making use of the goodwill of the claimants by misrepresenting to the public that its wine was champagne. A number of other drinks cases with similar facts followed.[64] In *Warnink v. Townend*, Lord Diplock approved the extended form of passing off. *Warnink v. Townend* was also significant because the misrepresentation which occurred was based not on a misrepresentation as to the geographic origins of the goods but rather on their make-up. Here the defendant held out his drink as "advocaat" although it was wine rather than spirit based, when traditionally advocaat was made from spirits. The claimants were makers of the drink in Holland. Passing off was found, even though the defendant made no claim that its goods originated in Holland. A further expansion of the

---

[59] Court of Appeal, 1989 R.P.C. 455 – *Bristol Conservatries Ltd. v. Conservatories Custom Built Ltd.* Often described as the "reverse" form of passing off, it may be viewed as approximating a tort of unfair competition since it can be seen to be based on a simple misappropriation of the claimant's goodwill. CARTY, "Inverse Passing Off: A Suitable Addition to Passing Off?," 15 E.I.P.R. 370 (1993). *See* also CARTY, *supra* note 26, at 196, where she argues that such a view is unwarranted since it is still necessary to prove the classic trinity of goodwill, misrepresentation and damage.

[60] High Court of Justice, 1991 F.S.R. 145 – *Mirage Studios v. Counter-Feat Clothing*; High Court, 2002 F.S.R. 60 HC – *Irvine and another v. Talksport Ltd.*; Court of Appeal, 2003 F.S.R. 35 CA – *Irvine v. Talksport*; *see* SCANLAN, "Personality, Endorsement and Everything: The Modern Law of Passing Off and the Myth of the Personality Right," 25 E.I.P.R. 563 (2003).

[61] Court of Appeal, 2000 R.P.C. 669 – *Dawnay Day & Co. Ltd v. Cantor Fitzgerald International.*

[62] *Warnink v. Townend* as per Lord Diplock, *supra* note 8.

[63] High Court of Justice, 1983 F.S.R. 155 – *Lego Systems A/S v. Lego M. Lemelstrich.*

[64] For example, High Court of Justice, 1968 F.S.R. 625 – *Vine Products Ltd v. Mackenzie & Co Ltd. (No.5)*, the "sherry" case.

extended form of passing off is generally held to have occurred with *Chocosuisse v Cadbury* (2000) in the Court of Appeal. The defendant's packaging implied that its chocolate was made in Switzerland when it was not. The claimants made chocolate in Switzerland. The Court of Appeal held that there was passing off even though there was no agreement among the public as to the attributes of Swiss chocolate. It was also held in this case that there was no need for a claimant to have built up good will in a product which is the subject of the action. New producers should also be assumed to have a stake in the manufacturers' goodwill.

It has been argued that the extended form of passing off has stretched the tort by expanding it to cover goodwill in a generic product rather than an individual business.[65] However, the better view is that the extended form of passing off, since it continues to require a misrepresentation which damages the claimants' goodwill, remains within the classic definition of the tort. Far more contentious has been the expansion of the tort to cover damage to the name or get-up of the product as such rather than to the claimant's business goodwill. The leading case is *Taittinger v. Allbev* (1993).[66] In this case, the defendant sold a cheap, non-alcoholic drink under the name "Elderflower Champagne", in a champagne-style bottle. The claimants were champagne producers. In its judgment, the Court of Appeal recognised that the claimants' business goodwill would be damaged by the defendant's misrepresentation. But the Court went further and added that the defendant's actions would also "erode" the "singularity" and "exclusiveness" of the "description *Champagne*" and so cause damage to the claimants of "an insidious but serious kind".[67] A number of commentators have suggested that by recognising "dilution" to the claimant's brand name as a head of damage, without the need for either customer confusion or damage to its business goodwill, the Court in *Taittinger* moved passing off into the territory of unfair competition.[68] Three years later in *Harrods v. Harrodian*, Lord Bingham in the Court of Appeal professed himself uncomfortable with a head of damage which did not rely on a misrepresentation but rather a simple association made by the public between the defendant's product and that of the claimant. Nonetheless, a number of cases since *Harrods* have found damage by dilution.[69]

The apparent development of passing off towards recognising dilution as a head of damage has attracted criticism. In her article, "Dilution and Passing Off: Cause for Concern"[70], Carty suggests that the tort had shifted away from protecting the

---

65 DWORKIN, *supra* note 10, at 244. Carty also warns that the extended form of passing off might lead to an "overextension" of the tort leading it into the territory of "unfair trading". CARTY, *supra* note 26, at 195.

66 High Court of Justice, 1993 F.S.R. 641 – *Taittinger SA v. Allbev Ltd.*

67 *Supra* note 66, as per Lord Bingham at 677.

68 *See* for example, CARTY, *supra* note 26, at 220. *See* also RUSSELL, "The Elderflower Champagne Case: Is this a Further Expansion of the Tort of Passing Off?," 15 E.I.P.R. 379 (1993). For an alternative view, *see* ROBERTSON & HORTON, *supra* note 1, at 569.

69 For example *Dawnay Day v. Cantor Fitzgerald, supra* note 61; also 2004 R.P.C. 36 – *Sir Robert McAlpine Ltd. v. Alfred McAlpine Plc.* In *Harrods*, in a minority opinion, Sir Michael Kerr endorsed the view of "dilution" taken by the Court of Appeal in *Taittinger.*

70 CARTY, "Dilution and passing off: Cause for Concern," 112 L.Q.R. 632-666 (1996).

public interest of customers in not being deceived towards protecting "trade mark value per se". She suggests that, as a consequence, passing off is in danger of being transformed into a tort of "misappropriation".[71] According to Carty, such a transformation would undermine the traditional justification which has been offered for passing off which she identifies as the protection of competitive markets by ensuring that the consumer obtains reliable information in order to make efficient and rational market choices.[72] The introduction of the "dilution" concept into passing off and the controversy it has aroused raises the question of to what extent the UK courts are moving towards developing a general tort of unfair competition. It is this issue which will be addressed in the following section.

3. The Future of Unfair Competition Law in the UK: The Courts, Competition and Comparative Advertising

We have argued thus far that in the UK historically there has been no general tort of unfair competition. Some developments, particularly in the law of passing off, such as the recognition of dilution as a head of damage or the comments of Aldous LJ in *Arsenal v. Reed*, have led some to conclude that the common law is moving towards the development of such a tort. In the final part of this essay, we will consider whether the common law in the UK is likely to develop something which, in other jurisdictions, would be recognised as a general tort of unfair competition. We will suggest that such a development is unlikely. To understand why this is so, it is first necessary to acknowledge the traditionally cautious attitude with which the UK courts have brought towards the regulation of competition generally. A number of concerns underlie this caution. For example, the penchant of the courts for developing the law through analogy, has militated against their fashioning a broad tort of unfair competition. As Lord Oliver noted in *Reckitt & Coleman v. Borden* in relation to passing off: "This is not a branch of the law in which reference to other cases is of any real assistance except analogically."[73] In addition, Cornish and Llewelyn have noted that following the widespread recognition of the idea of sanctity of contract in the nineteenth century, the courts were reluctant to impose obligations which went beyond the voluntary agreement, such as strictures against unfair competition or a right to privacy.[74] Another factor which has traditionally inhibited the courts from shaping broad legal principles has been their reluctance to make law where Parliament has failed to do so. This reluctance has manifested itself both in relation to unfair competition and more recently in the development of a right of personality.[75]

---

[71] CARTY, *supra* note 70, at 634.

[72] CARTY, *supra* note 70, at 655. *See* also CARTY, *supra* note 26, at 235-237.

[73] *Reckitt & Coleman v. Borden, supra* note 46, at 406; *see* also CORNISH & LLEWELYN, *supra* note 1, at 15-17.

[74] CORNISH & LLEWELYN, *supra* note 1, at 16.

[75] For the latter point, *see* Court of Appeal, 1999 R.P.C. 567 CA – *Elvis Presley Trade Marks, Re. See* also DAVIS, "The King is Dead, Long Live the King," Case note, 2000 Cambridge Law Journal 33-36. Cornish and LLewelyn point out that this reluctance intensified over the course of the twentieth century with the introduction of universal suffrage.

It has been argued that the UK courts are reluctant to intervene in the regulation of competition generally. They have traditionally taken the view that the public interest will be best served by robust competition between traders in an open market.[76] Thus, according to a recent Government report relating to the implementation of the Unfair Commercial Practices Directive: "English law tends to prioritise different values to those favoured by other European legal systems. First, as a matter of doctrinal form, English contract law prefers specific provisions to general clauses; and, secondly, as a matter of doctrinal substance, the default values of English contract law are those of self-reliance and individualism rather than mutuality and co-operation."[77] The same generalization might be made about the courts' attitude to the economic torts. As Jacob J. noted in *Hodgkinson v. Wards Mobility*, "the common law…leans against monopolies".[78] As a result the courts have been slow to recognise and to protect new forms of value, which might be harmed by unfair competition, for example through developing a general tort of "misappropriation". Instead, to the extent that the courts have sought to shape competitive practices, they have done so, as we have seen, through the development of a number of specific torts, such as passing off or malicious falsehood.[79] Alternatively, it might be said that the courts have confined their regulation of competitive practices to the protection of recognised forms of value, such as for example intellectual property rights and, in the case of passing off, goodwill.[80] Except at the margins, in the past they have not generally interpreted the common law in a way so as to protect the economic interests of traders' more generally or to recognise new forms of legally protectable value, such as might reside in, for example, a personality right.[81] This minimalist approach to the regulation of competition was summarised by Lord Scarman in the passing-off case, *Cadbury-Schweppes v. The Pub Squash* (1981).[82] He noted:

> "But competition must remain free; and competition is safeguarded by the necessity for the plaintiff to prove that he has built up an "intangible property right" in the advertised descriptions of his product, or, in other words, that he has succeeded by such methods in giving his product a distinctive character accepted by the market. A defendant, however, does no wrong by entering a market created by another and there competing with its creator. The line may be difficult to draw; but, unless it is drawn, competition will be stifled."

It follows from this approach that judges have also been slow to view the courts as providing an appropriate forum for drawing a line between what might be deemed acceptable or unacceptable competitive practices.[83]

---

[76] *See* for example, ROBERTSON & HORTON, *supra* note 1, at 569.
[77] DTI, *supra* note 21, at 6.
[78] *Hodgkinson v. Ward Mobility*, *supra* note 9, at 173.
[79] CARTY, *supra* note 26, at 1-2.
[80] CORNISH & LLEWELYN, *supra* note 1, at 14.
[81] For example, Elvis Presley Trade Marks.
[82] *Cadbury-Schweppes v. The Pub Squash*, *supra* note 7, at 491.
[83] SANDERS, *supra* note 1, at 55. *See* for example, dicta of Buckley LJ in *Bulmer v. Bollinger, supra* note 6, at 25.

Nonetheless, it is also the case that even as the courts have consistently identified a public interest in the encouragement of robust competition, successive governments have over this same period passed an increasing amount of legislation intended to protect the consumer against unfair trade practices. Further legislation will of course follow the implementation of the Unfair Commercial Practices Directive. In *Warnink v. Townend*, Lord Diplock had suggested that the recognition by Parliament of what he termed "the need for more rigorous standards of commercial honesty" should be taken into consideration by judges in deciding whether to extend the reach of economic torts such as passing off. In the area of unfair trading (most notably in relation to passing off), he suggested that legislation and the development of the common law, "ought to proceed upon a parallel rather than a diverging course…".[84] This might suggest that following the implementation of the Directive, the statute law which regulates consumer/business relations and the common law which regulates the relationship between traders might well converge through the development of general tort of unfair competition. It is submitted that a brief consideration of how the UK courts have interpreted the provisions in the TMA 1994 which regulate comparative advertising suggest that such an outcome is unlikely. The relevant provision of the Act is as follows:

> Section 10 (6) Nothing in the preceding provisions of this section [on infringement] shall be construed as preventing the use of the registered mark by any person for the purpose of identifying goods or services as those of the proprietor or licensee.
>
> But any such use otherwise than in accordance with honest practices in industrial or commercial matters shall be treated as infringing the registered trade mark if the use without due cause takes unfair advantage of, or is detrimental to, the distinctive character or repute of the trade mark.

The section did not derive from the EU Trade Marks Directive[85] but has domestic origins. Its inclusion in the TMA 1994 also preceded the implementation in the UK of the Comparative Advertising Directive although the courts have held it is compatible with the Act.[86] On the face of it, the comparative advertising provisions of the TMA 1994 would seem to be designed to regulate unfair competition, to prevent consumer deception and to protect the registered mark from dilution. Indeed, actions under these provisions have almost invariably been brought in tandem with a claim for malicious falsehood. In successive cases, however, the UK courts have interpreted Section 10 (6) in a manner which ensures it will have a minimal impact on the

---

84 *Warnink v. Townend, supra* note 8, at 743.

85 First Council Directive 89/104/EEC of December 21, 1988 to approximate the laws of the Member States relating to trade marks.

86 Directive 97/55 of the European Parliament and Council, amending Directive 84/450, concerning misleading advertising so as to include comparative advertising. On the relationship between the provision and the Directive *see* 2000 F.S.R. 541 – *British Airways plc v. Ryanair Ltd.* and High Court of Justice, 2005 ETMR 61 – *O2 Ltd., O2 (UK) Ltd. v. Hutchinson 3G UK Ltd.*

regulation of competition for all the traditional reasons. Thus, in the leading case, *British Airways v. Ryanair* (2000)[87], Mr. Justice Jacob summarised the approach that the UK courts have taken to the interpretation of the provisions on comparative advertising. He noted that the purpose of Section 10 (6) was a positive one: to permit comparative advertising as long as the use of the competitor's mark was not "seriously misleading."[88] Honesty is to be gauged by what is reasonably to be expected by the relevant public of advertisements for the goods or services in issue.[89] In gauging the public's response, the court should take account of the fact that the public is used to "hyperbole" or puffery in advertising. Indeed, the "average consumer" has become "hardened" to it.[90] Nor should the court put itself in the position of making fine judgements as to where the line between fair and unfair competition might be drawn. According to Mr. Justice Jacob, it is not necessary to embark on a "minute textual examination" of the advertisement, nor generally to "try and enforce through the back door of trade mark legislation a more puritanical standard than the general public would expect from advertising copy".[91] Finally, in comparative advertising cases thus far, the courts have failed to exhibit any marked concern for the possible "dilution" to the value of the claimant's mark which might arise from the manner of the defendant's use of it. For example, in *British Airways v. Ryanair*, the defendant referred to the claimant company as "Bastards". According to Mr. Justice Jacob while this amounted to "vulgar abuse", it would be caught neither by the provisions of the TMA 1994 nor the tort of malicious falsehood.[92]

The manner in which the UK courts have interpreted the comparative advertising provisions of the TMA 1994 suggests that they will continue to privilege the protection of market freedom over the protection of traders from unfair competition where the two might conflict.[93] This appears to be the case even though, away from

---

87 *British Airways v. Ryanair, supra* note 86.

88 Particularly at the stage of a pre-trial injunction. *British Airways v. Ryanair, supra* note 86, at 551.

89 *British Airways v. Ryanair, supra* note 86, at 552; *see* also *Barclays Bank v. RBS Advanta, supra* note 39.

90 *British Airways v. Ryanair, supra* note 86, at 552; *see* also *Barclays Bank v. RBS Advanta, supra* note 39.

91 *British Airways v. Ryanair, supra* note 86, at 552; *see* also *Barclays Bank v. RBS Advanta, supra* note 39 and *Vodafone v. Orange*.

92 He noted at 554 that it might be caught by the voluntary code of the ASA; but he also suggested this it is possible to denigrate a competitor's mark without being dishonest. The courts' failure to recognise the dilution aspects of the comparative advertising provisions of the TMA 1994 has been criticised by CARTY, in her article, "Registered Trade Marks and Permissible Comparative Advertising," 24 E.I.P.R. 294 (2002).

93 This approach was confirmed in the recent Court of Appeal decision, *O2 Holdings v Hutchison 3G* (2007). The issue arose as to when the use of a mark in comparative advertising, which isconfusingly similar to another's registered trade mark, is necessary or idispensable for the purpose of complying with the Comparative Advertising Directive. According to Lord Justice Jacob: "To construe the CAD as not permitting that would not be to interpret it 'in the sense most favourable' to comparative advertising". The questions has now been addressed to the ECJ. Court of Appeal, 2007 ETMR 284 – *O2 Holdings Ltd. (formerly O2Ltd) v Hutchison 3G Ltd.*

the common law, legislation is providing increasing protection for consumers against unfair trade practices. As a result, it is submitted that the signs are not propitious for those who would favour the development by the UK courts of a general tort of unfair competition in the future. It appears that the courts will continue to interpret unfair competition narrowly. They will recognise it as addressing relations between traders rather than between traders and consumers and they will locate the general public interest in nurturing robust competition rather than in protecting traders or indeed the general public from information, which while it may be dishonest or mistaken, will not be deceptive. In light of these conclusions it is possible to reinterpret Lord Justice Aldous's comment in *Arsenal v. Reed*. It may not suggest that the UK common law is now sufficiently expansive to accommodate a general tort of unfair competition. Rather it can be taken to mean the reverse: that the ambit of passing off continues to set strict limits as to how far the courts are willing to move in the direction of developing such a tort.

The Legal Framework of Unfair Market Practices in Hungary*

Judit Firniksz

1. Legal and Institutional Framework

Act LVII of 1996 on Prohibition of Unfair and Restrictive Market Practices (henceforth: Hungarian Competition Act) has a rather specific nature since it covers provisions relating to both competition-restricting practices (antitrust law) and unfair market practices of undertakings. The common rationale behind this composition of competition rules is set by the preamble of the Competition Act: "The public interest attached to the maintenance of competition on the market ensuring efficiency and social progress, the interests of undertakings complying with the requirements of business fairness and the interests of consumers require the State to protect by law fairness and freedom of economic competition". This phrasing refers to the preamble of Act XX of 1949 – the Constitution of the Republic of Hungary declaring social market economy as an overall aim as well as to Article 9 of the Hungarian Constitution stating that the Republic of Hungary recognises and supports the right to enterprise and the freedom of economic competition. Based on this constitutional framework, competition rules create a system of so-called "institutional protection" directed towards the institution of economic competition, and the free and undistorted competition process.

Besides the substantive law provisions, the Competition Act also establishes the institutional framework for the implementation of competition law. The procedural tasks regarding unfair competition provisions are shared: The so-called Chapter II cases, i.e. the unfair market practices or B2B relations belong to the jurisdiction of the civil court, while the Hungarian Competition Authority (Gazdasági Versenyhivatal, henceforth: GVH) proceeds in cases regarding unfair manipulation of consumer choice, i.e. B2C relations.

The GVH is a public budgetary institution of national competence which has no regional offices. It is independent of the Government, with a reporting obligation to the Parliament. The competition supervision procedure consists of two stages; the investigations are performed by the Investigation Sections, while the decisions are made by the Competition Council, a decision-making body set up within the organisational structure of the GVH.

As one of the latest institutional developments in the GVH the Consumer Section was set up last September which is a "functional" department specialised in consumer choice-related cases. Furthermore, the GVH was designated as a compe-

---

* Presentation made at the Conference on Unfair Competition Law organised by the Max Planck Institute for Intellectual Property, Competition and Tax Law, Budapest, June 16 to 18, 2005.

tent authority according to the provisions laid down in the Regulation on Consumer Protection Cooperation (Regulation No 2006/2004 of the European Parliament and of the Council of October 27, 2004 on cooperation between national authorities responsible for the enforcement of consumer protection laws).

Apparently, unfair competition does not constitute an independent field of law with its own specific legislation as it does for instance in Germany with its (recently reformed) "Act against Unfair Competition". Nevertheless, we have to add that unfair competition has deep roots in the Hungarian legal tradition. Since the second half of the 19th century several acts contained rules on unfair commercial practices and by 1923 a uniform law was created, Act No. V of 1923 on Unfair Competition, which can be considered as a definitive source of the present legal background of unfair competition.

2. Distinction Between B2B And B2C Relations

As mentioned before, the provisions regarding unfair competition are contained in two successive chapters of the Competition Act. The codification technique is similar: An introductory-type of general clause is followed by a list of typical infringements.

According to the general clause regarding unfair market practices, it is prohibited to engage in unfair economic activities. The legislative examples listed by the Act can be characterised by the following keywords: (1) injury of reputation, (2) injury of business secrets, (3) unfair calls for a boycott, (4) imitation, (5) infringement of the fairness of bidding.

The chapter on unfair influencing of consumer choice (Chapter III) distinguishes between consumer fraud and aggressive commercial practices. In this structure Chapter III of the Act contains provisions prohibiting both deceiving consumers in economic competition and applying business methods which restrict, without justification, the freedom of consumers' choice.

The Competition Act defines the situations in which deception of consumers shall be presumed. These include those where

> false declarations are made or facts are declared in a manner which is likely to deceive with respect to the price or essential features of the goods, including in particular, their composition, the effects of their use on health or the environment, as well as their handling, origin, source or method of procurement; if the designation of goods is likely to deceive, or if any other information which is likely to deceive pertaining to the essential features of the goods is disseminated,
>
> it is concealed that the goods fail to meet legal or other usual requirements for such types of goods, or that the use of the goods requires conditions which are significantly different from what is usual,
>
> information that is deceptive or may possibly be deceptive is given about factors related to the sale and distribution of the goods influencing the decision

of consumers, in particular, about the method of distribution, terms of payment, gifts associated with the goods, discounts, or the chance of winning,

a false impression of a particularly advantageous purchase is created.

To these rules two explanatory remarks are to be added: (1) The term "consumer" for the purposes of the Competition Act means a customer, purchaser or user (Art. 8), (2) the meaning generally accepted in daily life or in the respective trade or sector shall be taken as a guide when establishing whether information presumably deceives consumers.

3. Misleading and Comparative Advertising

From a merely practical point of view, misleading advertising can also be considered as a specific form of consumer fraud. Act LVIII of 1997 on Business Advertising Activity contains the harmonised provisions prohibiting misleading advertisement and the criteria set for comparative advertisements.

Consumer complaints against misleading and/or misleading comparative advertising activity are made very often. (Misleading priority claims in advertising may be mentioned as one of the recent hot topics, which may obviously affect consumer choice and at the same time damage competitors' goodwill.)

Separation of B2B and B2C dimensions can be detected also in the relevant provisions of the Act on Business Advertising Activity and competences are shared between the civil court and the GVH, respectively. Comparative advertising cases fall under the jurisdiction of the civil courts if this behaviour (1) may injure the reputation, name, merchandise, brand name or any other marking of a competitor (2) may cause a confusion between the advertiser and another company or the name, merchandise, brand name or any other feature of a competitor, (3) may produce any unfair advantage deriving from the reputation of a competitor, (4) may violate the provision of the Competition Act on the prohibition of imitating the merchandise of a competitor or imitating the characteristics of such merchandise. The GVH has powers to establish whether the requirements set forth for the comparative advertisement are satisfied, nevertheless, the court has also jurisdiction if such matter arises as a part of a case that belongs otherwise under its jurisdiction.

Misleading advertising and misleading comparative advertising fall under the law enforcement activity of the GVH. As an important procedural aspect we have to emphasise that in the GVH's proceedings, when evaluating misleading or comparative advertising cases, the rules of the Competition Act are to be applied, with a very limited number of deviations laid down in the Act on Business Advertising Activity. Finally, we have to add the definition given for the term "consumer" for the purposes of the Act on Business Advertising Activity: All private individuals, legal entities, and economic associations without legal entity towards whom or which advertising is directed.

4. The Structure of Protected Interests

While carrying out procedures, we are constantly aware of moving around in a network of interrelating interests. It has to be realised that the effects on the consumers' and the traders' interests can be considered as two inseparable aspects of market behaviour. Most market practices affect both consumers and competitors at the very same time and, especially as for information-handling type of problems, competition and consumer policies are two closely related areas in a legal and in an economic sense.

In view of the fact that consumers' and competitors' interests are often difficult to separate, the interrelationship between the interests is also reflected in the legal framework. As mentioned before, the general clause of Chapter II of the Competition Act contains the prohibition of unfair economic activities. This provision also emphasises the aspect of consumer interests as follows: „It shall be prohibited to engage in unfair economic activities, particularly in a manner which infringes or jeopardises the legitimate interest of competitors or consumers or is contrary to the requirements of business fairness".

Chapter III of the Competition Act covers practices which are of such a nature as to harm consumers' economic interests directly and may have an indirect effect on the competitors' interests, on competition itself. As Art. 70 of the Act says, the decision to initiate a procedure is based on three prerequisites: firstly the activity presumably violates the provisions of the Competition Act, secondly the procedure falls within the competence of the GVH and last but not least the procedure is necessary to safeguard the public interest. One necessary pre-condition has to be underlined: The GVH is not in a position to handle individual cases of consumer fraud. Only those kinds of market behaviour can fall under the scope of its activity which may have as a consequence affecting the public interest attached to the maintenance of an undistorted competition process (e.g. by potentially affecting the transactional decisions of a significant number of consumers).

In practice, it is often rather difficult to make a clear distinction between the B2B and the B2C dimensions, a decision in each case has to be preceded by a careful analysis. Nevertheless, the Competition Act does not preclude the possibility of parallel procedures.

5. Connected Fields of Law

When outlining the relations to other fields of law, I would like to focus on some recent experiences gained by handling consumer choice cases. In the law enforcement activity of the GVH, a competition authority, a significant number of the relevant questions arise from *antitrust* fields. For instance, possible conjunctions between consumer fraud (Art. 8 of the Competition Act) and abuse of a dominant position (Art. 21 of the Competition Act) cases arose in the last 6 months when the GVH presumed several companies abusing more than one article of the Hungarian Competition Act at the same time, with one or more actions. Most of these cases were detected in the IT field – possibly because numerous complaints have recently been made in this market segment.

Supposedly, while identifying and revealing these cases, we get closer to our goal – to create an information environment enabling consumers to make conscious choices in possession of sufficient and relevant information. Basically, lack of information is the key factor that links deception of consumers and abuse of a dominant position: consumers are not provided with sufficient and relevant information during the period of making their choice – by this the final decision of the consumers might be manipulated. After having chosen, insufficient information may hinder consumers in evaluating switching costs, i.e. information problems may cause the consumer to be captured in a detrimental situation.

We have to emphasise that fraud might happen before, while abuse of a dominant power might happen after the consumer makes his or her choice. Nevertheless, the two aspects might be substantively connected and deception might lead to a situation where consumers are "trapped" and are not able to switch from one company to another. In addition, abuse of a dominant position could serve as a basis for misleading information-handling techniques or practices aimed at raising the level of "information noise" on the market – causing exaggerated switching costs. In this context we have to underline that informed consumer choice, made upon consideration of product characteristics, prices and substitutes, is a prerequisite for the operation of the market economy, and that informed consumer choice is the cornerstone of inter-firm competition, a precondition for the success of competition policy.

One of the central concepts of *civil law* is the coordinate relation between equal parties. Rephrasing this situation in the language of economics, it resembles the situation in which partners have perfect information in the bargain process. We may state that it happens very rarely that consumers have the possibility to make a transactional decision in the possession of perfect information. The concept of information asymmetry causes many concerns also in contractual relations. As a consequence, the unequal bargaining power of the parties based on information asymmetry has led to rules safeguarding contractual intent. For some types of consumer contracts specific information disclosure rules were set and "cooling off" periods were guaranteed (e.g. time-sharing contracts, distant selling, etc). These cases relating to information problems in the pre-contractual period properly should be decided by the courts, but the complaints lodged with the GVH very often contain problems of this nature. The GVH has powers to offer proposals de lege ferenda as a part of its competition advocacy activity; the experiences gained through these complaints can be channelled into the law-making process.

Last but not least, it has to be mentioned that Act IV of 1978, i.e. the Criminal Code also contains anti-fraud provisions and several parallel procedures have recently been initiated. As to the main difference, it has to be pointed out that the criminal law rule against consumer fraud contains an additional element on the subjective side: deceptive behaviour has to be committed for the purpose of rendering a product more desirable.

6. Sanctions

A differentiated system of sanctioning is revealed by the unfair competition provisions. Should cases that fall under the jurisdiction of the civil court emerge, Art. 86 of the Competition Act contains the possible court orders the interested party may demand in his or her claim: (1) Establishment of the violation, (2) termination of the violation and the prohibition of continued violation by the offender, (3) amends made by the offender – through making an announcement or in some other appropriate manner – and, if necessary, sufficient publicity must be given to the announcement, (4) termination of the infringing state of affairs, restitution of the situation preceding the infringement etc., (5) damages subject to the provisions of the civil law.

According to Art. 77 of the Competition Act, in the administrative procedure of the GVH the following legal consequences can be applied: The Competition Council may (1) establish that the conduct is unlawful, (2) order a situation violating the act to be eliminated, (3) prohibit the continuation of the conduct which violates the provisions of the act, (3) order a corrective announcement to be published in respect of previous information which is likely to deceive, (4) impose an administrative fine up to ten per cent of the undertaking's net turnover in the preceding business year. Though the set of sanctions contains both reparatory (e.g. announcement of rectification) and repressive (e.g. administrative fines) elements, the repressive feature can be considered as dominant in practice.

As an ultima ratio, the Criminal Code contains some unfair competition-related criminal sanctions; according to Art. 296 imitation is a felony offense, which can be punished with imprisonment of up to three years, while Art. 296/A states deception of consumers to be a misdemeanor offense punishable with the following: Imprisonment of up to two years, labour in the public interest or a fine.

7. Conclusion

Based on this short outline of the legal framework of unfair commercial practices in Hungary, the conclusion may be drawn that the framework created in the period of economic transition has proved its effectiveness in assuring a competition-friendly market environment and contains the basic concepts, which prepare it to integrate Community law developments in this field.

The Law Against Unfair Competition in the Czech Republic

Petr Hajn

1. Is the Law against Unfair Competition Regarded as a Separate Field of Law in the Czech Republic?

The law against unfair competition is now regarded as a relatively independent part of commercial law in the Czech Republic. This is true above all in legislation (see below) and in the academic field – in the curricula of the legal faculties. In the academic institutions and in a number of new private universities, this law is considered within the context of intellectual property law.

2. What is the Legal Basis?

In legislation, the provisions concerning unfair competition are contained in the Commercial Code (Law No. 53/1991 with subsequent amendments – hereinafter the CC). This solution is based on technical legal factors rather than subject-based reasons. Originally, a uniform regulation was planned to include antitrust law. There were also proposals for the reintroduction of the rules of unfair competition from the pre-war period (Law No. 111/1927). The latter regulation was very strongly influenced by the traditional Act against Unfair Competition in Germany.

However, this old regulation was in part used, with many civil law (but only civil law) provisions being included in the CC. As a result, the good and detailed judicial practice from the pre-war period can be applied. It is also possible to take account of the old and more recent German as well as Austrian judicial practice as a source of inspiration for academics, attorneys and judges, as occurs occasionally.

The provisions for unfair competition consist of the following sections:

- (i) General provisions on commercial competition (participation in economic competition) (Sec. 41-43 CC).
- (ii) General clause against unfair competition (Sec. 44 CC).
- (iii) Special factual constellations of unfair competition (Sec. 45-52 CC).
- (iv) Provisions concerning penalties for unfair competition and some special procedural law provisions (Sec. 53-54 CC).

2.1 Sec. 41 of the CC defines competitors as "*natural and legal persons participating in commercial competition, even if they are not entrepreneurs*". This wording allows the competitor to be defined very broadly and the concept of the competitor to be applied ad hoc.

The general provisions also lay down that "*competitors have the right to the free development of their competitive activity in the interest of acquiring a commercial advantage, and can combine to carry out this activity; however, they are obliged to comply with the legally binding rules of commercial competition and not to abuse their participation in competition*".

What is interesting in this wording is that it first mentions the right to the free development of competitive activity and regards the restrictions on this activity as being of secondary importance. This wording can be construed in accordance with the Constitution (similar to the paper by Professor Hilty at Budapest Conference 2005). It can also be interpreted socio-biologically. I myself have attempted such an interpretation, and in the book "*Competitive behaviour and the law against unfair competition*" (Masaryk University, 2000). I developed the following consideration: *Human competitive behaviour is very strongly biologically determined. In order to secure the transmission of our genes to the next generation, nature has provided us with competitive tools and competitive behaviour, in particular a certain amount of aggression and the ability to "act competitively". Competitive behaviour is also a result of the cultural development of humanity and the "secondary needs" it has inspired, the satisfaction of which is not achieved by the existing sources. The cultural development of humanity is hugely accelerated by man's imitative behaviour.*

The legal regulation of competition cannot entirely suppress the biologically and culturally determined features of human conduct, but can only correct them to a certain extent. The law must permit human competitive behaviour a reasonable amount of aggression, guile and innovation through imitation (as permitted by the wording of Sec. 41 CC). The law cannot arrange the rules of the "competitive game" such that all competition disputes end in a draw.

The general provisions concerning commercial competition also regulate the equal status of Czechs and foreigners in their participation in commercial competition. The rule on the conflict of legal systems reads: "*Unless the contrary follows from international treaties by which the Czech Republic is bound and which are published in the Official Gazette, the provisions of this Chapter (Sec. 41-54 CC, author's comment) are not applicable to acts to the extent that they have effects abroad.*"

2.2 The general clause (Sec. 44 Para. 1 CC) defines unfair competition as "*an activity in commercial competition that runs counter to honest practices in competition and is capable of damaging other competitors or consumers*". The general clause expressly prohibits unfair competition.

It must be pointed out that the definition of unfair competition deals with honest practices in competition and not with general civil law (Roman) honest practices.

The general clause contains the general conditions that must always be satisfied by a specific activity (which means in the application of individual specific factual constellations) if such an activity is to be qualified as unfair.

The general clause can also be applied autonomously. Thus, alongside the specific factual constellations, Czech judicial practice can also develop case groups based on the general clause (known as judicial constellations of unfair competition), as has already been the case.

2.3 Sec. 44 Para. 2 of the CC lists specific factual constellations of unfair competition as indicative examples of unfair competition within the meaning of Sec. 44 Para. 1 (the general clause). The typical cases of unfair competition are thus:

(i) Misleading advertising
(ii) Misleading labelling of goods and services,
(iii) Creation of a likelihood of confusion,
(iv) Parasitic exploitation of the reputation of the enterprise, goods or services of another competitor,
(v) Bribery,
(vi) Disparagement,
(vii) Comparative advertising,
(viii) Infringement of business secrecy,
(ix) Endangering the health of consumers and the environment.

These constellations are regulated in more detail and in the usual manner in the other provisions.

2.4 In disputes based on unfair competition, the persons entitled to file an action are defined very generally as *persons whose rights are infringed or endangered by unfair competition* (Sec. 53 CC). The same provision also defines the persons against whom an action may be filed, referring to them simply as *infringers*. These persons can make use of *legal remedies for protection against unfair competition. They can require the infringer to discontinue the unfair activity and eliminate the contested condition. In addition they can also claim reasonable satisfaction, which may be granted in the form of money, as well as damages and the surrender of the unjust enrichment.*

The provision also deals with the activities of consumer and competition protection organisations. The rights (but only these rights) to require an infringer to discontinue the unlawful activity and eliminate the contested condition can also be asserted by legal persons who are entitled to defend the interest of competitors or consumers (Sec. 54 Para. 1 CC). A few (not numerous) such organisations (such as "Ars aequi et boni") are also active in the Czech Republic.

Consumer defence goes a little further than in the EC Directive on Misleading Advertising. *If a consumer asserts a right to require an infringer to discontinue the unfair competitive activities or eliminate an infringement of competition in the case of Sec. 44-47 and 52, the infringer must always prove that he has not effected any activity within the meaning of unfair competition. This also applies to the obligation to pay damages when it is a question of determining whether losses have resulted from an activity in the sense of unfair competition and to the right to reasonable compensation and the surrender of unjust enrichment; the burden of proof for the amount of losses caused, the extent and the significance of another loss, the character and the extent of the unjust enrichment is always borne by the plaintiff, even if he is a consumer.*

3. What Interests are Protected? Does Czech Law Emphasise More the Parallels Between the Interests of Entrepreneurs and Consumers or Does it Regard Them Separately?

Czech law considers that the interest of entrepreneurs and consumers run in parallel (see the wording cited above from the general clause). The regulation of unfair competition does not expressly refer to the interests of the general public. The defence of these interests can be derived from the general provision concerning economic competition. Old judicial practice, which is once again being cited, also stated that the courts should prevent the brutalisation of competitive practice.

4. What is the Relationship to Antitrust Law, Intellectual Property Law, the Law of Torts and Contract Law?

Sec. 42 Para. 1 of the CC mentions abuses of participation in commercial competition, specifically "dishonest competitive activities and unlawful restrictions of economic competition" (the brief mention of antitrust law in the CC was sufficient for the legal faculties to teach antitrust law as a part of commercial law).

Sec. 42 Para. 2 of the CC lays down that "unlawful restrictions of commercial competition are regulated by a special law" (Law No. 143/2001 Sam. on the Defence of Competition). Sec. 1 Para. 7 of this Act expressly states that this law does not deal with unfair competition. Both parts of competition law are thus dealt with separately; a number of cases (such as boycotts) can be assessed according to both legal sources.

On the relationship between unfair competition law and intellectual property law, reference can be made to the provision concerning misleading labelling (Sec. 46 Para. 2 CC), which lays down that *this provision does not affect the rights and obligations resulting from registered indications of origin, protected trademarks, protected plant varieties and animal varieties, as laid down in special legislation.*

Conversely there are old as well as current decisions that hold that what is permitted according to intellectual property law can be in conflict with honest practices in competition.

A simple penal provision (a general clause against unfair competition) is contained in Sec. 149 of the Penal Code. However, this provision is not applied very often and a more detailed regulation is expected in the future.

The administrative law regulation of competition can be found above all in Law No. 40/1995 Sam. (Advertising Act). Unfair competition law can also be found in Law No. 634/1992 Sam. on the Defence of the Consumer and in Law No. 231/2001 Sam. (the regulation of the activities of the electronic media). All these provisions have been amended on several occasions, the EC Directives on advertising, electronic media and the defence of the consumer having being implemented in the Czech legal system.

Relatively many cases can be judged in parallel under criminal or administrative law and under private law (as a judicial factual constellation under the general clause). The same also applies to the relationship between unfair competition law and contract law. Judicial practice tends to emphasise their separation.

5. How is Unfair Competition Penalized? Are the Major Penalties of a Civil Law, Administrative Law or Criminal Law Nature?

The penalties for unfair competition have already been mentioned above. The civil law penalties are the ones most frequently used. All penalties against unfair competition in the CC are based on objective responsibility; such a solution is not very practical for damages, and there have been almost no decisions in which damages have been awarded. Conversely, the courts have relatively often made use of reasonable satisfaction in monetary form (for intangible losses).

6. Is a Public Authority Involved in Preventing Unfair Competition?

There is no specific authority or organisation responsible for preventing unfair competition. In the Czech Republic, a number of organisations for the defence of consumers operate, but tend to pursue more an informational function. There is also the Advertising Council that deals with ethics in advertising.

The Legal Regulation of Unfair Competition in the Slovak Republic

Anton Škreko

This article deals with the legal regulation of unfair competition in the Slovak Republic regarding the general inclusion of unfair competition law in the system of laws in Slovakia and its special division into the law against illegal restriction of economic competition and unfair competition law. The conception of unfair competition law in the Slovakian legal system, and in the relation to other branches of law is considered as well.

1. Introduction

The need for the protection of the free market and of those operating in the free market space is evident in the nature of a free market economy itself. In the Constitution (No. 460/1992 Col.) Art. 55, the Slovak Republic declares that the economy of the Slovak Republic is based on the principles of a socially- and ecologically-oriented market economy and that the Slovak Republic protects and supports economic competition. The details are about to be settled in the special acts.

The free market creates a milieu of natural competition, which emanates on the one hand from the competitive struggle of competitors (in the relevant market), and on the other hand from the relationship between consumers and competitors. There is a clear demand on the part of society for the regulation of these relationships.[1] This regulation will always be determined by the fact that competition (competitive struggle) cannot be approved or strictly prohibited by the law, which is also evident in the nature of a market economy.

Legal regulation will, of course, only be reasonable if there is particular tension between human behaviour and higher cultural demands on human behaviour. As soon as the legal claims on human behaviour stray too far from the reality of this behaviour (reality conditioned also biologically), the tension changes into the overstraining – regulation fails to work and loses its relevance.[2] Competitive behaviour in human action emerges by itself, just as in the competitive struggle between competitors in the relevant free-market space. The law regulates this behaviour in particular, but there is a call for the flexible reaction of the legislature to the development of the market and the behaviour of those operating in this market.

---

1 To be compared in general, STRAUS, "Industrial Property Legislation as an Element in Market Economies", AIPPI Annuaire 1992/III – XXXV Congress – Tokyo 1992, 327 (also in Slovakian: STRAUS, "Legislatíva v oblasti priemyselného vlastníctva ako prvok v trhovom hospodárstve," 1994 Právny obzor Nr. 1).

2 HAJN, "Competition Conduct and Unfair competition Law (Soutìžní chování a právo proti nekalé soutìži)" 24 (2000).

The effect of higher cultural (moral) rules and principles of society on competition law should be understood in the specific relationship towards economic competition; traditional competition law is about to cultivate the manners (standards) of competitive conduct without concern for the development of the intellectual capacity of society.[3]

2. Competitive Relationship

A competitive relationship does not represent a legal relationship. It means that it is a factual relationship, but of course bears legal relevance. This special relationship originates between the subjects engaged in economic competition that is caused by the endeavour for economic profit and is not caused by the legal permission of competition.[4] The law declares only the freedom of the subjects to develop and expand the competitive conduct attempting to gain economic profit. This conduct has to meet the legally-binding rules of economic competition, which should be understood in a wider sense as the legal provisions. In this sense, we are talking about the rules of honest trade practices, professional principles, and so on.

Common obligation relationships (win/win strategy) cannot be considered as a relationship of economic competition (also if such a relationship could emerge in economic competition). A strategy where one side always wins and the other loses is applied in economic competition,[5] which is also typical for the competitive relationship.

The subjects of the competitive relationship could be defined from their correlation to each other in the market place. The law defines the subjects quite broadly, so that all possible subjects would be involved in the manner of complex protection of the market and free competition. A competitive relationship can emerge between entrepreneurs (legal persons or natural persons permitted to conduct business by special act), but also between other subjects such as shareholders, natural persons performing free professions (e.g. artists),[6] and of course the consumer in relation to particular competitors (entrepreneurs) on the one hand and in relation (in the competitive struggle) towards other consumers on the side of demand.

The object of the competitive relationship is the conduct of the subjects in competition approved by law and common competition principles aiming for success in competition, which is often represented by gaining economic advantage while the competitor (rival) loses, while at the same time fulfilling honest trade practices.

---

3 *See* HAJN, "Concurrence of the Authors Rights and Competition Law in Advertising (K souběhu autorského a soutìžního práva v reklamì)," in: "Intellectual Property in the Process of the Transformation of the Law System (Duševné vlastníctvo v procese transformácie právneho systému)" Collection from the International Conference: VI. Luby Legal Days 138 (1997).

4 ELIÁŠ, BEJČEK, HAJN, JEŽEK, "Course of the Commercial Law, General Part, Competition Law (Kurs obchodního práva, Obecná část, Soutěžní právo)" 294 (3rd ed. 2002).

5 *See* in detail, HAJN, *supra* note 2, at 35.

6 *See also* OVEČKOVÁ, "Commentary on the Commercial Code (Obchodný zákonník – komentár)" 104a *et seq.* (1995).

3. Legal Treatment of the Protection of Economic Competition

The need for protection emanates from illegal conduct, which impairs or endangers the social function of economic competition by restricting, eliminating or misrepresenting it. An internal division is given through the division of the acts of restriction and elimination on the one hand, and on the acts of misrepresentation on the other hand. The acts classified in the former group deal with the law against illegal restriction of economic competition (also called cartel or antitrust law); the acts classified in the latter group deal with the law against unfair competition. The relationships originating in the first group (the law against illegal restriction of economic competition) should be seen on the vertical level with characteristic subordination principle (public sphere/public law); the law against unfair competition is characteristic of the equivalence of the subjects, and this law should be understood in the horizontal plane, thus the relationships are of a civil law nature.[7]

Antitrust law is concerned with the preservation of the freedom of competition by combating restraints on trade and abuses of economic power. Unfair competition law, on the other hand, is concerned with ensuring fairness in competition by forcing all participants to play according to the same rules.

Antitrust law has a broader scope than unfair competition law as can be seen in the range of the subjects. It involves not only the concrete, particular subjects of the competitive relationship, but also involves a range of not-so-clearly defined individual subjects of economic competition, and consumers as well. This means that antitrust law plays a far more important role in prevention than does unfair competition law. Therefore, in antitrust law, the preventive function is more important than the repressive function, while in unfair competition law the opposite is the case. Antitrust law also bears a protective function in relation to the national economy (public interest).[8] Generally, we can say that in the regulation of competition law, antitrust law bears the public law interest and that unfair competition law bears the private (civil) law interest.

The both groups are not strictly separated and some acts could be, depending on the case, considered as acts breaching the law against illegal restriction of economic competition or unfair competition law.

As to the legal conception of the above-mentioned two groups of laws, these are separated into two different legal acts. The law against illegal restriction of economic competition is regulated in the Special Act No. 136/2001 Col., and on the protection of economic competition also called the Antitrust Act. The regulation of unfair competition can be found in the Commercial Code (hereinafter "CC") act No. 513/1991 Col., Chapter 5.

---

7 KNAP, KUNZ, OPLTOVÁ, "Industrial Rights in International Relations (Průmyslová práva v mezinárodních vztazích)" 207208 (1988); ŠVIDROŇ, "Basis of the Intellectual Property Law (Základy práva duševného vlastníctva)" 214–217 (2000).

8 Knap, Kunz, Opltová, "Industrial Rights in International Relations" 208–209 (1988).

This division is based on the legal tradition of the former Czechoslovakia, where such a separation already existed in the two specific acts in the period of the so-called "First Republic" (1918–1939).[9]

The connection of these legal regulations can also be seen in the text of the CC, where illegal restriction of economic competition is divided into the above-mentioned two groups and in the case of illegal restriction of economic competition the CC refers to the Special Act on the Protection of Economic Competition.

Legal regulation of economic competition in its Special Act deals particularly with the protection of the market against two basic forms of illegal restriction of economic competition: contracts restricting competition (so-called cartel contracts), and the abuse of a dominant position on the market. Control of the merger of businesses – concentration – that could have a negative effect on the market in the sense of strengthening the dominant position of particular businesses is regulated as well.[10]

It has to be mentioned that the Act for the Protection of Economic Competition also regulates antitrust proceedings held by the Antitrust Office (Protimonopolný úrad) of the Slovak Republic, which is the central authority of the State administration for the field of protection of economic competition. These proceedings have an administrative nature, regulated by the particular administrative statutes.

4. Unfair Competition

The regulation of unfair competition[11] is based on the principle that every illegal (prohibited) use of the efforts of others, ideas and invested resources in economic competition goes against good faith.[12]

As mentioned, unfair competition is regulated in the CC, one of the basic private law statutes in the Slovak Republic. Regarding the dualism of private law in Slovakia (i.e. separate legal regulation of general civil law (Civil Code No. 40/1964 Coll., in the wording of its later amendments, hereinafter "CivC") and commercial law (CC), the question of the application of good faith in the field of unfair competition should be considered. This question already arises from the general clause of unfair competition.

As to the theoretical conception of the legal sources, good faith by itself does not represent the source of law in Slovakia. The independent sources of law in this respect are only the legal rules, which refer to good faith.[13] In a simplified way, we can say that good faith is based on the moral principles of the society, and therefore

[9] *See also* OVEČKOVÁ, "Commentary on the Commercial Code" 104b (1995); in the period of the First Republic the protection against unfair competition was included in Act No. 111/1927 Col. – Act against unfair competition and the protection against other forms of restriction of competition was included in Act No. 141/1933 Col. – Cartel and Private Monopolies Act.

[10] *See also* OVEČKOVÁ, "Commentary on the Commercial Code (Obchodný zákonník – komentár)" 96–97 (2005).

[11] *See also* ŠVIDROŇ, "Intellectual Property – Slovak Republic," in: "International Encyclopaedia of Laws" 190–194 (2001).

[12] VOJČÍK, "Industrial Property Law (Právo priemyselného vlastníctva)" 300 (1998).

it should be a coherent part of the relationships which emerge between the members of society and should be reflected in their behaviour. As to this construction, legal acts that go against good faith are absolutely invalid (Sec. 39 CivC). In contrast, commercial law (regulated basically in the CC – as to the dualism of private law) operates with terms such as honest trade practises, or in unfair competition, standard practises of competition ("principles of fair business conduct" Sec. 265 CC).[14] The inhomogeneous use of the concept of good faith in Slovakian private law can be seen in the above-mentioned facts when honest trade practises as well standard practises of competition will always mean more limited terms than good conduct generally.[15] This inconsistency is given through the nature of competitive conduct in the market economy where a stronger subject (in an economic sense) defeats the weaker one. However, this "victory", even if not approved by the moral convictions of the society, should be reached honestly, respecting the rules of competition.

The protection against unfair competition is based on the principle of territoriality, which means that such protection can only be accorded in the case that unfair business practises (unfair deeds) were committed within the territory of the Slovak Republic or the effects of such an action appeared in the Slovak Republic. If the effects of said action performed in the Slovak Republic territory, appeared abroad, there will be no sanction according to Slovakian law, but rather the legal regulations of the place of appearance will be valid (where international treaties do not provide otherwise).[16]

Unfair competition law protects the particular interests of competitors (mentioned in the section on competitive relationships) as well consumers, who are enabled to take legal action against deeds of unfair competition in particular cases.[17] Foreign subjects (foreign entrepreneurs) may take part in economic competition in the Slovak Republic. They have the same position as domestic competitors if they operate a business in Slovakia in accordance with the legal regulations stipulated in the CC. If such a foreign subject does not operate his business in Slovakia, he is protected by international treaties, which are also binding for the Slovak Republic.[18] If there is no such a treaty, he is protected on the basis of national treatment.

---

[13] *See also* LAZAR, "Basis of the Civil Law 1 (Základy občianskeho hmotného práva 1)" 91 (2004).

[14] *See* LAZAR, "´Bonos Mores` in Civil Law (´Dobré mravy` v občianskom práve)" 110123 (1993). OVEČKOVÁ, "Decency in Business Relations (Slušnosť v obchodnoprávnych vzťahoch)" 166177 (1993). HAJN, "´Bonos Mores` in Trademark Application Proceeding (Hledisko ´dobrých mravů` při zápisu ochranné známky)," in: VYPARINA, (ed.), "Collection from Conference: Protection of Intellectual Property IV (Zborník z celoštátneho seminára Ochrana duševného vlastníctva VI)" 64–69 (1999).

[15] Also in ŠVIDROŇ, in: LAZAR, "Basis of the Civil Law 2" 475 (2004).

[16] *See* SUCHOŽA, "Commercial Code and Connected Acts – Commentary (Obchodný zákonník a súvisiace predpisy – komentár)" 103 (2003).

[17] *See also* ELIÁŠ, BEJČEK, HAJN, JEŽEK, *supra* note 4, at 289.

[18] Slovak Republic as one of two successor states of the former Czechoslovakia has been a Member State of the Paris Union since 1993 (Paris Convention for the Protection of Industrial Property from the year 1883, in the Stockholm version from 1967).

4.1 Legal Regulation of Unfair Competition

The legal regulation of unfair competition[19] is built on two connected pillars: the general clause which declares that unfair competition shall mean such competitive conduct that is contrary to the standard practises of competition and that may be detrimental to other competitors or consumers; and on the special facts of unfair competition.

The meaning of the general clause is twofold. First of all, it is clear that the legal features of unfair competition that are declared in the general clause such as conduct in economic competition in conflict with the standard practises of competition and its capability to cause harm to competitors and consumers, should always be fulfilled simultaneously and accumulatively, even in the case of some of the special cases of unfair competition. Actions of particular cases of unfair competition will be considered as unfair competition only if the features from the general clause are met. The second meaning of the general clause lies in the fact that every action (conduct) that meets the legal features should be considered as unfair competition, even if it does not meet the particular legal requirement of the specific case of unfair competition.[20]

With respect to particular torts of unfair competition, it has to be mentioned that the CC only gives us a demonstrative list of examples, consisting of: deceptive advertising, deceptive description of goods and services, misrepresentation, benefiting from the exploitation of a competitor's reputation, bribery, defamation, breach of trade secrets, and the endangerment of health and the environment.

Act No. 147/2001 Col. (Advertising Act) should also be mentioned as one of the sources of law in the field of unfair competition. It regulates advertising requirements in general, specific requirements for the advertising of some special products (such as tobacco or pharmaceutical products), and the protection of consumers and entrepreneurs from the offences of deceptive and forbidden comparative advertising. The Advertising Act stipulates the supervision over the law by State authorities, namely: the Agriculture and Food Inspection of the Slovak Republic, the State Institute for Pharmaceutical Product Control, the State Institute for Veterinary Medicine Control, and for the remaining cases, the Slovak Trade Inspection.

The relationship between the CC and the Advertising Act[21] is actually seen in the offence of deceptive advertising[22] (Sec. 45 CC). The regulations of the Advertising Act are considered as the regulations of the Special Act (Special Law) and the CC and are intended to be used as a subsidiary. In practise, this means that the regulation of advertising is to be found in the Advertising Act in general, except the regulation of deceptive advertising, mentioned in the Advertising Act as well, but regulated in the CC.

[19] Sec. 44–52 CC.

[20] Also in Eliáš, Bejček, Hajn, Ježek,

[21] It has to be mentioned that the Advertising Act is of public law nature.

[22] *See* also: OVEČKOVÁ, "Commentary on the Commercial Code (Obchodný zákonník komentár)" 102-104 (2005).

4.2 Protection against the Unfair Competition

If a competitor has infringed his primary legal duty not to engage in unfair competition, and has fulfilled the general clause of unfair competition and possibly fulfilled one of the forms of unfair competition, he commits the offence of unfair competition and the secondary duty emerges from the liability of the perpetrator towards the injured party (the subject whose rights were endangered or impaired). The secondary duty is the obligation of the liable subject (perpetrator) not to engage in unfair competition and to eliminate the consequences of his unfair conduct. Injured parties are also entitled to demand appropriate restitution, indemnities and the forfeiture of unjustified gains.

In the case of acts of unfair competition, the law (CC) enables injured parties request an injunction (before the court) against activities of conduct of unfair competition on the part of the perpetrator, to demand a remedy for the objectionable state of affairs, to demand appropriate relief that may be granted in cash, indemnities and the forfeiture of the unjustified gains.

Particular claims concerning its use should be separated from each other. The injunction has a preventive effect and aims at the continuation of illegal action or such actions in the future which are threatening at the time when this claim is used. On the other hand, a demand for remedy is aimed at eliminating the source of the consequences of illegal actions which have already arisen.[23]

Active permission to use these claims is granted to persons whose rights were endangered or impaired, in particular competitors and consumers.

Consumers also have the possibility to claim protection against unfair competition practises. However this possibility is somewhat restricted and consumers can use such claims only in cases (cases of unfair competition) of deceptive advertising, the deceptive description of goods and services, misrepresentation, endangerment of health and the environment, and the general clause.

The law also provides for the active permission to claim protection for special legal persons, who are authorized to protect the interests of competitors and consumers. This active permission is, however, restricted to the protection of the rights that could be endangered or impaired by the commission of unfair competition in the form of deceptive advertising, the deceptive description of goods and services, misrepresentation, endangerment of health and the environment, and the general clause. These legal persons can only bring forth demands for forbearance and remedy since these legal persons do not represent the interests of specific, individual subjects.[24]

The prohibition of the accumulation legal actions is also one of the precepts in the Slovakian regulation of unfair competition. If a court proceeding has already begun (or has already been officially concluded), and it concerns a case that falls into the scope of this precept, other similar legal actions containing the same claims

---

[23] *See* also DEDIČ, FOREJT, KNAP, "Commercial Code with Commentary for Legal and Business Practice (Obchodný zákonník s podrobným komentárom pre právnu a podnikateľskú prax)" 75 (1992).

[24] *See also* SUCHOŽA, *supra* note 16, at 117–118.

are prohibited. Persons with the same claims may join such legal actions as secondary claimants. Final court decisions concerning these claims are effective for other legitimate persons as well. The prohibition of the accumulation of legal actions is restricted (according to the law) to the demands for forbearance and restitution. Every competitor or consumer (or other subject of competition) should themselves claim appropriate satisfaction, recompense and the forfeiture of groundless enrichment in a separate action.[25]

4.3 Relationship of Unfair Competition Law to other Branches of Law

The legal regulation of unfair competition in the Slovakian legal system can be specified (as mentioned above) in the field (branch) of private (civil) law, and especially in the branch of commercial law. This fact does not exclude some connections with public law as well: the Consumer Protection Act[26] refers to the claiming of consumers' rights in this field and to the application of the rules included in the CC.

The relation of unfair competition to public law (excluding the law against illegal restriction of economic competition, which was explained above) can also be seen in the connection to criminal law. The Criminal Act[27] in its special section defines the criminal acts of the misuse of participation in economic competition. The legal requirements of this offence are met when someone misuses participation in economic competition in such a way that he infringes on goodwill or endangers the running or development of a particular business through actions of unfair competition. The sanction is imprisonment or a fine or forfeiture of the object.

If we defined unfair competition law as a part of the branch of commercial law, its relation to intellectual property law, which is part of private law (and considered nowadays in the Slovakian legal system as a hybrid branch of law[28]), should be specified. Regarding the WIPO Establishment Convention,[29] the rights included in the law of the protection against unfair competition should be considered as the subject matter of the protection of intellectual property. As to the Paris Convention,[30] one of the assignments of the protection of industrial property is the suppression of unfair competition. Article 10bis considers every competitive act that counters honest trade practises in industry or business should be understood as unfair competition and therefore prohibited by law. In particular, all acts of such a nature as to create confusion by any means regarding the business, the goods, or the industrial or commercial activities of a competitor should be prohibited. Likewise, false allegations in the course of trade of such a nature as to discredit the business, the goods, or the industrial or commercial activities of a competitor should be prohibited. Finally regarding indications or allegations, the use of which in the course of trade would be liable to mislead the public as to the nature, the manufacturing process, the charac-

---

[25] *Ibid.*, at 118.

[26] Consumer Protection Act No. 634/1992 Col.

[27] Criminal Act No. 140/1961 Col.

[28] More in ŠVIDROŇ, *supra* note 15, at 368.

[29] Published in Col. as No. 69/1975 Col.

[30] Published in Col. as No. 64/1975 Col.

teristics, the suitability for their purpose or the quantity of the goods should be prohibited.

The Slovak Republic has, as one of the legal successors to the former Czechoslovakia which was among the signatories of the above-mentioned conventions, has joined these conventions and their obligations. Therefore, in order to be systematically correct, considering this criterion, unfair competition law even if formally regulated in the CC should be classified as a part of intellectual property rights. A further argument for such a classification is also the fact that each of the intellectual property rights[31] (authors' rights, trade mark, or patent rights, etc.) could be protected and enforced using the rules of unfair competition law. From the opposite point of view, acts of unfair competition are often breaches of the above-mentioned rights. However, it is indeed correct to consider competition law in relation to intellectual property law as a somehow independent area that is internally divided into the law against illegal restriction of economic competition and unfair competition law.[32]

5. Conclusion

Finally we can summarise that unfair competition law in the Slovak Republic has its legal foundation in one of the basic codes of private law, namely in the Commercial Code; however, Slovakian legal doctrine – following the Paris Convention as well as the WIPO Establishment Convention – also treats it as a part of the law of intellectual property (in legal science as well as in legal education); the law against unfair competition is not considered to be an independent branch of the Slovakian legal system.

The legal foundation of the unfair competition regulation is found, on the one hand, in the CC, and on the other in international documents (conventions) binding for the Slovak Republic.[33]

The protection of the interests of competitors, consumers and other subjects is stressed in unfair competition law. The interests of competitors (entrepreneurs) and consumers are protected in the particular offences of unfair competition and parallel in the general clause. In cases of benefiting from the exploitation of a competitor's reputation, bribery, defamation and breach of trade secrets, the interests of entrepreneurs are protected independently, separated from the interests of consumers.

The relation of unfair competition law to antitrust law is given through the basic division on the law against illegal restriction of economic competition and unfair competition law. This division can be seen in the relation to the public (law against

[31] Intellectual property rights are divided into two groups of rights: authors rights (and neighbouring rights) and industrial property rights.

[32] *See* also KNAP, KUNZ, OPLTOVÁ, *supra* note 7.

[33] Regarding the international measurement, we should not forget the TRIPS Agreement, where Art. 40 regulates the control of anti-competition practice in licences, while this regulation lingers on the edge of the public and private level of protection of economic competition. *See also* ŠVIDROŇ, *supra* note 15, at 476.

illegal restriction of economic competition) and the sphere of private (unfair competition law).

As to the facts mentioned above, we can say that the nature of legal sanctions in unfair competition law is private (civil), represented by the possibility of bringing legal actions before the courts, which of course does not exclude the criminal dimension and administrative fines[34] as well.

34 This type of sanction can be found in the Advertising Act – Sec. 11. Concerning this issue *see also* OVEČKOVÁ, "Commentary on the Commercial Code" 104 (2005).

Unfair Competition Law in Slovenia*

Peter Grilc

1. Constitutional and Legislative Framework

The basis of competition law in Slovenia is represented by a series of constitutional provisions enabling the independence of legal entities.[1] The main constitutional provisions are as follows: Art. 33, private property rights; Art. 49, rights on the freedom of employment; Art. 74, freedom of commercial initiative; Art. 74(2) the prohibition of unfair competition; and Art. 74(4) on certain acts restricting competition. Article 74(4) is a quite a nomotechnical curiosity in comparative constitutional law. Even though the Constitution introduced a negative definition for the restriction of competition (i.e. the following acts are shall be prohibited ...), restrictions may not be considered as absolute because the subsumption is left over to the law.

The most important provisions concerning unfair competition (without the aim of enumerating a complete list of laws) are represented by the Protection of Competition Act (*Zakon o varstvu konkurence* (ZVK), OJ 18/1993) as a central legislative act and the Consumer Protection Act (*Zakon o varstvu potrošnikov* (ZVPot), OJ 20/1998).

The main, important provisions *stricto sensu* in the competition area (without the aim of a complete enumeration) are the following: the Prevention of the Restriction of Competition Act (*Zakon o prepreèevanju omejevanja konkurence* (ZPOmK), 1999); the Media Act (*Zakon o medijih* (ZMed), 2001); the Restriction of the Use of Tobacco Products Act (*Zakon o omejevanju uporabe tobaènih izdelkov* (ZOUTI), 1996); the Medicaments and Medicine Expedients Act (*Zakon o zdravilih in medicinskih pripomoèkih* (ZZMP), 1999); the Cosmetics Products Act (*Zakon o kozmetiènih proizvodih* (ZKozP), 2000); the Tracking of State Aids Act (*Zakon o spremljanju državnih pomoèi* (ZSDrP), 2004); the Civil Procedure Act (*Zakon o pravdnem postopku* (ZPP), 1999); the Administrative Procedure Act (*Zakon o splošnem upravnem postopku* (ZUP), 1999); and the Obligation Code (*Obligacijski zakonik* (OZ), 2001)[2]

---

* This text is based on the author's contribution at the Max Planck Symposium "Das Recht gegen unlauteren Wettbewerb in den neuen Mitgliedstaaten: Impulse für Europa?", held in Budapest (June 16-18, 2005) and on a text published in EKEY (ed.), "Wettbewerbsrecht Heidelberger Kommentar" 1006-1015 (2005).

[1] ZABEL, "Tržno pravo" (1999); ZABEL, "Uvod v gospodarsko pogodbeno pravo" (1986).

[2] Other important laws related to competition, especially with advertising. The following list is a result of a legislative query using the descriptors *advertis[ing, ments] (in slov. oglašev*) and/or commercial*[s] (in slov. reklam*), not translated and altogether with more than 50 laws: *ZVK – zakon o varstvu konkurence, ZVPot zakon o varstvu potrošnikov, ZPOmK zakon o prepreèevanju omejevanja konkurence, Zmed zakon o medijih, Zakon o ratifikaciji Evropske konvencije o èezmejni televiziji, ZOUTI zakon o omejevanju uporabe tobaènih izdelkov, ZZMP*

2. Sources and Comparative Law Matrix

The historical, traditional and methodological background and matrix of Slovenian law against unfair competition[3] are based on German and Austrian models.[4] In the last decade, EU Directives have exerted a great influence, especially in the area where the unfair competition matrix enters into consumer protection legislation. The above sources and matrix are dealt with in detail in a further text. In a general sense, legislation acts as a tool for the following basic goals:

(i) Legislation prohibits violations concerning both classical areas (unfair competition with a general clause in Art. 13 ZVK; antitrust concentrations as defined in Arts. 5, 10, 11 ZPOmK with catalogues of typical offences of fair and workable competition as a legislative approach). It is not only the parties who are protected by the legislation but competition as itself; the latter sees the consumer as a protected person.

---

zakon o zdravilih in medicinskih pripomoèkih, ZKozP zakon o kozmetiènih proizvodih, ZZdr zakon o zdravilih, ZKem zakon o kemikalijah, ZJG zakon o javnih glasilih, ZOdv – zakon o odvetništvu, ZSpo – zakon o športu, ZPSto zakon o poštnih storitvah, ZZVR zakon o zdravstvenem varstvu rastlin, ZIL – zakon o industrijski lastnini, ZASP – zakon o avtorski in sorodnih pravicahZZUZIS – zakon o zdravstveni ustreznosti živil in izdelkov ter snovi, ki prihajajo v stik z živili, ZPotK – zakon o potrošniških kreditih, ZPSPD zakon o predhodnih sestavinah za prepovedane droge, ZVolK zakon o volilni kampanji, ZJN zakon o javnih naroèilih, ZJC zakon o javnih cestah, ZKmet zakon o kmetijstvu, ZRTVS zakon o RTV Slovenija, KZ kazenski zakonik, CZ carinski zakon, ZTVP – zakon o trgu vrednostnih papirjev, ZISDU – zakon o investicijskih skladih in družbah za upravljanje, ZPSPID – zakon o prvem pokojninskem skladu RS in preoblikovanju PID, OZ – obligacijski zakonik, ZZavar – zakon o zavarovalništvu, ZVCP – zakon o varnosti cestnega prometa, ZIS zakon o igrah na sreèo, ZDDPO zakon o davku od dobièka pravnih oseb, ZIZ zakon o izvršbi in zavarovanju, ZDDV zakon o DDV, ZLet zakon o letalstvu, ZGSH zakon o grbu, zastavi in himni RS, ZMZPP zakon o mednarodnem zasebnem pravu in postopku, ZON zakon o ohranjanju narave, ZOSRL zakon o obligacijskih in stvarnopravnih razmerjih v letalskem prometu, ZMR zakon o morskem ribištvu, ZZODPM zakon o delovnem podroèju ministrstev, ZAGA zakon o arhivskiem gradivu in arhivih, ZPDZC zakon o prepreèevanju dela in zaposlovanja na èrno, ZPPŽP zakon o prevoznih pogodbah v železniškem prometu, ZUT zakon o upravnih taksah, ZKL zakon o Kobilarni Lipica, ZRPSJ zakon o regijskem parku Škocjanske jame, ZPCP zakon o prevozih v cestnem prometu, Zakon o ratifikaciji Konvencije o poenotenju nekaterih pravil za letalski prevoz, Zakon o ratifikaciji Konvencije med RS in Italijo / RS in Kanado / RS in Èeško o izogibanju dvojnega obdavèenja, Zakon o ratifikaciji Sporazuma o mednarodnem cestnem prometu med RS in Španijo, Zakon o ratifikaciji Sporazuma med RS in Francijo / RS in Španijo / RS in Ciprom / RS in Èeško o letalskem prometu, Zakon o ratifikaciji Konvencije o zaèasnem uvozu.

3 A brief historical background. 1930: the first general law against unfair competition with a secondary general clause; 1962: Regulation of Business Relations on the Market Act (a relatively modern law, primary general clause and *exempli causa* added typical acts of unfair competition); 1974: Unfair Competition and Monopoly Agreements Act; 1975: Basics of Conducting Business by the Organizations in the Area of Commerce and Services and on the System of Measures Against Destruction of Common Federal Market Act; 1990: Commerce Act; 1993: Protection of Competition Act (ZVK).

4 Further ZABEL, *supra* note 2, at 343-353.

(ii) The prohibition of unfair competition is absolute (Art. 74 of the Constitution) and restrictions of competition are permitted only insofar as allowed by law.
(iii) The catalogue of typical restrictions of fair and workable competition as already known in comparative law is known in national legislation, enabling the application of views, jurisprudence and of the administrative practice.
(iv) Foreign legal entities shall, from the aspect of rights and obligations, be equal to domestic natural and legal persons.
(v) Administrative protection and judicial protection shall be ensured.

The protection of the Competition Act, dealing with protection against unfair competition is, as already stated above, only a part of Slovenian competition law.[5] The competent authority for the protection of competition within the framework of the Prevention of the Restriction of Competition Act (ZPOmK) shall be the Protection of Competition Office (*Urad za varstvo konkurence*, ZPOmK 4, 14, 15). Unfair competition actions before regular courts are ensured (ZVK 26, 27); the law also enables supervision by the inspectors of the Market Inspectorate of RS, who act as representatives of the State (ZVK 28).

3. Unfair Competition; Protection of Competition Act (ZVK)[6]

Chapter III of the ZVK is based on the basic characteristics of classical legislation dealing with unfair competition, deriving from the German legal and legislative tradition. There is a great deal of historical and substantive similarity between Slovenian and German law. It is obvious that expertise in German legislation, and especially in legal practice, would make the interpretation of the ZVK much easier.

From the nomotechnical aspect, the system on the national protection against unfair competition is based on the "general clause" (*Generalklausel*), consisting of a series of elements (Art. 13 (2)). A list of several acts of unfair competition (Art. 13 (3)) follows the general clause; the enumeration is based on the *exempli causa* principle. Only if all of the elements from the general clause are fulfilled, is there an act of unfair competition.

---

5 Outline of the competition legislation system: (i) Unfair Competition; Act on Protection of Competition (13), Media Act, Consumers Protection Act, a series of sectorial laws (several enumerated *supra* note 2); (ii) Cartels; Prevention of the Restriction of Competition Act (5); (iii) Monopolizing through the abuse of a dominant position ; Prevention of the Restriction of Competition Act (12); (iv) Concentrations; Prevention of the Restriction of Competition Act (11-13); (v) Public monopolies; Commercial Public Services Act and several sectorial laws; (vi) State aids; ZSDrP; (vii) Restriction of competition with authoritative acts and through the acts of institutions of the state ; Prevention of the Restriction of Competition Act.

6 Commentary on the ZVK, ZABEL, ILEŠIÈ, ILEŠIÈ & GRILC, "Zakon o varstvu konkurence s komentarjem" (1993).

Article 13[7]

1. Unfair competition shall hereby be prohibited.
2. Unfair competition is deemed to be *acts* committed by the *undertaking* at the market, which are not compatible with *good commercial practices* while performing *commercial activities* and which result or may result in causing *damage.*[8]
3. …

The elements of the general clause are good commercial practices that create a borderline between fair and unfair competition. The notion of good commercial practices within the meaning of the provision is a legal standard. The contents of this legal standard shall be defined in each individual case and is widely known as *gute Sitten*, social ethics, morality, fairness, *correttezza professionale*, *Treu und Glauben*. The court would define the contents *in concreto* itself; nevertheless, inquiries are available through chambers of commerce, trade associations, and other associations, etc.

Individual acts of unfair competition are enumerated in Para. 3 of Art. 13 as *exempli causa* only; therefore, the list is not closed and each and every act from the list should firstly fulfil all the conditions from the general clause: advertising, publicity or offering of the goods while quoting data or expressions which confuse or may confuse on the market, or with abuse of credulity or non-information of consumers; advertising, publicity or offering of the goods while quoting data or expressions which uses the reputation of another business or the reputation of its products or services; advertising, publicity or offering of goods or depreciation of another business or using national, ethnical, political or religious appurtenance; divulging data of other business if this data causes harm or may harm its reputation and activities; passing off or the concealment of defects in goods or otherwise misleading consumers; and the advertising of fictitious clearance sales or fictitious lowered prices.[9] To summarise, we could establish that all classical forms of unfair compe-

---

[7] 1. Unfair competition is prohibited. 2. Unfair competition is the activity of an enterprise on the market in breach of honest business practices that causes or could cause damage to others on the market.

[8] A short description of components of the general clause: *acts* committed by the (performance / non-performance / permission (allowance)); *undertaking* at the market (very broad meaning of the undertaking; including commercial companies, cooperatives, individuals, trade unions performing commercial activity); *good commercial practices* (defined in the full text above); while performing *commercial activities* (all commercial activities); and which result or may result in causing *damage* (possibility; actual (existing) damage).

[9] Full translation of original text into English: "Advertising of products or services with details that do not correspond to the truth, or the use of misleading or deceptive details and statements on the market, or the misuse of consumer ignorance or credulity; advertising or the offering of products or services using details or statements that exploit the image of another enterprise, its products or services, or if the quality of the products of another enterprise are valued or undervalued; advertising of products or services or the disparagement of another enterprise by means of a reference to nationality, race, political or religious membership; the use of details of another enterprise if such impairs or could impair the image or business activities of the enterprise; the

tition are known to the ZVK. As enumerated in Para. 3, they are relatively old. Comparative advertising is allowed following the changes of the Consumer Protection Act (on the basis of Directive 84/450/EEC). The relationship between the general clause and individual acts as enumerated *exempli causa* shows that each individual act should fulfil all elements from the general clause; the acts in Para. 3 are enumerated mostly for pedagogical reasons and add information only.

4. Legal Protection

Unfair competition is prohibited because it runs contrary to the standard of fair market performance. Additionally, if an act of unfair competition may be qualified as an intervention into the rights of a third party, the holder of that right should be entitled to claim the protection (e.g. individual intellectual property rights; copyright, trade mark, geographical origin). The holder of the right is entitled to put into force claims deriving from the system in which that right is based and claims within the system of unfair competition protection. Claims are mainly identical in both systems, since they cover the prohibition of further acts, restitution, actions for damages, publication of the judgment, destruction of items. Nevertheless, conditions for claims from both systems are not the same. It is easier to put into force the claim for the reason of encroachment into someone's right, since only the proof of the existence of the right and the proof for the reason of encroachment into the right is demanded; there is no need to prove the existence of all the elements of the general clause from Art. 13 (2) of the ZVK. In particular, the proof that standard commercial practices have been violated could be very problematic. On the other hand, legal protection within the system of unfair competition legislation could be easier, especially in the event that the existence of the right is problematic. The plaintiff may choose the title (system) for legal protection; the limitation is the accumulation of both proceedings.

---

sale of products with labelling or details that lead or can lead to a deception as to origin, production, quantity, quality or other quality of the product; the concealment of product or service defects or other deception of consumers; inducement to breach of contract in a business relationship between other enterprises or the hampering of such relationships; illegitimate breaches of contract with enterprises with the aim of concluding the same or a similar contract with another enterprise; advertising of apparent special offers or apparent price reductions or similar actions that mislead consumers as to price; illegitimate use of company names, trademarks or other identifiers of the enterprise irrespective of whether the other enterprise has issued its consent or not, if such causes or could cause deception or the misleading of the market; donating or promising gifts, financial or other benefits to another enterprise, its employees or a person active within the other enterprise so that the donor would acquire benefits to the disadvantage of another enterprise or consumers; unauthorised use of services of the representative of another enterprise; enticement of the purchasers of products or services by donations or promises of prize winnings or other financial advantages or benefits, the value of which is substantially above the actual value of the product or service, the purchaser being granted the possibility of winning a prize (premium transactions); unlawful acquisition of business secrets of another enterprise or unauthorised exploitation of confidential business secrets of another enterprise."

4.1 Private law

According to Art. 13 (1) of the ZVK, unfair competition shall be prohibited. Sanctions for violation of the prohibition are defined in Chapters VII (Arts. 26-28) and VIII of the ZVK. The plaintiff is entitled to a civil procedure action. He may demand prohibition of further acts, restitution, action for damages, publication of the judgment, and destruction of items that were subject to the offence. In the event the act of unfair competition was committed via the media or something similar, or the act caused harm to a larger number of market participants, the market participant may demand the judgment be published in the media (Art. 26). If damage was inflicted through an act of unfair competition, the person that inflicts the damage shall be obliged to reimburse him/her according to the rules set down by the Obligation Code (Art. 27 of the ZVK in connection with Art. 131 of the Obligation Code[10]).

4.2 Inspectorial System

The inspector competent for the market (Market Inspector), acting within the Market Inspectorate of the Republic of Slovenia (a part of the Ministry for Commerce) is entitled to supervise application of the ZVK and to issue appropriate measures and orders (Art. 28). He is entitled to act *ex officio* or on request of the plaintiff. In this respect, the inspector may temporarily prohibit acts of unfair competition, which are subject to private or criminal proceeding; the inspector is entitled to file the case with the misdemeanour judge.

4.3 Case Law

The quantity of national court decisions is not very significant; nevertheless, judgements and argumentation reveal a high level of reasoning. Public legal data bases contain mainly the Supreme Court of Slovenia, Higher Courts and the Administrative Court of Slovenia judgements.[11]

---

[10] Obligation Code: Art. 131 (Basis for Liability). (1) Any person that inflicts damage on another shall be obliged to reimburse him/her, unless it is proved that the damage was incurred without the culpability of the former. (2) Persons shall be liable for material damage and activities that result in major risk of damage to the environment, irrespective of culpability. (3) Persons shall also be liable for damage irrespective of culpability in other cases defined by law. Article 132 (Damage). Damage comprises the diminution of property (ordinary damage), the prevention of the appreciation of property (lost profits), the infliction of physical or mental distress or fear with respect to another person, and encroachment upon the reputation of a legal person.

[11] A deeper analysis is substituted by a table of cases as per June 1, 2004 related with Art. 13 of the ZVK: Supreme Court, January 8, 1997, decision No. 12396, *(prohibition of temporal ballot of coupons in the casino);* Supreme Court, September 25, 1997, decision No. 12631 *(prohibition of temporal ballot of coupons in the casino);* Supreme Court, April 17, 2003, decision No. 15306 *(temporal prohibition of unfair competition);* Supreme Court, October 15, 1998, decision No. 40199 *(trade mark relating case – imitation);* Supreme Court, March 9, 2000, decision No. 40301 *(illegal acquisition of business secrecy);* Supreme Court, December 23, 1999, decision No. 40311 *(unfair competition);* Supreme Court, March 9, 2000, decision No. 40353 *(unfair competition and sale of goods);* Supreme Court, June 20, 2002, decision No. 40585 *(un-*

5. Other Legislation

5.1 Consumers Protection Act (ZVPot)

Chapter III of the ZVPot deals with the advertising of goods and services (Arts. 12-15), introduced by a type of general clause (advertising should not be contrary to the law, it should not be indecent or misleading). The law demands that advertisements should be in the Slovenian language with the only exception that another law allows a different solution. Article 12 (a) defines indecent advertising (advertisements which could insult consumers, readers, listeners or viewers or content which is contrary to morality). In relation to unfair competition, Art. 12 (b) is of significance since it prohibits misleading advertising in the same way as Directive 84/450/EEC[12] (Para. 1). The definition of misleading advertising is subject to Para. 2. Comparative advertising is allowed under the conditions as set down in Art. 12 (c) and is based on the above-mentioned Directive and on the Directive on Comparative Advertising. Following Art. 12 (c), the provisions of Chapter III on advertising shall be used for advertisements which are not also limited to consumers. Article 12 (d) sets down rules for the burden of proof; according to the circumstances and having in mind the interests of advertisers, consumers, or other parties of the procedure, the court may order an advertiser to submit proof corroborating that the statements made in advertisements are true. In special circumstances, a deadline of eight days for the submission of evidence could be ordered. Article 15 prohibits content of advertisements which cause or could cause physical, psychical or other damage to children. It prohibits content of advertisements which could take advantage of children's trust or lack of experience. Article 15 (a) demands that all advertisements which are part of the information society should clearly signify this is the advertisement (Para. 1). If special offers, such as premiums, rebates, gifts, etc. are offered in an advertisement, conditions for acquisition should be clearly defined (Para. 2).

---

11 *fair competition and securities);* Supreme Court, November 21, 2002, decision No. 40589 *(firm; advertising of business activities);* Ljubljana High Court, December 6, 1995, I Cpg 1518/1995 *(unfair competition and trade mark);* Ljubljana High Court, December 13, 1995, I Cpg 436/1994 *(protection of firm);* Kranj High Court, October 7, 1999, I Cpg 14/1999; Kranj High Court, October 7, 1999, I Cpg 15/1999 *(sales);* Ljubljana High Court, January 13, 2000, I Cpg 1459/1999 *(unfair competition);* Ljubljana High Court, April 6, 2000, I Cpg 1399/1999 *(unfair competition and damages);* Ljubljana High Court, April 6, 2000, I Cpg 170/2000 *(unfair competition and intellectual property rights);* Ljubljana High Court, May 25, 2000, I Cpg I 102/2000 *(trade mark, right of personality);* Ljubljana High Court, April 12, 2001, I Cpg 386/2001 *(trade mark);* Ljubljana High Court, September 21, 2001, I Cpg 943/2001 *(Unfair competition and intellectual property rights; good commercial practices);* Administrative Court of Slovenia, October 9, 2002, 1590/2001 *(unfair competition; preliminary ruling);* Administrative Court of Slovenia, December 10, 2002, U 79/2000; February 12, 2003, U 1622/2000 *(Market Inspector's measure);* Administrative Court of Slovenia, May 8, 2003, UPRS U 287/2000 *(human rights, constitutional right to freedom of entrepreneurial action).*

12 Directive 84/450/EEC of September 10, 1984 relating to the approximation of the laws, regulations and administrative provisions of the Member States concerning misleading advertising, OJ L250/17, September 19, 1984.

5.2 Media Act (ZMed)

The Media Act deals with the basic principles of advertising in the media. Article 47 (3) prohibits advertising that does not respect human dignity, which is contrary to racial, sexual and national non-discrimination or religious or political intolerance. It prohibits advertisements that could cause harm to the health and safety of humans, to the protection of the environment or cultural heritage, which could insult religious or political beliefs, or which could cause harm to the consumer. The law prohibits disguised (Art. 47 (1)) and subliminal advertising (Art. 47 (2)). Except where otherwise provided in special legislation, the advertising of alcoholic beverages in media shall be prohibited (Art. 47 (4)). Advertising of tobacco, medicaments and health services shall be regulated by special laws (Art. 48).[13] Special attention is devoted to children (the prohibition of advertisements including acts of violence, pornography or other similar contents in which children are acting or children are their object; the prohibition of dangerous situations, etc; Art. 49).

5.3 Tobacco Products Act (ZOUTI), Cosmetics Products Act (ZKOzP), Medicaments and Medicine Expedients Act (ZZMP)

The Tobacco Products Act, ZOUTI (OJ 57/1996) was put into force even before Directive 98/43/EC. As to the **Cosmetics Products Act (ZKOzP)**, Art. 15 prohibits misleading advertising of cosmetic products (especially in the way which could, by use of words or their contexts, of trade marks, of pictures or of other marks – misleadingly inform consumers that these cosmetic products have healing effects or other effects which are not true). Advertising and information on medicaments and medicine expedients are dealt with in Arts. 68-72 of the **Medicaments and Medicine Expedients Act (ZZMP)**. For other laws, see footnote 2.

5.4 Autonomous Regulation – Code of Slovenian Advertising Association (OKSOZ)

The OKSOZ is a supplement to the above-mentioned regulation in the area of advertising and the system of dissemination of other commercial information. By its nature, the OKSOZ is a self-regulatory, autonomous document. Its main contents are rules and principles for advertising.[14] The ambit of the code is comparable to similar codes in comparative law. For further information consult <http://

---

[13] *Infra*; Tobacco Products Act (ZOUTI) and Medicaments and Medicine Expedients Act (ZZMP).

[14] The role of advertising in Slovenia; other definitions; rules concerning advertising (Arts. 1-31; constitutional provisions, legality, decency, honesty, truth, form of presentation, responsibility of society and consumers, privacy, religious sentiments, safety, children and younger persons, trade marks related rights, imitation, third persons, advertising with reference to prices, references to prizes, warranties, environmental argumentation); special provisions (Arts. 21-32; alcoholic beverages, medicaments, health foods, special goods, spas, schools and seminars, sale by instalments and credit, sale and catalogues, lottery, employment; political advertising); final provisions.

www.soz.si/> (*Slovenska oglaševalska zbornica* / Slovenian Advertising Association; member of EACA, WFA, IAB Europe).

6. The Future

For several reasons (annulment of a substantial part of the original ZVK resulted in the present ZVK as a framework; consumer protection legislation has only partially filled the gap; other reasons of nomotechnical and legislative-political nature[15]) a general new law regulating protection against unfair competition would be welcome along with nomotechnical adaptation. It is not expected that the new law would come into force within the next four or five years.

15 It seems that the Unfair Commercial Practices Directive (Directive 2005/29/EC concerning unfair business-to-consumer commercial practices in the internal market and amending Directive 84/450/EEC, Directives 97/7/EC, 98/27/EC and 2002/65/EC and Regulation (EC) No. 2006/2004) will be enacted in another separate law.

Poland: Unfair Competition Law

Ryszard Skubisz and Janusz Szwaja

1. Introduction

With respect to the topic of this article, reference must be made to two extraordinarily important events in recent Polish history: above all to the unusual phenomenon of the 20th century in the form of the major social movement "Solidarnosc", which triggered radical political changes in Poland and in other countries of eastern and central Europe. The consequence of this movement was the transformation of the centrally controlled economy into an economic system based on private property and competition. Market economy institutions have been created in Poland. The privatisation process of state enterprises has continued without interruption, with the result that today the majority of these businesses are present on the market as private economy enterprises. This event also had extensive consequences for the development of the Polish legal system. This includes the "rebirth" of the Law on the Combating of Unfair Competition, which was devoid of all importance in the period of the centrally controlled real socialist economy. Even though the Law against Unfair Competition of 1926[1] remained formally in effect, it was enforced neither by the ordinary courts nor by the state arbitration commissions that were responsible for settling disputes between the various state-owned enterprises (i.e. nationalised enterprise, cooperatives, etc.). The situation only changed towards the end of the 1980s. A second historically important event was Poland's accession to the European Union on May 1, 2004. Irrespective of the important consequence of this fact in the short and long term, Poland's membership of the EU represents an opportunity to complete the market economy developments of recent years while making use of the collection of legal instruments common to all the Member States of the European Community. This also concerns unfair competition law.

2. The Legislative Framework of Unfair Competition Law

In Polish legal theory, a traditional distinction is made between the law against unfair competition in the narrower sense and unfair competition law in the broader sense.[2] Unfair competition law in the narrower sense comprises regulations in the Act on the Combating of Unfair Competition dated April 19, 1993,[3] which replaced the 1926 Act. Unfair competition law in the broader sense also includes the legal provisions contained in a number of special regulations. The Polish Act on the Combating of

---

[1] 56 Dziennik Ustaw (Official Gazette) Item 467 (1930).

[2] SKUBISZ, "Das Recht des unlauteren Wettbewerbs in Polen," 1994 GRUR Int. 681 *et seq.*

[3] Uniform text in 153 Dziennik Ustaw (Official Gazette) Item 1503 (2003) with subsequent amendments.

Unfair Competition is structured according to the standard of German law, which was implemented in the countries of eastern and central Europe. Art. 3 (1) of the Act contains the actus reus of unfair competition (general clause). Art. 3 (2) then lists as examples the individual special actus reus. Art. 3 (1) lays down that unfair competitive activity is unlawful and dishonest if it endangers or infringes the interests of other entrepreneurs or customers. Art. 3 (2) lists as examples the following unfair competitive activities: misleading corporate designation, incorrect or fraudulent indication of the geographical origin of goods or services, misleading labelling of goods or services, infringement of business secrecy, inducement to breach of contract, slavish imitation, defamation or dishonest praise, impediment of market access, bribery of the holders of public offices, organisation of pyramid sales systems and the operation and management of business activities in the consortium system. These are accordingly identified as typical unfair competitive acts. The legislature qualified as unfair competitive acts these forms of undesirable market behaviour that occur most frequently in business practice. Of the said unfair competitive acts, the prohibition of unlawful and dishonest advertising (Art. 16 of the Act)[4] is the most important in practice. The provision of Art. 3 of the Act allows the development of other (unspecified) forbidden competitive activities in judicial practice.[5] As of today, case-law has developed the following forms of dishonest market behaviour: the use in the course of business of signs or symbols to which only entrepreneurs from specific professions are entitled,[6] unauthorised use of another's radio concepts,[7] advertising for goods that are not available at all or only in insufficient quantities.[8]

Competition law in the broader sense includes provisions for specific fields of business. The most important are the Act on Education without Alcohol and the Combating of Alcohol Addiction dated October 26, 1982,[9] the Press Act dated January 26, 1984,[10] the Act on Games of Chance and Competitions dated July 29, 1992,[11] the Broadcasting Act dated December 29, 1992,[12] the Act on Protection against the Consequences of the Consumption of Tobacco and Tobacco Products dated November 9, 1995,[13] the Act on the Public Trading in Securities dated August 21, 1997,[14] the Pharmaceuticals Act dated September 6,

---

[4] *Cf.* SKUBISZ, in: SZWAJA, "Ustawa o zwalczaniu nieuczciwej konkurencji. Komentarz (Act on the Combating of Unfair Competition. Commentary)" 621 *et seq.* (2006). WISZNIEWSKA, "Polskie prawo reklamy (Polish Advertising Law)" 28 *et seq.* (1998).

[5] *Cf.* SZWAJA, in: SZWAJA, *supra* note 4, at 170 *et seq.*

[6] Decision of the Warsaw Court of Appeal dated November 14, 1996, I Acr 890/96, 9 OSA Item 36 (1998) – *Taxi case.*

[7] Decision of the Supreme Court dated February 23, 1995, III CZP 12/95, 5 OSN Item 80 (1995).

[8] Decision of the Supreme Court dated October 20, 1978, IV CR 402/78, 7-8 OSN Item 154 (1979) – *Polmozbyt case.*

[9] Uniform text in 147 Dziennik Ustaw (Official Gazette) Item 1231 (2002) with amendments.

[10] 5 Dziennik Ustaw (Official Gazette) Item 24 (1984).

[11] Uniform text in 4 Dziennik Ustaw (Official Gazette) Item 27 (2004) with amendments.

[12] Uniform text in 253 Dziennik Ustaw (Official Gazette) Item 2531 (2004) with amendments.

[13] 10 Dziennik Ustaw (Official Gazette) Item 55 (1996) with amendments.

[14] Uniform text in 111 Dziennik Ustaw (Official Gazette) Item 937 (2005).

2001,[15] the Act on the Production of Ethyl Alcohol and the Manufacture of Tobacco products dated March 2, 2001,[16] the Act concerning the Provision of Electronic Services dated July 18, 2002[17] and the Act on Alcoholic Beverages dated September 13, 2002.[18]

A reference to the Constitution of the Republic of Poland dated April 2, 1997[19] is necessary to determine the position in the legal system hierarchy occupied by a provision in the field of unfair competition law. The Act on the Combating of Unfair Competition as an ordinary statutory regulation must not contain provisions incompatible with the Constitution. The construction of the Act should also lead to results that are compatible with the Constitution. For the construction of the provisions of the Act on the Combating of Unfair Competition, the provision of Art. 20 of the Constitution is of fundamental importance, providing that the social market economy is based on the freedom of business activity and on private property and forms the basis of the economic system in the Republic of Poland. The principle of freedom of business is regulated in detail in the Act on the Freedom of Business Activity dated July 2, 2004.[20] Freedom of business means that as a matter of principle any natural or legal person can commence and pursue a business activity in any field and within limits that they themselves decide. There is thus no general regulation of the business activity of entrepreneurs, which means that there is competition between enterprises. However, the Constitution permits restrictions on business activity. Art. 22 lays down that the restriction may only be imposed by virtue of the law in the form of a statute and only on the grounds of a not insubstantial public interest. The said provision determines the general constitutional compatibility of the Act against Unfair Competition. The factual constellations of unfair competition are after all antisocial market activities. The prohibitions of the Act are therefore intended to protect the interests of consumers, and consumer interest protection is one of the functions of the public authorities laid down in Art. 76 of the Constitution.

3. The Act on the Combating of Unfair Competition

The Act on the Combating of Unfair Competition is a complex piece of legislation, basically regulating the extensive and complex field of corporate relationships. The consequence of this basic assumption is that the character of the provisions contained in the Act is highly differentiated. The Act contains not only substantive civil law provisions but also provisions that can be classified as falling under international private law, civil procedural law, criminal procedural law and criminal law. A clear majority of the provisions of the Act, including the general clause, are of a civil law nature. In the light of this complex structure, the Act as a whole cannot be regarded as a special law as against the provisions of the Civil Code dated April 23,

[15] Uniform text in 53 Dziennik Ustaw (Official Gazette) Item 533 (2004) with amendments.

[16] 31 Dziennik Ustaw (Official Gazette) Item 353 (2001).

[17] 144 Dziennik Ustaw (Official Gazette) Item 1204 (2002) with amendments.

[18] 166 Dziennik Ustaw (Official Gazette) Item 1362 (2002) with amendments.

[19] 78 Dziennik Ustaw (Official Gazette) Item 483 (1997).

[20] 173 Dziennik Ustaw (Official Gazette) Item 1807 (2004).

1964.[21] There is no doubt that some of the provisions of the Act have the character of a special law as against the corresponding provisions and legal institutions regulated in the Civil Code. There are also a number of civil law provisions that apply to the scope of application of the Act on the Combating of Unfair Competition. This is the case in particular for the concept of competition law tort and criminal law responsibility. The individual competition law torts are torts within the meaning of the Civil Code. The tortious character also involves responsibility based directly on Art. 3 of the Act on the Combating of Unfair Competition. Consequently, with the exception of cases in which a special provision exempts the plaintiff from the burden of proof that the defendant has committed an unfair competitive act, the enterprise concerned is as a matter of principle obliged to provide evidence of the tort and set out the circumstances that are decisive for the legal assessment of the actus reus. It is the unlawfulness of the defendant's conduct in the course of business that determines whether the assumption of a specific and typical competitive tort or of the general clause is confirmed.

An enterprise's claims based on unfair competitive activities are of a civil law nature. The scope of the provisions of the Act relating to claims is not sufficient and for this reason the corresponding provisions of the Civil Code and other civil law regulations apply. In some cases, in particular with a claim for damages and a claim to the surrender of the unjustified enrichment, the Act on the Combating of Unfair Competition refers directly to "general principles", which judicial practice and theory interpret beyond doubt as a reference to the provisions of the Civil Code.

Pursuant to Art. 1 of the Act, its express purpose is to prevent and combat unfair competition in the interests of the public, entrepreneurs and customers, in particular consumers. Theory unanimously assumes that all three types of interests are of equal importance.

The public interest is in preventing or combating unfair competition. Competition is after all the basic factor for economic development. Competition can achieve its basic function if it is honest and not distorted. The public interest protected by the Act against Unfair Competition is not the same as the interests of the individual state enterprises or trading companies with state participation. The state enterprises and the trading companies fully owned by the state are entitled to competition law protection in accordance with their role as market operators. They are treated in the same way as other enterprises if they participate as entrepreneurs in business activities. Art. 1 of the Act on the Combating of Unfair Competition corresponds with the provision in Art. 76 of the Polish Constitution, which lays down that public authorities must protect consumers against measures that might damage their health, privacy and security and against unfair competitive activities, and that the scope of protection is determined by legislation. In addition, there are parallels between the provision of Art. 1 of the Act on the Combating of Unfair Competition and the meaning and purpose of the Act concerning the Protection of Competition and Consumers dated February 16, 2007.[22] The latter lays down the preconditions for the

[21] 16 Dziennik Ustaw (Official Gazette) Item 93 (1964).

[22] not yet published in the Official Gazette, text available on http://orka.sejm.gov.pl/opinie5.nsf/nazwa/1110_u.pdf.

encouragement and protection of competition in the interest of the public, entrepreneurs and consumers. It regulates the principles and methods for combating anti-competitive practices and anti-competitive agreements between entrepreneurs and business federations. According to the reasoning behind both statutory provisions, the aim is to achieve genuine, free, honest and undistorted competition. The construction of both acts should aim at the harmonisation of the resulting requirements and prohibitions for the effective achievement of the objectives. For this reason, judicial practice and theory reject attempts to use the provisions of the Act against Unfair Competition as a means of excluding competition in order to maintain a dominant position on the market[23] or to enforce the protection of a monopoly.[24]

The Act on the Combating of Unfair Competition contains the definition of the concept of the entrepreneur. Pursuant to Art. 2 of the Act, an entrepreneur is any natural or legal person and organisational unit without legal personality that participates in business activities, even if such activity is only secondary. The qualification of a specific business entity as an entrepreneur must also take into account the definition of the entrepreneur as contained in the aforementioned Act concerning the Protection of Competition and Consumers, the Act on Freedom of Business Activity and Art. 43^1 of the Civil Code. Art. 43^1 of the Civil Code lays down that an entrepreneur is a natural person, a legal person or an organisational unit without legal personality that has been granted legal personality by virtue of the law and that pursues a professional or business activity for its own account. In general, the two pieces of legislation contain parallel provisions.

The Act on the Combating of Unfair Competition contains no definition of the consumer or the customer. The concept of the consumer is currently defined in the Civil Code in accordance with Community law. Pursuant to Art. 22^1 of the Civil Code, a consumer is defined as a natural person who effects transactions without any direct connection with his professional or business activity. The customer is defined neither in the Act against Unfair Competition nor in the Civil Code. In the opinion of theory, the term "customer" is broader than that of the consumer. Customers are not only consumers but also other customers, including entrepreneurs who acquire means of production or services or goods for resale for the purpose of their own business activity (e.g. production). Customers also include collective consumers that acquire goods or services in order to carry out their non-commercial functions as laid down in their articles of association or the law (e.g. state authorities, educational institutions, public hospitals and charitable associations).

4. The System of Sanctions in Unfair Competition Law

The system of penalties for competition law torts is well developed in Polish law. The penalties include criminal law, civil law and administrative law penalties. The

---

23 Decision of the Lublin Court of Appeal dated September 30, 1998, 1 Apel. – Lubl. Item 1 (1999).

24 Decision of the Supreme Court dated February 2, 2001, IV CKN 255/00, 11 OSP Item 162 (2001); comment by KÊPIŃSKI.

Act on the Combating of Unfair Competition itself provides for penalties in the form of civil law claims and criminal penalties.

Practice has shown that civil law penalties are of a greater importance. Their purpose is based on the fact that competition law allows civil law claims to entrepreneurs whose interest have been threatened or infringed by unfair competitive activities. The Act on the Combating of Unfair Competition provides for the following claims:

(i) Termination of the unlawful act,
(ii) Elimination of the consequences of the unlawful act,
(iii) The issue of a declaration of a corresponding content and in a corresponding form,
(iv) Compensation for the losses incurred by the injured party according to the general principles,
(v) Surrender of unjustly acquired advantages according to the general principles,
(vi) Payment of a specific amount of money to social purposes and for the promotion of Polish culture or the cultural heritage – if the unfair competitive activity was deliberate.

In addition, upon application by the entitled party, the court can decide on the products and their packaging, the advertising material and other objects that are in direct connection with the anti-competitive activity committed. In particular, the court can decide that they are to be destroyed or offset against compensation.

These claims can be asserted for any (specified or non-specified) competition law tort provided that the preconditions of the claim are satisfied.[25]

The remedies provided by the Act on the Combating of Unfair Competition are often cumulative. The plaintiff, i.e. as a rule the entrepreneur affected, bears the burden of proof that the defendant committed an unfair competitive activity and must provide evidence that this also satisfies the preconditions for this anti-competitive act necessary for the claim to be upheld.

The first two claims mentioned, i.e. the claim to the termination of the unlawful acts and the claim to the elimination of the consequences of the unlawful acts, do not depend on the perpetrator's guilt. The entrepreneur affected is only obliged to prove that the defendant committed an unfair competitive activity and that this activity threatens or infringes his interests.

The claim to the issue of a declaration likewise does not as a matter of principle depend on fault. As a rule, the existence of fault, in particular evidence of the perpetrator's bad faith, will influence the contents of the perpetrator's declaration. The decision of the court determines the content of the declaration to be

---

[25] On the claims based on Art. 18 of the Act, *see* SZWAJA, in: SZWAJA, *supra* note 4, at 826 *et seq*; GADEK, "Generalna klauzula odpowiedzialnosci za czyn nieuczciwej konkurencji (Art. 3 u.z.n.k.) (General clause on responsibility for competition torts. Art. 3 Act on the Combating of Unfair Competition)" 164 *et seq.* (Prace Instytutu Prawa Własnosci Intelektualnej UJ, z. 85) (2003).

issued. The court is also at liberty to determine the number of copies and the manner in which the declaration is to be issued. As a rule, the court requires the publication of the declaration in one or two daily newspapers or magazines. If the defendant does not comply with the court's decision, the entrepreneur who prevailed in the judicial proceedings can himself publish the decision in the newspapers or magazines specified by the court and then claim refund of the costs from the defendant.

The claims to the refund of damage caused and the surrender of the unjustly acquired advantages are subject to general principles (Art. 18 (1) sentence 3, Act on the Combating of Unfair Competition). Legal theory is unanimous that this provision refers to the corresponding provisions of the Civil Code. Consequently, the entrepreneur affected must, when asserting a claim to damages, prove that the defendant committed an unfair competitive activity, that fault can be ascribed to the defendant, that this activity caused the plaintiff to suffer a loss and that there is a reasonable connection between the loss and the perpetrator's activity and the amount of the loss. The finding of the extent of the loss and the determination of the compensation as a rule causes practical difficulties. If it proves impossible or difficult to provide precise evidence of the circumstances, the court can decide on a reasonable amount at its own discretion after examining all the circumstances of the case. Such a decision is permissible pursuant to Art. 32 of the Law dated November 17, 1964 – the Code of Civil Procedure.[26]

Theory has reservations about the claim to the surrender of unjustly acquired advantages and in this connection about the application of the provisions of the Civil Code concerning unjust enrichment. The prevailing opinion is that the claim is subject to the provisions of the Civil Code. However, the transfer of the financial advantages from the assets of the party affected to the assets of the infringing party is regarded as the benefits acquired by the infringing party as a result of the unlawful intervention in the scope of the rights and interests of the entrepreneur affected. Even in this case, if it is not possible or extremely difficult to provide precise evidence of the amount of the claim, the court can decide on a reasonable amount to solve all the circumstances of the case (Art. 322, Civil Code).

In 2000, the claim to the payment of a reasonable amount for charitable purposes or for the promotion of culture was inserted in the Act. The power for deciding on such payment and the amount thereof lies with the court. The introduction of this claim, which is similar to the concept of the "administrative fine" under German law, was sharply criticised in the literature, which argued that this institution was superfluous. In addition, the preconditions for the court's decision were worded too broadly, with the result that the court could decide not only in cases where the infringing party acted deliberately but also if the infringing party could be shown to have acted negligently. In practical terms, this solution does not appear to be of any importance since the entrepreneurs do not make use of the possibility.

Until recently, the interlocutory injunction was regulated by a special provision (Art. 21, Act on the Combating of Unfair Competition) that was repealed on Febru-

[26] 43 Dziennik Ustaw (Official Gazette) Item 296 (1964).

ary 17, 2005. The interlocutory injunction based on unfair competitive activity is now covered by the general provisions of Arts. 730 et seq. of the Code of Civil Procedure.

In practice, entrepreneurs as a rule ask the court to decide on the injunction against the unlawful activity and the issue of the declaration, which is sometimes regarded as a means to eliminate (at least practically) the consequences of the anti-competitive activity. The claim for damages is likewise often asserted, but in practice there are serious difficulties in proving the amount of the losses incurred by the entrepreneur affected. Without exception, the courts require the plaintiff to provide evidence of the amount of damages in accordance with the principal of the burden of proof (Art. 6, Civil Code).

Actions for claims based on anti-competitive activities are examined by ordinary courts and the Supreme Court. Jurisdiction for such cases at first instance lies with the municipal courts or the district courts, depending on the amount at issue. Second instance jurisdiction lies with the district courts or the appeal courts, as the case may be. The decision of the second instance court is as a rule final. If regulations permit, there is the possibility of filing an appeal on a point of law to the Supreme Court, which then acts as third-instance court. The Code of Civil Procedure applies in proceedings before the ordinary courts and the Supreme Court. A decision is rendered almost every day by the ordinary courts on the basis of the civil law regulations of the Act on the Combating of Unfair Competition, an indication of the substantial practical importance of these provisions.

The Act grants rights above all to entrepreneurs. However, it also contains provisions that allow certain rights to associations of entrepreneurs. Pursuant to Art. 19 (1), sentence 2, and (2) in conjunction with Art. 18 (1) sentences 1, 2, 3 and 6 of the Act, these are national and regional associations whose objective is to safeguard the interests of entrepreneurs. They can assert claims if anti-competitive offences have been committed that threaten or infringe the interests of the entrepreneurs in a trade sector or a region. In practical terms, this provision is of little importance.

In contrast to entrepreneurs, customers and consumers are granted few rights by the law. In particular, they cannot use the provisions of the Act on the Combating of Unfair Competition to file individual actions. Competition law does not provide for an actio popularis class action. However, they are not entirely denied the protection of the law. Customers can assert their claims on the basis of other regulations, in particular the Civil Code, the Act on the Protection of Certain Consumer Rights and Responsibility for Damage resulting from the Use of a Dangerous Product dated March 2, 2000,[27] and the Act concerning Special Conditions in Consumer Sales and Amending the Civil Code dated July 27, 2002.[28]

The Act on the Combating of Unfair Competition also grants certain rights to the Chairman of the Competition and Consumer Protection Office, who by virtue of Art. 19 (1) sentence 3 and (2) in conjunction with Art. 18 (1) sentences 1, 2, 3 and

---

[27] 22 Dziennik Ustaw (Official Gazette) Item 271 (2000).

[28] 141 Dziennik Ustaw (Official Gazette) Item 1176 (2002).

6 of the Act, is entitled to assert the claims provided for in the Act if an unfair competitive act threatens or infringes consumer interests. The Chairman of this competition and consumer authority can also take the measures provided for by the Act for the protection of competition and consumers.

A number of unfair competitive activities specified in detail in the Act on the Combating of Unfair Competition are subject to criminal law penalties (Arts. 26-30, Act on the Combating of Unfair Competition).[29] If an anti-competitive activity is unlawful and at the same time satisfies the preconditions of one of the regulations in the Penal Code, the offender can be made criminally liable in accordance with the applicable regulation. For this reason, criminal proceedings can be filed against unfair competitive activities that are not specified individually as crimes or offences in the Act on the Combating of Unfair Competition. The penalties for individual offences are highly differentiated, ranging from a fine to three months to eight years imprisonment. The preparatory proceedings in matters provided for in the Act on the Combating of Unfair Competition are conducted by the state attorney upon application by the affected party. Criminal cases are heard by the ordinary courts.

As stated above, the Act against Unfair Competition does not provide for criminal penalties. Such penalties are, however, to be found in the provisions of unfair competition law in the broader sense (such as in the Pharmaceuticals Act). Monitoring powers in the field of the advertising of pharmaceuticals are held by the Chief Inspector for Pharmaceutical Products. If necessary, he can issue a decision forbidding the unlawful advertising and order the publication of this decision or a correction of the misleading advertising. He is also responsible for ordering the elimination of the offending circumstances. An analysis of the decisions of the Chief Inspector for Pharmaceutical Products shows that the protection of the law against prohibited advertising functions very well. In the relatively short period of time since the Pharmaceuticals Act entered into effect, the pharmaceuticals authority has developed a very rich body of judicial practice on pharmaceuticals advertising. Powers of monitoring in the area determined by the law are held by the Inspectorate for Trade Quality of Agricultural Products and Foodstuffs (the Inspectorate). This power includes the monitoring of the packaging, labelling and presentation of agricultural products and foodstuffs (Art. 23 (2) sentence 2). The consequences of this monitoring include the inspector being able to issue a decision prohibiting the marketing of products that do not satisfy the criteria of trade quality or even to have the products destroyed at the owner's expense (Art. 30 (1) sentences 1 and 5). The Act also provides for criminal responsibility for the marketing of agricultural products that do not comply with trade quality (Art. 40 (1)).

The Act on the Combating of Unfair Competition contains no provisions concerning contracts concluded in connection with or under the influence of an anti-competitive offence (e.g. deception as a result of an indication of geographical origin). Nor is there much judicial practice in this field. Similarly, there is hardly anything in the literature on this issue. In this context, it would be necessary to deter-

---

[29] Details in MOZGAWA, "Zwalczanie nieuczciwej konkurencji srodkami prawa karnego (Prevention of Unfair Competition with Criminal Law Measures)" (1997).

mine whether the commission of the anticompetitive offence could be seen as a reason for the nullification of the contract as a result of the unlawfulness or as a result of the infringement of the principles of social life. Both circumstances lead to the nullification of the contract concluded (Art. 58 Sec. 1 and Sec. 2 of the Civil Code). Unfair competitive activities are invalid within the meaning of the Act on the Combating of Unfair Competition and the Civil Code, but the commission of an unfair competition offence of itself is not sufficient ground for declaring the contract invalid. The same applies to defects in the declaration of intent, the consequences of which for the transactions are regulated in the provisions of Sec. 82-88 of the Civil Code. However, individual cases could occur in which real circumstances satisfy both the conditions of the unfair competition regulation defining an anti-competitive offence and of the provision of the Civil Code that allows the withdrawal from the effects of the declaration of intent (e.g. acceptance of an offer) on the grounds of customer deception or the coercion (see Arts. 84, 86 and 87 of the Civil Code). The affected party can then withdraw from the consequences of his declaration of intent, but on the grounds, to the extent and in the manner provided for in the Civil Code. Naturally, the party affected, if he is a consumer, is entitled to the protection of the law on the basis of the provisions concerning the conclusion of contracts involving customers. The Act on the Combating of Unfair Competition contains regulations concerning neither prohibitions on competition nor contracts that impose such prohibitions. However, the conclusion of such contracts is permissible. The relationships between entrepreneurs and employees are based on corresponding provisions of the Employment Code. Such contracts are currently concluded relatively often. Judicial practice has also developed with respect to such contracts. In other legal relationships, the provisions of the Civil Code concerning the freedom of contract provide the basis for the imposition of prohibitions on competition. An infringement of the contractual prohibition on competition can under certain circumstances be regarded as an unfair competitive activity.

The Act on the Combating of Unfair Competition does not provide for the establishment of special state administrative bodies whose aim is to combat or prevent unfair competition. Proposals on the establishment of an authority submitted during the work on competition law in 1991 and 1992 were not taken up. This does not mean that the state authorities and self-administration and professional administration bodies cannot influence the form of competition law principles and their application in practice. In the field of statutory powers, individual ministries and central government authorities, including the Patent Office, are required to perform certain functions. Alongside granting patent protection and trade mark rights, the Patent Office decides on disputes that are of huge importance for competitive transparency (e.g. disputes based on the conflict between a company name and a trade mark).

Broadly defined functions and a field of jurisdiction corresponding to these functions is held by the Competition and Consumer Protection Office, in particular its Chairman. This authority is the central state authority responsible for matters of competition protection and the collective interests of consumers. The Act on Competition and Consumer Protection contains a Chapter III a on practices that infringe the collective interests of consumers. The infringement of the duty to inform, misleading and dishonest advertising and other acts that infringing the collective interests of consumers are regarded as practices that infringe the collective interests of consumers pursuant to Art. 23 a (2) of the Act. If it is found that an entrepreneur has committed dishonest practices, the Chairman of the Competition and Consumer Authority can in administrative proceedings issue a decision on the unlawful practice that infringes the collective interest of consumers and order the termination of such activities. The proceedings can also be commenced upon application by consumer associations and the consumer ombudsmen who work within the local district self-administration bodies. In his decision, the Chairman of the Competition and Consumer Authority can specify the means necessary to eliminate the lasting effects of the infringement of the collective interests of consumers and to enforce the decision. In particular, he can oblige the entrepreneur to issue a single or a repeated declaration with a content specified in the decision and to publish the decision entirely or in part at the entrepreneur's expense (Art. 23 c (1) and (2), Competition and Consumer Protection Act). An appeal against the decision of the Chairman of the Competition and Consumer Authority lies with the Warsaw District Court as competition and consumer court on the basis of special proceedings regulated in the Code of Civil Procedure. The proceedings before the higher instances, i.e. before the Warsaw Court of Appeals and the Supreme Court, are subject to the general principles of the Code of Civil Procedure. In the appeal proceedings, the Chairman of the Competition and Consumer Authority is a party to the proceedings.

In practice, the Chairman of the Competition and Consumer Protection Office makes relatively frequent use of the possibilities granted to him by the law. As a rule, the entrepreneurs terminate their practices following a request by the Chairman. The activity of the Chairman of the Competition and Consumer Authority has now, as practice has shown, become an effective instrument for the protection of consumers.

5. The Relationship Between Unfair Competition Law and Industrial Property Law

Of considerable practical importance is the relationship between unfair competition law and copyright law and the provisions in the field of patent law, trade mark law and other aspects of industrial property law. The Copyright and Related Rights Act dated February 4, 1994[30] applies in Poland. This Act, however, does not contain any particular provisions concerning their relationship with the Act on the Combating of Unfair Competition. This problem was left to judicial practice and legal theory to solve. It is generally assumed that in the field of copyright, the 1994 Act applies. This is because this Act contains complex provisions concerning copyright works. The provisions of the Act on the Combating of Unfair Competition can only provide legal protection outside the scope of application of copyright. Thus the Act on the

[30] Uniform text in 80 Dziennik Ustaw (Official Gazette) Item 904 (2000) with amendments.

Combating of Unfair Competition provides supplementary protection in its relationship to the subject matter of copyright protection.[31]

The field of industrial property law is subject to the Industrial Property Act dated June 30, 2000.[32] This law is complex because, with the exception of unfair competition law, it covers the entire field of industrial property. Like the Copyright Act, this Act contains no express provisions that regulate its relationship to the Act on the Combating of Unfair Competition.

On the basis of the view adopted by judicial practice and teaching, it is possible to identify an approach that has now prevailed. In the field of the previous regulations concerning inventions, utility models and industrial designs, the provisions of the Act on Industrial Property apply. The latter are complex in character. For this reason, the application of the provisions of the Act on the Combating of Unfair Competition in this field is not possible. The Supreme Court has held that the provisions of the law on inventions exclude the application of the Act on the Combating of Unfair Competition concerning activities that are based on the production of a product according to a legally protected utility model.[33]

In contrast, in the field of trade marks, the provisions of both acts can be applied in parallel. One and the same constellation of facts can be qualified as satisfying both the conditions of the Industrial Property Act (e.g. Art. 296 (1)) and the provisions of the Act on the Combating of Unfair Competition (e.g. Art. 10). There is nothing to prevent the provisions of the latter Act being applied to the protection under this Act, provided that the conditions for a specific unfair competitive activity are satisfied (supplementary legal protection).[34]

---

31 The Warsaw Appeal Court held that, given that copyright and the Act against Unfair Competition enjoy the same status in the ranking of legal sources, it is to be assumed that the provisions of the Act against Unfair Competition play a supplementary role in the sense that they provide the protection of the law outside copyright law, and the claims deriving from the Act against Unfair Competition can be asserted if a third party infringes the rights in any manner other than that regulated by the scope of application of copyright law. One form of unfair competition was the attempt to exploit the image or achievements of another where the infringing party acts unlawfully (decision of the Warsaw Court of Appeal dated December 8, 1994, I ACr 789/94). The Supreme Court held that the conduct of a radio broadcaster can be regarded as unfair competition if it satisfies the conditions of the general clause of the Act against Unfair Competition (decision of the Supreme Court dated February, 23 1995, III CZP 12/95, III CZP 12/95, 5 OSN Item 80 (1995), 3 OSP Item 55 (1996) with in part critical comments by CZAJKOWSKA-DĄBROWSKA, 9-10 Palestra 189 (1995) with critical comments by KASPRZYK).

32 Uniform text in 119 Dziennik Ustaw (Official Gazette) Item 1117 (2003) with amendments.

33 Decision of the Supreme Court dated November 28, 1998, No. I CKN 904/97, 5 OSNC Item 97 (1997); in part acknowledging the comments by KÊPIŇSKI on this decision: 59 OSP Item 91 (1999).

34 *Cf.* SKUBISZ, "Prawo znaków towarowych. Komentarz (Trade Mark Law, Commentary)" 287 *et seq.* (1997). In judicial practice *see* for instance decision of the Białystok Court of Appeal dated March 11, 1999, I ACa 430/99, 11-12 OSA Item 57, 92.

6. The Relationship Between Unfair Competition and Antitrust Law

The Act on the Protection of Competition and Consumers contains a provision in the field of antitrust law and an extensive regulation of consumer protection. Antitrust law (the main part of the Act on Competition and Consumer Protection) and the Act on the Combating of Unfair Competition together form competition law. In accordance with the legislative tradition of the 1920s, the subject matter of the legislation is contained in two separate acts. In general, the antitrust section of the Act on Competition and Consumer Protection regulates the principles and proceedings for combating monopoly practices by enterprises and associations of enterprises.[35] These objectives in part overlap with the objectives of the Act on the Combating of Unfair Competition. However, the direct objectives methods, enforcement and procedural rules of the two acts are different. Some typical competition offences can simultaneously constitute prohibited monopoly practices, while conversely an infringement of the statutory prohibition on cartels can be an unlawful act within the meaning of Art. 3 of the Act on the Combating of Unfair Competition.[36] It appears neither possible nor necessary to make a precise separation between the cases covered by the two acts. As a result, there may in practice be situations where a single constellation of facts satisfies the conditions of both acts.[37] The overlapping of the provisions leads to a jurisdictional conflict that in practice is very difficult to solve.

The main part of the Competition and Consumer Protection Act concerns antitrust law, the aim of which is to protect competition against distortion in the form of measures taken by entrepreneurs.[38] Antitrust law is intended to ensure that heterogeneous offers by entrepreneurs are available at the same time on the same market for the same consumers. The Act prohibits any measures by entrepreneurs that prevent other entrepreneurs participating in competition. The subject matter of the protection granted by the provisions of the Competition and Consumer Protection Act is the existence of the competitive mechanism as such.[39] It is irrelevant how this mechanism works. Unlike antitrust law, unfair competition law protects the honest character of entrepreneurial competition to the benefit of the consumer. Unfair competition law does not protect the mechanism of competition but rather the manner of the existence of competition on the market. As follows from the synthetic combination of the two branches of competition law, the market behaviour of an entrepreneur need not endanger the mechanism of competition within the meaning

---

35 MODZELEWSKA-WĄCHAL, "Ustawa o ochronie konkurencji i konsumentów. Komentarz (Competition and Consumer Protection Act. Commentary)" 11 (2002).

36 SZWAJA, in: SZWAJA, *supra* note 4, at 80.

37 SKOCZNY, in: *ibid*, 555-556.

38 MODZELEWSKA-WĄCHAL, *supra* note 35, at 11. GRONOWSKI, "Polskie prawo antymonopolowe zarys wykładu (Polish Antitrust Law)" 54 (1998); decision of the Competition and Consumer Protection Court dated November 16, 2005 No. XVII Ama 97/04, Dz.Urz.UOKiK of 2006 No. 1 Item 16.

39 MIĄSIK, "Reguła rozsądku w prawie antymonopolowym. Studium prawnoporównawcze (The Rule of Reason in Antitrust Law. A Comparative Law Study)" 32 (2004).

of the provisions of the Competition and Consumer Protection Act but at the same time may infringe the honesty of competition within the meaning of the Act on the Combating of Unfair Competition. At the same time, market behaviour that infringes the provisions of the Competition and Consumer Protection Act infringes the principles of honest competition within the meaning of the Act on the Combating of Unfair Competition, being a measure that damages or endangers another market participant.[40]

The interaction between the provisions of the Competition and Consumer Protection Act and the Act on the Combating of Unfair Competition also results from the interests that are protected by the two acts. Pursuant to Art. 1 of the Competition and Consumer Protection Act, the Act determines the conditions for the development and protection of competition as well as the principles for the coordination of the protection of entrepreneur and consumer interests in the public interest. The provisions of the Act are accordingly applied in the public interest.[41] An infringement of the prohibitions set out therein is not of itself sufficient for the application of the regulations (prohibition on agreements restricting competition, prohibition on the abuse of a dominant market position, prohibition on concentration). This infringement must additionally be incompatible with the public interest.[42] The concept of public interest is vague. It is assumed that there is an infringement of the public interest if a wide circle of persons is affected by the consequences of the conduct in breach of antitrust law or if such conduct has other negative consequences on the market.[43] A different interpretation of the public interest is also possible, according to which the provisions of the Act are always intended to apply if the conduct of an entrepreneur or of entrepreneurs threatens or distorts the mechanisms of competition.[44] The public interest is based on the securing of this mechanism within the economy. The expression of the concern for the public interest is found in the principle of de *minimis non curat preator.* There is no infringement of the provisions of the Act if the entrepreneur's measures are not perceptible on the

---

[40] Decision of the Antimonopoly Court dated September 19, 1991 No. XVII Amr 9/91, OG of 1992, No. 3 Item. 54.

[41] Decisions of the Supreme Court dated February 26, 2004 No. III SK 1/04, 18 OSNP 323 (2004) and August 27, 2003 No. I CKN 527/01, unpublished; decisions of the Competition and Consumer Protection Court dated November 16, 2005 No. XVII Ama 97/04, Dz.Urz.UOKiK of 2006 No. 1 Item 16; March 21, 2005 No. XVII Ama 16/04, Dz.Urz.UOKiK of 2005 No. 2 Item 27 and December 1, 2005, No. XVII Ama 69/04, 7-8 Wokanda 104 (2006).

[42] MODZELEWSKA-WĄCHAL, *supra* note 35, at 13-14.

[43] Decision of the Supreme Court dated August 27, 2003 No. I CKN 527/01, unpublished; decision of the District Court in Warsaw dated December 11, 1996 No. XVII Ama 59/96, unpublished. For an examination of the case law on public interest, *see*: KASTELNIK, "Pojêcie "interes publiczny" w orzecznictwie Sądu Antymonopolowego (The notion of public interest in the case law of the Antimonopoly Court)," 10 Glosa 13 (2004), at 14.

[44] Decision of the Supreme Court dated February 26, 2004 No. III SK 1/04, 18 OSNP 323 (2004); decisions of the Competition and Consumer Protection Court dated November 16, 2005 No. XVII Ama 97/04, Dz.Urz.UOKiK of 2006 No. 1 Item 16; March 21, 2005 No. XVII Ama 16/04, Dz.Urz.UOKiK of 2005 No. 2 Item 27 and December 1, 2005, No. XVII Ama 69/04, 7-8 Wokanda 104 (2006).

market. Unlike the Competition and Consumer Protection Act, the Act on the Combating of Unfair Competition protects the interests of entrepreneurs, consumers and the general public. The Act on the Combating of Unfair Competition can accordingly be applied in any individual case where one of these protected interests is threatened or infringed.[45] The scope of application of the Act's regulations is thus broader than that of the Competition and Consumer Protection Act. In particular, the Act on the Combating of Unfair Competition applies in the event of an infringement of the individual interests of a specific entrepreneur. An infringement against the public interest or that of consumers is only occasionally the basis for the application of the provisions of the Act. From the point of view of the Act on the Combating of Unfair Competition, it is irrelevant whether the entrepreneur's market behaviour has an effect on the market. It is sufficient that it is perceptible for one market participant. Nor is it necessary for the circle of persons affected by unfair conduct to be broader.

The types of interests protected by the provisions of the Competition and Consumer Protection Act and the Act on the Combating of Unfair Competition have the following effect on the interaction between the two pieces of legislation. If a specific conduct by an entrepreneur does not infringe the public interest, it is to be regarded as compatible with the provisions of the Competition and Consumer Protection Act. If a specific conduct does not infringe the public interest within the meaning of the Act on the Combating of Unfair Competition, it is not possible for the provisions of this Act to be applied by bodies acting in public law proceedings. However, there is nothing to prevent the application of the provisions of the Act on the Combating of Unfair Competition on the grounds of an infringement of the individual interests of an entrepreneur. From this it follows that the same conduct can be regarded as both a prohibited monopoly practice within the meaning of the Competition and Consumer Protection Act (infringement of the public interest) and a competition offence (infringement of the individual interest). On the other hand, it is possible for one and the same conduct to be regarded as not being unlawful within the meaning of the Competition and Consumer Protection Act (no infringement of the public interest) but as being an unfair competitive activity. This follows not only from the different regulatory scope of the two acts but also from the different procedural rules in the event of an infringement of their regulations. The prohibitions of the Competition and Consumer Protection Act are dealt with in public law proceedings by the Chairman of the Competition and Consumer Protection Authority. These proceedings are of an administrative law character. Appeal against the decision of the Chairman of the Authority lies with the Warsaw District Court – the court for the protection of competition and consumers. The jurisdiction of this court only comprises the examination of the appeals against the decisions of the Chairman of the Office for Competition and Consumer Protection. In contrast, the provisions of the Act on the Combating of Unfair Competition are applied before the ordinary courts.

---

45 SZWAJA, in: SZWAJA, *supra* note 4, at 77-79; SKOCZNY, *ibid*, 556-557.

From all this it follows that the provisions of the two acts supplement each other.[46] The parallel application of the two acts is possible if the same conduct constitutes an interference with the mechanism of competition (antitrust law) and at the same time is an unfair competition activity (competition law). The same conduct can also be the subject matter of differing examinations from the perspective of the provisions of the Competition and Consumer Protection Act and the Act on the Combating of Unfair Competition, since the former applies in the interests of all market participants while the latter is in practice mainly an instrument for the protection of the interests of an individual entrepreneur.

7. Conclusion

Art 4 of the Act against Unfair Competition lays down that foreign natural and legal persons can claim the rights granted by the Act on the Combating of Unfair Competition on the basis of international treaties in force in Poland or on the basis of reciprocity. The wording of this provision justifies its being classified amongst what is known as "alien law", i.e. the regulations that regulate the legal position of foreigners in Poland. The principles for the commencement and pursuit of a business activity by members of foreign states in Poland are regulated in particular in the provisions of the above-mentioned 2004 Act on Business Freedom.

In the field of intellectual property law, which also includes competition law, situations with an "alien element" also involve the provisions of international treaties, in particular the Paris Convention[47] and TRIPS[48], both of which have been ratified by Poland. For this reason, natural and legal persons that are nationals of the Member States of the Paris Convention and the TRIPS agreement can assert the rights in Poland. This applies in particular to natural and legal persons from all the Member States of the European Union. Natural and legal persons from countries that are not Member States of the Paris Convention or the TRIPS Agreement, of which there are very few, can enjoy the protection of the Act on the Combating of Unfair Competition on the principle of reciprocity.

Foreign natural and legal persons pursuing a business activity in Poland are obliged to comply with the requirements of Polish law. In particular, they are required to behave in accordance with the principles of fair competition, honest practices and consideration of consumer interests (Art. 17 of the Act on the Free Pursuit of Business Activity). They should comply with the provisions of the Act on Combating Unfair Competition, because otherwise they can be made liable under

---

[46] PODRECKI, "Stosunek ustawy o zwalczaniu nieuczciwej konkurencji do ustawy o przeciwdziałaniu praktykom monopolistycznym (Relationship between Competition Law and the Act on the Combating of Monopoly Practices)" 23 (1994).

[47] Paris Convention dated March 20, 1883 as amended by the Stockholm Act of July 14, 1967 (9 Dziennik Ustaw (Official Gazette) Item 51 (1975)).

[48] Agreement on Trade-Related Aspects of Intellectual Property – Schedule 1 c to the Document on the Foundation of the World Trade Organization (WTO) signed in Marrakech on April 15, 1994 (32 Dziennik Ustaw (Official Gazette) Item 143 (1996)).

civil or criminal law on the basis of the relevant provisions, including the Act against Unfair Competition.

The latter Act grants foreign natural and legal persons the protection of the law according to the principle of assimilation, where such is provided for in the international treaties binding on Poland, or is necessary on the basis of substantive reciprocity. However, this rule does not help to determine when Polish law, in particular the Act on the Combating of Unfair Competition, is to apply to a specific legal relationship. Regulations that limit and determine the scope of application and applicability of the legal systems of different countries and determine which of the conflicting and competing legal systems is to be applied are above all to be found in the Act on International Private Law of November 12, 1965.[49] This Act contains, like many regulations in other countries, no particular provisions concerning unfair competition constellations. The determination of the applicable law is found by application of the general principles of this Act. The starting point is the finding that the factual constellations covered by unfair competition are unlawful and as such must be regarded as torts under civil law. The general rule refers to the *lex loci delicti commissi* as being the law applicable to the tort. Art. 31 (1) of the Act on International Private Law refers to the applicable law as being the law of the country in which the event that is the source of the obligation took place in accordance with the *lex loci actus*. In the literature, it is argued that the legislature has left it to the courts to determine whether the applicable law is to be regarded as being the law of the country in which the infringing party acted or the law of the country in which the effects of the deed were felt. The court can thus select the applicable law by applying either the principle of *lex loci actus* or the *lex locus damni* rule. The court can also apply the law that has the closest connection to the offence committed and its effects. Accordingly, the court can determine according to the proper-law-of-the-court rule. As such, the court can recognise the law of the country in which the conflict of the parties' interests took place according to the rule of the market-effect principle (the place of the conflict of competitive interest).

This brief assessment of the Polish law on the combating of unfair competition can in our opinion be summarised as follows:

(i) The Polish legislation is related to the legal model used in eastern and central Europe.
(ii) It is doubtful whether the provision concerning the protection of the collective interests of consumers should be introduced into the Competition and Consumer Protection Act.
(iii) The civil law instruments are of fundamental importance for combating unfair competition, while the penal instruments have no substantial practical importance. Use is often made of administrative law penalties.
(iv) The President of the Office for Competition and Consumer Protection makes use of the powers granted to him by law. Practice has shown that entrepreneurs discontinue their dishonest practices after a corresponding

[49] 46 Dziennik Ustaw (Official Gazette) Item 290 (1965).

request. The activity of the Office, as experience shows, has become an effective means for protecting consumer interests.

(v) The provisions of the Act on the Combating of Unfair Competition currently in force correspond in full to the provisions of Community law and the regulations of the international treaties of which Poland is a member. They are also compatible with the provisions of international (multilateral) and bilateral treaties of which Poland is a signatory.

Unfair Competition Law in the Baltic States

Vytautas Mizaras

1. General Presentation

1.1 Summary of the Legal Situation in the Field of Unfair Competition Law

The legal institution of unfair competition law is protected and regulated in all three Baltic States by Art. 10bis of the Paris Convention for the Protection of Industrial Property and by a number of specific pieces of legislation. Unfair competition law in Estonia, Latvia and Lithuania is essentially characterised by the following features:

Firstly, none of the three Baltic States have a comprehensive act against unfair competition;

Secondly, the legal provisions that provide protection against unfair competition in Estonia, Latvia and Lithuania are regarded as part of the field of competition law (only with respect to regulation);

Thirdly, there are also a number of specific provisions in individual pieces of legislation and in general civil law.

The competition laws of the three Baltic States cover both the provisions concerning the competitive system and the rules against unfair competition.

Irrespective of the fact that unfair competition law is part of the field of competition law, no comprehensive analysis of this aspect can be found in the legal theory of any of the three Baltic States.

1.2 Sources of the Law

There are four different groups of sources for unfair competition law that can be distinguished in Estonia, Latvia and Lithuania:

1. Art. 10bis of the Paris Convention for the Protection of Industrial Property;[1]

2. The competition laws (the Competition Act of the Republic of Estonia dated June 5, 2001, the Competition Act of the Republic of Latvia dated

1 Paris Convention for the Protection of Industrial Property dated March 20, 1883, entered into effect on May 22, 1994 in Lithuania, September 7, 1993 in Latvia and August 24, 1994 in Estonia.

October 4, 2001 and the Competition Act of the Republic of Lithuania dated March 23, 1999);

3. Other legislation:

3.1 The general civil codes (the 2001 Estonian Act on the Law of Obligations, the 2000 Lithuanian Civil Code);

3.2 Other specific acts and other regulations:

3.2.1 Advertising Acts (Estonia dated June 11, 1997, Latvia dated December 20, 1999, Lithuania dated July 18, 2000);

3.2.2 Consumer Protection Acts (Estonia dated 1993, Latvia dated 1999 and Lithuania dated 2000);

3.3 Other specific acts and regulations (e.g. the 1996 Lithuanian Act on the Dissemination of Information to the Public, which contains the provisions concerning radio and television advertising, or the 1995 Estonian Radio Act, containing provisions on advertising in radio and television, and the Lithuanian Pharmaceuticals Act, which provides for specific rules for pharmaceuticals advertising).

2. Definition and the Factual Constellations of Unfair Competition

2.1 General Clauses

Some of the legislation in the field of unfair competition law in the Baltic States contains general clauses that define a standard for fair competitive behaviour and are for this reason of central importance.

Such a general clause is to be found in the Lithuanian Civil Code, Art. 1.137 (4) of which reads: *"The exercise of civic rights shall not be used unfairly and unlawfully to restrict competition and to abuse a dominant position on the market."* Another general clause is to be found in Art. 16 (1) of the Lithuanian Competition Act, which prohibits any competitive act that runs counter to decent practices in trade or commerce.

Art. 18 (2) of the Latvian Competition Act, like the afore-mentioned provision of the Lithuanian act, contains a general clause that defines unfair competitive activity as being conduct leading to an infringement of statutory provisions or fair trading practices, and that might lead to an obstacle to or a restriction or distortion of competition.

Art. 50 (1) of the Estonian Competition Act also contains a general clause that defines conduct as unfair if it infringes honest practices or customs.

These examples from the statutory provisions of individual Baltic States show that all the general clauses in the legislation are very similar. In principle, the laws of the three Baltic States contain not only the same definition of unfair competitive conduct on the basis of the general clauses but also have a similar list of specific unfair competitive activities.

2.2 Individual Unfair Competition Law Actus Reus

As already stated, the general provisions are given specific content by means of lists of unfair competitive activities. Individual constellations of unfair competitive conduct are provided for in individual articles of the Estonian, Latvian and Lithuanian competition acts and in other legislation.

2.2.1 Exploitation of Another's Achievements, Likelihood of Confusion, Imitation

The specific provisions concerning the exploitation of another's achievements, likelihood of confusion and imitation are contained in the Latvian and the Lithuanian competition acts. The Estonian act does not contain such an express specific provision. The provisions contained in the Latvian and Lithuanian competition acts concerning the exploitation of another's achievements, likelihood of confusion and imitation are very closely related to general trade mark protection. Art. 16 (2) No. 1 and No. 5 of the Lithuanian Competition Act prohibits the unauthorised use of a sign that is identical or similar to another enterprise's registered trade mark, famous trade mark, older trade mark, name or other distinguishing sign if the use of this sign (a) means that there is a likelihood of confusion for the public with this enterprise or its activity or (b) impairs the distinctive character of the older trade mark or sign, or (c) unfairly exploits or impairs the esteem of the older trade mark or the reputation of this enterprise. Unauthorised imitations of the products or product packaging of another enterprise in which the external shape, packaging colour or other distinctive feature is imitated are prohibited if such imitations lead to a likelihood of confusion or if the reputation of the other enterprise is exploited. Similar provisions are also to be found in Art. 18 of the Latvian Competition Act.

2.2.2 Disparagement and Defamation

The allegation or dissemination of untruths about other tradesmen is unfair competitive conduct pursuant to Art. 16 (2) Nos. 2 and 6 of the Lithuanian Competition Act. The untruths can concern a person in the enterprise or the manager, the goods or the commercial services.

Similar provisions are contained in Art. 18 (3) No. 3 of the Latvian Act and Art. 50 of the Estonian Act.

2.2.3 Deception

Art. 16 (2) Nos. 2 and 6 of the Lithuanian Competition Act prohibits not only the allegation or dissemination of untruths about other tradesmen but also, without exception, misleading indications about business conditions for the purposes of competition in the course of business. Misleading advertising is also prohibited pursuant to Art. 5 (1) of the Lithuanian Advertising Act. At the same time, misleading advertising constitutes an infringement of competition law pursuant to the Lithuanian Competition Act (Art. 16 (1) No. 7).

Misleading advertising is also prohibited pursuant to Art. 8 of the Latvian Advertising Act and Art. 4 of the Estonian Advertising Act. Art. 50 of the Estonian Competition Act lays down that the publication of misleading indications constitutes an infringement of competition law.

2.2.4 Disclosure of Secrecy

Although the protection of business secrets is provided for in the three Baltic States, the Lithuanian legislation not only applies a general prohibition on the disclosure of secrets but also provides a fairly clear definition of the business secret.

One definition of the business secret is contained in Art. 1.116 of the Lithuanian Civil Code. Pursuant to Para. 1 thereof, information is a business secret if it has actual or potential business value because it is unknown to third parties and because it is not freely accessible as a result of the reasonable efforts to keep it secret by its owner or by other persons to whom the owner has entrusted this information. The persons who have acquired information deemed to be a business secret without authorisation are liable to damages. Damages are also payable by employees who in breach of the employment relationship disclose the business secret, and by a party to another contract who in breach of the contract discloses the business secret entrusted to him. The Lithuanian Civil Code also defines the loss as being the costs incurred in creating, perfecting and using the business secret and any lost earnings. Earnings acquired through the unlawful use of a business secret are deemed to be unjustified enrichment.

In Lithuanian unfair competition law, the protection of the business secret is also laid down by Art. 16 (1) No. 3 of the Competition Act. Pursuant to Art. 16 (3) of the Act, former employees are subject to an obligation to maintain secrecy for the period of one year.

In Latvia and Estonia, business secrets are protected by Art. 18 (2) of the Latvian Competition Act and Art. 50 (2) and Art. 52 of the Estonian Competition Act respectively. The use of confidential information about a competitor is prohibited if this information has been acquired unlawfully. The same also applies to the misuse of confidential information by a competitor's employee or representative if this employee or representative has been induced to act in the interest of the inducing person or a third party.

2.2.5 Regulation of Advertising

In all three Baltic States there are separate advertising acts[2] containing general and broad advertising rules. Despite the general and uniform provisions of these acts, there are additional rules in certain specific pieces of legislation concerning the advertising of specific products (e.g. alcohol, tobacco goods, pharmaceuticals etc.) or specific activities (e.g. radio or television).

---

2 *See* Section 1.2 of this paper.

In Lithuania, for instance, specific provisions are contained in the Act on the Control of Tobacco Products dated December 20, 1995 (Arts. 17-18), the Act on the Control of Alcohol, new version dated March 9, 2003 (last amended on November 20, 2004) (Arts. 28-29), the Act on Pharmaceutical Activity dated January 31, 1991 (last amended on April 29, 2004) and in the Regulation on the Advertising for Medical Products dated May 30, 2000.

Similar specific legislation also applies in other Baltic States (e.g. the 1999 Latvian Act on the Control of Alcohol or the 1995 Estonian Radio Act).

In terms of contents, many legal regulations on advertising derive from the European Directives. The definitions of advertising[3] and of misleading advertising correspond with the wording of Art. 2 (1) and (2) of Directive 84/450/EEC. The definition of comparative advertising (Art. 2 (5), Art. 6 (1) Nos. 1-8 of the Lithuanian Advertising Act, Art. 9 of the Latvian Advertising Act, Art. 4^1 of the Estonian Advertising Act) and the conditions under which comparative advertising is permissible are derived from Directive 84/450/EEC as amended by Directive 97/55/EC.

2.2.6 Information Obligations

Pursuant to Art. 6.353 of the Lithuanian Civil Code, the vendor is obliged on the label or in another manner to provide the consumer with the necessary, true and general information about the goods sold, the price (including all taxes), quality, manner of use and safety, the quality guarantee period, the useful life and other qualities of the object and its use, taking into account the type of object, its purpose, the person of the consumer and the requirements of the retail trade. The vendor who infringes this duty to provide information is obliged to compensate the purchaser for any losses incurred.

The provisions concerning price details are set out in Art. 6.353 (3)-(7) of the Lithuanian Civil Code. They are based on the 1997 Directive on Consumer Protection in the Indication of Prices of Products Offered to Consumers. The Lithuanian Consumer Protection Act also contains regulations concerning information obligations (Art. 5). As a result, there is a dual regulation of the information obligations in the Republic of Lithuania.

In Estonia and Latvia, information obligations are regulated in the consumer protection legislation. This aspect is covered by Art. 4 of the Estonian Consumer Protection Act and Art. 4 of the Latvian act.

2.2.7 Specific Sales Methods, Direct Marketing

According to Lithuanian law, telephone advertising or advertising by fax or e-mail is only to be directed to consumers who have expressly or implicitly given their consent to this type of advertising or who have requested such advertising (opt-in principle (c.f. Art. 13. (1) of the Lithuanian Advertising Act)). All other kinds of direct

---

[3] Pursuant to Art. 2 (7) of the Lithuanian Advertising Act, advertising is any statement in the pursuit of a trade, commerce, craft or liberal profession aimed at promoting the sale of goods or the provision of services including immovables, rights and obligations.

marketing to individual consumers is subject to the opt-out principle provided for in Art. 13 (2) of the Lithuanian Advertising Act.

Doorstep selling and distance selling are regulated in Arts. 6.357 and 6.366-6.367 of the Lithuanian Civil Code, which essentially follow the contents of the corresponding EC Directives.

In Estonia, doorstep selling, distance selling and the forms of direct marketing are regulated in the Estonian Code of Obligations, and in Latvia in the Latvian Consumer Protection Act.

2.2.8 The Sending of Unsolicited Goods

Art. 6.368 of the Lithuanian Civil Code forbids the sending of goods to consumers without their consent if payment for the goods is demanded. If the goods are supplied without the consumer's consent, the consumer is entitled at his choice to use these goods free of charge (similar to Art. 9 of the 1997 Distance Selling Directive).

2.2.9 Sales Promotion

Specific provisions on sales promotions are only to be found in the Lithuanian Civil Code, Art. 6.350 (3) of which lays down that the following is prohibited in retail sales contracts:

(a) A provision that the purchase contract is only concluded if a specific quantity of the goods is purchased at the same time or subject to other conditions;

(b) Giving the purchaser immediately after conclusion of the purchase contract or at a specific time the right to receive gifts or a supplement to a product, with the exception of advertising bonuses or accessories for the product purchased;

(c) Influencing the purchaser by importunately offering products or services, offering supposed price reductions in price lists, on price labels, in displays and shop windows, and advertising with means that are in conflict with honest practices or public order.

The Latvian Advertising Act only regulates the specific conditions for advertising special offers. The advertising must contain particular details about the subject matter and duration of the offer, including its starting and final dates, and the conditions under which the offer can be taken up (Art. 6 (2) of the Latvian Advertising Act).

3. Protected Interests

In the legal theory of the three Baltic States, there is no discussion about the subjects of protection of unfair competition law. Such a discussion should analyse the question of whose interests – those of competitors, consumers or both – are meant to enjoy the protection of the regulations concerning fair competitive practices. The present essay argues that the regulation of unfair competition law in the Baltic States, particularly in Lithuania, is intended not only to protect traders against their competitors' dishonest conduct but also to protect consumers against all forms of deception.

In Lithuanian judicial practice, it is sometimes stated that honest competition not only serves the freedom of business activity but also ensures the normal activity and interests of the subjects of business.[4] In addition, it serves to safeguard consumer interests, particularly where this is combined with a lawful reference to the origin and quality of the goods.[5]

4. Relationship to Other Related Fields of Law

As already mentioned, the competition legislation of the three Baltic States provides for two objectives of the regulations, the promotion of free competition and protection against unfair commercial practices. This means that competition law comprises not only the classical institution of antitrust law but also the protection of the law against unfair competition. However, the provisions against unfair competition are included in competition law only because of the two said regulatory objectives of the legislation, which are identified as being separate objectives. The specific institutions of competition law (agreements restricting competition, protection against the abuse of a dominant position, merger control) are construed and applied separately from the rules against unfair competition.

In the context of intellectual property rights, the following two aspects should be emphasised:

> *Firstly*, Art. 10bis of the Paris Convention for the Protection of Industrial Property, according to which the protection of fair competition is a part of industrial property law, applies in all three Baltic States;
>
> *Secondly*, the provisions concerning the exploitation of another's achievements, likelihood of confusion and imitation are closely related to the provisions on the protection of intellectual property.

If Lithuanian judicial practice is taken as an example, there are many cases involving the unlawful use of trade marks or the unlawful imitation of the design of products that invoke the corresponding unfair competition law regulations.

It is important to note that any unfair competitive conduct can be interpreted as an infringement of the requirements laid down in the legislation. If such conduct leads to losses, damages can be claimed on the basis of the general provisions of tort law.

The claim is based on a general clause in Art. 6.263 (1) of the Lithuanian Civil Code: "Every person is obliged to comply with the rules of conduct such that their actions (acts and omissions) do not cause losses to the other person."

---

4 *See* the decision of the Supreme Court of the Republic of Lithuania, April 25, 2005, Case No. 3K-3-259/2005 – *UAB "Ekspedita" v. UAB "Chemtransa"*.

5 *See* the decision of the Supreme Court of the Republic of Lithuania, March 23, 2005, Case No. 3K-3-150/2005 – *Unilever N.V. v. UAB "Varta"*.

5. Remedies, Penalties and Procedure

5.1 General Characteristics

Penalties for unfair competitive practices are imposed by both civil law and administrative law.

5.1.1 Civil Law Penalties

According to the competition legislation of Estonia, Latvia and Lithuania, the person injured by unfair competitive practices can claim from the infringing party an injunction, damages and counter statement, and, under certain conditions, the confiscation or the destruction of the goods or their packaging. According to the Lithuanian Competition Act, these rights, with the exception of the claim to damages, can also be asserted by professional or consumer organisations. If the interests of a larger number of consumers or competitors are impaired by unfair practices, the Competition Board can initiate its own investigations.

5.1.2 Administrative Law Penalties

The Competition Boards can impose substantial fines and other penalties.

5.1.3 Procedure

Compliance with the competition law regulations is monitored in all three Baltic States by Competition Boards and Consumer Protection Boards. The Competition Boards are responsible for identifying infringements of competition law and can impose legal obligations and administrative fines on the infringing party. In Lithuania, the Competition Board can issue injunctions, demand counter-statements and impose administrative penalties. The consumer protection authorities impose administrative penalties for infringements of consumer rights. These authorities monitor the market and in the event of infringements of the law can impose fines, issue injunctions or, in Lithuania, file a class action. The ordinary courts have jurisdiction for the civil law actions.

5.2 Special Features of Lithuanian Damages Law

In cases of the exploitation of another's achievements, likelihood of confusion or imitation, it is recognised in Lithuanian legal practice that infringements of fair competitive practice law can also be subjected to the penalties provided for in intellectual property legislation. Lithuanian intellectual property law provides not only for compensatory damages but also for the payment of monetary compensation.

Pursuant to Art. 77 (1) No. 7 and Art. 79 (6) of the Lithuanian Copyright Act, Art. 50 (1) No. 4 and Art. 51 (3) of the Lithuanian Trade Mark Act and Art. 47 (1) No. 4 and Art. 48 (3) of the Lithuanian Design Act, the injured party can, instead of damages, claim monetary compensation from the infringing party. This claim is only provided for by Lithuanian intellectual property law, since general Lithuanian civil law does not recognise such a claim.

The amount of the monetary compensation is determined by the court in the specific case. However, the calculation criteria are laid down by the legislature. Pursuant to Art. 79 (6) of the Lithuanian Copyright Act, the injured party can, instead of damages, claim from the infringing party monetary compensation to the amount of 10 to 1000 times the amount of the minimum living wage.[6]

The monetary compensation for infringements of trade mark rights and design rights is increased by up to 200 percent and, in the event of deliberate action, up to 300 percent, based on the lawful sales price of a particular work or subject of protection. The differences in the calculation methods of compensation in the various intellectual property laws are explained neither by judicial practice nor in the legal theory of Lithuania.

It should be noted that the claim to payment of monetary compensation is relatively broadly applied in Lithuanian judicial practice. The claim in Lithuanian legal theory can be compared with American statutory damages. For this reason, in court practice the objectives of compensation are construed similarly to American statutory damages. Its effect is justified primarily by the fact that it allows the injured party to receive compensation in cases in which the actual losses cannot be determined or can only be determined with difficulty. Secondly, the compensation of infringements serves as a deterrent.[7] The difference between the compensation and the actual losses is, however, due to the fact that in the case of the claim to compensation there is no need to prove a specific actual amount of losses, since these are calculated on the basis of the amount specified in the law. The accumulation of both claims is not possible – the plaintiff must decide between the claim for damages and monetary compensation.

The penalty just described is to be understood simply as a legal remedy with the character of a penal sanction. This does not correspond to civil law claims. Such a protective measure is obviously in conflict with the principle of proportionality and exceeds the deterrent purpose of the regulations for the protection of intellectual property.

6 The minimum living wage amounts to 125 Litas (approx. EUR 36) per month.

7 *See* the decision of the Supreme Court of the Republic of Lithuania, December 17, 2001, Case No. 2a-352/2001 – *Microsoft, Adobe Systems Incorporated, Symantec v. UAB "Sagra"*.

Programme

The Law Against Unfair Competition in the New Member States: An Impetus for Europe?

Friday, 17 June 2005

Introduction to the Subject

9.00 a.m.	Welcome Address
	The Law Against Unfair Competition and Its Interfaces (Prof. Hilty)
	International Unfair Competition Law (Dr. Henning-Bodewig)
	Protection Against Unfair Competition at the International Level – The Paris Convention, the 1996 Model Provisions and the Current Work of the WIPO (M. Höpperger)
	The Law Against Unfair Competition and the EC Treaty (Prof. Glöckner)
	The ECJ's Case Law (Prof. Glöckner)
11.00 – 11.30 a.m.	Secondary Unfair Competition Law (Dr. Henning-Bodewig)
	The Unfair Commercial Practices Directive (Prof. Schuhmacher)
11.30 – 01.30 p.m.	The Approaches of the "Old" Member States to Regulation; Belgian Report: Example of an Integrated Approach (Prof. Stuyck)
	Brief Report on Italian Unfair Competition Law (Prof. Auteri)
	The Scandinavian Model of Unfair Competition Law (Dr. Bakardjieva Engelbrekt)
	Unfair Competition Law in the United Kingdom (Prof. Llewelyn)
03.00 p.m.	The Approaches of the Acceding Member States (Round Table Discussion on Issues relating to protective purposes, the relation to the IP Laws, Antitrust Law, the sanctions)
	Hungary: Dr. Firniksz, Hungarian Competition Authority Czechia: Prof. Hajn Slovakia: Dr. Škreko

	Slowenia: Prof. Grilc Poland: Prof. Skubisz Baltic States: Dr. Vytautas Mizara
Until 05.30 p.m.	Discussion

Saturday, 18 June 2005

The Acceding Countries' Laws as "Factor Tipping the Scales"?

09.00 a.m.	Summary of the Results (Prof. Hilty, Dr. Henning-Bodewig) Chances of a Future Community Law (Final Discussions with all Speakers)
12. 30 p.m.	End of Session

Speakers:

Prof. Dr. Paolo Auteri	University of Pavia, Judge of the Giuri, Italy
Dr. Antonina Bakardjieva Engelbrekt	University of Stockholm, Sweden
Dr. Judit Firniksz	Office for Economic Competition, Hungary
Prof. Dr. Jochen Glöckner	University of Constanze, Germany
Prof. Dr. Peter Grilc	University of Ljubljana, Slovenia
Prof. Dr. Petr Hajn	University of Brno, Czech Republic
Dr. Frauke Henning-Bodewig	Max-Planck-Institute, Germany
Prof. Dr. Reto M. Hilty	Max-Planck-Institute, Germany
Marcus Höppberger	WIPO, Geneva
Dr. Vytautas Mizaras	University Vilnius, Lithuania
Prof. Dr. Ryszard Skubisz	University Marii Curie-Sklodowskiej of Lublin, Poland
Prof. Dr. David Llewelyn	King's College London, UK; IP Academy Singapore
Prof. Dr. Wolfgang Schuhmacher	University Salzburg, Austria
Prof. Dr. Jules Stuyck	University of Leuven, Belgium
Dr. Škreko	University of Trnava, Slovakia

The Symposium was held at the Central European University (CEU) in Budapest from 17 to 18 June 2005.

Minutes of the Discussion on Friday, 17.5.2005

Prof. Hilty opened the discussion with the comment that unfair competition law in Europe was at first sight a patchwork, but that much that seems to be different is in reality not so far apart. The current phase of harmonisation was a particularly critical one, since it would decide whether legal uniformity could be established in Europe in the field of unfair competition law. The following discussion, as **Dr. Henning-Bodewig** emphasised, should concentrate on the main issues involved in achieving this harmonisation and not get lost in detailed problems.

Prof. Dietz began by pointing out that Prof. Hajn at the Ringberg MPI symposium in 1991 had already insisted that the statement "where there is competition, there is also unfair competition" also applied conversely to the countries of Eastern Europe, "where there is unfair competition, there is competition". **Prof. Szwaja** expressed his astonishment that the stimuli in unfair competition law were now coming from the east; the more recent harmonisation projects of the Commission showed that there was apparently little trust in the national judges.

Prof. Skubisz raised the question whether the new harmonisation projects would not lead to the over-regulation of unfair competition law, with the Commission merely creating work for itself and denying free competition the necessary scope for development. This was rejected by **Prof. Glöckner**, who gave a practical example. A few years ago, he was asked by an American company about the apparently simple issue of the marketing possibilities for a product in Germany, Austria and Switzerland. But the answer was anything other than simple, because of the different unfair competition requirements in these countries, and for this reason the company decided not to advertise the product. Harmonisation at Community level was thus not simply for its own sake but was urgently required from the point of view of the companies affected. **Dr. Bakardjieva-Engelbrekt** agreed with this in principal, but referred critically to the love of detail that was particularly apparent in Germany. An excessive regulatory density made it seem impossible to achieve a common position in all 25 Member States.

Prof. Stuyck agreed in principle with Prof. Glöckner on the question of the advantages of legal uniformity, but emphasised the problems of practical implementation. General clauses in particular were interpreted differently in the various Member States, with the result that even uniform regulations could not create complete legal certainty. On the mania for regulation, **Prof. Boytha** stated that a free market economy was not the same as absolute freedom. It was worth reflecting on Prof. Hilty's idea that investment protection could represent a justification for the provisions of unfair competition law. The absence of rules led to the undermining of the possibility of free competition. Granting exclusive rights was necessary for a certain period of time – as elsewhere in intellectual property law. In clarification, he referred to the historical development of copyright.

Dr. Henning-Bodewig emphasised the fact that there were no fundamental doubts about the benefits of harmonisation, but that in the recent past there had been considerable deficits in the quality of the work at Community level. There had been no considerations as to how the regulations adopted at increasingly shorter intervals were affecting the Community regulations already in force. This was particularly clear with the Directive against Unfair Commercial Practices, in particular the blacklist. Without taking account of system and coherence, it included everything that the Commission had found cause to object to. In addition, the multitude of vague legal concepts used meant that its interpretation was unpredictable, which was diametrically opposed to the aim of legal certainty. Instead of numerous poorly coordinated detailed provisions, attention should be given more to the question of what aspects really required harmonisation. **Prof. Hilty** added that this criticism of the Commission was shared by many and that it was precisely the function of the academic world to think ahead and not just to criticise the regulations adopted. There was no point in waiting till the horse had bolted before criticizing.

Mr. Schrock first addressed Prof. Glöckner's statement, which showed that the Commission was mainly motivated by business interests. As an example, one could take the Coca Cola advertising campaign that was to be transmitted to over 200 countries. For the legislature, it was not always easy to implement the various directives from Brussels. It was precisely in order to avoid the passive post-hoc critical attitude referred to by Prof. Hilty that the new Act against Unfair Competition was adopted in Germany. In this way, it became possible to use national legislation to influence European development.

Prof. Schuhmacher, in conclusion, once again addressed the problem of the Annex to the Directive on Unfair Commercial Practices, and asked how far it actually made the application of the law easier. After all, the Annex contained binding requirements for the Member States. **Prof. Hilty** and **Dr. Henning-Bodewig** proposed that this question be examined in more detail during the next day's discussion.

Minutes of the Discussion on Saturday, 18.5.2005

Prof. Hilty and **Dr. Henning-Bodewig** welcomed the participants and opened the discussion. In order to give this a structure, Prof. Hilty proposed beginning by examining the question of what an ideal European unfair competition law might be like. This "ideal" could then form the basis for a second stage, a comparison with existing law and the identification of possible deficits. The discussion of the different national regulations should initially be left out of consideration in order to avoid a mere repetition of the previous day's lectures.

Prof. Skubisz asked whether this discussion of the unfair competition law "ideal" should ignore only secondary European law or whether primary law should also be left out of consideration. **Prof. Hilty** emphasised the fact that European primary law could naturally not be called into question; the aim was not to re-invent the European Union.

Prof. Traple once again referred to Prof. Hilty's lecture on the previous day. She raised the criticism that unfair competition law could not be interpreted simply as the protection of investments, but that fair conduct was at the point of focus, as was also laid down in the Paris Convention. Although **Prof. Hilty** principally agreed with these considerations, he pointed out that it would probably prove impossible to achieve a Europe-wide harmonisation of a standard focusing on the notion of unfairness. Moreover, one should not fail to take account of more recent legislative tendencies which could, in fact, be seen as being aimed at the protection of investments.

Returning to the starting point of the discussion, the "ideal" of unfair competition law, **Dr. Henning-Bodewig** repeated the question of what absolutely must, from the point of view of the participants, be regulated at European level and what a list of the most necessary harmonisation provisions might be like.

Prof. Glöckner, referring to the Directive on Unfair Commercial Practices, commented, at the same time returning to a point made by Prof. Schuhmacher the day before. Criticism was to be directed to the fact that the most important things in the Directive were in the Annex. In addition, this blacklist was admittedly binding on the user of the law, but there still remained the problem of interpretation addressed by Dr. Henning-Bodewig. The courts would have to interpret the definitions of factual constellations that contained a large number of vague legal concepts, which merely shifted the problems. After all, although the implementation of the Directive was, by virtue of its legal character, the responsibility of the national legislatures, the "clarification function" of the Annex desired by the Commission would also have to be taken into account in its implementation in national law, and thus restricted the national freedom to determine.

Prof. Cornish took this opportunity to explain the fundamental British scepticism concerning the benefits of excessive protection. As early as 1973, at the Conference on Legal Harmonisation in Hamburg under Prof. Ulmer, the discussion turned on what was apparently still the central question today of how excessive protection could be prevented and whether protection in the field of "B2B" and "B2C" should be integrated in legislation. From the British point of view, the action by the competitor involved the risk that this competitor was merely pursuing his own interests and that ultimately too much protection would be granted, which in turn would restrict free competition. In England, consumers were sufficiently protected by criminal law and public authorities, with the result that there was no need for a competitor action to the benefit of consumers. The regulation of the two fields of protection "B2B" and "B2C" was to be found in a number of pieces of legislation in England; the choice of this should be left to national law.

Prof. Hilty replied that it was not a question of presenting or defending national models, since this only created contrasts without addressing the question of what aspects could and ought to be harmonised. **Dr. Henning-Bodewig** added that almost every national system worked well in the individual country. However, the differences in the systems led to obstacles to cross-border trade that had to be reduced. This some sort of harmonisation was unavoidable.

Prof. Szwaja agreed with the fundamental need for European regulation, particularly in the light of the new Union members. These countries still had little experience with preventing unfair competition and were therefore reliant on help from Brussels. The recently adopted Directive against Unfair Commercial Practices, however, laid down an excessively strict standard for the new countries. A possible solution could be that the old Union countries should agree on their lowest common denominator and the resulting regulations could be used as the basis for a European unfair competition law.

Prof. Hilty, recapitulating, stated that as a result one purpose of harmonisation could be to give the new Member States a guideline. In addition, however, attention should be paid when creating a common unfair competition law to maintaining sufficient scope for the development of the free market.

Prof. Stuyck then raised the deliberately provocative thesis that there was actually no need for a directive on harmonisation. The argument of trade barriers could be countered by the fact that the Directive merely established new obstacles. Concerning the much-discussed issue of consumer confidence, it could be stated that consumers did not even expect to find the same legal situation everywhere in Europe. And finally, the advantage of legal certainty was always combined with the disadvantage of possible excess regulation. The ECJ could ensure sufficient minimum standards.

Prof. Grilc agreed to the extent that there were in the countries of Europe a large number of different legal traditions that had each developed their own approaches and values. Harmonisation would have to respect these differences and should not attempt to eliminate all legal traditions. It would be preferable to allow the individual states a certain degree of freedom in their reliance on the courts and the systems of values, and not to impose on them a large number of blacklist constellations. As far as concerned Prof. Stuyck's thesis about the function of the ECJ, one should remember that the duration of proceedings before this court was very long, 26 to 28 months; it would be worth considering creating a special court with a kind of summary proceedings.

In reply, **Prof. Vida** defended the Directive on Unfair Commercial Practices. In the preparations for Hungary joining the EU, he had been responsible for adjusting patent and trademark law, and despite much resistance this adjustment of Hungarian law had subsequently proved to be very beneficial. Harmonisation was thus fundamentally important and constituted the right approach. It was astonishing that it was precisely the Germans who were calling into question the achievements of the Directive, since the new German Act against Unfair Competition of 2004 was only insignificantly different. In any event, the Directive was now a fact and had to be implemented. For the future, however, it would be desirable for the Commission to at least discuss with the countries that expected difficulties in implementation before a regulation was adopted.

Prof. Wiebe referred to the preceding contributions by Prof. Grilc and Prof. Vida and reported on a conference held on IT law a few weeks previously. Two main objections from the new members of the Union against European harmonisation had become apparent. Firstly, European legislation was proceeding too quickly and did not leave the individual countries sufficient time for reception. Secondly, not enough account was taken of specific national features. **Prof. Schuhmacher** commented that although he regarded complete harmonisation as necessary because of the aim of a common internal market, this objective was at the time not to be achieved at a stroke, with the result that a policy of small stages would have to be accepted. **Prof. Glöckner** also commented positively on the benefits of complete harmonisation and specifically objected to Prof. Stuyck's thesis. He doubted whether the four fundamental European freedoms in conjunction with a large number of decisions in individual cases could achieve sufficient harmonisation. This would merely create an unmanageable collection of rules that would not prevent the individual Member States from pursuing different objectives within the limits of the framework provided. Every cross-border marketing therefore led to considerable costs on the part of the companies affected. In addition, although he was in favour of civil law monitoring of unfair competition, he was not opposed to the establishment of a supervisory authority that would act as a complement to this.

Mr. Höppberger also spoke in favour of harmonisation, since it was only in this way that legal certainty and predictability could be achieved. However, there was little willingness in most countries to depart from their own familiar approach. It would be preferable to take the best from each system and bring it together. In specific terms, consideration should also be given to the approach of self-regulation, which seemed to function very well in some countries.

Prof. Skubisz also emphasised the fact that the free internal market required the harmonisation of unfair competition law. However, this would encounter resistance because every entrepreneur was largely satisfied with the legal rules in his own country and was not willing to depart from this familiar system. Standardisation of unfair competition law must in any event take place by means of binding regulations wherever particularly important fields were affected; directives still left far too much scope for country-specific interpretation.

Dr. Henning-Bodewig pointed out that the in part considerable differences in the enforcement of unfair competition rules should not be ignored in the course of harmonisation. The enforcement of rules was deeply rooted in the generally national system, and was therefore difficult to harmonise. Thus in Germany, unfair competition law was essentially enforced by means of a number of interlocutory injunction proceedings by the parties involved, while in England the public authorities and considerable self-regulation played a major role. It could not be said generally that self-regulation or civil law enforcement by interlocutory injunction represented the "correct" instrument for enforcement; nor, as could frequently be read, could the "thousands of judicial proceedings" in Germany be compared with the handful of proceedings in Great Britain, and conclusions drawn from this. On the contrary, it must be asked what functions the individual enforcement measures actually had within the system as a whole and what aspects of the enforcement, despite the different legal traditions that needed to be respected, could be harmonised; this required a careful comparison of the laws.

Mr. Schrock emphasised that in the light of the need for uniformity, it was indeed necessary to distinguish between substantive law and enforcement. Given the very different legal traditions, it was doubtful whether harmonisation of the enforcement of rights could be carried out successfully. Among the substantive provisions, there were some that concerned immediately obvious misconduct and others than required cultural valuation. The first group was relatively easy to harmonise, while the second group involved difficulties. However, here too, uniform standards could and should be established, in particular in core sectors, but the limits of harmonisation and a policy of small stages also needed to be accepted.

Returning to the question of the necessity of harmonisation, **Prof. Dietz** pointed out that the new members of the European Union expected assistance from Brussels because they had still comparatively little experience with the problems of unfair competition and its prevention. In some of these countries there was no or only marginally relevant judicial practice to which they could have recourse. In the light of the situation, the expectations these countries had of the EU were different to those of the old EU countries.

In summary, **Prof. Hilty** pointed out that a time axis was of relevance for harmonisation. In the short term, harmonisation by directives served as an aid for the new countries of the Union, while in the long term the focus was more on the need for legal certainty and an internal market without obstacles. The fundamental conflict was no doubt in the implementation of the internal market on the one hand and the conflict between national cultures on the other hand. This conflict of interests had to be solved by balancing the interests involved in each individual case. For this reason, however, one should not ignore the European legal principle of subsidiarity, according to which harmonisation was not for its own sake but must lead to additional value.

After the break, **Dr. Henning-Bodewig** put the question of what should happen if national interests were in the individual case diametrically opposed to the interests of the internal market. **Prof. Hilty** added that according to the comments so far, there was apparently a conflict of objectives between the desire for the completion of the internal market and the attempt to retain the cultural features of the individual countries.

Concentrating particularly on the common features, **Dr. Senftleben** then proposed the theory that unfair competition law was ideal for harmonisation since in any event the countries of continental Europe all agreed on working with a general clause, broadly accepted the triple purpose of protection and had now reached agreement on the model consumer. In his opinion, it might be appropriate to take up the idea of the protection of investment and differentiate from there. However, in any event a certain freedom of action at national level should be ensured. The self-regulation referred to on several occasions was preferable to state regulation if effective monitoring by the industry could be ensured. **Dr. Bakardjieva-Engelbrekt** agreed with this statement to the extent that there were in unfair competition law indeed a number of aspects that made harmonisation easier. However, one should not ignore the fact that, as Dr. Henning-Bodewig had already pointed out, the enforcement of rights in the countries in question revealed considerable differences and that the harmonisation of the sanctions of the rights would for instance have far-reaching consequences for established institutions. Harmonisation of the enforcement of the rights was therefore improbable in the near future. Thus the problem remained that despite uniform substantive law there would in the final analysis continue to be substantive law differences as a result of the different enforcement.

Prof. Glöckner emphasised the fact that if only certain fields were harmonised there would have to be a convincing criterion for distinguishing that would provide the answer to the question of what areas were not to be harmonised. However, there was no such criterion at present. In his opinion, the only starting point could be the legal costs of companies when marketing across borders. Once this objective was lost from view, harmonisation achieved nothing. **Prof. Stuyck** objected and drew precisely the opposite conclusion from Prof. Glöckner's statement, namely that in the absence of a clear possibility for differentiation, harmonisation should be completely abandoned. It was doubtful whether there was really a significant number of cross-border marketing activities. He personally was only aware of one single case from Belgium. It was regrettable that there was no economic analysis of unfair competition law; this was urgently necessary since otherwise legal principles would be created without their economic effects being known.

Summarising, **Dr. Henning-Bodewig** stated that a fundamental distinction was to be made between the "old" Member States that were suffering under the flood of regulations from Brussels and the new Member States that expected detailed assistance from Brussels. The common factor in both groups was, however, the wish for legal certainty. To this extent, it was of relevance that most of the old Member States already had extensive judicial practice that had been systematised by the courts and jurisprudence ("case groups") and could easily be used to give content to a broad general clause. In contrast, the new countries still lacked such judicial practice and needed a much more detailed guideline. One way of satisfying these different requirements could for instance be a "framework directive" on unfair competition law, which would be supplemented by a specific list of examples; this would have to provide the new Member States with concrete aids to interpretation without immediately containing binding law.

Prof. Schuhmacher objected, referring to antitrust law. The provisions in this law were by no means without obligation and – contrary to the view expressed by Prof. Glöckner on the previous day – were not simple or "rough-hewn". On the contrary, the guidelines created a very differentiated system. In addition, however, guidelines that were not binding could not achieve genuine legal uniformity, because the fact that they were not binding precisely did not lead to a uniform application and enforcement of the legal principles they contained. For this reason, a binding directive was necessary.

Prof. Glöckner replied that he had by no means called antitrust law a simple legal field. However, the term "rough-hewn" used by him was appropriate since there were only four factual constellations. Leaving that aside, antitrust law, however, had also shown that a general clause was viable within the European framework. However, account must be taken of the fact that for almost forty years the EU had had sole responsibility for enforcement and it was only after this long period of adjustment that this responsibility was also allowed to the members states. The situation was different in unfair competition law, with the result that there was a uniform judicial practice that could be used to interpret the Directive.

Mr. Baechler pointed out that the protection of investments was to the core in competition protection. In each case, it was necessary to examine whether the abandonment of certain protective regulations would in fact lead to a loss of welfare. Examples could be the exploitation of reputation or slavish imitation. The question arose whether in the light of the fact that these constellations existed throughout Europe there was at all a need for harmonisation and to what extent there should at the same time be a general protection of investments.

With respect to the need for regulations, **Dr. Sambuc** recalled the discussion in the 19th century about the benefits of patent protection. At the time, it had not been certain whether such protection would achieve an increase in welfare or not. Since the patent system, however, appeared to work, it was retained. The same applied to the current discussion in the field of unfair competition law and the existing regulations. The latter also had the benefit of mitigating the "all or nothing principle" of protection. As far as concerned the basic question of the harmonisation of unfair competition law, there was doubt whether standardised legal regulations would also lead to standardised law. Every regulation had to be subsumed and interpreted, which given the different cultural backgrounds of the judges in the various countries would again lead to differences and hence legal uncertainty. Even with the German Act against Unfair Competition, for instance, it was rarely possible to predict exactly how a decision would fall. The laws and the directions resulting did not of themselves lead to a harmonisation of living law.

Dr. Bakardjieva-Engelbrekt was admittedly positive about the harmonisation of constellations such as the exploitation of reputation, but reminded the meeting that in unfair competition law there was still the important difference between collective and individual rights, which made harmonisation more difficult. **Prof. Dietz** took this occasion to discuss once again the different models of enforcement. In Bulgaria and some of the new Union countries, unfair competition law was for instance enforced by public authorities, which had proven to be very effective. This suggested that it was possibly preferable in small countries to create a supervisory authority, while in large countries this function could be assumed by competitors. A directive should therefore leave both possibilities open in order to allow the structure that was appropriate in the specific case.

Summarising, **Prof. Hilty** stated that in Europe there was an incredible density of regulations. Accordingly, as in copyright, one should think about the possibility of an "umbrella" directive in competition law, too, that would cover the entire field of law comprehensively. In substantive terms, a distinction could be made between infringements of unfair competition law that called into question the operation of the market (objective constellations) and where there was agreement in terms of value judgements, and those that concerned moral issues, where harmonisation was not even desired. If this division was feasible, it would appear appropriate to harmonise at least the objective field to begin with.

Prof. Stuyck replied that this did not solve the actual problem – namely to find out what specifically fell within the said "objective constellations". In addition, it was necessary to determine whether the "umbrella" directive covered both B2B and B2C constellations or whether this should be dealt with in separate regulations. **Prof. Hilty** replied that his proposal served to address the said problem of differentiation. For this, it was necessary to create harmonisation on the basis of superordinate objectives, and for this reason it could not be based on different views of the feature "unfair", but objectively on where the market had failed and such failure could be remedied. **Prof. Auteri** pointed out that there was already a large number of Europe constellations in the objective areas, and that it was no accident that harmonisation had made particular progress in these areas. With respect to the large number of existing regulations, **Prof. Hilty** added that this was precisely the problem. The large number of unadjusted small-scale regulations was to be replaced by a comprehensive regulation within the framework of an "umbrella" Directive, so that not every new need for protection required the adoption of a new regulation.

Concerning the question of the form of a general clause, **Prof. Wiebe** emphasised that the ethical aspects could not be ignored entirely. However, this was based to a large part on different cultural ideas and was therefore unsuitable for harmonisation "from above" by means of a directive. Harmonisation in this sector was only possible "from below" over time.

Prof. Glöckner argued against the idea of an "umbrella" directive since this would not lead to legal uniformity amongst the 25 members and hence would not create legal certainty for companies active across borders. The problem would merely be shifted to the subsequent directives that would be needed to give it specific content. However, in fact, the relationship between competitor protection and the protection of "honest practices" was not without problems. It was only an approach based on improving the business situation, i.e. an economic approach, that provided the possibility of a justification for harmonisation. However, if honest practices were to be abandoned, the clauses would have to be drafted very narrowly, since otherwise genuine harmonisation would not take place.

Ms. Reppelmund recalled that the Directive on Unfair Commercial Practices had initially indeed been planned as a "framework directive", which in her opinion would also have been the right approach. Since the various directorates of the Commission, however, had attempted to outdo each other and – in accordance with their limited powers – had then developed separate regulations for B2B and B2C after all, it was no longer possible to speak of a "great project". In a number of areas, however, there was agreement that standardisation had to take place, for instance in the case of aggressive commercial practices and deception. The approach ultimately adopted could overall be regarded as entirely passable, since competitors were after all given the right of action and the initial exclusive focus on consumers had been some what mitigated.

Dr. Henning-Bodewig once again set out the advantages of a "framework directive". The recently adopted Directive on Unfair Commercial Practices again revealed the problem of extremely detailed regulations limited according to factual constellation and that overall led to complicated solutions. She agreed with Prof. Auteri that in certain case groups harmonisation had progressed far already. What was missing, however, was the attempt to combine these piecemeal regulations into a comprehensive system of rules. The focus ought to be on system and coherence, since only in this way would there be no further need for additional "small-scale" provisions with ever more problems of differentiation. A framework directive would have to set out the basic lines clearly and convincingly, with supplementary detailed provisions providing legal certainty in the individual case. Regrettably, however, system and coherence had no longer been a declared objective for the Commission's harmonisation process. This has already come back to haunt us in the form of a complicated overlapping and in part contradictory undergrowth of regulations at Community level.

Prof. Auteri agreed that coherence and system were important objectives and in the final analysis a framework directive was probably necessary. However, there might be reservations whether the time for such harmonisation was already ripe. **Prof. Hilty** replied that in the current situation it was no doubt difficult to prepare a comprehensive umbrella directive and to push it through against all resistance. However, it was the function of scholars to think ahead and to provide a stimulus for development. In addition, work on such a directive could take years, with the result that considerations should already be started now.

Prof. Glöckner agreed with this. In Germany, the unfair competition law general clause was created over a hundred years ago and aberrations have been repeatedly observed and eliminated in a case-by-case development. This showed that the process required considerable time. The time was now ripe for a uniform European regulation, because otherwise businesses would continue to suffer from the differences in the law. The world did not take account of the deadlocked situation in Europe. For this reason, it was now time to think ahead and draft appropriate regulations.

Returning to the objection of a lack of coherence, **Prof. Dietz** reported that the EU had already recognised this problem in copyright and that the Commission was indeed applying efforts to develop a systematic solution. Reasonable solutions that were accepted by a plurality of countries had almost always been adopted. Nor should it be forgotten, finally, that European legislation indirectly had global effects; this was another reason why the creation of good-quality laws was worth the effort.

Prof. Hilty and **Dr. Henning-Bodewig** thanked all the participants and stated that much had been learned from one another. A publication would be made of the presentations and the discussion in order to advance the debate. It was, however, necessary to continue working in this sector and to try to regain greater influence on the development of the law. Therefore it would be desirable to meet again in the foreseeable future. Special thanks were expressed to everyone who had been involved in the preparation of the symposium, in particular Prof. Messmann and Dr. Bacher.

MIX
Papier aus verantwortungsvollen Quellen
Paper from responsible sources
FSC® C105338
FSC
www.fsc.org

If you have any concerns about our products,
you can contact us on
ProductSafety@springernature.com

In case Publisher is established outside the EU,
the EU authorized representative is:
Springer Nature Customer Service Center GmbH
Europaplatz 3, 69115 Heidelberg, Germany

Printed by Libri Plureos GmbH
in Hamburg, Germany